8-16-72

ANAGOGIC QUALITIES OF LITERATURE

YEARBOOK OF COMPARATIVE CRITICISM

VOLUME IV

Anagogic Qualities of Literature

Edited by

Joseph P. Strelka

THE PENNSYLVANIA STATE UNIVERSITY PRESS

University Park & London 1971

Library of Congress Catalog Card Number 79-136962
International Standard Book Number 0-271-01145-9
Printed in the United States of America
Designed by Marilyn Shobaken

CONTENTS

PREFACE

THE ESSAYS OF THIS VOLUME ARE DEVOTED TO THE ANAGOGIC QUALITIES of literature, which is to say they deal with the relationships between literature and mystic or esoteric traditions and with the means and methods which literary criticism uses to reveal and to describe those relationships. Thus, in the context of our title the term "anagogic" stands for "mystic" or "esoteric" in its broadest sense in order to avoid misunderstanding, since "mystic" is sometimes restricted to experiences, texts, and traditions within Judeo-Christian cultures. Here, however, as well as in most of the essays of this volume, the words anagogic and mystic are sometimes used interchangeably and therefore cover a very broad scale of phenomena ranging from Christian mysticism to Zen Buddhism. As Garma C. C. Chang put it, "If mysticism is defined, in its broadest sense, as the 'Doctrine that direct knowledge of God or spiritual truth is attainable through immediate intuition,' Tibetan Tantrism can also be considered as a form of mysticism."[1] He hastens of course to point out the complex problems of this definition, since its meaning depends again upon what one understands by the terms "knowledge," "God," "spiritual truth," and "intuition." But here the "intimate union with ultimate reality"[2] of the Chinese Wei-Chin scholars and Neo-Taoists can fit as well into our context as Jewish chassidism might.

There are, of course, many differences in patterns and forms as well as in degrees of profundity among and within the different traditions. Trying to order and to catalogue some basic patterns here is perhaps even more difficult than Mircea Eliade's purely religious undertaking in his book *Patterns in Comparative Religion.*[3] Some anthologies of mysticism, which are still far from covering a universal range of all world traditions, show this point very clearly.[4]

However, as a significant binding link one very important, basic similarity exists among all the traditions in question when they are viewed as sources of literary works. As Zenkei Shibayama defined it,

"Five years ago. . . . I made my first lecture trip to the United States. Since then on four different occasions I have had the privilege of talking with students and professors at several American colleges and universities. On each trip, as we came to know each other better, I have come to realize more clearly the differences and unique characteristics of Eastern and Western traditions. We should not too easily conclude that there is just one Truth and that East and West are after all the same. If, however, we are awakened to our true humanity, we will realize that at the bottom of all differences there is the fountainhead which is the basis for the happiness of all mankind."[5]

It is clear that this happiness in its ultimate depth does not rely on rational moral rules or external social surroundings and relationships, even though they may be connected with it in an indirect way. The essential values of literature may perhaps lie first of all in its anagogic qualities and their adequate aesthetic forms and expressions, all of which have their last source in the "fountainhead."

If one may say "Zen presents a unique spiritual culture in the East, highly refined in its long history and traditions, and . . . it has universal and fundamental values that can contribute toward creating a new spiritual culture in our time,"[6] then the same would hold true for most —if not all—other esoteric traditions, if one could only reach deep enough to arrive "at the bottom of all differences."

This fountainhead can and should in my opinion be one of the most important if not the most important criterion for value in literature as well as in literary criticism. It certainly may be discovered and shown in "realistic" literary works of art as well as in "idealistic" ones. The practical side of the problem is, however, very difficult to solve. First of all, there are many ways of misunderstanding central problems and only a few ways of deeper understanding, and it is not by accident that the religious practice of almost all these traditions has either declined to a point where they are almost dying out, or they have been endangered by superficial and mistakenly fashionable forms of realization. Secondly, the literary work of art and especially the great work happens to be a very complex and complicated phenomenon and nothing could be more wrong than to expect it to point directly towards certain rational, clear, and unambiguously formulated values. Works of art are usually sublimated to a symbolical complexity. They may deal at different or even on many levels with these qualities and may take a "positive" or a "negative" approach in order to reach the same goal.

The following essays therefore can in this respect be no more than essays in the literal meaning of the word, each of them dealing with one or several model cases. But beyond the contributions of the individual essays, the collection as a whole is an attempt to create an experimental field which might point toward this "fountainhead" and indicate how it could be put to use for literary works or for literary criticism. There can be no doubt that these are only some preliminary steps aimed in the direction of building a new foundation for literary criticism, but the criticism which is intended will focus on nothing less than the totality of world literature and will encompass a simultaneity of aesthetic, ethical, philosophical, and religious values for mankind as a whole.

In his later essays the Austrian writer Hermann Broch, who died in American exile, compiled some important suggestions for an initial framework of such a theory of literature. Broch stated that literature is an art designed to grasp and express a totality[7] and to search for a new scheme of basic human values;[8] he espoused the idea of a simultaneous universal value-system;[9] and finally, he insisted upon the unity of apparently dualistic or even polar antitheses such as death and life, or rational and irrational. Along with this approach he encouraged the quest for self-realization.[10]

Stanley Romaine Hopper not only tried to show how mysticism as a means—in the broad sense used by Kenneth Burke—can bring a "solution to the poet's dilemma," but also with his anthology *Spiritual Problems in Contemporary Literature* he set an example of how this general idea can influence a new theory of literary criticism.[11] Burke himself even distinguished different patterns by which literature might lead upwards, in an anagogic way, in what he calls "the range of mountings."[12]

The common background of anagogic qualities in literature may stem from the magic and mythic origins of literature as such, a background which anthropologists have shown to contain similar features throughout the world. Herder, for example, was already quite aware of the fact that those early stages survived in clandestine channels and that they kept on providing living sources of literary power. Great developments and changes of the utmost importance have taken place, however, not only in the transition from myth to mysticism but also in the transition of different forms of mysticism into their complete secularization and back into new religious quests.

In this matter, Horst Rüdiger has shown with the model case of Winckelmann and his aesthetics of German classicism how the anagogic idea of "elevation," found in Homer, was cleansed of all religious overtones and made a completely secular term in order to characterize the "highest" or "golden style" and thus to formulate a system of artistic styles.[13] There exists a broad scale of forms of secularization as well as of forms of mysticism, and some of them seem only to touch the external, orthodox form of a particular denomination but never the inmost religious striving as such. Hence Hermann Broch could write, "Und tatsächlich war es ja auch immer so, dass das lebendig Religiöse gleichzeitig der Träger humaner Bildung gewesen ist. Bildung in diesem Sinne aber hat auch die Aufgabe, das polyhistorische Wissensgut der jeweiligen Zeit auszuwählen, es unter die Leitung eines obersten Wertes zu stellen, es gewissermassen ethisch fruchtbar zu machen und damit den Menschen, dem die Bildung übermittelt wird als das aufzubauen, was er ist, was er sein soll: Persönlichkeit."[14]

At least one function and goal of literature becomes clear here, that is, the process and development of individuation and self-realization. Although limited to the symbol of the "muse" and its interpretation from a Jungian viewpoint, one of the first essays of this volume focuses on an important problem of this process, the problem of literary creativity. But in spite of all limitations, this opening essay by Mario Jacobi points to one of the central problems in dealing with the anagogic qualities of literature and at the same time indicates their essential role for literature in general.

In contemporary literary criticism the term "anagogic" is nowhere used so often and has nowhere such an important meaning as in the critical work of Northrop Frye. However, it is there seen more as an aspect of criticism than of literature, although Frye states that anagoge is to be "discovered chiefly in the more uninhibited utterances of poets themselves" and is usually found in "direct connection with religion."[15] Frye furthermore does not distinguish between the exoteric and the esoteric sides of religions, even though he implies an esoteric viewpoint when he states that the literary symbol seen anagogically "is a monad, all symbols being united in a single infinite and eternal verbal symbol which is, as *dianoia*, the *Logos*, and, as *mythos*, total creative act."[16] The significance of a specific level of symbolism in connection with literature's anagogic qualities is shown in yet another basic essay of this volume, in the contribution of O. K. Nambiar.

Frye's use of the term "anagogic" is similar to but not identical with the use of the word in our context. Frye is of course methodologically correct in pointing out the autonomy of both forms, those of religion as well as those of literature, when he states: "The close resemblance between the conceptions of anagogic criticism and those of religion has led many to assume that they can only be related by making one supreme and the other subordinate. Those who choose religion, like Coleridge, will, like him, try to make criticism a natural theology; those who choose culture, like Arnold, will try to reduce religion to objectified cultural myth. But for the purity of each the autonomy of each must be guaranteed."[17] Something, however, should be added here. Of course both forms, be it religion and culture or be it religion and literature, are in a certain way autonomous and yet are both bound in their patterns and development by temporary social and historical developments; but on the other hand both are driven by the same timeless powers of that perennial "fountainhead" which embraces both. Ultimately, both forms are expressions of powers stemming from this fountainhead, and it is these powers which, beyond all ephemeral changes and differentiations, serve to make the anagogic "anagogic."

JOSEPH P. STRELKA

November, 1970

Notes

1. Garma C. C. Chang, *Teachings of Tibetan Yoga* (New Hyde Park, New York, 1963), p. 11.
2. Wing-Tsit Chan, trans. and comp., *A Source Book in Chinese Philosophy* (Princeton, 1963), p. 315.
3. Mircea Eliade, *Patterns in Comparative Religion* (London and New York, 1958).
4. Cf., for example, *The Mystic Vision*, Papers from the Eranos Yearbooks, vol. 6, Bollingen Series XXX, Joseph Campbell, ed. (Princeton, 1968).
5. Zenkei Shibayama, *A Flower does not talk* (Rutland, Vermont, and Tokyo, 1970), p. 6.
6. Ibid., p. 5.
7. Hermann Broch, *Erkennen und Handeln* (Zürich, 1955), p. 83–89; *Die Schuldlosen* (Zürich, 1950), pp. 359–365.
8. Broch, *Erkennen und Handeln*, pp. 203–255.
9. Broch, *Erkennen und Handeln*, pp. 172–181; *Dichten und Erkennen* (Zürich, 1955), pp. 211–238, 311–350.
10. Broch, *Dichten und Erkennen*, pp. 239–275.
11. Stanley Romaine Hopper, *Spiritual Problems in Contemporary Literature* (Eromstown, N.Y. and London, 1957). The essay, "Mysticism as a Solution to the Poets Dilemma" is on pp. 95–115 in this book.
12. Hopper, *Spiritual Problems in Contemporary Literature*, p. 108.

13. Horst Rüdiger, "Winckelmann's Personality," in *Johann Joachim Winckelmann 1768/1968*, edited by Internationes, (Bad Godesberg, 1968), p. 20–39. See also Walter Mueller-Seidel, *Probleme der literarischen Wertung*, ch. 2 about "Das Hoehere," (Stuttgart, 1965), p. 59–85.
14. Broch: *Dichten und Erkennen*, p. 236.
15. Northrop Frye, *Anatomy of Criticism*, (New York, 1966), p. 122.
16. Frye, p. 121.
17. Ibid, pp. 126 f.

GENERAL PROBLEMS

Stanley Romaine Hopper

"LE CRI DE MERLIN!" OR INTERPRETATION AND THE METALOGICAL

> When the stone was finished, I looked at it again, wondering about it and asking myself what lay behind my impulse to carve it.
> The stone stands outside the Tower, and is like an explanation of it. It is a manifestation of the occupant, but one which remains incomprehensible to others. Do you know what I wanted to chisel in the back face of the stone? "*Le cri de Merlin*!"
>
> —C. G. Jung

THE CONTEMPORARY LITERARY ARTIST PARTICIPATES RADICALLY, EVEN agonistically, in the deep revision of the Western consciousness that is going on about us. He is thrust, by the nature of his calling, into that resonating void between that which has ceased to be and that which is not yet: and there, like Eliot's penitent in the place "where three dreams cross," he suffers his ambivalent beseeching—"And let my cry come unto Thee."[1]

This cry is not unrelated to that of Merlin in Jung's surprising anecdote. Jung dedicated his Tower at Bollingen in 1950. His "stone" had been ordered to serve as a cornerstone, but, when delivered, it was a square block instead of a triangular stone. The mason would have rejected it; but Jung exclaimed, "No, that is my stone. I must have it."

On one side of it he carved the verse of the alchemist, Arnaldus de Villanova (d. 1313):

> Here stands the mean, uncomely stone,
> 'Tis very cheap in price!
> The more it is despised by fools,
> The more loved by the wise.[2]

It is the alchemist's stone, the *lapis*, which, "despised and rejected," is referred to here.[3] The Grail itself, in the text of Wolfram von Eschenbach, is referred to as a stone, as the *lapis exilis*. When Jung looked upon the stone, he tells us, it reminded him of Merlin's life in the forest of Broceliande, after he had vanished from the Table Round. "Men still hear his cries, so the legend runs, but they cannot understand or interpret them."[4]

From these fragments it is clear that Jung's anecdote is double-pointed. As an analogy and as a confessional identification of himself with Merlin, it tells us a great deal about Jung; but as an anecdote or cryptic charade, it tells us a great deal about ourselves and about our time. From either perspective it says much and says little, and also says much in little. It is an "explanation" and a "manifestation," but it remains "incomprehensible." It is a conundrum. Yet it is precisely on these terms that it promises to be useful. "The dreams clash and are shattered,"[5] as Pound says, which in itself, as a parable of our times, is salutary.

I

If we take first the anecdote as analogy, Jung explains to us that Merlin "represents an attempt by the medieval unconscious to create a parallel figure to Parsifal." He regards Parsifal as a Christian hero, and Merlin as his "dark brother." Merlin, the anti-type to Parsifal, was the son of the devil and a pure virgin; but the twelfth century's categories for thought (even anagogic thought) provided no means whereby Merlin's depth significance could be grasped in this way. Hence, Merlin "ended in exile" and his cry still sounded in the forest (Gawain, questing there, recognized the voice as that of Merlin) after his person had vanished to be seen no more. "This cry that no one could understand," argues Jung, "implies that he lives on in unredeemed form. His story is not yet finished, and he still walks abroad."[6]

But if Merlin still walks abroad, it may well be in forms so strange and unexpected that we can scarcely recognize him.

Jung's special interpretation of this gnomic parable now follows. Merlin's secret was carried on in alchemy, represented primarily by the figure of Mercurius; and, in our time, Jung himself has carried it further by way of his psychology of the unconscious—which, as he is careful to point out, is still not understood because people as a rule are reluctant to come into very close quarters with the unconscious.

The *ad hominem* elements in this interpretation are apparent. Nevertheless, Merlin was not a persistent figure in Jung's writing. There are but two other references to him, I believe, in Jung's published works, both of these occurring in his essay on *The Phenomenology of the Spirit in Fairy Tales.* Merlin is presented in these passages as an image of the Wise Old Man—something of a seer, guru, magician, doctor, priest, teacher, shaman, and the like, images in every way agreeable, we must suppose, to Jung in this sudden appraisal of his life's role. These images are favorable, positive, "pointing upwards"; but, in his theory of archetypes, Jung makes due allowance for their negative characteristics. The archetypes may also be unfavorable, negative, chthonic, "pointing downwards." Taken together (the positive *and* the negative) they symbolize "the spiritual factor." They exhibit also the basic characteristics of the unconscious, "whose contents are without exception paradoxical or antinomial by nature, not excluding the category of being."[7] Thus the Wise Old Man may appear at times as good incarnate; at others he is the wicked magician, the bewitching wizard with his bag of tricks.

It is not essential that we should concur altogether in Jung's evaluation of his Merlin role in the first half of our century. Certainly contemporary literature, in all its forms, and in both its conscious appropriation and in its unconscious confirmation, substantiates impressively his claim; and criticism which makes any pretense at being thorough will seem parochial and limited, no matter how sophisticated in formal ways, if it omits from its account the insight and wisdom (including a revision of its categories) made possible by Jung and other explorers in the field of human consciousness. Jung's main point is clear: something was omitted from the medieval way of seeing things which made it partial and one-sided. Jung summarizes this ascetic excess in the figure of Parsifal.

I should wish to go further. It would seem that the defect was in the classical-Christian intellectualistic commitment itself, which was subtly rationalistic, literalistic (or allegorical), dualistic, and dogmatic. For this, Merlin was the compensatory antitype, along with certain mystics, tricksters, troubadours, and literary moralists who fell eccentrically outside the larger synthesis, or who, like Reynard the Fox and Tyl Eulenspiegel, tampered with its large sobrieties in a mode of spoofery and Rabelaisian effrontery that kept the Aristotelian intellect on its hierarchical ladder in some slight and dubious (or virtuous) imbalance. The symbol system elaborated from that matrix was compendious and splendid, and there was magic in it for a time, the mysteries were present there; but something was omitted or repressed in it, the symbols hardened and became overt, and at last they crumbled and have fallen now into the deep collective unconscious.

Today, we begin to see the thrusting up of fresh symbolic designations—strange, as art is strange, cryptic as our literature undertakes a quest for sacred objects that it knows not how to name. The literary artist today knows that something has gone from our traditional culture consciousness. Something is gone from our common life and from our common symbols. Our heritage of Wisdom, so to speak, has vanished from our ways of thinking and seeing. Like Arthur and his knights, we stand bereft and desolate, with our lances and our arms akimbo. We feel abashed and disconcerted, insofar as we remain clad in our medieval trappings, when the hunting horns have died and the mythic procession of a former world has swept around our table like the fairy figures conjured up by Merlin as a challenge to the Table Round. At times we feel, when our poetry is candid, that we have also lost the meaning of the hunt. We stand, as we say, "between the times," where "meaning" has gone from us. It is present neither in the "broken images" of the archetypal canon of our classical inheritance, nor in the empirical "objectivities" that would replace them. We occupy, as Joseph Campbell has so trenchantly put it, "this precious moment between two engrams." We appear, he says,

> to have broken the celestial enchantment that enthralled mankind for six thousand years, and to be offering, now, a new Alpha and Omega: a new image, a new engram, for the center of our mandala. . . .[8]

Our task now is to penetrate, if possible, "to that void 'between two thoughts' from which the symbols come. . . ." It is here, we would suggest, that Merlin's cry can still be heard.

II

If we turn now from the more obvious analogies whereby Jung adroitly celebrates his life's achievements and notes the over-intellectualization of the Western consciousness, we are struck by what is enigmatic in it, by what is unsaid (and which constitutes its lure), by the clearing that it makes or opens up within our thinking. It comes before us now as anecdote, leading straightway to its unexpected conundrum of "the cry." As analogy, or allegory, it is about Jung and his sense of what has been omitted from the Western consciousness. But when heard as anecdote, Jung becomes a person in its drama. The little drama is not *about him*; it is about *us*! We are distributed or refracted (like "persons in the drama") into all the drama's parts, becoming Jung, Parsifal, Merlin, the medieval consciousness in its pageantry of quest, just as we are also the failure of its ideal, and Merlin's "exile," and Gawain's shadow hearing Merlin's cryptic cry. We are this, very likely, by analogy and metaphoric identification: but, as distinct from conventional rhetoric, we are this by analogies internal to the movement of the anecdote and by analogies internal to ourselves in our "own" predicament. We are this, by anagogic identification, by an identification in depth: almost as though traditional rhetoric, sustained by classical intellectualism and a dualistic religious consciousness were suddenly internalized, and the ancient questing for the Grail had now become the necessary search in deepest inwardness for "meaning" and identity. Or (to use an image which will seem at first to mix the metaphor, but which in terms of psychological verity does not), it is as though the "cry" were only now just *surfacing*—coming to awareness, that is, in our uncertain consciousness.

For it is not Merlin, but Merlin's "cry," that makes of this anecdote a conundrum, making it on the one hand a parable of our time's condition, and on the other a *koan* interrogating me and riddling me out of my clichés of conventional commitment and drawing me upon Baudelaire's "*Gouffre*" or Pascal's "abyss." Suddenly, if I am not prepared for this, "Je ne vois qu'infini par toutes les fenêtres. . . ."[9] or, at the very least, the cry sounds cryptic and strange. It is cryptic, because Merlin is largely lost to us (Dr. Seuss and the Wizard of Oz are nearer), and his "cry" means nothing. Yet this "cry" solicits me. My "consciousness" keeps returning to it, as it does to the unknown, sensing a secret there. At the same time, as Jung surmised, the "cry" retains its riddle effectively within itself, which also is a lure to the unconscious. It is spoken in French, which adds nothing to its content; it simply removes the secret one step further from us, adding one more transparency, making it strange, more cabbalistic, more enticingly concealed in its own internal meaning. And it is strange because our epoch seems so radically disenchanted with the medieval scheme of things, as though the *modus intellectualis* of the Platonic-Christian hierarchical principle and the Aristotelian rhetoric implicit in it had at last run out. "No symbolism is acceptable," the modern poet says.[10] "Get the meaning across and then quit!" advises Ezra Pound.[11]

But then, that is just the problem. The question as to what is meaningful, or the question as to how (and in what way) things mean, or the question as to what the question is that we are asking when we ask what is meaningful—all this is just the question. "Getting it across" expresses our impatience with the former rhetorics, but it is a real problem whether Pound's demand does not itself unwittingly pertain to our traditional rhetoric (only crisper and mounted disjunctly in a seeming *collage*). "I cannot make it cohere," he laments in Canto CXVI, whereas a new way of seeing (i.e., "making it new") requires a new *logos*, a new grammar of awareness.

"Thought" reaches here its own impasse. It is at the end of its classical "tether"—to borrow a metaphor from Plato's *Meno*, where the question is posed in its acutest form. Or, in the idiom of Wallace Stevens:

> . . . there lies at the end of thought
> A foyer of the spirit in a landscape
> Of the mind, in which we sit
> And wear humanity's bleak crown.[12]

It has slowly been borne in upon us that we occupy today such a "crude foyer" of the spirit which lies at the end of "thought." Deprived suddenly of the former reference systems, we feel paradoxically both released and frustrate: the place, or *topos*, at which the Western consciousness has arrived seems barren, and the crown that rewards our sophistication's breakthrough seems bleak.

This bleakness may be of two kinds. It may be the bleakness of *The Waste Land,* an aridity of spirit we have come to understand quite well. Its cross-stitch anecdote—*April is the cruellest month* out of Chaucer and Gawain at the empty chapel—has been rehearsed now many times, and its cry, "*shantih,*" still turns inward on the Thunder's emptiness.[13] Aridity is plain, the drouth is tangible; it presupposes its symbolic opposite.

The other bleakness is more difficult. It is more radical. On the one hand, "no symbolism is acceptable." But on the other, the surfacing of Merlin's "cry" in the literature of our time signifies that we realize today more keenly than we have ever done that we live within a symbolic reality. Whether we think of this in terms of "standpoint" philosphy, or a philosophy of symbolic forms, or mythopoiesis, or "world hypotheses," or "master images," or archetypes of the unconscious, or radical metaphor, or "models," or "fields," or "frames of reference," or "language games," or "the global village," or the "house of being," the same point is being made. Our "thinking"—religious, philosophical, literary—belongs to "that prodigious net of numinous creation in which man is captured, although he himself has brought it forth" (Erich Neumann).[14] This is the puzzling paradox of our present *topos.* On the one hand we perceive the failure of the former symbol systems. What a pity, says Ezra Pound,

> . . . that poets have used symbol and metaphor and no man learned anything from them for their speaking in figures.[15]

But on the other hand we have become aware of the ubiquity of the "as" structures of knowing—the *as*-structures *as "a constitutive state for understanding, existential* and *a priori.*"[16]

Here again, we appear to have reached a certain impasse. On the one hand, symbolic or metaphoric speaking seems unavoidable; on the other, our awareness that our language is at bottom metaphorical seems to pull the rug from under speech as having any dependable *meaning* whatsoever. "Every concept," as Santayana once remarked, "is framed in its own irony."[17]

Let us note, however, *en passant,* that our use of the phrase *dependable meaning* obscures the problem at issue here, prevents it in fact from arising. For the question at issue is precisely what modes of speech are meaningful (the former reference systems having dropped away), and what it is precisely that we are asking for when we ask that such meaning should be "dependable." This fluctuation, this unconscious reinstatement of former criteria in the light of a radical question, is not surprising; it is, in fact, to be expected in the time of the "between," and is an evidence of it. In the time when

> The grail broken
> the light gone from the glass,
> we would make it
> anew.

From the thought of the smasht gold or silver cup
once raised to the lips
we would raise *shadows* to hold the blood the drinkers
desire so. . . .[18]

Clearly something of Merlin's "cry" can be heard here; but, as Jung says, it is not understood! That is, today's poet is caught in the above dilemma. He would raise *shadows* of former verities, symbol systems, reference syndromes, to hold the blood (of the crucified? of mutilated humanity? of death? of sacrifice? of healing? of reality?) for which our time secretly longs. But one feels how these *shadows* are lost like Merlin in the enchanted forest of former correspondences, analogues now lapsed and wishful, unless radically recast. If the poet stopped here, his speech would be already enervated from within by the movement of recession of the symbol system that contains his words. But in what follows, the poet undertakes to pass from the knowledge that "There was a land and a time in which we were . . ." to the recognition that

There *is* [italics mine] a land and a time—Morgan le Fay's—
marsh and river country, her smoky strand
in whose lewd files I too have passt. to
tell the beads of that story again.

This is an important passage, for in it the poet attempts to transpose his key, to move from his initial *analogy* with the grail quest (while also retaining it as "objective correlative") over to an *anecdote* of passage—the poet's passage as the necessary hero of our time, questing for "the maiden carrying the bleeding head" and dreading much the unavoidable encounter (within) with the "red man" of these dismaying times—"For I dread me sore to pass this forest. . . ." What ensues becomes the crucial part (for if the poem succeeds it must ensue in each of us):

. . . They brought forth
certain wonders he did not remember what
and among those shadows
the shadowy cup passt.

Thus the poem ends in irony or in conundrum. If the former, it remains caught within the net of the former hierarchical analogue (among its shadows); if the latter, the problem and its parabolic enigma is passed along to me, the reader. I must appropriate it to my own consciousness and question not the poem but myself as confronted with its deeper anecdotal cry. Jung's view is thus confirmed. The medieval consciousness, with its projected symbols, did not comprehend the Merlin dimension, and the shadowy cup passed.

Today also, a re-projection of the former symbol patterns becomes a projection of symbols twice removed. But to bring *this* to awareness is also to raise *shadows* in the Jungian sense of the term. It is to bring the repressed side of the collective psyche into consciousness which awareness may itself turn out to contain what the poet later calls "the blood of the Real." Thus the *translation* of yesterday's symbolic structures into a new anagogy in depth (by way of the parabolic conundrum) may effect a breakthrough into new awareness.

But does this poem of Robert Duncan's achieve this? Does it effect the translation which such a breakthrough must require? Or does it remain trapped within its own reflexivity and become emptied through a perpetual return upon its own internal irony? It observes that a world —a symbol system—is gone from us. The poet today would make it new. He would at least raise shadows of that former glory to hold the blood of the Real. But if the poet is to manage this, he must traverse within himself those "lewd files" in our present world if the "beads" of that story are to be told again.

Interestingly enough, a very recent study of the meaning of modern art has appraised the work of Jung in almost identical terms, arguing that his conception of man provides his readers with an ideal that "promises release from the burdens of individuality"; and that

> It is here, rather than in his scholarly achievement, that the source of Jung's popularity must be sought. Jung is another *ludi magister*, manipulating symbols that are almost dead in order to catch an echo of the language of the dead gods. Where gods have become silent, man can at least dream of them, and in his dreams recover their shadows.[19]

Were we to accept this appraisal, we should have to say that Duncan's poem and Jung's depth psychology are both vitiated or enervated in the same way—by the attempt to make vivid, through craft and adroit manipulation, symbols that have died and whose echoes only can be caught by their shadows in our dreams. Jung's appeal to "*le cri de Merlin*!" would seem to be the very epitome of this wishful compromise —if read as *analogy* and *not* as *anecdote*. As anecdote, however, Merlin's cry deprives me of my classical sanctuary (the perspective from which the above appraisal is made, though the mystery of Merlin's cry is hiding undetected behind almost every term of the appraisal). Jung's point is that *Merlin* (as literalistic myth) is dispensable, whereas his cry is not. But the criticism does point to a problem, a problem that is *resident in our language as such*. Quite simply, the language of the Western consciousness is predominantly Hellenic and Aristotelian, and the *modus intellectualis*—whether as grammar, or as logic, or as metaphysics—is internal to it. It is a question whether this language is susceptible of mutations as radical as those now required of it: required that is by a new cosmological setting and a new understanding of man. To this problem we must now turn.

On Robert Duncan's behalf, however, let us note that the way of the poet for him is no "release from the burdens of individuality"; for, while he would acknowledge that the poet may (perhaps must) indeed be a *magister ludi* ("there is trickery in the very nature of creation itself; innovation can only come from what we do not know"),[20] he combines the Hellenic *poiein* ("making a world of the poem") with the Celtic view of the poet as bard ("the chant that enchants, the myth or tale as *spell*. . . ") plus a "Jewish" strand—"where song comes to David's lips, not fashioned, but as the voice moves him." And there is yet a fourth part—a Judaeo-Christian part, more central even than all the rest, held radically against the background of a universe which "strives to be what it truly is to be"; or, in theological language, "God strives in all Creation to come to Himself." His viewpoint is, on the one hand, incarnational, holding that "the Word is for me living Flesh, and the body of my own thought and feeling, my own presence, becomes the vehicle for the process of genetic information". And, on the other, this view is an acceptance in "a new key" of the theological anagogical anecdote in depth, in which the poet "greets as truth," in its deepest mythic poetic sense, the "proclamation of the Son" which identifies the Wrathful Father of the Old Testament with the "First Person of Love. As Chaos, the Yawning Abyss, is First Person of form. And the Poet, too, like the Son, in this myth of Love or Form, must go deep into the reality of His own Nature, into the Fathering Chaos or Wrath, to suffer His own Nature. In this mystery of the art, the Son's cry to the Father might be too the cry of the artist to the form he obeys."[21]

Here too "*Le cri de Merlin*!" is being heard; but it is not yet understood.

III

To precipitate the problem abruptly (it being conceded that there is a depleting circularity, or benumbing reflexivity in the foregoing *recueil* of inflections gathered about a voice that has vanished and a "cry" that is not yet understood), there is a fine statement by Martin Heidegger which occurs at the end of one of his key meditations on "Identity and Difference." Here he argues that our

> difficulty lies in language. Our Western languages are languages of metaphysical thinking, each in its own way. It must remain an open question whether the nature of Western languages is in itself marked with the exclusive brand of metaphysics, and thus marked permanently by onto-theo-logic, or whether these languages offer other possibilities of utterance —and that means at the same time of a telling silence.[22]

Now certainly we cannot hope to undertake an exposition of Heidegger's quest for a "fundamental ontology" in the compass of this brief essay; but there is no question whatever that Heidegger's question about our Western languages is related directly to the questions concerning Western logic and metaphysics, and these in turn presuppose the Aristotelian "principle of identity" which lies at their base, and this question lies directly in the path of our problem. "I cannot make it cohere," Ezra Pound complains. But he is trying to "make it new," to make language speak in ways it has not been speaking, to petition other models of meaning, to see whether our Western languages "offer other possibilities of utterance," to explore ("I dread me sore to pass this forest") other modes of coherence. All of this Pound dimly sees (though its meaning is not yet understood): he seeks "to affirm the gold thread in the pattern," and

> . . . it coheres all right
> even if my notes do not cohere.[23]

The cry that he hears is what coheres: that which lies behind, beyond, within, and around what he is talking about is what coheres. He alludes to it, and attempts to capture it, in many ways. In this context, it is "the great acorn of light."[24] It coheres all right, but not in the ways of "Western metaphysics."

In quite a different idiom Wallace Stevens confesses to the same difficulty:

> I cannot bring a world quite round,
> Although I patch it as I can.
>
> I sing a hero's head, large eye
> And bearded bronze, but not a man,

Although I patch him as I can
And reach through him almost to man. . . .[25]

Yet this passion for "other possibilities of utterance," for fresh visions of order, is essential to his calling.

Oh! Blessed rage for order, pale Ramon,
The maker's rage to order words of the sea,
Words of the fragrant portals, dimly-starred,
And of ourselves and of our origins,
In ghostlier demarcations, keener sounds.[26]

Heidegger's initial point is that if we are to explore radically and so place ourselves in the position of discovering "other possibilities of utterance," we must first of all *step back* from the modes of Western metaphysics. This is a matter of great difficulty, for this is what we "know." But we are helped today into this possibility by the recession of the former symbolic systems, by what Nietzsche called the "death of God," or by the fallaciousness of what Kierkegaard termed "Christendom" (as distinct from Christianity). We are helped by inhabiting the time of the "between"—the time in which, as Heidegger quotes from Hölderlin, "God's failure helps." For the "God" of Western metaphysics (or of onto-theo-logical thinking) has prevented God's *logos* from being heard; or, if heard by someone wandering or questing through the forest, it has not been understood, has indeed been misunderstood and misconstrued by being thought in the framework of Western metaphysics. A "transformation of the frame" is essential, for the frame, as Heidegger points out, "is more real than all of atomic energy and the whole world of machinery, etc."[27] The "frame" sets the "horizon" within which we see all that we see: it is made up of our uncriticized assumptions as well as of our picture of relations.

The "step back" and the "transformation" of the frame must be brought about by our letting go of the very "attitude" of "representational thinking" implicit in the rationalistic modes of Western metaphysics. This step is like a "leap" out of the attitude, since one cannot argue one's way out of the dilemma on the basis of the assumptions one is trying to gain a release from.

Is this leap, Heidegger asks, necessarily then a leap or a spring into an abyss (such as that of Baudelaire, or Pascal, noted above)? And he answers,

> Yes, as long as we represent the spring in the horizon of metaphysical thinking.

But the answer may also be

> No, insofar as we spring and let go. Where to? To where we already have access: the belonging to Being.[28]

Now this is the point in which, literarily speaking, the dreams cross or collide and are shattered; this is the either/or of present ambiguities and ironies so characteristic of contemporary letters; this is the Rubicon of contemporary consciousness, the pass at Thermopylae, the point of no return, or the point where we

> "Blind eyes and shadows"
> [are] to enter the presence at sunrise
> up out of hell, from the labyrinth
> the path wide as a hair. . . .[29]

This is the point which Stevens refers to (in a poem on metaphor) as "the change of key . . . the difficult difference."[30]

This is the point also at which contemporary literature exhibits everywhere its agony of passage, and where we see in our literary evidences how the step back from the modes of Western metaphysics is being made. What Heidegger describes as the necessary step back is already taking place (has indeed already taken place up to a point in poetry, drama, and the novel). But it is "not yet understood," and perhaps will not be understood until it is seen how the problem of language so posed relates intrinsically to the metaphysical problem of identity.

One cannot do justice to Heidegger's analysis here, but a quick summary is essential, inasmuch as the key to the history of Western thought is to be found in this principle. Parmenides' famous *Fragment*,[31] τὸ γάρ ἀυτὸ νοεῖν ἐστιν τε και εἶναι, was construed historically as "Thinking and Being are the same"—thus projecting Western metaphysics along intellectualistic lines. This identification of thought with Being had the effect (decisive for the Western tradition) of dissociating thinking and its projected structures from Being, which, to Heidegger, was a misconstruction of Parmenides' saying. This led to a "forgetting of Being" in the West, and a separation of thought from its ground.

For Heidegger, what is intended here (in Parmenides) is the expression of a *relation* between Being and thinking, in which Being is to be grasped by man through a *setting before one* of that which is *as* it is; but at the same time Being is a relation in which *that which is as it is* is springing up, growing, emerging (since *being* derives from the Greek root, φύω).[32] Both terms of the relation are necessary (Parmenides, Fr. B); it supposes a λέγειν (a speaking or saying that is also a gathering, an arranging) as much as a grasping of the thing in its being.[33] Such a oneness is a unity, or a belonging-together, of opposites. Being comes out of hiding, as it were, precisely in this occurrence of the coming together of thought and being after the manner of their original and primordial oneness.

To put it more simply, in the classical view, identity is regarded as a characteristic of Being; but in Heidegger's view it is regarded as a property of the "event of appropriation." To effect this shift I must step back from the principle as a statement about identity and spring into the belonging-togetherness of man and being, into "the essential origin of identity."[34] Once this "spring" has been made, or once the radical difference between the two orientations for thought is grasped, thinking itself will have undergone a *transformation*, such a transformation in fact as our modern poets have been trying to effect. For, as Heidegger recognizes, "in the event of appropriation vibrates the active nature of what speaks as language, which at one time was called the house of Being."

The focus here upon language is clearly central, for the "event of appropriation" is "that realm, vibrating within itself," whereby both man and Being come to occurrence first by "reaching each other in their nature" and then by "losing those qualities with which metaphysics has endowed them." This is effected through language from which thinking "receives the tools" for the kind of "self-suspended structure" which makes the spring into the relation possible. For, says Heidegger,

> language is the most delicate and thus the most susceptible vibration holding everything within the suspended structure of the appropriation. We dwell in the appropriation inasmuch as our active nature is given over to language.[35]

In the same way, man (no longer objectified as a "rational animal") comes to know who he is and what he is:

> For we begin to learn what man is only when we analyze that point where man steps into the ring of being for a "set-to" (*Auseinandersetzung*) with things (*Seienden*); for only then does man project something new, only then does he poetize in a primordial fashion (*ursprünglich dichtet*).[36]

Being, in the "event of appropriation," is, so to speak, a coming to utterance.

But—another paradox! Only as the step back procures for us a greater and greater distance from the clichéd frames (in this case, of metaphysics) "does *what is near* [my italics] give itself as such," only then "does nearness achieve its first radiance."[37] Only then do we become aware that "we do not reside sufficiently . . . where in reality we already are."[38]

Heidegger is aware of the difficulties in this manner of speaking. He knows that in order really to think of Being profoundly we must think of it *in its difference* with beings (which is not the same as abstracting from particulars). Being itself (as the mystics tell us) overwhelms us (comes over us); but, as Heidegger says, Being *beings*, it is transitive, it *arrives*, it arrives in beings. And we establish here, in our thinking (as we try to represent this relation), a difference, a "between"—between Being and beings. Here, paradoxically, Being *overwhelms* in its unconcealing coming-over; but in beings it *arrives* in a manner that keeps itself concealed in unconcealedness.[39] In this paradoxical realization we see that that which overwhelms and that which arrives are at once held apart from each other (by our representation of difference, of the "between") and made to face each other by reason of the nearness, the belonging together of that unity of opposites which is more primordial than the difference inherent in my representation of that which arrives. Thus we have, via Heidegger:

the overwhelming   the arrival of Being
of Being   in beings
held apart and held toward
one another
in
the perdurance of the two
in unconcealing keeping in
concealment.[40]

This interesting paradigm, when translated from the jargon of formal thinking to that of modern poetry, may very well appear as follows:

heaven   earth
in the center
in
juniper. . . .

The poetry is Pound's again.[41] It is doubtless what Pound is trying to say. But, though the cry is heard, it is not yet understood. It could also be put in another way, in the form of the anecdote, or in the form of utterance which contains "a telling silence":

> A student asked his Zen master: "If the Buddha is more than Siddhartha Gotama, who lived many centuries ago, then tell me, please, what is the real nature of the Buddha?"
> The teacher replied: "The blossoming branch of a plum tree."

IV

There is a sense, now, in which we have taken the "step back" from "Western metaphysics," of which Heidegger speaks—aided by Jung's conundrum accepted as anecdote, by Heidegger's translation of the principle of identity into the "new key" of eventful appropriation, and by the *koan* technique of dramatizing the impropriety of the basic irrelevance, amounting to unconscious but systematic evasion, of our conventional questions. The "cry" in contemporary letters can now, at least, be heard.

It is not a small matter. "Who, if I cried, would hear me among the angelic orders?" pleads Rilke; and the *Elegies*, and the *Sonnets* too, are a response to this cry. It is the "Hail, cry hail!" of the sometimes "scrawny cry" of Stevens' poetry. It is Hopkin's "inscape" and Joyce's "epiphany" and Yeats' struggle with the "*daimon*," and Lorca's wrestle with the "*duende*." It is the utterance, sometimes in anguish, sometimes in joy, that comes from the poet's penetration into that "between" described with such difficulty by Heidegger. The cry is one of anguish when the "between" appears as an Abyss; but when one discovers that it is precisely out of the Abyss that Being comes into presence, the cry becomes one of emergent joy. This means that the modes of the Western consciousness are today being radically qualified in the direction of new ways of seeing. It also means that the creative artist stands between yesterday's clichéd rhetorical requirements and his call to go questing for new possibilities of utterance. It is for this reason that the art of our time "is turned inward" and "inclines toward a radical spiritualism,"[42] or why the artist attempts, as Kandinsky says, to reach "the secret soul" or "the inner being of things."[43] Paradoxically, it makes for what some critics have called a "new realism."

Three aspects of this turn to new vision may be noted.

First, there is the sense of a new immediateness. The presentation of the *juniper* and the *blossoming branch of the plum tree* are attempts to let the thing *be*—what it is and as it is, unadorned and unembellished by any Aristotelian metaphors of likeness; it is also an attempt to get us to *see* the thing as it is and for what it is. By the same token there is no "analogy of being" operative here, as in Plato or Plotinus, inviting us to "mount upwards" from image to image until we grasp ecstatically "that form entire," that "Beauty absolute" which is the otherworldly goal of the hierarchical vision. Not that there is no Plotinus in Ezra Pound; there is, in fact, a great deal, but for him the "body is inside the soul," and not vice versa.[44] His *light* symbolism (one of the central clues to his "coherence"), while numinous and mystical, does not lead away from the object, but points *into* the object, as it were, in order to unconceal there (to import the Heideggerian terms) the arrival of Being.

> Lux enim—
>   versus this tempest.
> The marble form in the pine wood,
>   The shrine seen and not seen
> From the roots of sequoias[45]

Though he owes much to Dante, and to other practitioners in light, he complains that

> Their mania is a lusting for farness
> Blind to the olive leaf,
>   not seeing the oak's veins.[46]

What he aims at is "exactness," without that metaphorical fusion of things that we see in Baudelaire's "évangile des correspondences,"[47] or in Mallarme's strategies of indirection. When Pound uses a straight metaphor he manages to preserve the discreteness and independence of the terms in the comparison:

> The water-bug's mittens
>   petal the rock beneath. . . .[48]

Here the likeness of *mittens* is extended metaphorically *through* the term *petal* used as a verb, making the comparison both vivid and explicit without compromising the integrity, at any point, of the particulars used in the comparison. Thus we have a coinciding of opposites, setting up a creative and liberating tension between the terms distributed in ideographic placements upon the page. We do indeed have a *coincidentia oppositorum* (so central to Heraclitus, to Nicholas of Cusa, to Pascal, and to Coleridge); but whereas Coleridge holds that the poet "diffuses a tone and spirit of unity, that blends, and (as it were) fuses, each into each," by the power of imagination,[49] Pound sets up by way of his ideographic language a system of relations which interact in a "field" of tensions and resonances, and in such a way as to effect recognitions or awareness of the dynamic dance of relations (in the zone where Being arrives) making new all those things in the relation. Actually the new is sought here through the relations but also beyond the relation. Pound does not always succeed in this (and the same is often true of W. C. Williams, E. E. Cummings, and Robert Duncan as above). Sometimes the objects on his page lie dormant, without interaction, integers of difference that set up no resonance of relation. Ideally, Pound's lesser ideographs would combine into larger and larger ideographic inclusions, until the entire poem would have the contour and pattern of a single ideogram. (Just as, in The Rikugien Garden in Tokyo, the paths and flowers and trees are placed superbly about an interior pool, which pool is shaped like the Chinese character for "mind." *Rikugien* refers to the six principles for composing Oriental poems.) The dimension of inwardness is often lacking in Pound's occasionally arbitrary locutions. He says: "God's eye art 'ou, do not surrender perception."[50] But perception is not recognition. Recognition without perception is empty; perception without recognition is blind. Recognition comes through penetration into that "between," where Being is unconcealed in the concealment of beings. But this penetration is not secured merely by my *perceiving* the "difference"; rather, as Heidegger says, I must "leap" into this between, and "see as God sees" (Rilke), or, in the case of the poem, stand *within* the magnetic field of the elements in tension, and see as the poem sees. As Rilke puts it, "Who pours himself forth as a spring, him Cognizance knows"[51]—or, recognition re-cognizes (*den erkennt die Erkennung*). What is miraculous here in the moment of recognition is the sudden sense of identification with that which is beyond conceptualization. It is not unlike the story of Pythagoras, who at Delphi caught sight of the shield of Achilles, which was the votive offering, and swooned with the cry, "My shield!"

V

But this implies an anagogy in depth. This comes increasingly before us when we consider the second aspect of the turn in modern literature to a new vision: to its sense of "presencing." "Reality is presential," wrote Philip Wheelwright.[52] "By this I mean something fairly close to what Rudolph Otto has called 'the numinous.' "[53] This is the metalogical element in contemporary letters that we have been noting from the beginning of this essay, and which I associate also with Northrop Frye's statement:

> When poet and critic pass from the archetypal to the anagogic phase, they enter a phase of which only religion, or something as infinite in its range as religion, can possibly form an external goal.[54]

I quarrel only with the term 'external" in the phrase "external goal." For neither the goal of the poem nor the goal of religion is external. Should the metaphor of the "kingdom" be taken as religion's goal, it is a kingdom of the spirit, held inwardly, not sociologically. Should the metaphor of "literary universe" be taken as the poem's goal of "total identity" then the poem is itself a radical metaphor and the "cry" of Being—the place (topos) where Being as Logos comes to utterance. To distinguish poetry and religion at this point of anagogic depth is philosophically arbitrary; that is, the distinction participates in "Western metaphysics." It shuns the leap into the "between," where Identity remains a characteristic of Being instead of becoming an event of appropriation. In the old rhetoric *logic* presides via syllogistic exactness; in the new grammar Logos presides as utterance in the realm of the "difference" between Being and beings: it *presences* there as *Mythos* or as radical metaphor containing the opposites—an unconcealing that at the same time necessarily conceals.[55] Nevertheless it can surely be said that "the literary universe . . . is a universe in which everything is potentially identical with everything else."[56] I only add that contemporary literature is effecting a *translatio* of this awareness into ontology itself, which means that at its depth one may take the part for the whole (the *pars pro toto* principle), that everything *is* in its depth identical with everything else anagogically, that "it [God, or the universe] is an infinite sphere of which the center is everywhere and the circumference is nowhere."[57] Therefore, as Pound says, one speaks of *juniper*, of the *oak's veins*, of the *shrine* seen and not seen from the *roots of the sequoias*. It is the same insight that led Giordano Bruno to hold that divinity was "within us even more than we ourselves are within ourselves";[58] and

De Quincy: ". . . thus the least things in the universe must be secret mirrors to the greatest."[59]

The comparison with Baudelaire once more obtrudes. As the shrine is to the roots of the sequoias (in Pound's metaphor), so "La Nature est un temple" would seem to be to Baudelaire's "forêt de symboles." Yet there is a difference—that between the energic continuum of today's world picture and that more stratified view of the classic "eternal-temporal" equation.

Dame Edith Sitwell would seem to be on the track of it, though she appeals not to the correspondences of Baudelaire, but to those of Swedenborg.

> Seeing the immense design of the world, one image of wonder mirrored by another image of wonder—the patterns of fern and of feather by the frost on the windowpane, the six rays of the snowflake mirrored in the rock-crystal's six-rayed eternity. . . . Are not these the correspondences . . . whereby we may speak with angels?[60]

But there is a literalism about these comparisons, a geometric rather than an anagogic resemblance; thus her metaphors function conventionally:

> . . . like the planets, those bright bees
> That move in heaven about their honeycombs of light,
> And are forms of Time that imitate the eternal. . . .[61]

Kandinsky's "secret soul" or "inner being of things" does not come to presence here. "A presence," says Wheelwright, "is a mystery—not an enigma that arouses our curiosity, but a mystery that claims our awe. Every presence has an irreducible core of mystery, so long as it retains its presential character."[62] This is fine, so far as the irreducible core is concerned; but a dimension is excluded here. Must we not say, rather, that a presence is a mystery in which both an enigma *and* a mystery are present?

We remember Heraclitus' saying, that "Nature is a riddle" (*gryphos*) —not a temple, or a forest of symbols. Or Jorge Luis Borges, whose work is itself an enigma of quest, preoccupied with dreams, fictions, labyrinths, time, and the inner secrets of things, believed that "the world is a book and the book is a world, and both are labyrinthine and enclose enigmas designed to be understood and participated in by man."[63] In his essay, significantly entitled, "The Mirror of Enigmas," he quotes from Saint Paul: "Videmus nunc per speculum in aenigmate. . . ." (1 Cor. 13:12). He notes how central this thought was to Leon Bloy, and how Bloy returned to it again and again in his fragmentary writings. He cites several of these references, for example:

> The statement by St. Paul: *Videmus nunc per speculum in aenigmate* would be a skylight through which one might submerge himself in the true Abyss, which is the soul of man. The terrifying immensity of the firmament's abysses is an illusion, an external reflection of *our own* abysses, perceived "in a mirror." We should invert our eyes and practice a sublime astronomy in the infinitude of our hearts. . . .

Or again:

> Everything is a symbol, even the most piercing pain. We are dreamers who shout in our sleep. . . . We now see, St. Paul maintains, *per speculum in aenigmate*, literally: 'in an enigma by means of a mirror'. . . .

Thus "we see everything backwards. . . ." Borges approves this, suggesting first that these judgments are "perhaps inevitable within the Christian doctrine," and secondly that Bloy has done nothing more than "*apply to the whole Creation*" (italics mine) the method applied by the Jewish Cabalists to the reading of the Scriptures.[64] Borges does likewise.

> "In a riddle whose answer is chess," [asks a character in one of his stories,] "what is the only prohibited word?"
>
> I thought a moment and replied, "The word *chess*."
>
> "Precisely," said Albert.

Albert then goes on to add something very interesting about this narrative in which he is a character: "*The Garden of Forking Paths* is an enormous riddle, or parable, whose theme is time. . . ."[65] There is a sense in which, for Borges, the world itself is the Garden of Forking Paths—a riddle, a parable—whose cryptic theme to be deciphered is time. But the riddle of time is caught up in the *unspoken* riddle of illusion and reality. Borges is fascinated with the conundrums of Zeno, such as the hare and the tortoise, as a parable of appearance and reality. We see it refracted even in a brief passage from an entirely different context:

> Intolerably, I dreamt of an exiguous and nitid labyrinth: in the center was a water jar; my hands almost touched it, my eyes could not see it, but so intricate and perplexed were the curves that I knew I would die before reaching it.[66]

What is the water jar? What does it signify? As a dream image does it signify the deep psyche's center—or the dreamer's goal, his "water of life?" Is it the secret of the real, from which the dreamer must drink? Is it comparable to the treasure image, hid in a cave, for which the dreamer seeks? Is the labyrinth in which it is situated—with its rights and lefts, forwards and backwards, to and fro of daily life—the twistings and turnings of our objectivizing consciousness, which always seems almost to touch life's center, but paradoxically never does and so remains frustrate and baffled? Yet, despite the water's being hedged in by the labyrinth, it is near, very near (nearer than I am to myself?): my hands almost touched it.

What we observe in all of this is that Borges' parables and fictions, like those of Kafka, are antimetaphorical in the conventional sense of that term. They have become a kind of metaphor themselves. Their only frame of reference is themselves. They are anecdotal, implying movement; but the movement is parabolic, returning upon its own center. Thus, as Beda Allemann has pointed out in the case of Kafka, "the parable as a whole is a kind of absolute metaphor."[67]

But again, let us note how the "step back" from conventional patterns is effected: how the parable enforces the enigma, how the enigma brings me into the presence of the mystery. The mystery *presences* from the interplay of the relations between the words, out of the field of opposites put in play by the anecdote. It may, indeed, achieve *only* the step back and so leave me poised precariously and ironically over the enigma as the Abyss; but if it has achieved an anagogical movement in depth, then a *translatio* should occur, and the "No" of the horizon of Western metaphysics be converted into the "Yes" of the event of appropriation.

VI

The term *anagoge* refers, in its dictionary sense, to the spiritual or mystical significance or interpretation of words. It means literally in terms of its Greek components to "lead upwards." This view was compatible with the medieval world-view, since such language pointed beyond itself and towards mystical theology. We have been suggesting an anagoge in depth, as responding to the peculiar needs of the literary artist in our times. Our argument has moved from analogy and archetype to the anagogical, attempting in each case to describe rhetorical factors which in contemporary practice supervene over classical modes of meaning. This supervention, which is still not understood, is complex as well as radical. It must effect first the *step back* of which we have spoken by way of Heidegger, making us aware of the changed perspectives, and releasing us from the commitments already present as "built into" our western grammar. We have also suggested that an anagoge in depth points into the zone of tensions between the opposites, into the field of resonances set up by the terms of the art-work. This is comparable, psychologically and mythically, to a *step down*, for it must engage the unconscious if the third step, and the most meaningful one, is to accrue. This is the *step through* into the *newness* of the whole where the presencing of Being is experienced. This is that "creative advance" of which Whitehead has spoken; it is the realm, ontologically, of radical innovation. This is the point most difficult for the classical consciousness, constrained as it is by its mathematical analogies and models. Northrop Frye notes well that, anagogically, "the symbol is a monad, all symbols being united in a single infinite and eternal verbal symbol which is, as *dianoia*, the Logos, and, as *mythos*, total creative act."[68] Applying this to criticism, he remarks

> The anagogic view of criticism thus leads to the conception of literature as existing in its own universe, no longer a commentary on life or reality, but containing life and reality in a system of verbal relationships.[69]

But there is, in what remains *unsaid* in the second of these statements, the strong shadow of a classical reticence which is reluctant to go all the way with the implications of the first.

By contrast, the language of Gaston Bachelard is instructive. After citing with approval Pierre-Jean Jouve's claim that "Poetry is a soul inaugurating a form," and stressing this inaugural power and the soul's "dwelling" in it, he goes on to remark of the poetic image:

> It becomes a new being in our language, expressing us by making us what it expresses; in other words, it is at once a becoming of expression, and a becoming of our being. Here expression creates being.[70]

Then, as if wishing to leave no doubt as to his intention, he says flatly that his statement defines the level of ontology towards which he is working: "I believe that everything specifically human in man is *logos*."[71]

This is also the level of ontology towards which my own thesis has been moving. The transformation of consciousness must be thoroughgoing, the Euclidean frame must be broken, and the "debris," as Wittgenstein says, be cleared away. All of which means that, in addition to the sense of immediateness and the sense of presencing which the artist today is attempting to bring forth, there must also be the movement *through*, the sense of radical innovation.

Whitehead asserts this dimension very clearly. For him creativity is "the universal of universals characterizing ultimate matter of fact. It is the ultimate principle by which the many, which are the universe disjunctively, become the one actual occasion, which is the universe conjunctively."[72] The poem is precisely such an occasion, not merely its analogue. "The ultimate metaphysical principle," writes Whitehead again, "is the advance from disjunction to conjunction, creating a novel entity other than the entities given in disjunction."[73] This is the matrix out of which the Logos speaks, the point where *dianoia* and *mythos* are renewed, and where expression or utterance is one with the deepest level of ontology. "Expression," for Whitehead, "is the one fundamental sacrament. It is the outward and visible sign of an inward and spiritual grace."[74]

An anagogical criticism, however, will note first, how in the art-work all three steps are—or are not—performed *at the same time*, and second, how the poem, as the occasion of this creative metamorphosis, retains within its anecdote, or within itself as the absolute metaphor of itself, the unconcealing-concealing mystery of Being's coming to presence within it. As metaphor, or as anecdote, it will point through the pairs of opposites it holds in tension to that "sphere which is no sphere," the realm of "the Manifest-Hidden," called "Moving-in-secret."[75] The poem will conserve in its parable the mystery of inwardness:

> Jesus said: The Kingdom is like a man
> who had a
> treasure hidden in his field, without knowing it.
> And after he died, he left it to his
> son. The son did not know about it, he accepted
> that field, he sold it. And he who bought it,
> he went, while he was plowing
> he found the treasure.[76]

And as for Merlin, it is said that he withdrew into the power that was himself. He met Niniane ("symbol of the spellbinding energy of life itself") in the forest of Broceliande. He taught her his magical arts, and she enchanted him with his own craft.

> . . . he allows the forest, the abyss, to swallow him back, and he becomes

> again the magic wood and all its trees. For he is lord of the forest and its essence, whereas the knights of the Round Table are children of men, lords of castles, and heroes of the world. The unconscious, through Merlin, has manifested itself to the world in revealing symbols, and sinks again into its own primeval stillness.[77]

But the point is "the whitethorn hedge blossoms imperishably, and in it Merlin is living still."[78] His cry is still being heard. Merlin, in the idiom of the broken canon, is expendable; but his cry is not. In the new quest of letters today we begin to see how "The poem is the cry of its occasion."[79]

Notes

1. *Ash Wednesday,* VI (New York: G. P. Putnam's Sons, 1930), p. 29.
2. C. G. Jung, *Memories, Dreams, Reflections,* ed. Aniela Jaffe, trans. Richard and Clara Winston (New York: Pantheon Books, 1963), p. 227.
3. Arnold of Villanova, in *Rosarium philosophorum* (*Artis Auriferae*), II, Part xxi (Basel, 1593), p. 210; cited by Jung, *Psychology and Alchemy,* in *The Collected Works,* Vol. 12, Bollingen Series XX (New York: Pantheon Books, 1953), pp. 78, 171, n. 117. Cf. Joseph Campbell, *The Masks of God, Creative Mythology,* Vol. IV, p. 429, *et passim* for a discussion of the Grail texts.
4. *Memories, Dreams, Reflections,* p. 228.
5. Ezra Pound, *Drafts and Fragments of Cantos CX–CXVII* (New York: A New Directions Book, 1968), p. 32.
6. *Psychology and Alchemy,* p. 228.
7. C. G. Jung, *Archetypes of the Collective Unconscious,* trans. R. F. C. Hull, in *The Collected Works,* vol. 9, pt. 1, Bollingen Series XX (New York: Pantheon Books 1959), pp. 227, 245.
8. Joseph Campbell, "The Symbol Without Meaning," in *The Flight of the Wild Gander* (New York: The Viking Press, 1969), p. 156.
9. Charles Baudelaire, "Le Gouffre," *Oeuvres Complètes* (Bruges: Bibliotheque de la Pleiade, 1961), p. 172.
10. William Carlos Williams, *Selected Letters,* ed. John C. Thirlwall (New York: McDowell, Obolensky, 1957), p. 213.
11. Ezra Pound, *Section: Rock-Drill, 85–95 de los cantares* (New York: A New Directions Book, 1956), p. 41.
12. Wallace Stevens, "Crude Foyer," in *The Collected Poems of Wallace Stevens* (New York: Alfred A. Knopf, 1954), p. 305.
13. T. S. Eliot, "What the Thunder Said," *The Waste Land,* V, *The Collected Poems 1909–1935* (New York: Harcourt, Brace and Co., 1936), pp. 86–90.
14. Erich Neumann, *Art and the Creative Unconscious,* trans. Ralph Manheim, Bollingen Series LXI (New York: Pantheon Books, 1959), p. 128.

15. Ezra Pound, *Drafts and Fragments*, Addendum for Canto C, p. 29.
16. Martin Heidegger, *Being and Time*, trans. John Macquarrie and Edward Robinson (London: SCM Press, 1962), p. 190, italics his.
17. Quoted by Philip Wheelwright in "The Archetypal Symbol," in *Perspectives in Literary Criticism*, Yearbook of Comparative Criticism, Vol. I, ed. Joseph Strelka (University Park and London: The Pennsylvania State University Press, 1968), p. 241.
18. Robert Duncan, "Shadows," in *Bending the Bow* (New York: New Directions, 1968), p. 31.
19. Kirsten Harries, *The Meaning of Modern Art* (Evanston: Northwestern University Press, 1968), p. 130.
20. Robert Duncan, "The Truth and Life of Myth in Poetry," in *Parable Myth and Language,* ed. Tony Stoneburner (Cambridge, Mass.: Church Society for College Work, 1968), p. 44.
21. Ibid, pp. 43, 38.
22. Martin Heidegger, *Identity and Difference* (New York: Harper and Row, 1969), p. 73.
23. Pound, Canto CXVI, *Drafts and Fragments*, p. 27.
24. Ibid., p. 25.
25. Stevens, "The Man With the Blue Guitar," in *Collected Poems*, p. 165.
26. Stevens, "The Idea of Order in Key West," in *Collected Poems*, p. 130.
27. Heidegger, *Identity and Difference*, p. 35.
28. Ibid., p. 32.
29. Pound, Canto 93, *Section: Rock-Drill,* p. 92.
30. Stevens, "The Pure Good of Theory," in *Collected Poems*, p. 332.
31. Parmenides, B 3 (Diels *Vor-Sokratiker*); cf. John Burnet, *Early Greek Philosophy* (London: Adam and Charles Black, 1892), p. 185.
32. Cf. George Joseph Seidel, *Martin Heidegger and the Pre-Socratics* (Lincoln: University of Nebraska Press, 1964), p. 63.
33. Ibid., p. 69.
34. Heidegger, *Identity and Difference*, p. 40.
35. Ibid., pp. 37–39.
36. So Seidel, p. 70, paraphrasing Heidegger's *Einfuhrung in die Metaphysik*, p. 110.
37. Heidegger, *Identity and Difference*, p. 64.
38. Ibid., p. 33.
39. Ibid., p. 65.
40. Ibid., p. 65, et passim.
41. Pound, Canto CX, *Drafts and Fragments*, p. 8.
42. Neumann, *Art and the Creative Unconscious*, pp. 116, 127.
43. Walter Hess, *Dokumente zum Verständnis der modernen Malerei* (Hamburg: Rowohlt, 1956), p. 87, as cited in K. Harries, p. 103.
44. Pound, Canto CXII, *Drafts and Fragments*, p. 18.
45. Ibid., Canto CX, p. 11.
46. Pound, Canto 107, *Thrones* (New York: New Directions, n.d.), p. 114.
47. Cf. André Rousseaux, *Le Monde Classique*, ed. Albin Michel (Paris, 1941), p. 215.
48. Pound, Canto 91, *Section: Rock-Drill*, p. 76.
49. Samuel Taylor Coleridge, *Biographia Literaria*, ed. John Calvin Metcalf (New York: The Macmillan Co., 1926), ch. 14, p. 197.
50. Pound, Canto CXIII, *Drafts and Fragments*, p. 20.

51. R. M. Rilke, *Sonnets to Orpheus*, trans. M. D. Herter Norton (New York: W. W. Norton and Co., 1942), p. 93.
52. Philip Wheelwright, *Metaphor and Reality* (Bloomington: Indiana University Press, 1962), p. 154.
53. Ibid., p. 135.
54. Northrop Frye, *The Anatomy of Criticism* (Princeton: Princeton University Press, 1957), p. 125.
55. Northrop Frye, in his invaluable study, indicates that in his theory of symbols (advancing through the literal, formal, mythical-archetypal, and anagogic phases), "we have been going up a sequence parallel to that of medieval criticism" (Ibid., p. 115). It is this "going up" of his medieval criticism that leaves his analysis attached, despite its brilliant innovations, to classical rhetoric. Thus "radical metaphor" is less than *radical*, and an anagogy in depth is not realized.
56. Ibid., p. 124.
57. Pascal, *Pensees*, No. 72 (*et al.*, from Parmenides to Montaigne).
58. Quoted in Jorge Luis Borges, *Labyrinths* (New York: A New Directions Book, 1964), p. 191.
59. Quoted in Borges, *Labyrinths*, p. 209.
60. Edith Sitwell, *The Canticle of the Rose, Poems 1917–1949* (New York: The Vanguard Press, 1949), pp. xv–xvi.
61. Sitwell, *Canticle of the Rose*, "Out of School," p. 258.
62. Wheelwright, p. 158.
63. Borges, *Introduction* by James E. Irby, p. xix.
64. Ibid., pp. 209–211.
65. Ibid., p. 27.
66. Ibid., p. 107.
67. Beda Allemann, "Metaphor and Antimetaphor," in *Interpretation: The Poetry of Meaning*, ed. Stanley Romaine Hopper and David L. Miller (New York: Harcourt, Brace and World, 1967), p. 114.
68. Frye, p. 121.
69. Ibid., p. 122.
70. Gaston Bachelard, *The Poetics of Space* (New York: The Orion Press, 1964), pp. xviii–xix.
71. Ibid.
72. Alfred North Whitehead, *Process and Reality* (New York: The Macmillan Co., 1929), p. 31.
73. Ibid., p. 32. This Whiteheadian perspective will be seen to correlate significantly, as introduced here, with the *coincidentia oppositorum* line of thinkers (from Heraclitus, through Nicholas of Cusa and others, to Jung): it adds the important dimension of the movement *through* the opposites in the novelties of creative advance.
74. Alfred North Whitehead, *Modes of Thought* (New York: G. P. Putnam's Sons, 1958), p. 86.
75. Mundaka Upanisad, 2. 2. 1.
76. *The Gospel According to Thomas*, Coptic Text, trans. A. Guillaumont, H. C. Puech, G. Quispel, W. Till, and Yassah 'Abd Al Masih (New York: Harper and Brothers, 1959), Log. 98. 31–99. 1, p. 55.
77. Heinrich Zimmer, *The King and the Corpse*, ed. Joseph Campbell (New York: Meridian Books, 1960), p. 198.
78. Ibid., p. 200.
79. Wallace Stevens, "An Ordinary Evening in New Haven," *Collected Poems*, p. 473.

Mario Jacoby

THE MUSE AS A SYMBOL OF LITERARY CREATIVITY

THERE ARE VARIOUS POSSIBLE SPONTANEOUS ASSOCIATIONS WHICH COME to mind when one hears the word "Muse." One might think of lovely ethereal young women with long curled hair singing in beautiful harmony with voices like silver and playing the harp or the cithara with the most gracious movements. Or is this just my own fantasy? Am I confusing them with singing angels in the Christian paradise, and do I find them somehow fascinating and ridiculous at the same time for this reason? The sublime and the ridiculous are very close neighbors. However that may be, "muse" sounds like music, museum, sublime, harmonious, out-of-this-world—with a tinge of boredom and of antiquated serenity. I cannot help being reminded of my school days in the "Gymnasium" where one had to learn the names of all nine muses by heart and where those teachers who were classical scholars celebrated a cult of the muse with religious awe. I loved it and was bored by it; it also seemed funny. Perhaps the cult of the muse and the somehow pompous admiration of ancient Greece is a specific German tradition—Winckelmann's "noble simplicity and quiet grandeur" (*edle Einfalt und stille Grösse*), the classical period in German literature, etc. In the German language we have many more terms derived from "muse" than in English—like *ein musischer Mensch, ein Musensohn, Musentempel, Musenalmanach, Musenquell,* and so forth. The English equivalent of these terms has nothing to do with the word "muse."

Just what is the muse? Is she a phenomenon which belongs to a certain historical period in Greece, admired still by classical scholars, historians, and lovers of antiquity; or is she something alive, at any time, relevant for any process of literary creativity? This is the question that interests me.

Ancient poets of Greece like Homer or Hesiod believed that they received their vocation and their actual inspiration from the muse. Hesiod begins his poem on theogony as follows:

> The muses once taught Hesiod to sing in verse
> while tending his sheep by Mount Helikon's slopes,
> but first the stern ladies would scold me with words,
> the Olympian muses, the daughters of terrible Zeus:
> 'You fumbling peasants, you oafs, you are nothing
>   but stomachs.
> Our song is rich in illusion, truth's glittering sister,
> but if we wish, we can also prophesy truly.'
> Thus spoke the daughters of Zeus, the Great, the
>   Mighty in Words.
> A wand they would give me, a branch of laurel in
>   bud newly plucked,
> and breathing upon me thus they bestowed upon me
>   the power of foretelling song.
> Now I must herald the past and the future,
> the Olympians' praise I must hail, the immortals;
> the beginning and end of my song must be filled
> with their being.

And Homer's Odyssey begins:

> Sing me the deeds, O Muse, of the much traveled hero, he who strayed far after Troy's destruction. . . .

The muse evokes in human beings what is called enthusiasm. *Enthusiasmos* in Greek comes from *entheos*, "the god within." Enthusiasm is thus a state where the poet is visited by a god, where a god becomes alive in him. In this state it is really the muse herself which sings through the poet; the poet is only her tool. *Enthusiasmos* means that the boundaries of the ego consciousness become open for the experience of a divine will which takes hold over the poet with all its might. Plato holds that great poets speak in enthusiasm, in an inspired state, and not by means of their own craftmanship (*techne*). This passage from *Ion* shows that even in his day philosophers were aware of the problem of inspiration and its relation to craftmanship. The poet-singer in the Homeric period, called *aoidos*, recited and sang spontaneously what the muse called him to do. We would say he was improvising to a great extent on occasions of common festivities. The name "poet"—*poietes*—is derived from *poiein*, "to make or to produce something." Here the accent lies more on the activity of the poet to write his verses. The term *poietes* we find only since the end of the fifth century before Christ when poems were written down. At this moment writing becomes also a craftmanship, a *techne*, which is at the free disposal of the poet. Perhaps he felt independent of the muse. But according to Plato, this is not true poetry, and there is a myth which tells us of the danger of the human attitude which tries to dispose of the muses. Thamyris, who was a great singer and poet, thought that his art was greater than the art of the muses. He even went so far as to enter into competition with the muses, but of course he could not win. The muses punished him severely, for they blinded him and made him forget how to play the harp. If the poet is not fully devoted to the muses, his art becomes sterile, blind, and meaningless.

The muses have their definite place in the Olympian cosmos. In a hymn of Pindar we find a myth which gives us a reason for the existence of the muses. When Zeus had put all things in their right order, he celebrated his wedding and asked the Olympian deities whether they thought that his creation was complete or whether they still missed and needed something. The gods asked him to create some divine beings who would praise his great deeds and his universe, and embellish it by means of words and music.

It seems that the gods are not satisfied that the universe and life simply exist; they also need for its completion the expression of this existing in words and music. The muses have the task of praising the deeds of Zeus and bringing the existence of the whole to conscious attention. As divine beings they know the secrets of the immortal gods and the mysteries of the past and the future. Once they bestow on the human poet the power of prophetic song, his song must be filled with divine being. In this way they act as a link between the divine and the human realm through the poet.

By uniting with Mnemosyne ("remembrance") Zeus created the muses. Remembrance, who was considered to be a well, is the mother of the muses. The parents of Mnemosyne are Ouranos and Gaia, the primordial gods of heaven and earth. So we can say that the muses are associated with the remembrance of primeval creation, of the last and deepest mysteries.

I think all these myths pertaining to the muses are full of deep meaning in themselves. The question now arises for the psychologist: how does it come about that myths can touch us with such wisdom, and what are myths from a psychological point of view? I shall confine myself to the myths of the muse. It is an empirical fact that certain human beings can feel a strong urge to express something by means of poetry, music, painting, or some other means. It seems to be a great inner necessity; the creative drive can really take possession of the whole personality of an artist. This is a phenomenon experienced by creative artists for which modern depth psychology does not find a convincing explanation and probably never will. Freud operated with the idea that the creative work of a writer is a wish fulfillment of infantile sexual impulses in a sublimated form. But at the same time he knew that this kind of psychoanalytical interpretation could not really explain the mystery of artistic creation and admitted, "Before the problem of the creative artist, analysis must, alas, lay down its arms."[1] The power of the creative urge and the source of inspiration are for us equally inexplicable factors. They were, moreover, unknown and mysterious to the ancient Greeks. Now it is a psychological fact that man is never satisfied with the statement "I do not know." Whenever he comes to the limits of his knowledge about facts, imagination takes over. Myths are really imaginings about the realm of life which can be experienced but is beyond the reach of conscious or scientific explanation. Unexplained facts and experiences are felt as mysteries and bring forth imagination about superhuman powers, a mythology about the divine; and thus we can say that man believes, in a religious way, in his own imagination. This is the argument of any enlightment. But—there is a great "but." It is true that religious myths of all times are manifestations of man's fantasy and imagination; this explains the abundance of god images and different religions. Also, the contents of religious belief change with the growth of consciousness throughout our history. Myths are products of man's imagination, but that does not say that he produces them actively and of his own free will. We cannot control consciously what enters our head, what occurs to our minds. "It occurred to me" is an expression of our experience. Fantasies, imagination, and associations happen to us whether we are conscious of them or not; dreams are fantasies which occur during sleep when our conscious mind is extinguished for the night. The phenomenon of dreaming is a proof that psychic life in the form of fantasies has its autonomy and is only in a loose way connected with conscious mental activity. Thus depth psychology became much interested in dreams. Freud called the dream the "*via regia*," the royal highway to the unconscious. Thousands of dreams were studied by Freud and Jung to penetrate deeply into the hidden secrets of the unconscious mind, its activity and influence on our consciousness. Both Freud and Jung noticed how often dreams resemble motifs from mythology, from fairy tales, and from folklore. As Jung explained: "I had often observed patients whose dreams pointed to a rich store of fantasy material. . . . The variety defies description. I can only say there is probably no motif in any known mythology that does not at some time appear in these configurations. If there was any conscious knowledge of mythological motifs worth mentioning in my patients, it is left far behind by the ingenuities of creative fantasy. In general, my patients had only a minimal knowledge of mythology."[2] These are most interesting facts. They imply that unconscious fantasy has the ability to create spontaneously mythological motifs of which our conscious mind is unaware. The myth-creating factor is unconscious and therefore not under the control of our conscious will. Thus we cannot do justice to the full impact of religious myths when we say that religion is nothing but man's imagination about the unknown. It is imagination, but the latter happens to him and is not at his command. Man can experience it as inspiration or even revelation, but the myth-creating factor, the source of inspiration or revelation, is unknown. We may call this unknown factor "X" which produces creative fantasy "the archetype" as C. G. Jung does. But Jung admits that his concept of the archetype is merely a scientific hypothesis for the unconscious potential and its ability to produce images and ideas. As Goethe says, "All supreme productivity, every important observation, every invention, every great idea that bears fruit and has lasting effect, stands not in anyone's power and is above all earthly force. Man must regard these things as gifts from on high, as pure children of God, and he must receive and venerate them with joyful gratitude. It is related to the daemonic which can overpower him and do with him as it pleases and to which he gives himself up unconsciously, while believing himself to be active under his own power. In such cases man can often be regarded as the tool of a higher world government, as a vessel that has been found worthy to receive a divine influence."[3]

Is it astonishing, after all this, that for the Greeks this unknown and mysterious source of artistic creation was depicted as the divine figure of the muse? The muse is the source of inspiration for the ancient Greek poet; she bestows upon him the power of song. She is the image of his unconscious creative potentiality which, as he rightly feels, is not in his own power. But he believes in her divine creative power if he opens himself to her, evokes her, and lets her enter into himself so that he enters into the state of *enthusiasmos*.

You will recall that my lecture is entitled "The Muse as a Symbol of

Literary Creativity," but in the experience of ancient Greek poets the muse was probably not a symbol but a real divine being to be believed in. What do I mean now when I speak of the muse as a symbol?

The word "symbol" comes from the Greek *symballein* which literally means "to throw together." A *symbolon* in ancient Greece was a fragment of a cube or some other object which could be fitted back together with the other half of the object. Friends would each take one such half to seal a friendship that often extended to every member of their respective families. The pieces were used as means of identification and were handed down through generations in each family. If two halves fitted together to make a whole, the bearer of the fragment was legitimately identified and made welcome.

From this original concrete meaning the *symbolon* came to stand for a contract or agreement in the legal world. In the aesthetic sphere it came to mean what in German is aptly called *Sinn-bild* ("sense-image" or "image of meaning"). An image becomes a symbol when he who looks at it sees in it *a meaning beyond* that which it depicts. This meaning varies within the image; it shines through it. An image which strikes us as a living symbol points beyond itself and appears rich in meaning. For C. G. Jung a symbol is "the best possible description or formula of a relatively unknown fact . . . which cannot conceivably, therefore, be more clearly or characteristically represented."[4] Goethe, too, gave thought to the symbol. He wrote: "This is truly symbolic: when the specific represents the general, not as a dream or shadow, but as the living and immediate experience of the unfathomable."[5]

The main characteristic of a living symbol is thus its conveyance of the unfathomable. It carries a meaning which cannot be described in rational language since it consists of a hunch, an undefined feeling. As soon as this hidden meaning can be defined and described exactly the symbol ceases to be alive. It then becomes an allegory or a sign. Sigmund Freud used the word "symbol" very frequently in his interpretation of dreams; for example, he reduced all long-shaped objects occurring in a dream to so-called symbols of the masculine genital organ and all round objects to symbols of the vagina. All movements in a dream, like climbing stairs or traveling by train, stand for sexual intercourse. But all adults know what a penis, a vagina, or sexual intercourse is. By reducing the unfathomable to something known, to sexuality and its organs, symbols lose the full impact of their significance, they become signs. But on the other hand we know that the image of sexual organs can really be experienced symbolically. In the ancient so-called phallus cults an oversized sculpture of the masculine genital organ belonging to a god—usually Hermes—was worshipped, very often by sterile women. This phallus was a symbol of creation and procreation in a spiritual and physical sense. Creation and procreation are, after all, miracles in human experience; thus the phallus can have a living symbolic quality.

Jung says, "Whether something is a symbol or not depends first of all on the way in which our consciousness approaches it."[6] It is possible for our consciousness to remain closed to the wealth of meaning contained in a symbol and to reduce its meaning to some well-worn, generally known facts. When this happens, the symbol loses its depth; it no longer points to the unfathomable, to that which transcends our consciousness; it becomes a mere sign.

What then does it mean if I consider the muse as a symbol? As we have already said, for an ancient Greek poet the muse was a fact. He believed that a lovely divine female figure bestowed the power of song on him or inhabited him in a state of *enthusiasmos*—perhaps we may say an anagogic state. To us it is clear that the muse was a symbol for the secret of his own unconscious creative potentiality, but he was unaware of this. He projected his own unconscious creativeness into the divine figure of the muse which came down from Mount Olympus to inspire him. This belief seems archaic and naïve to us, but he explained his condition of being inspired to sing and to write in this way and was not aware that the muse is a symbol, an image produced by the myth-creating factor of the human unconscious.

When we learn in school about the muses, we think that belief in them is naïve, poetic, lovely, or slightly funny. The muse belongs to Greece and hardly anyone today (except perhaps the German classical scholar Walter F. Otto) still believes in her, for the muse has become for us a symbol of the past and is not something alive, a living symbol. Is it possible, however, that the muse can still be a living symbol for a modern artist? We said that the muse is a lovely divine woman concerned with the remembrance of primeval creation and its mysteries. As a symbol she is thus an image of the mysterious woman in the psyche of the man. C. G. Jung discovered that all the psychically feminine tendencies of a man are symbolized by feminine figures in dreams. Usually a boy is educated and developed according to patterns which are considered masculine: a boy should not cry, should not be too softhearted, should be brave, disciplined, intelligent, and think logically. He should be active, not a passive dreamer; he should be able to fight in life's struggle to protect his wife and children, and so on. This is more or less the conventional image of masculinity. But fortunately men also have to a greater or lesser extent a feminine side, and women a masculine one. In the development of the boy his feminine side is often repressed because of the collective masculine ego ideal which he introjects. A lot of aggressive masculine behavior demonstrated by men serves really as a defense mechanism against their despised feminine passivity, open receptivity, and irrational feelings. Jung called the feminine side of men the "Anima" which actually means "soul." Even when the anima is unconscious and repressed, it still exercises its influence upon the man in the form of irrational moods, depressive feelings, bad temper, and so forth. We know, for example, that the strong and militaristic German chancellor Bismarck would have sudden attacks at home when he would cry like a baby for hours.

The man who is consciously identified with masculinity experiences his soul as feminine because it involves all the experience of moods, feelings, irrational hunches, wanted and unwanted emotions, and fears. It is a threat against his masculine stability but at the same time a valuable potential for deep experiences even when accompanied by emotional crisis. The feminine is the image of his soul, but at first unconscious. Now it is a recognized psychological principle that we meet unconscious contents first in the form of projection. The anima tends to appear in a projected form, namely as a woman the man falls in love with. The projection of the soul image of the anima in men and the animus in women is, according to Jung, the psychological basis for the attraction of the two sexes. The choice of the beloved occurs according to the kind of anima image a man carries unconsciously in him. He sees a woman who has a certain similarity to this inner image, and his anima is constellated: he has found the woman of his dreams. And then what often happens? As his beloved is very much a projection of his own inner image, he expects unquestionably that she will behave according to his imagination, his wishes, and his needs. He has certain expectations—often unconscious—about how she should dress, cook, behave, walk, kiss, and so on. And those expectations lead sooner or later to a severe disappointment: his beloved corresponds only partly to his anima-expectations. She is, after all, a human being of flesh and blood with her own problems, needs, and expectations, with her own law of self-development. Most crises in marriage or partnership arise from this disappointing and disturbing gap between the projection of the anima image and the concrete being of the partner. In order to avoid the muddles described by Edward Albee in his play *Who's Afraid of Virginia Woolf*, one must know how to differentiate between the inner anima image with its expectations and the real woman. In psychology we call this process "taking back the projection," becoming conscious of the influence of one's own inner anima image.

I would say that the muse can be a symbol of the anima and its mysterious influences upon the poet. With a simple everyday observation I should like to exemplify what I mean: one can often observe a transformation in a young man once he falls in love. His feelings and emotions grow more intense; he experiences great inner happiness—or perhaps intense sadness or world weariness; he feels inspired to write passionate love letters to his beloved every day, and poems may come quite spontaneously in such a state. Even if his love is unanswered, there is very often a great need for expression. Love can thus be something inspiring, and psychical energy is set free. The man in love imagines that this inspiration comes from his beloved; she is *la femme inspiratrice*, the inspiring woman. But what happens in reality is that in the love situation his own anima becomes active in him; the creative fantasy of the unconscious comes into movement. In German we would say *Er wird von der Muse geküsst*—"he is kissed by the muse." This example shows us that by means of anima projection the man falls in love. He experiences thus a relationship to a partner and at the same time he may discover a new side of himself. He may suddenly become a poet of sorts and have the feeling of being inspired. Jung thought therefore that the anima has a psychological function, the function of relationship. It relates on the one hand to a real woman who becomes fascinating through projection; on the other hand it relates the ego consciousness of the man to his own inner potentials, to his anagogic state, to his deeper self.

It is, however, self-evident that the inspiring activity, the influence of the anima alone, does not make a poet. The literary output of such an emotional state may be well-meant in its clumsiness, touching in its naïveté; the inspiration may take on a pompous or sentimental form. The Greeks knew that poets produce their works by means of *physis* and *enthusiasmos* (Plato, *Apology*). *Physis* we may translate in this connection as "natural gift or natural talent." The combination of natural talent and actual inspiration is necessary. Nevertheless it is apparent that the muse can play a role in the experience of any man.

As a matter of fact, the anima as an inspiring real woman or as a literary fantasy figure plays a great part in creative work—I think of Dante's Beatrice, of Hölderlin's Diotima, Beethoven's immortal beloved, or Goethe's Frau v. Stein. Lou Andreas-Salomé was inspiring to Nietzsche and Rainer Maria Rilke. Alma Mahler-Werfel fascinated four great artists in the course of her life: Gustav Mahler, Walter

Gropius, Franz Werfel, and Oskar Kokoschka. The other day a lady who had known Alma Mahler in Vienna told me, "You know, she was a real muse to those men."

Years ago I met in Paris the woman painter and writer Loulou Lazart. She was at that time an old but still charming and strong woman. In her youth she had been for a time the mistress of the poet Rainer Maria Rilke. Now as an old woman she occupied herself with writing a book about him; she had also translated some of his poems into French in a very sensitive and masterly way. She told me about her relationship with Rilke and said that it was at times really intolerable. When he was with her he sometimes got up in the middle of the night and disappeared. But the next day she would receive from a different town a most passionate and beautiful love letter. Psychologically this is interesting for us since it shows that at certain times the need for literary expression of his love was greater than the wish to experience the physical nearness of his beloved. In such moments she played the part of catalyst evoking the inner anima muse.

The anima muse does not always need a love relationship with a woman in order to come into play, although this is a frequent and evident pattern. It has often a tinge of romanticism as we find in many biographies of artists. But the muse also finds other secret and subtle ways to operate. We find, for instance, a good many homosexuals among creative artists; they cannot fall in love with a woman, but all the same they can produce fine works. They seem rather to identify with the anima muse--and we know from mythology that the muse worshipped with her song the beauty of Apollo.

Some poets or writers seem unable to form any close relationship with another human being. They have to live lonely lives to serve their inner muse who jealously never lets them out of her grip.

We have said that the muse is a symbol of the anima in man, an image of feeling-relationship. In Greek mythology the muse knows the secrets of the immortal gods and the mysteries of the past and the future. Through the poet she brings this knowledge to conscious attention in the form of song and poems; she acts as a link between the divine and the human realms and has a relating function—thus she is from a psychological point of view a symbol of the anima.

But the immortal Greek gods are dead for us, in spite of their immortality. Christianity took over with its quite different representations; but if we believe Nietzsche, the Christian god is also dead; now we even have a modern "God is dead" theology. But have the immortals really died, or have they just transformed themselves into different representations? Psychologically speaking they always have been symbols of an unknown, unconscious reality which nevertheless finds manifestation. The form of the symbols changes, yet the reality they point to seems immortal, belonging to the essence of man's being. In modern times the realm of the gods has received different names such as *Ding an sich*, *Urgrund des Seins* ("primal ground of being"), *die Transzendenz* ("the transcendent"), because we know that god images are really anthropomorphic. For Jung the realm of the gods, the transcendent, is a psychical fact. The creative primal ground of man's mental life is in himself, in his unconscious. It is greater and more powerful than his conscious ego and therefore not under the control of the ego. That means we can find the gods neither on Mount Olympus nor in heaven, but in ourselves. Eastern religions and Christian mystics have always known that, for their religious activity consists in inner meditation, not in praying to a "Thou" far away in heaven. Thus, if the Greeks thought that the muse brings the human poet in contact with the wisdom of the gods, we would say that the anima, the experience of the unconscious, can lead him to essential sources of human existence. Gerhart Hauptmann wrote, "Poetry evokes out of words the resonance of the primordial word."[7]

In the Greek myth the muses are, through their mother Mnemosyne, the well of remembrance, associated with primeval entities, the primordial gods Ouranos and Gaia. Emil Staiger explains these relationships in his theory of poetry: "Der lyrische Dichter vergegenwärtigt das Vergangene so wenig wie das, was jetzt geschieht. Beides vielmehr ist ihm gleich nah und näher als alle Gegenwart. Er geht darin auf, d.h. er 'erinnert'. Erinnerung soll der Name sein für das Fehlen des Abstandes zwischen Subjekt und Objekt, für das lyrische Ineinander. Gegenwärtiges, Vergangenes, ja sogar Künftiges kann in lyrischer Dichtung erinnert werden."[8]

Rainer Maria Rilke wrote in one of his famous letters to a young poet: "Describe your sorrows and desires, passing thoughts and the belief in some sort of beauty—describe all these with loving, quiet, humble sincerity, and use to express yourself the things in your environment, the images from your dreams, and the objects of your memory. If your daily life seems poor, do not blame it; blame yourself, tell yourself that you are not poet enough to call forth its riches; for to the creator there is no poverty and no poor indifferent place. And even if you were in some prison the walls of which let none of the sounds of the world come to your senses—would you not then still have your childhood, that precious, kingly possession, that treasure house of memories?"[9]

We are reminded also of Proust's "A la recherche du temps perdu" —again an indication of the mythological belief that remembrance is the maternal source of the muse. But remembrance is different from the memory of plain facts. Plato calls it the inner memory: in his view the soul lives in its pre-existent life in the realm of pure ideas. If now an idea comes into man's mind, this is an *anamnesis*, the soul's remembrance of its pre-existent state.

We know from depth psychology that dreams often have a much greater capacity of remembrance than our conscious mind. Events or impressions from our childhood which we had forgotten may suddenly appear. And sometimes there appear very impressive dreams of a mythological or religious kind where the dreamer is plainly astonished that themes of this kind come into his nightly fantasy. In reality "he never would have dreamt of such things." Jung published many of those great or archetypal dreams, as he called them. Jung himself thought at first that dreams of this kind must be unconscious memories not of events and impressions of the dreamer's individual life but memories of a more archaic state of mankind. Freud, too, discovered "phylogenetic material" in the unconscious and wrote: "Furthermore dreams bring to light material which cannot have originated either from the dreamer's adult life or from his forgotten childhood. We are obliged to regard it as a part of the archaic heritage which a child brings with him into the world, before any experience of his own, influenced by the experiences of his ancestors. We find the counterpart of this phylogenetic material in the earliest human legends and in surviving customs. Thus dreams constitute a source of human prehistory which is not to be despised."[10] Later on Jung thought that the factor which creates and arranges fantasy and mythological imagination is the unconscious archetype inherent in the psyche of man. The phenomenon of mythological dreaming must therefore not be dependent on unconscious memories of an archaic heredity; it simply belongs to the psychic functioning of man and can appear spontaneously at any time under certain conditions. In this case remembrance would have more the meaning of the German *Erinnerung* in the sense of *Inne-werden*, "to perceive, to become aware of."

Inspiration we can define as an occurrence in which new ideas invade the boundaries of one's ego consciousness carrying an emotional energy which strives for expression. The Greek poet felt he was visited by the muse; from a psychological point of view we would say today that the unconscious became activated and some of its contents intruded into the realm of consciousness. The ego of the writer feels that this event happens more or less independently of his own will. In "Big Sur and the Oranges of Hieronymus Bosch" Henry Miller tells us: "Whole sentences poured in on me. Then paragraphs. Then pages. . . . It is a phenomenon that always astounds me, no matter how often it happens. Try to bring it about and you fail miserably. Try to squelch it and you become more victimized. During the year or so that I was occupied with *Plexus* the inundation was almost continuons. Huge blocks—particularly the dream parts—came to me just as they appear in print and without any effort on my part, except that of equating my own rhythm with that of the mysterious dictator who had me in his thrall."[11]

Modern rationalism has devaluated the idea that there is a divine or irrational unconscious power which inspires the poet. The French poet Paul Valéry, for instance, attacked the inspiration theory. Mallarmé used the image of the workshop in which the poet constructs his works; Gottfried Benn spoke of a "laboratory of words." Critical reflection and analytical thinking, working by means of a refined artistic skill, are the principles of such literary directions. In contrast to these principles, which put their accent on rational processes, we have the movements of the Dadaists, the Surrealists, and lastly the modern attempts of psychedelic art. We find in our day an increased fascination with the unconscious. Hashish and LSD are means by which one can break out of the prison of rationalism and undertake a trip into the imaginative wealth of the unconscious. It is considered as something fascinating and inspiring. I do not want to judge those attempts which obviously can have many negative and dangerous side effects. But these phenomena which exert such an attraction demonstrate the need to overcome the relatively narrow boundaries of rational ego consciousness in order to experience the reality of the unconscious.

It seems to me that poet and writer both need visions, imaginations, ideas which come up spontaneously from the unconscious, as well as refined skill and critical reflection. Karl Schmid, professor of German literature in Zurich, writes in this connection that the unconscious may be called creative because it can bring something up from the "impersonal realm of the Mothers into the person. This is true for everybody and at all times for the unconscious. The artist, however, is creative in a specific sense because he can bring forth what the unconscious brings up; he can express in collective terms what came upon him from the unconscious. This bringing forth is probably the decisive thing; here the artist finds his dignity. The act of bringing forth is as essential for a work of art as the primary spark coming from the unconscious. The specific artistic act, however, is one of consciousness. It cannot be stressed too much that what the artist experiences and does is quite a cool and hard sort of business. A dreaming unconscious inwardness which we as laymen tend to see as the really artistic mood is nothing but a projection of the non-artist into the artist. We love our inwardness, the joy of feelings, of dreams, all these fair compensations for our habitual clever adaptation to the outer world. The inwardness of the artist, however, is his hell. His joy means bringing forth, forming, bringing into existence. The creative process is not only a happening, it is also an act. It is not the unconscious of the poet that is creative. Only the poet is creative, thanks of course to his unconscious, but also in opposition to the unconscious and beyond the unconscious."[12]

The difficult question of which is more important for the creative process—creative impulses on the one hand, skill and critical reflection on the other—will find different answers according to the poet's personality and the spirit of his time. It seems clear, however, that the experience which the Greeks explained by the influence of the muses is an essential part of literary creativity at all times. The muse was a divine being for the Greeks, although debased to a cliché later on in history. From a psychological point of view we might call her a symbol of the poet's relation to his creative unconscious potential. She is therefore immortal, disguised under the many names we give to creative impulses and ideas which have their decisive influence over the poet. The myth of Thamyris who tried to dispose of the muses has its overall validity; he was punished by blindness, and the daughters of Mnemosyne took away his capacity of remembrance—he forgot how to play the harp. Nobody can be truly creative by means of his rational consciousness alone—the inner muse always remains a power beyond the complete control of the poet.

Notes

1. Sigmund Freud, *The Standard Edition of the Complete Psychological Works* (London, 1959), vol. 9, p. 153.
2. C. G. Jung, *Collected Works* (Princeton, 1960), vol. 8, pp. 154–55.
3. J. W. Goethe, *Conversations of Goethe with Eckermann* (New York, 1960).
4. C. G. Jung, *Collected Works*, vol. 6, p. 618.
5. J. W. Goethe, *Maximen und Reflexionen* (Weimar: Schriften der Goethegesellschaft, 1907), vol. 21, p. 314.
6. C. G. Jung, *Collected Works*, vol. 6, p. 603.
7. Ibid., vol. 15, p. 80.
8. Emil Staiger, *Grundbegrtiffe der Poetik* (Zürich, 1961), p. 62.
9. R. M. Rilke, *Briefe an einen jungen Dichter* (Leipzig, 1932), first letter.

10. S. Freud, *Complete Psychological Works* (London, 1964), vol. 23, pp. 166–67.
11. Henry Miller, *Big Sur* (New York, 1957).
12. Karl Schmid, "Tiefenpsychologie und Literaturgeschichte," *Neue Zürcher Zeitung*, 21 März 1965.

O. K. Nambiar

SPIRIT—PSYCHE—SYMBOL—SONG

ST. JOHN'S INSPIRED VERSE: "IN THE BEGINNING WAS THE WORD, AND the Word was with God, and the Word was God," recalls a similar inspired declaration heard earlier in the Vedas:

> Prajāpathi [Brahman] only was then this. [Prajāpathīr vai idam āsīt.] Vāk ["word," Latin "vox"] was second to Him. [Tasya vāg dvitīya āsīt. "The Word potentially in Him issued forth as His power."] And the Word is the Supreme Brahman. [Vāg vai Paramam Brahma.][1]

The Word is said to be the first spontaneous creative activity of God; similarly the first spontaneous creative activity of man is speech in its most elementary form.

What is meant by the term *Vāk* or Word? How does it arise? What are the stages by which it evolves into the universe of names and forms? A gist of the Hindu speculations on this subject is given as follows.

Word or Vāk has two aspects. One is the Cosmic aspect, the creative Word as the seed of the manifested universe of name and form; the other is the microcosmic aspect, and in particular, the biological aspect where we consider it as the divine creative energy expressing itself in and through man. Considered in this last aspect, Word includes and means the manifold works of man which fill the earth, though it stands for speech in its narrow and specialized application. All kinds of creative expressions of the spirit in man, his thoughts and deeds, laws and institutions, art, religion, science, language and literature, and indeed all his aims and aspirations and the tools and means he devises to realise them are comprised in the term Word. For these are but the results of the wide-ranging operations of the eternal spirit expressing itself in and through the human instrument. Of these myriads of forms of creative expression, I wish to confine myself to the area of literary expression, which I have further limited to religious and mystical poetry—the poetry of the spirit. I choose mystical and religious poetry because here the spirit expresses itself spontaneously, directly, and integrally. Here it springs from the common spiritual ground, and suffers the least contamination from the action of what is extraneous or accidental. Here we have archetypal images and universal symbols and an idiom more or less the same all over the world. Here we have evidence of inner experiences strikingly similar, whatever the religious culture in which we find them recorded. These symbols, rightly interpreted, are a key to our understanding of the common ground and substrate of all mystico-religious experience from which the poetry of the spirit takes origin. Religious scriptures and mystical poetry are therefore a vital area for our exploration. Later, I shall deal with a few concepts and symbols taken from the poetry of the spirit belonging to different religious cultures to show their close kinship and parallelism as evidence of their emergence from a common ground and soil shared by mankind universally. We shall examine whether the similarity we notice has any connection with the structure and mechanism of the mind and psyche of man, which must be the same for all, everywhere, every age.

By Word is meant a creative stress. The word we hear and speak is the gross end-product of a multiphased movement of creative energy, which gets subtler and subtler as we trace it back to its root and origin in human consciousness. The gist of the Hindu speculations on this subject is as follows.

The Ultimate Reality—the Vedic Brahman and the Siva of the Āgamās represent this—is expressed in the metaphysical formula Sad-Chid-Ānanda or, Being (existence)–Consciousness–Bliss. This Ultimate Reality, Brahman, is the creator, the ground of creation, and also comprises the stuff of creation. In the Brahman (or Siva-state), Consciousness, absorbed in itself, is in a state of Bliss. It is a Cosmic closed circuit —an *ouroboros*,[2] the serpent swallowing its tail. All creation is potentially in Brahma. It is the Supreme Consciousness in a quiescent state, the three Gunas[3] are in Him in equipoise, the Word or power of creation (Shakti) was in Him and the Word was He.

Hindu speculations start with the assumption that creation arose from a self-produced causal stress in Brahman. The stress is his own power and condenses a will-center upsetting the balance of the three Gunas. From this will-center surges out a creative movement like waves on the sea. Seemingly different from the sea, the wave is but a modification in the stuff of the sea. Similarly, creation is described as a modification in the stuff of Brahma accomplished by its own potential power now brought into play. We have now Supreme Consciousness in two states, both as stasis and dynamis, the will center and creative ideation, resulting in a 'seeming' differentiation into subject and object. Brahman sees the universe objectified out of Himself by His own Shakti. When this projection ceases and His Shakti or power merges back into Him, the universe ceases to be. In the Supreme Consciousness there is nothing added now, as there was nothing taken away then, by these developments, for the creative power of Brahma and the stuff of creation all were only movements in Brahman. The power of Brahman returns from the dynamic to the static state. The wave subsides in the sea out of which it arose.

As above, so below. In man this union brings about Yōga, according to Hindu thought, the chief goal both of man's life and of evolutionary movement. In the Cosmic scheme, the Word returns to the Will, which in its turn melts into the Supreme Consciousness. The vast fabric of creation dissolves marking the apocalyptic end of the eonic cycle.

The Saiva Āgamās describe the Supreme power by a hyphenated Siva-Shakti, fusing Siva, the masculine principle, with Shakti, his power conceived as a feminine power. Shakti, the womb of creation, is also the nourisher of it. Shakti is the Word and issues forth from Him to project the phenomenal universe of name and form. Her Cosmic chore begins with each immense cycle of creation and ends with dissolution. Siva is the power of consciousness, Shakti the Word as creative power. In the microcosmic view, Siva and Shakti are no longer united but polarized. They are present in every individual body, Siva as the spirit and Shakti as the mind-life-matter constituents of man. In Tantric speculations, the Siva principle is said to reside in the head and the seat of the Shakti principle is in the body anchored to the Mūladhāra or spinal base. The whole drift of evolution is the reunion of Shakti with Siva; Shakti the creative evolutionary power yearns to be reunited to her lover and lord. This union of Siva and Shakti achieved in the body is the same as the attainment of Yoga.

In song after song in the religious literature of man this tense theme of yearning and reunion has been sung—Sankara's *Ānanda Lahari*, *The Songs of Solomon*, the Sufi songs of *Leila and Majnun*, and the Radha-Krishna and Siva-Parvathi themes.

> He is the Mahādēva, white like pure crystal and is the effulgent first cause, and she is Parā, the lovely woman of beauteous body, whose limbs are listless by reason of her great passion. [Bṛhat—Sri Karma.]

I have always felt—I say this subject to correction by those who are better informed in Christian esoterics and theology—that St. John of the Cross grasped this truth of Siva-Shakti union and knew their respective situations in the human body. In one of his spiritual canticles he sings:

Man shall be as God hereafter;
God shall be as human kind;
He shall eat and drink with mortals;
And commune with mortal mind.

He shall tarry in their presence,
Be with them continually,
Till this present dispensation
Ended and consum'd shall be.

Then 'mid melody eternal
Bride and Bridegroom shall be wed,
Two already close united,
She the body, He the head.

All the Bride's component members
Shall partake in that great rite
And those members are the righteous
Which in her He will unite.[4]

Hindu speculations regarding the Cosmic phases through which the Causal Word moves creatively to manifest the universe are too elaborate and far afield to fit into this essay. We shall confine ourselves to Vāg or Word as it rises in the human consciousness and the phases through which it finds expression in human speech. The process as it takes place in man is said to be a pale replica of the process by which the Divine Word became the Logos, the manifested universe. Besides, it is a continuation of the Cosmic process beginning at the stage where the Cosmic process ends. From the human viewpoint the last phase of the divine Word is described as Parā Vāk ("the word beyond"). In the evolution of the word in man, the first stage is the Parā Vāk which is the last phase of the Cosmic evolution of the Word.

In man there are four stages in the movement of the Word from its genesis as an idea to its expression in speech. When a thought or idea arises in the ground of consciousness, it is at first *indistinct and vague.* As it grows in definiteness, consciousness *perceives* it as an *object.* Next there is an intermediate stage before the final act of vocal utterance. In this intermediate stage the means (images, symbols, signs) for expressing the thought or idea in the terms of the sounds of speech (a symbolic phonal transcription) are sought in the field of the individual's experience, and found. It is in this stage that the *thought unites with the sound.* It has to be understood that the sound at this stage is not yet articulate, but only potentially present in an undifferentiated form. Articulation takes place in the last stage when the vocal instruments come into play.

This movement of the word from idea to speech (and this is a willed movement) with its four stages is said to be a weak replica of the cosmic movement of the Divine Word by which the divine idea manifests as the universe. "Four are the steps measured by Vāk. The wise Brāhmin knows them; three being hidden in the cave[5] do not issue. The fourth is spoken by men in their speech." So the *Sruti.* In the *Sarada-Tilaka,* a Tāntric work, we read:

> First Parā and then came Pasyanti, Madhyama and Vaikhari sabda. It is in this order that Kundalini Shakti [see next section of this essay] who is Ichha [will], Jnana [knowledge] and Kriya [action], who is both energy and consciousness [Tejō-rūpa and Chid-rūpa] and possessed of Gunas [attributes or qualities],[6] creates the Garland of Letters [the sounds of speech].

In the *Yōga Kundalini Upanishad* the movement is described metaphorically:

> That Vāk sprouts in Parā, gives forth leaves in Pasyanti, buds in Madhyama and blossoms in Vaikhari.

Parā ("beyond"), the first stage, is only an ideational stir in the consciousness field, and in Pasyanti ("seeing"), the second stage, the idea becomes defined and perceived, when the idea is held in the light of the mind. These two are activities of the psyche and forms of energy, like wireless waves in ether. Next comes the *Madhyama* stage (literally, the "middle" stage) when Vāk energy assumes Nāda (Nāda rūpini, "undifferentiated sound"). Last is *Vaikhari* where, using the vocal apparatus, she issues forth as the articulated speech we use and hear—syllables, words, and sentences.

These are the four steps. Mallinātha in his excellent commentary on

Kalidasa's profound Kāvya, *Kumara Sambhava*, (2–17–[58]) writes:

> Vaikhari manifests the words, Madhyama is perceived through the mind, Pasyanti throws light on the idea, and the subtle voice Parā is identified with the Causal Brahman.

The spirit wills, an idea rises, takes specific form in the psyche, and moves towards utterance producing the sound symbols required for manifestation as speech. Spirit-psyche-symbol-utterance are indeed the four steps Vāg takes to manifest herself.

According to Kundalini theory of *chakras*, the Parā stage has its psychic center in Mūladhāra (base of the spine), Pasyanti in Swādhistāna (region below the navel) and upwards, Madhyama is in Anāhata (heart) and upwards, and Vaikhari is in the throat. Higher above reigns the silence of the spirit.

Earlier I made a passing reference to Kundalini Shakti. Described as the Mother Energy, she is the creative evolutionary force at work in the universe and in man. It both creates and powers man's physical, vital, mental, and psychic bodies and supports him in the three states of wakefulness, dream, and sleep. She is also the power which leads him to the fourth state of yogic consciousness—the Turya state.

It is further stated that this energy is normally quiescent or asleep in man. Her seat is at the base of the spinal column when our normal consciousness functions. When awake or aroused, certain higher centers of consciousness are vitalized into activity, our awareness becomes heightened and its range broadened. Modes of awareness become modified. The "sleeper" awakes to an apprehension of the Higher Reality. This is the Yōga state.

The name Kundalini is given to it because it is imagined or actually perceived by the inner eye of the yōgi as a spiral of fiery red light when it is static. When aroused—whether this happens naturally or by meditational techniques—it straightens out, makes a "hissing" sound like an angry serpent and ascends along the central neural channel, seeking to reach the opposite pole in the cranium. It is curious that the tree-snake symbol and the myths developed out of them are present in the religious speculations of different races.[7]

Considered in terms of the psycho-physical energetics of the human system, the process seems to consist in the phased withdrawal of all radially distributed *prānās* or vital energies to the central axis, the spinal cord. The sense instruments stop their functioning. The prānas are thus withdrawn and absorbed into the main energy-stream of Kundalini. In the ascent of the Kundalini, she "pierces" the six chakras or psycho-physical centers, and traverses the zones of matter, mind, and spirit. These centers or chakras are "strung like datura flowers, one above the other, on a string." Breaking "the three knots" she enters the life of the spirit, the yōga state. Breaking the first of the three knots (Brahma Granthi) gives entry from the zone of matter to the vital zone; the second (Vishnu Granthi) opens a way from the vital zone to the zone of the mind; and the third (Rudra Granthi), from the mind to the spirit. The Kundalini Shakti herself is modified as she makes this ascent. In the early stages of the ascent she is described as the serpent power, in the later phases she is Devi or Shakti, a goddess.

The chakras are said to be areas in the central nervous system connected to the sympathetic systems, and the three Granthis or knots have to do with the somatic, psychic, and spiritual areas of experience.

The chakras are called lotuses and have varying but definite numbers of petals and colours. Every petal carries a letter of the alphabet[8] and every chakra a seed-sound or Bīja-Letter, which has its powers and functions. The passage of the Kundalini energy through these chakras greatly enhances these powers. In the earlier stages of her ascent certain psychic and somatic experiences are described; in the later phases (after the fifth and sixth chakras) the subjective center of experience, the Ego, gradually dissolves into the Cosmic Consciousness. This is mythologized as the holy union of Kundalini Shakti with her lord and husband Siva, the Supreme spirit. This happens in the region of the cerebrum where the energies of the two poles meet. In song after song of ecstacy mystics all over the world have hymned this exalted state of union.

After the union takes place it brings a profound sense of bliss and peace to the yōgi, described as an inner experience of "a shower of nectar."[9] Thereafter, Kundalini retraces her movement back to her normal seat, through the chakras bringing to them a new life and light from a higher source. The psyche is reborn. The world scene remains the same as before, but one's attitudes, sense of values, and responses are now changed. Walt Whitman, the American sage, has described it in *Song of Myself*.

> Swiftly arose and spread around me the peace and
> knowledge that pass all the argument of the earth,
> And I know that the hand of God is the promise of my own,

And I know that the spirit of God is the brother of my own,
And that all men ever born are also my brothers,
and the women my sisters and lovers,
And that a kelson of the creation is love,
And limitless are leaves stiff or drooping in the fields,[10]
And brown ants in the little wells beneath them,
And messy scabs of the worm fence, heap'd stones,
elder, mullein and poke-weed.

Tensions are resolved in joy. He sees the whole universe as divine, the face of God in every face, perfect plan and purpose in every event, and beauty spread everywhere. Love flows out in all directions. Adam is restored to his lost Paradise. Along with this comes an urge to proclaim this discovery in song and speech and good works. This is sainthood.

The ascent of Kundalini is laya karma ("dissolution") and the descent, the Sṛshti ("recreation"). This is the rebirth or second birth of the religious mysteries.

What has been said so far is the briefest possible summary of Kundalini movement in relation to yōga. We have now to consider its movement in the creation of literary works.

The *Shad Chakra Nirūpana* describing the movement of Kundalini, visible to yogis as a "streak of young strong lightning," also mentions a sound which it is said to produce: "Her sweet murmur is like the indistinct 'hum' of swarms of love-mad bees. She produces melodious poetry and Bandha [a kind of literary composition] and all other compositions in prose or verse, in sequence or otherwise, in Sanskrit, Prakrit and other languages. It is she who maintains all beings of the world by inspiration and expiration, and shines in the cavity of the root-lotus [Mūladhāra chakra] like a chain of brilliant lights" (verses 10–11). *Sarada Tilaka* (Ch. I, v. 11–14) tells us that it is the Kundalini Shakti which is "in all living bodies that manifests itself in prose and verse by the aid of letters [Varnas] of the alphabet." It is consciousness power, and makes and uses its instruments of utterance. This humming sound contains potentially all the sounds and meanings of human speech and song. The earlier Parā stage of speech is nonvibratory, silent, unmanifested, stationary, and is located in the root-chakra. Pasyanti is said to be in Swādhisthāna and upwards. Madhyama (middle) is the stage where she becomes Nāda rupini, (assumes the form of sound). This is in the Anāhata lotus in the region of the heart. Then "she goes upward as a mere undifferentiated 'hum' [samjalpa matra avibhakta]" before she finds utterance in the mouth in the Vaikhari stage (between the heart and the mouth).

At the Madhyama stage, between self-manifestation and utterance, Kundalini energy moves into the external and internal instruments of speech (Bahyāntakaranātmika). The *Yōga Kundalini* tells us:

> Kundalini is subtle [sūkshma] and in the form of light and not an object of hearing. Then she goes up Sushumna Nādi. When she reaches the lotus of the heart she becomes Madhyama as a mere undifferentiated "hum." It is she who, appearing at the throat, chest, teeth, nose, palate, and head, assuming the form of letters [Varna], and issuing from the root of the tongue and lips becomes Vaikhari—the Mother of all sounds that we hear.

It is said that the Parā stage is silent and non-vibratory. When a thought reader *en rapport* with his subject, reads another's thoughts, he is probably tapping his subject's ideas at the Pasyanti or Madhyama levels where specific ideas take shape. The Vaikhari speech differs from man to man and from race to race due to numerous factors of which culture, education, environment, climate, and defects of speech organs are only the more apparent causes. Psycho-physiological factors also operate so that the inner movement of Sabda ("sound") and Artha ("meaning") slip from alignment resulting in phonetic and semantic shifts. It is at the Vaikhari stage that differences arise, illustrating the significance of the story of the confusion of tongues which fell on the builders of the Tower of Babel.

Applied to literature, Vaikhari is the stage where all poetry, prose, drama, and indeed all forms of literary expression, are manifested. The different forms and kinds, qualities and purposes these works reveal are due to Samskāra,[11] Gunas, the powers of the mind and spirit, and the social, ethical, and aesthetic values of their authors. It is in the poetry of the spirit that these differences are least manifest. This is illustrated by the selections from the poetry of the spirit presented in the penultimate section of this essay. It will be found that the concepts and symbols, the myth and idiom employed by mystics are the same in every race and every age, pointing to a common ground of inner experience. Before giving these examples, a word about the psychic mechanism involved in these operations will not be out of place.

In the fifty-two verses of *Shad Chakra Nirūpana* there are three specific references to the power of literary expression or uttered word, conferred by the awakened Kundalini passing through the chakras. At Swādhistāna Chakra, she is said to confer the power of "nectarlike words which flows in prose and verse as well as well-reasoned discourse" (v. 18). At the Anāhata chakra (v. 27) "one becomes capable of intense concentration and he is able to enter the minds of others" (empathy?). At Visuddha (v. 13) "one acquires wisdom and peace of mind, can know the past, present and future." At this stage he hears the seed-sound "Hum." "His words possess great power which the Gods are powerless to resist. . . . His words dispell sorrow and disease." Next, at Ājna, the Divine Light penetrates the human mind. All spiritual knowledge is gained here. Here is the seat of the Vedās (Scriptures). Beyond Ājna, the Ego, the lower self already attenuated, dissolves and spiritual life begins. Those rare saints and prophets who have risen to this height are able to pass the power of the spirit to our earth-life. Their words establish reality at every level. Their words create and transform.

As I said earlier, when the spirit expresses itself through the human organism, of necessity it uses the psychic and mental instruments evolved in the human body. The shape and structure of the inner Nādi[12] systems and the chakras are said to become visible to the clairvoyant vision of the yōgi when the Kundalini power reaches and energizes the Ājna chakra between the brows, called the third and "unpaired" eye of "spiritual illumination."[13] From Ājna he is said to be able to see the subtle channels, the chakras, their shapes and colours, the fields and flows of biopsychic energies, and hear the internal seed-sounds or Bīja Mantra.[14] The different Mandalās which are used in Hindu worship and psychotherapy are patterned on the basis of the inner configurations seen by the yōgi's inturned vision. From this arose the symbols of light, moon, inverted tree (symbols for the brain and the descending spinal cord), the three circles, the triangles, lotuses or rose, and several other symbols we come across in mystical literature. I shall illustrate this in another section of this essay.

THE SARASWATHI NĀDI

So far we have considered the mother-energy in its yogic movement along the principal channel, the Sushumna. We shall now consider its movement along another channel, the Saraswathi Nādi by which creative works of aesthetic appeal are produced, and in particular those of the spoken word. Hindu religious imagination conceives Saraswathi as the Goddess of speech, learning, and the fine arts. Poets invoke her blessing at the commencement of their major works. The name itself signifies "that which flows forth." She is conceived as the first offspring of Brahman (Supreme Consciousness) with whom Brahman united to create the universe. She is therefore poetically described as the daughter and wife of Brahman. I once heard an overzealous Christian missionary hold forth on this metaphor as an instance of the moral depravity of the Hindus! Forgive him.

The Nādi system is a subject elaborately dealt with in yōga works. Nādi (from Nād, "to move") are conduits of vital energies (prānās) which are themselves functionally and qualitatively differentiated. The network of innumerable Nādis resembles "the veins in the leaf of an Aswatha tree," some gross, and others subtle, like the Yōga Nādi (subtle or sūkshma). The prānās fall under two broad classifications, those belonging to the Moon Mandalā and those of the Sun Mandalā, the former connected with affective and spiritual experiences. The central Sushmna by which Kundalini is said to ascend is called the Nādi of Fire. Integral yōga is the total experience in which these three systems of the sun, moon, and fire unite.[15]

Of the principal Nādis which have a bearing on yōga, the most important three are called Ida, Pingala, and Sushumna. Ida (moon) to the left, and Pingala (sun) to the right of the spinal column are said to correspond to the two sympathetic cords; Sushumna is equated with the interior canal in the spinal cord. The chakras appear to be centers in the spinal cord from which branches spread out in the system. The prānās or energies are several. For the purpose of yōga, the most important are two, Prānā and Apāna, described by some as the positive and negative (afferent and efferent?). It is not our purpose to go into this subject in detail or depth; we are concerned here with the Saraswathi Nādi as it is said to be the channel of consciousness energy in creative art expression.

The Sushumna, which is the spinal cord, runs from the basic plexus (Mūladhāra) and reaches to the lotus of the thousand petals, the brain. Within Sushumna is the Vajra Nādi and inside it is the Chitrini Nādi (*Shad Chakra Nirūpana*, v. 1). Thus we have a three fold channel of energy: Chitrini ("nectar-dropping") represents pure intelligence (Suddha Bodha-svabhava) a faculty of consciousness, Sātvic in quality—the Moon principle. Vajrini, the principle of the Sun, stands for Rājasic quality. Sushumna is Tāmasic, of the principle of Fire. Further research is required to unravel the meaning of these terms, as well as the significance of the elaborate Mandalā structures called the chakras. A point of importance may be noted regarding the shape of the Ida and Pingala Nādis in relation to the central spinal cord: Ida and Pingala cross the spinal cord alternating from one side to the other forming the figure of the Caduceus, an important religious symbol among the ancient Egyptians, Sumerians, Hindus, and Romans. The two wings on top of the Caduceus represent the two-petalled lotus of the Ājna chakra, the sixth chakra. A point which may be mentioned here is that the petals of the chakras 'carry' the speech sounds of the alphabet. The letters thus distributed total the fifty letters of the alphabet. They exist as the seed forms of the sounds. The Sahasrara (thousand-petalled lotus) in the brain is said to be a twenty-fold multiplication of the fifty letters. (See v. 17 of Sri Sankara's *Ananda Lahari, Intoxication of Bliss.*)

Sarawathi Nādi, with which art and literary productions are linked, is situated outside and to the right of the Sushumna and stretches up to the tongue (the hypoglossal nerve of the cervical plexus). The Saraswathi Nādi appears to become vitalized by an inductive influence passed into it by the three-fold (Chitrini, Vajrini, Sushumna) emanation from the activated Kundalini in its upward movement bringing forth creative literary utterance in "compositions in verse and prose." These are instant and highly complicated operations calling into play the powers of the Nādi systems, taking what is needed for the creative work—sound, meaning, ideas, thoughts, symbols, images, words, emotions—from every repository, tapping every line and channel. In the poetry of the spirit there is a nearly total integration of utterance proceeding from a common unified source. The Scriptures, myths and epics, and mystical writings are examples of this kind of poetry, although they may contain, in the form in which they have been put together and given to us, features and elements derived from less unified areas of origin. But we can detect amidst it all the true ring of the poetry of the spirit. When the spirit calls to the spirit, words, images, and myth—having done their work—withdraw when the soul unites with the spirit.

If yōga is man's highest and most direct participation in the spirit, art experience is next to it, for it too—in whatever manner it comes to us—is a feeble and indirect experience of what is true, beautiful, and good.

The Saraswathi Nādi is only a channel for the flow of creative activity; the main energy comes from the aroused Kundalini in its ascent. The *Shad Chakra Nirūpana* (v. 10–11) says:

> Her sweet murmur is like the 'hum' of swarms of love-mad bees. She produces melodious poetry and Bandha and all other compositions in

> prose or verse, in sequence or otherwise, in Samskrita, Prakrita and other languages. It is she who maintains all the beings of the world by inspiration and expiration, and shines in the cavity of the root-lotus like a chain of brilliant lights. . . . (*Sarada Tilaka*, Ch. I, v. 10–11).

Sarada Tilaka (Ch. I, v. 11–14) tells us that ". . . that sound is called by those versed in the Āgamas, Sabda Brahman [consciousness power manifested as sound]. She is the awakener of eternal knowledge . . . greatly skilled in creation. She receives the continuous stream of ambrosia and illuminates the whole universe." Now I want to illustrate what has been said so far with a selection of mystico-religious poetry, using the symbolic key. From the vast amount of material available, often colored by mythological and theological elements, the pure poetry of the spirit has to be separated and allowance made for racial and personal factors. With this caution let us examine this area of symbols.

The Tree is a well-established symbol in mystical poetry. The Biblical Tree of Life and the Tree of Knowledge, the latter as a means of world experience and the former of life in the spirit, and the associated serpent symbol are seen in several religious scriptures. The mystic tree Yggdrasil, described in Scandinavian myths, was the most sacred and the greatest of all trees and linked the three planes of heaven, earth, and hell. Its branches spread all over the world and reached above to the heavens. It has three great roots; one of them reached heaven, another grew in the direction of the realm of the frost giants, and the third to the Under world. From beneath each of these roots rose a magical fountain whose waters had miraculous virtues, and from the tree itself fell a constant shower of honey-dew. A serpent named Nithhoggr lay at the Underworld fountain and gnawed at the root of Yggdrasil. High up on the tree sat a kingly eagle. The squirrel, Ratatoskar, was said to run up and down the tree, breeding strife between the serpent and the eagle sitting aloft.

Among the Druids, the Eagle was a symbol of their Supreme God and among the Romans, it was the emblem of Jupiter, the father of the Gods. The Yggdrasil tree, therefore, is an image of man in his vast-spreading and many-branched consciousness activity, reaching Godwards above to the heavens in one direction, and in another, down to the earth and farther down to hell. Perhaps the squirrel represents the frisking ego which oscillates between extremes of good and evil, between the spiritual and the material. It is a complex collocation of symbols that we find in the Yggdrasil tree of the Scandinavian myth. In the same myth the tree appears also to have served the same purpose of moral and intellectual progress and spiritual ascent which is represented in the Bible by the ladder Jacob saw in his dream (Gen. 28) with angels moving up and down along its rungs between Earth and Heaven. Again, in the Hindu list of sacred trees we find four evergreen trees (aswatha, banyan, and so on), which exuded a milky juice, all belonging to the Ficus group. We learn that the Sumerians of old believed in a Cosmic Tree which they called Eridu, situated at the center of the earth. It is said to be crystalline white and in it dwelt their God Tamuz, implying the notion that trees represented life forces which sustain all creation.[16] The Hindus look upon the sacred Aswatha tree as the seat of the God of Fire (life force). The Egyptian equivalent is the Sycamore—a tree which yields milk—worshipped in ancient days. In the *Egyptian Book of the Dead* are prayers addressed to the sycamore: "Hail Sycamore tree of the Goddess of Nūt. Grant thou to me the water and air which are in Thee."[17]

Among the several trees mentioned in Hindu myths, each symbolizing or in some way connected with one or the other of the deities of the Hindu pantheon, there are two trees which deserve special attention. The heavenly Kalpa Taru is the tree of wish fulfillment which gives man all he desires of worldly felicity. This tree, therefore, stands for all the material cravings of man. There is another tree, the aswatha or pepul mentioned in the Upanishads and repeatedly referred to in the later mythological and scriptural texts. This tree has "its roots above and branches below" spreading all over the world. There is a striking parallel in the Jewish *Book of Bahir*, which compares the system of Sephiroth, or the creative emanations microcosmically present in the human body, to "an inverted tree whose roots are above and the foliage below."[18] This is the tree of human consciousness, rooted in the brain, in the cerebrum, and its many-branched nervous system spreading to every part and extremety of the human body. It is by means of these numerous branches of the nervous system that consciousness activity is sustained and the whole phenomenal world is experienced: the withdrawal of consciousness activity from the periphery to the root in the brain is the process by which the yōgi attains the heightened consciousness of the divine. It is a disengagement of the consciousness activity from the senses. The Bodhi tree under which Buddha sat in meditation and received enlightenment is another tree highly venerated as the Tree of Enlightenment.

When Seth killed Osiris, the Egyptian God-hero, it was an erica tree which revealed to Isis the place where the body was concealed. Similarly the place of concealment of the body of the Master Builder in

Freemasonic legend was revealed by an acacia plant. In both these legends of resurrection to a higher and immortal life the symbolic plant plays an important part, a significance revealed also by the symbolic ivy of the Dionysian rites, the myrtle of the festival of Ceres, and the Druidic mistletoe. It is curious that the Rosicrucians have a tree symbol signifying the same concept. "The highest wisdom," writes Engelke in *Secret Symbols of the Rosicrucians*, "can be gained only by reaching back to the root of the tree whose branches represent the phenomenal world." Among the Akkadians mention is made of the tree, the Tintir, which is literally, Life-Tree, guarded by the spirits of good and evil. Among the Assyrians it was called the Asher—a name which signifies 'holy.' In Book VI of Virgil's *Aeneid*, there is the Golden Bough which admits Aeneas into the inner world of being where he converses with his father, Anchises, who represents the realm of the spirit. The legend of Aeneas suggests that entry into the realm of the spirit is possible only for one who has gained possession of the Golden Bough. It may also be mentioned here that before revealing divine wisdom God showed himself to Moses as a burning bush, specified in the Jewish Talmud as the wild acacia, which he was asked to approach barefoot. In the mythological story of Jason, the hero uses a branch of the oracular oak tree when he sails in quest of the Golden Fleece. In Babylonian myths, the serpent, venerated as the giver of life, is described as coiled round a mystical tree.

The Tree of Life (". . . tree which gives life," Apocalypse 2:7) by which man's spiritual life is gained, is associated with the symbol of the ladder which represents spiritual ascent (Jacob's Ladder, Mithraic Ladder of seven rungs, the Yupa or pole of Vedic and Shamanistic rituals, the ladder described by the poet Tulsi Das—these also stand for spiritual ascent). In one of his great religious songs the Veerasaiva mystic Nirūpādhi Siddha adopts the ladder symbol. He sings: "Be silent, rise by the ladder to your *Brahmarandhra* [the seat of mystical enlightenment in the cerebrum] and there enjoy supreme felicity." The Hindi poet and mystic, Tulsi Das, prays: "Take me by the ladder to the terrace where God is." The Tree of Life is the symbolic projection of the inner neural structures and the celebrated serpent of the myths, the energy movement experienced in them.

It seems that the tree, taken over from primitive worship, later became a symbol of intuitively grasped truths as man rose from ritual to philosophy. Viewed philosophically the tree is a symbol of the substance and power of the created universe—the *Mula Prakriti*. In a microcosmic view it represents the physiological structures of man, especially the nervous system rooted in the brain and branching and spreading out all over the body—the tree of the human psyche—with the branches as the channels of sensory activities. The withdrawal of all sensory activity into the mind and the repose of the mind in the cranial seat of consciousness is the psycho-physiological basis of yōga. The participation of the nervous system is indispensible in the yogic process.

The power and means of our spiritual ascent lie within ourselves. In Hata Yōga we have a descriptive account of the mechanism and the operation of the power. The symbols and their mythological elaborations take their shape and theme from the nature of man's inner experiences and reflect the very structure of the psycho-physiological mechanism through which he gains them. Variously described as The House of Net (*Egyptian Book of the Dead*), Linga Sarira (Hindus), Almond Tree (Old Testament), Vine (*The Song of Solomon*) and Creeper (Tantric poetry), the same truth appears in different allotropic modifications in the symbolism of mystical poetry.[19]

In symbology the vertical and the horizontal stand for the spiritual and the mundane respectively. The mountain (Mountain Kailasa, Hindu—Mount Carmel, Christian—Olympus, Greek) is the high seat of spiritual bliss. It is the seventh heaven of the religious mystics, because it is the seventh and highest region, the place of the *Sahasrara Padma* ("the lotus of a thousand petals") which the mystic's soul enters when the Kundalini Shakti has traversed the six chakras. The seventh heaven, the Seven Mansions (St. Theresa of Avila), the turret or tower (St. John of the Cross), and the mountain peak stand for the same idea. These symbols, it may be said, are interchangeable.

The Hindu lotus-experience is paralled by the Christian rose-experience. In the final effulgent experience of Dante, the Christian yōgi-poet, Beatrice (Shakti)[20] led the poet to a stage in his spiritual journey where he has a vision of "the three circles of light" (this is, according to yōga, the experience when Kundalini energizes the Ājna Chakra):

> O Light Supreme, that art so far exalted
> Above our mortal ken! Lend to my mind
> A little part of what thou didst appear. . . .
>
> I saw that in its depth there are enclosed,
> Bound up with love in one eternal book,
> The scattered leaves of all the universe. . . .

As though fused together in such a way
That what I speak of is a single Light.
The universal form of this commingling
I think I saw. . . .
For within the substance, deep and radiant,
Of that exalted Light, *I saw three rings*,
Of one dimension, yet of triple hue.
One seemed to be reflected by the next
As Iris by Iris, and the third
Seemed fire shed forth equally by both. . . .

In *Kāma Vilāsa Tantra* the great Kashmiri mystic, Lalleswari, describes these three circles of light seen by her:

Sadā Siva, Light itself, appears beyond the thunder,
The soul of power, omnipresent, etherial, blissful,
The gentle one, half-moon, the one who, seen as three,
Three lights, three circles, sun and moon and fire.
O Sivā! makes the world to be.[21]

In Tantric works and in Hindu mystical poetry there are frequent references to these three circles of light which we are told represent the three mandalās of the Sun, Moon, and Fire systems in man and relate to Pingala, Ida, and Sushumna Nādis respectively. Beyond Ājna Chakra, where these three Nādis unite, is the region of the thousand-petalled Lotus. Here Shakti merges with Siva, the beloved unites with the lover. It is interesting that Beatrice merged into the blazing vision of the Rose of Light and the poet himself becomes absorbed into it:

How vast indeed must be the amplitude
of this great rose in its remotest petals
So that the quantity and quality
Of all that joy to me was manifest.
For near or far means nothing in that region
And when God's power is thus immediate
The laws of nature are of no avail.[22]

In the *Mahā Nirvāna* Tantra (*The Great Liberation*) v. 61–62, we find the significance of these three lights elaborated as "Mukti or liberation is one's own union with these three lights," which the Tantra tells us are "Fire, Sun and Moon," respectively, centered in the chakras of the spinal base, the heart, and the head. In one of his deeply mystical poems, saint and poet Jnanadeva writes:

> It is only when the circles have been experienced that God can be realized. Hard to describe is this sweet experience. The first circle is of a white color, in the midst of it is a dazzling circle [color not mentioned]. "The still inner circle is of a red color and the *final* innermost is blue. This leads to truth, all else is ignorance.[23]
>
> (Jnanadeva's *Abhanga*, 59)

A contemporary Hindu saint, Sri Nitynanda Swami, states in his *Chidakasa-Gita* that these circles stand for the Ida (blue), Pingala (green), and Sushumna (red) Nādis. He further states that they are seen in the Chidakasa—the ether of consciousness, the firmament within—in the head above the Ājna Chakra. These inner experiences seem to vary slightly from text to text and in different persons point to differences in the psycho-physiological constitutions of the mystics.

The first effulgent vision of brilliant light (Walt Whitman's "Light untellable Lighting the very light," and "the million suns resplendant" of Hindu religious poetry), in which the mystic with the functions of his senses and mind suspended is lost in the supreme bliss of the Self, is the consummation of spiritual striving—mystical union. In the poetry of the spirit, of every land and age, we hear the exultant voice of the mystics proclaiming this experience in ecstatic poetry.[24]

Kalmeswara, the South Indian mystic, sums up the light experience in his canticle *Sada Belagutade Jyoti* (*The Light Shines Forever*):

Behold O friend,
This it is, here it is,
When, sitting all alone
An inexpressible light
Fills you to the full
Give praise to your Guru
For this supreme Gift.

These visual symbols are so numerous—lamp, cave, bees, rain of nectar, the pearl, star, forest, garden—that it is not possible to deal with all of them here. The visual symbols sometimes emerge as geometrical forms—triangles, squares, crescents, circles, a point—in spiritual poetry. A striking example of the universality of geometrical symbols for spiritual concepts may be seen in the symbols for the principles of earth (square), water (crescent or inverted triangle), fire (triangular), air (hexagon), ether or sky (circle). The equipoise of water (consciousness) and fire (life-force) principles is the celebrated Star of David (Seal of Solomon), the same as the Sri Chakra Mandalā of Hindu worship. The punctum, point, or Bindu is likewise the point and source of creation. Similarly the directions, east, west, north, and south have esoteric meaning. The subject is vast.

Besides these, there are sound symbols. One of the most striking instances of this inner sound symbol, described in detail in yogic texts, is found in *Song of Myself*. Its author, Walt Whitman, was a great yōgi—one whom Patanjali would call a yōgi by birth. I consider *Song of Myself* the finest and purest example of the poetry of the spirit that we have. Whitman's relevance in the context of the spiritual problems we face today will become apparent when we learn to look upon him as what he really was—a religious genius first, and a literary genius only incidentally. He brings independent experiential testimony which bears out some of the inner experiences described in religious literature.

In the *Song of Myself* Whitman describes the transforming spiritual experience he had. Let me quote the passage, section five of *Song of Myself*:

> I believe in you my soul, the other I am,
> must not abase itself to you
> And you must not be abased to the other.
> Loafe with me on the grass, loose the stop
> from your throat,
> Not words, not music, or rhymes I want,
> not custom or lecture, not even the best
> Only the lull I like, the hum of your valved voice.
> I mind how we once lay such a transparent
> summer morning,
> How you settled your head athwart my hips
> and gently turned over upon me,
> And parted the shirt from my bosom-bone, and
> plunged your tongue to my bare-stripped heart,
> And reach'd till you felt my beard, and reach'd
> till you held my feet.

This experience, Kundalini Yōga in every detail and symbol, brought him the highest spiritual state:

Swiftly arose and spread around me the peace and
  knowledge that pass all the arguments of the earth,
And I know that the hand of God is the promise of my own,
And that all men ever born are also my brothers,
  and the women my sisters and lovers,
And that a kelson of the creation is love,
And limitless are leaves stiff or drooping in the fields,
And brown ants in the little wells beneath them,
And mossy scabs of the worm fence, heap'd stones,
  elder, mullein and poke-weed.

The passage describes the arousing, the ascent, and the descent of Kundalini followed by a profound experience of unitive life based on love. Symbol for symbol, the description given here tallies with what is given in *Hata-Yōga-Pradeepika* and *Yōga Upanishad* and corresponds to the accounts given by Tirumoolar, Sri Ramakrishna, St. Teresa of Avila, Jalaluddin Rumi, and several other mystics. Here I shall confine myself to just one symbol, a sound symbol, "the hum of your valved voice."

Mystics mention hearing certain inner sounds when in deep meditation. Concentration on these sounds is one of the prescribed means of attaining samādhi. The sounds heard are of several kinds: at different stages of the ascent of the Kundalini, different sounds are heard and in a definite order. But it is also stated by yōgis that the sounds heard do not always follow the textbook schema and sometimes some of these sounds are skipped. It will be recalled here that when Mohammed the Prophet was asked how he knew that his words were from God, he said that he heard the sound of a bell before God spoke to his inner ear. Yogic works speak of the Anāhata sound heard as if rising from the region of the heart. We have already made a reference to "the humming of swarms of love-mad bees." The first sound heard when Kundalini is roused is said to resemble "the tinkling of bangles." Tirumoolar, the Tamil mystic and poet, refers to this and writes in *Tiru Mantiram*:

By faith I held her fast in my heart. She is a child of eight or ten years,[25] tender as a sapling, of the colour of coral, with budding breasts and fragrant hair—one sought by celestial beings—came to me (v. 1034).

She rapt in meditation, embodying all knowledge, came and filled me. (v. 1036).

> She, bejewelled, beautifully attired, came and stayed in the Golden Temple and was unified with the One. (v. 1037).
>
> She, manifesting Herself, gave me clear revelation and showed me the bright light. She filled me with bliss and raised me. (v. 1077).
>
> While I lay asleep, she, the Manōnmani, came. Her *bangles jingling* [italics mine], she laid her hand, cool and soft, on my heart and stroked my breast, even to the neck. She passed the cud of chewed betel leaves from her mouth to mine [a symbol standing for the passing of Wisdom from one to another], and said, "Do not sleep." Thus she showed me the way (v. 1083).

Tirumoolar refers to the schema of ten successive sounds (that is, according to Tantric classification) but in v. 2481 mentions hearing the sound of the bell and seeing "a brightness within. I felt I was with Him and enjoyed profound happiness." The Sarada Tilaka, a Tantric work of great authority, tells us: "the first sound heard is like the humming of bees, the next sound is like air passing through a hollow bamboo, and then is heard a bell-like sound. . . ."

St. John of the Cross refers to "certain extraordinary words" heard by the inner ear during meditation. Sri Ramakrishna also heard the Anāhata sound. St. Teresa of Avila (*Interior Castle*) writes: "For the spouse who is in the Seventh Mansion seems to be calling the soul in a way which involves no clear utterance or speech, and none of the inhabitants of the other mansions [the senses, imagination or the faculties] dares to stir, and . . . though perfectly formed, the words are not heard in the bodily ear, yet they are understood much more clearly than if they were so heard, and however determined one's resistance, it is impossible to fail to hear them. For when on the natural plane, we do not wish to hear, we can close our ears . . . but when God talks in this way to the soul, there is no such remedy. I have to listen whether I like it or not. . . ."[26]

These instances show that auditory experiences are of different kinds, some involving words, others only voice or sounds.

Whitman's experience appears to have an origin presumably at the Ājna Chakra level of Kundalini ascent, the place of the Bijā Mantra (seed-sound) "hum." The whole Kundalini movement is described here. It begins with the rotary movement of the spinal base ("How you settled your head athwart my hips / And gently turned upon me"). The aroused Kundalini moves up, reaches the heart and farther up to the throat ("and reach'd till you felt my beard"). Its descent ("till you held my feet") fills him from head to foot. It will be recalled that Tirumoolar speaks of the young girl of his vision stroking him from the heart to the neck, from Anāhata Chakra to the Visuddha Chakra, beyond which consciousness steps across the threshold from the mind to the spirit and no more images and symbols are present. I must not fail to mention an astonishing parallelism in the images employed by Whitman and Sri Ramakrishna; both were contemporaries but knew nothing of each other. Sri Ramakrishna says:

> Just before attaining this state of mind, it has been revealed to me how the Kundalini is aroused, how all this culminates in samādhi. This is a very secret experience. I saw a boy twenty two or twenty three years old, exactly resembling me [was this Sri Ramakrishna's age then?] enter the Sushumna nerve and commune with the lotuses, *touching them with his tongue* [italics mine]. He began with the center at the anus [Mūladhāra, spinal base] and passed through the centers [chakras] . . . the different lotuses of those centers—four-petalled, six-petalled, ten-petalled, and so forth—had been drooping. At his touch they stood erect. *When he reached the heart—I distinctly remember it—and communed with the Lotus there, touching it with his tongue* [italics mine], the twelve-petalled lotus, which was hanging its head down, stood erect and opened its petals. Then he came to the sixteen-petalled lotus in the throat and the two-petalled lotus in the forehead. And last of all, the thousand-petalled lotus in the head blossomed. Since then I have been in this state.[27]

This and Whitman's "And parted the shirt from my bosom-bone, and plunged your tongue to my bare-stript heart," are identical symbols emerging from the same spiritual experience, except that the Hindu saints' idiom is rich in Tantric terms.

The experience of physical sensation (touch, cold, warmth, and so on)—a means of tracing the movement of Kundalini—is what both these mystics have described. It is clearly mentioned in the works on Kundalini Yōga that the heart chakra (Anāhata) and the neck chakra (Visuddha) are two important centers where somatic pressures and pains are registered, marking stages of transition from the sensory to the mental (here, the heart) and from the mental to the spiritual areas of Being—what the Sāstras describe as the "breaking of the knots or granthis."[28]

These profound inner experiences gained in spiritual life appear to be connected both with the anatomy of the psyche and at certain definite points with the body. Sri Ramakrishna, who had knowledge of the traditionally established Tantric symbol system and thematics, and

Whitman, who did not have that advantage (or disadvantage?) but nevertheless had an undoubted Kundalini experience leading to Laya Yōga, both used symbols which were suggested by the very content and feature of the inner experience, and they come fairly close to an identity of experience. The tongue symbol seems to me a most extraordinary parallel.

The "lamp" symbol stands for the light of the Ātma or soul monad. Its location is generally stated to be in the heart. St. John of the Cross describes the experience in one of his well known *Songs of the Soul*:

> O happy night and blest!
> Secretely speeding, screen'd from mortal gaze,
> Unseen, on I prest,
> Lit by no earthly rays,
> Only by heart's inmost fire ablaze,
>
> 'Twas that *light* [italics mine] guided me,
> More surely than the noonday's brightest glare,
> To the place where none would be
> Save one that waited there—
> Well knew I whom or ere I forth did fare. . . .

In the *Maha Svacchandra Tantra* (v. 22–27) the Ātma (Jīvātma) is described as "the steady flame of lamp in a windless place." The *Shad Chakra Nirūpana* (v. 26) refers to the heart lotus (Anahata Chakra) as the seat of Jīvātma "which is like unto the steady tapering flame of a lamp in a windless place," a description which is improved later on (in v. 37) where the radiance seen in the Ājna Chakra is described. "He then sees the Light which is in the form of a flaming Lamp lustrous like the morning sun, glowing between the sky and the earth. Here the Lord manifests Himself in the fullness of His might. . . ."

I must make it clear that not all symbols handled in myth and poetry are thus produced. A great many we habitually use arise from the interaction of concepts and observed similitudes. Symbols, howsoever arisen, fall into affinitive patterns, and later run into thematic structures shaped by the very forces and urges which brought them forth. They form the heart and core of all religious myths, allegories, and parables. They have come down to us theologically distorted and poetically embellished. The value of a myth is in the spiritual truth it contains, and it is a grave error to take it as a literal fact or as a historical truth belonging to a definite place and time. Speaking of Greek myths, the Neo-Platonist Sallustius said, "These things never were; they always are." The universal mythological theme of the quest by a race hero, the difficulties faced and overcome, the triumphant return, are a projection of the eternal drama of the soul in the life of every individual and episodes in its pilgrimage to perfection. The legends of the Gnostic "Pearl," the Golden Fleece, the Holy Grail, the Promethean Fire, the Sougandhika Flower, the Fountain or the Well of the Water of Life, and similar variations of the theme of the soul's quest, sometimes presented as the yearning of the bride for her lord and husband, are but cultural modifications of the same old story. When a symbol becomes empty of the original spiritual experience out of which it arose, concepts and impressions gathered from life-experience fill the vacuum. The symbol structures get weakened and paraphrased into the idiom of our ordinary life-experience. Hence by the myths and parables the inner experiences of the soul in her spiritual striving are dramatized and projected to the external, time-space world. Often built round a race hero, the scenario also reflects the ethos and mores of a people.

The spiritual canticles, the Scriptures, religious poems, and epics are examples of different gradations and extensions of the poetry of the spirit. An analysis of the symbols used in them and their structures in light of the inner movements described here will give them a new and unsuspected dimension, a significance universally valid and acceptable. Spirit to psyche to symbol to song is the outward movement, and the inward movement is a retracing of the steps. The Sāstras tell us that by working our way back from Vaikhari to Madhyama and then to Pasyanti, we reach Parā—the Supreme Experience Beyond—the Supreme Bliss far above the reach of mere aesthetics.

Om Shantih, Shantih, Shantih

Notes

1. In the Veda (Satapatha Brahmana VI, I-I-8) it is further stated: "This Being, Prajapathi, willed, 'May I be many; may I be propagated.' He energized. Vāk was His. She was produced from Him (Vāg ēva sya srjyata) and pervaded all which exists."

2. *Ouroboros* stands for the "One and All" in Gnosticism (*Codex Marcianus*), and also the union between the Chthonian (Earth) principle represented by the serpent and the celestial principle usually represented as a bird (Christian dove, Hindu swan, Ancient Egyptian falcon, Roman eagle, etc.).
3. The three Gunas (or qualities) are the Satwa, Rajas, and Tamas. On the metaphysical level Satwa is the revealing power, Rajas the power of action, Tamas that of obscuration. Disequilibrium of these Gunas initiates the unfolding which is creation.
4. St. John of the Cross, "Of Creation," *Romance IV*; italics mine.
5. By "cave" is meant internal to the body, but the inner operation of the psyche is implied.
6. Gunas: Satwa, Rajas, and Tamas, as explained earlier.
7. It may be pointed out that the Kundalini concept is found described in veiled language in the Old Testament, in the Kabalistic and Hermetic systems. See my *New Light on Ancient Yoga* and *Yoga in the Temple*, in which I have worked out in detail the symbolic and conceptual correspondences.
8. The Jewish *Book of Creation* (*Sepher Yetzirah*) refers to a similar distribution of the Hebrew alphabet in different parts of the body. In combinations with the ten *sephroth* (singular, *sephira*), which roughly correspond to the chakras, they have creative power.
9. Sri Sankara's *Ananda Lahari Intoxication of Bliss*, v. 10, refers to this: "From your feet there issues forth a stream of nectar bedewing and cooling the nerves and structures of the body. . . . Thereafter you go back to your own home in the Mūladhāra and resume your sleep in the subtle aperture." Compare this with the Kabalistic concept of *Shepha*—the flow of grace from the higher to the lower level of Being. Rabbi Ben Jochai, speaking of the Mystery of the Mysteries, says:

   > His clothing is white and his aspect that of a countenance unveiled. . . . From his head he shakes a dew which awakens the dead and brings new life. It is this which nourishes the most exalted saints, the manna which descends. The aspect of this dew is white. . . .

   (Zohar, Part III, fol. 12, Franck's translation, p. 170.)

   Similarly Siva is conceived as white, "the color which contains all"; from his matted locks flows the divine, all-purifying waters of the Ganga by which the soul is raised to the higher life. Bhagiratha did penance to bring the celestial Ganga to the earth to revive the ashes and bones of the sons of Sagara. Hercules brought the stream to clean the Augean Stables. It is believed that the biophysiological basis of this is an endocrinal secretion, perhaps from the pineal body.

   Novalis refers to this in his *Hymn to the Night*:

   > The crystal rill which unperceived by the common sense drips in the dark bosom of the hill, breaks forth at the foot in the earthly stream; and whosoever has tasted it and stood on high on the high ridge that bounds the world and looked over into the new land . . . he surely no more returns to the toil and bustle of the world or to the world where light dwells in eternal unrest.

   (Freemantle and Auden, *The Protestant Mystics* [London, 1964], p. 212.)
10. The green leaf (life of spiritual joy) and dry leaf (sapless sense life); compare this with Allama Prabhu's lines:

    If a headless trunk will brouse
    On dry leaves

Is it a wonder, O Guheswara,
If one loses sight of green leaves?

(*Sunya Sampādane*, trans. Nandimath, Hiremath, and Menezes [Karanataka University, 1965], p. 75.)

11. Samskāra: Karmic traces which shape individual nature, genius, attitudes, etc.
12. Nādi (from *Nād*, "to move") is the channel of movement for vital or psychic energy: it sometimes corresponds to the nervous system.
13. The invisible sephiroth—called *Daath* in Kabal, the "third eye of Siva" among Hindus, and the *Aureus* symbol in ancient Egypt—are all shown as located between the eyes and universally stand for spiritual illumination and power.
14. The subject of mantras is far too large to deal with here.
15. Phenomenal life, spiritual life, and vital energy, respectively. The three mandalas are referred to on later pages. The lunar way is the way of intuition, imagination, and feeling, while the solar way that of reason, reflection, and objectivity.
16. Eugène Felicien Albert Goblet, comte D'Alviella, *The Migration of Symbols* (New York, 1956), p. 157.
17. Sir Ernst Alfred Thompson Wallis Budge, *Egyptian Book of the Dead* (New Hyde Park, N.Y., 1960), p. 315.
18. Werblowsky and Wigoder, *The Encyclopaedia of the Jewish Religion.*
19. The *Sunya Sampādane* (Ch. XX, v. 13) uses the creeper symbol (Solomon's Vine). The reference is clearly to the Nadi system: "Whichever way you look, behold a creeper, Basavanna! You pick it up, lo, a cluster. The Linga! Pick up the cluster and oh, the juice that brims from it."
20. In the *Vita Nuova* Dante describes Beatrice as "that most blessed one," "not a daughter of mortal man, but of God," and "youngest of Angels," one who governed his new Life of Love.
21. According to another version, the phenomenon of the three circles is related to the Nadis, Sushumna, Vajrini, and Chitrini, one inside the other. "Sushumna is fiery and outermost, inside it at the height of two fingers breadth is Vajrini, sunlike, and innermost is Chitrini, pale white like the moon." Another interpretation, more authentic and preferred by yōgis, is that they represent the "three knots," Brahma Granthi, Vishnu Granthi, and Rudra Granthi, by breaking which the zones of the senses, mind, and spirit are unified in the final integral experience in yōga.
22. Dante, *Divine Comedy, Paradiso,* Canto 30, trans. Lawrence Grant White.
23. The fourth circle (blue) that he refers to is later explained (Jnanadeva's *Abhanga*, 62):

    By the eye is the eye to be seen, and it is indeed the end of the void. It shines forth like a dark blue circle. In it rests the light form of God.

    Other mystics also have referred to this blue light and it comes from the divine source. Leaving out for the present speculations regarding this blue light, we are left with the three rings of light seen by mystics in an advanced stage of meditation.

24. Jnanadeva: "Even the sun's light is inferior to that of Atman" (*Abhanga*, 70). "His light is greater than the light of the sun and moon" (*Abhanga*, 69). "And it is wonderful that light is neither hot nor cold" (*Abhanga*, 67). "And beyond that light is God who is transcendant" (Abhanga 104). Of Tukaram, "God's light is

like the light of a million moons. . . . Tuka says that his vision is now satisfied" (*Abhanga*, 4026).

25. This recalls Dante's first vision of Beatrice. He is himself nine years old when the glorious Lady of the mind first appears to him. Beatrice also is "almost at the beginning of her ninth year." It is said that Tirumoolar's first mystical onset came when he was about that age. Could this vision be what Jung calls the *anima*?
26. From *Interior Castle*, in *Complete works of St. Teresa of Avila*, ed. and trans. E. Allison Peers (London, 1946), vol. 2, p. 276, and vol. 1, p. 156–157.
27. Mahendra Nath Guptra, *The Gospel of Sri Ramakrishna Paramahamsa* (New York, 1942).
28. "Raja yoga is above the neck"—Sri Nityananda in *Chidākāsa Gita*.

INDIVIDUAL STUDIES ON SPECIFIC LITERARY AND RELIGIOUS TRADITIONS

Gwendolyn Bays

THE ORPHIC VISION OF NERVAL, BAUDELAIRE, AND RIMBAUD

ORPHEUS, THE SON OF CALLIOPE, THE MUSE OF POETRY, BY APOLLO, WAS celebrated as the initiator of the Egyptian and Dionysian mysteries in Greece. Music and poetry thus wedded were conceived by the ancients as revealers of eternal truth. The sweet singer, whose magic lyre charmed wild beasts and even stones, who descended into hell in his attempt to rescue love from the kingdom of death, was finally destroyed by the priestesses of the night, the Bacchantes. By his death, according to Edouard Schuré, France and Greece were converted to the Orphic and Dionysian mysteries, and Orpheus' soul became the soul of Greece.[1]

Although poetry and truth were thus mythologically and ideally joined in the very origins of Greece, an opposition developed by the time of Pindar, and was expressed later by Plato in the *Ion* and the *Republic*, against the esthetic Homeric conception of the poet as a sorcerer or an entertainer. In Plato's opinion Homeric poetry not only stirs the passions and therefore blinds men to truth, but it possesses a power which may be compared with the forces of magic (*Republic*, Book X). Although few today would agree with Plato in his attack on Homer, his insight into Homeric art is accurate. It is perhaps not without some semantic significance that the most frequent Homeric word for poet is *'αοιδος*, "singer," while his song is referred to as *κηλθμός*, "enchantment" signifying that the poet's chief function is to charm his listeners. It was only among later Greek writers that the word for poet was replaced by *ποιητής*, which carries the connotation of "craftsman." Similarly among the Romans the word *vates* ("seer") was replaced by *poeta*. In spite of the Platonic attack, the Homeric idea of the poet as entertainer seems to have persisted, for the poet and grammarian Apollonius of Rhodes, writing a century and a half after Plato, uses the verb *θέλγειν*, "to charm," in describing the process of creating poetry —the same word which Homer chose to describe Hermes putting Odysseus' men to sleep in the episode of the Sirens.

The real significance of the Homeric as opposed to the Platonic theory of artistic creation, however, consists in more than the difference between the ancient world's way of expressing a conception akin to the view of art for art's sake (the Homeric theory) and the idea of art as a means of communicating truth (the Platonic theory). The Homeric conception implies that the poet is a magician whose chants have hypnotic effects, and the poetic process therefore involves a lowering of consciousness. The Platonic theory suggests exactly the opposite; instead of having soporific effects, the creative process is compared by Plato to a Bacchic frenzy; a heightening or quickening of the waking consciousness is suggested rather than a slowing down, as the case was supposed in the Homeric idea.

Much importance was attached by the ancients to the "ecstatic" or Homeric theory of artistic creation, which after Plotinus fell into a long oblivion lasting really until the Romantic movement. Artistic excellence, in the Plotinian doctrine, depends upon the quality of the artist's vision, which improves only as he develops spiritually. In the sixth book of the *Enneads* Plotinus compares the mystic and the sculptor, both of whom must "cut away what is gross, straighten what is crooked, lighten what is too heavy" until the good has been "enthroned in a stainless shrine." Plotinus described the nature of his visionary experiences in these terms: "We may know we have had the vision when the Soul has suddenly taken light. This light is from the Supreme. . . . He comes bringing light; the light is proof of the advent. Thus the Soul unlit remains without vision; lit, it possesses what is sought. And this is the true end set before the Soul, to take that light, to see the Supreme by the Supreme . . . just as it is by the sun's own light that we see the sun."[2]

Thus in the minds of the ancients there existed a distinction between two kinds of seers—the nocturnal or the orphic, the artist who descends into the underworld (the Unconscious) and charms the wild beasts there; and the Platonic-Plotinian, whose experience was later cultivated by medieval Christian mystics. Whatever judgment one may wish to make of other aspects of Freudian psychology, this distinction between a waking consciousness and a sleeping or "unconsciousness" state can hardly be denied, for it is within the experience of us all.

The existence of a barrier between the realm of sleep and that of waking was perceived by both Homer and Virgil, and both made a distinction between the two kinds of visionary experiences. In the celebrated imagery of the gates of ivory and the gates of horn they represented this fundamental poetic insight (Odyssey XIX, 562–567; Aeneid VI, 893–896). Through the portal of horn, leading into the realm of the dead, came nothing but truth, whereas through the gate "of gleaming ivory" false dreams often came to men. Thus the ancients wisely saw that dreams can be the bearers of both truth and error, for in the light of modern knowledge is it not true that misevaluations of the past can lead men to errors which are often embodied in their dreams? Or, conversely, that dreams may be representations of the highest truths?

This conviction is central in the poetry of Nerval, Baudelaire, and Rimbaud. Using the Homeric metaphors Nerval expressed his intuition of the barrier between the conscious and the unconscious in *Aurélia*: "Le rêve est une seconde vie. Je n'ai pu percer sans frémir ces portes d'ivoire ou de corne qui nous séparent du monde invisible." After entering these gates Nerval leads us down a staircase and summarizes his explorations at the end of *Aurélia* as "a descent into hell." Likewise Rimbaud calls his hashish investigations "a season in hell." In *Les Paradis artificiels*, Baudelaire uses two metaphors to describe the unconscious: the palimpsest and the abyss (*le gouffre*). In the first he compares the mind, as it appears under the drug, to an immense palimpsest, a medieval parchment manuscript, with innumerable layers of writings of which nothing is ever lost. From the point of view of modern psychological knowledge the metaphor is remarkably accurate. Just as a sudden accident has been known to illuminate suddenly all the darkened layers or the forgotten incidents, so, Baudelaire continues, the drug brings back the past. The metaphor of the abyss, which he uses in *Les Fleurs du mal* to symbolize both death and sleep, represents in *Les Paradis artificiels* the plunge into the unconscious. One has the pleasant sensation of an immense expanse of water (*un gouffre limpide*) and of being pulled under "comme le pêcheur dans la vieille fable de l'Ondine." Describing the effects of opium on De Quincey, Baudelaire writes: "Il lui semblait, chaque nuit, qu'il descendait indéfiniment dans des abîmes sans lumière, au-delà de toute profondeur connue, sans espérance de pouvoir remonter."[3]

In addition to the darkness and the abyss, Baudelaire has the sensation of plunging through water: "L'eau devint l'élément obsédant. Nous avons déjà noté, dans notre travail sur le haschisch, cette étonnante prédilection du cerveau pour l'élément liquide et pour ses mystérieuses séductions."[4]

These two passages cited above should be compared with the following from Nerval's *Aurélia*, in which the same experience of the abyss and the water is related: "Cependant, la nuit s'épaississait peu à peu, et les aspects, les sons et le sentiment des lieux se confondaient dans mon esprit somnolent; *je crus tomber dans un abîme* qui traversait le globe. Je me sentais emproté sans souffrance par un courant de métal fondu, et *mille fleuves pareils*, dont les teintes indiquaient les différences chimiques, sillonnaient *le sein de la terre* comme les vaisseaux et les veines qui serpentent parmi les lobes du cerveau."[5]

The Freudian overtones of this passage, in which Nerval describes a moment before going to sleep, seem very obvious and even more suggestive of the birth process than those cited from Baudelaire. Descent, darkness, and water are all mentioned here just as they are in *Les Paradis artificiels*. Regarding the metaphor of water Jung says: "Water is the commonest symbol for the unconscious."[6]

The *Illuminations* of Rimbaud open with the poem "Après le Déluge" in which the waters of the Flood have just subsided. This poem is followed by a second one, "Enfance," with a crytic reference to darkness in the symbol of the "idole, yeux noirs et crin jaune, sans parents." This image, which has not been previously explained by any of Rimbaud's critics, becomes clear if it is related to the "noire idole" of Baudelaire's *Paradis artificiels*. In several passages Baudelaire, quoting De Quincey, calls opium "la noire idole" and his taking of the drug a "prostration devant la noire idole" or the *Mater Tenebrarum*. The word *crin* used by Rimbaud, which may be poetically translated "hair," actually means either "a horse's mane" or the fibrous stem of a plant such as hemp from which opium comes.

After their initial plunge into the unconscious, the seer poets found themselves in the domain of childhood. The past has become present. In a passage which reminds us of some modern book of psychology, Baudelaire insists upon the powerful effect of childhood impressions and their enduring quality: "La passion et la maladie n'ont pas de chimie assez puissante pour brûler ces immortelles empreintes." As an example of the difference between the ordinary power of memory to recall the past and the recall which takes place under opium, Baudelaire cites De Quincey's memory of his sister Elizabeth's death. As an elderly man De Quincey relived these events in their entirety with all details present, even his own childish desire to join his sister, since she could not return to him. Baudelaire refers to this most interesting passage from De Quincey: "Of this, at least, I feel assured that there is no such thing as ultimate forgetting; traces once impressed upon the memory are indestructible; a thousand accidents may and will interpose a veil between our present consciousness and the secret inscriptions on the mind. Accidents of the same sort will also rend away this veil. But alike whether veiled or unveiled, the inscription remains forever."[7]

With Rimbaud's "Après le Déluge" and "Enfance" the reader enters a luminous world of enchantment. The two poems should be read simultaneously because their atmosphere is similar and because both refer to the event of the Flood. One receives the impression of having just stepped through the looking glass into a fresh new world, still glistening from primordial rains which have not yet stopped and bright with rainbows, magic flowers, and precious stones which are alive, as all things are, in the world of childhood. The poet suggests that we are in a state of dreams by saying that at the edge of the forest "les fleurs de rêve tintment, éclatent, éclairent" (from "Enfance"). This is a country inhabited by all the fabulous persons encountered in children's fairy tales: giantesses sultanas, princesses, "superb black women" ("superbes noires dans la mousse vert-de-gris"), Bluebeard, the girl with the lips like oranges ("la fille à la lèvre d'orange"), and the witch who lights her embers in an earthen pot and will not tell her secrets ("la sorcière qui allume sa braise dans le pot de terre, ne voudra jamais nous raconter ce qu'elle sait, et que nous ignorons"). As one would expect in a child's paradise, it is filled with many animals: beavers, a rabbit, a spider, a bird, and "beasts of fabulous elegance" ("des bêtes d'une élégance fabuleuse circulaient"). Abruptly the scene changes from an outdoor to an indoor setting. Children in mourning are sitting inside a house looking at picture books while outside the last rains of the Flood are beating against the window. One of the children gets up and goes out, swinging his arms as a signal to weather-vanes and steeplecocks, who understand him immediately, for communication between man and other creatures was immediate in these early times. This would seem to be clearly a dream representation of birth—not only of the individual, but of man himself upon a new earth. The poetic symbols of blood and milk lend further support to the interpretation of this as a symbol of birth. Nor should it be overlooked that the children who are about to arrive are in mourning.

We should like to decipher this series of images thus: the child upon his arrival into the world is exactly comparable to Man as he appeared on the earth after the Flood; both are surrounded with wonder and mystery, both seek explanations which Nature of herself cannot give since she is at once a part of that mystery. The only knowledge which exists in this primitive age of innocence is that of legends and fairy tales, or of Magic and Alchemy, that heavenly wisdom which Enoch was supposed to have obtained from the angels before the Flood, the last few remnants of which survived on the Ark. Believing as he did that "it is this present age which has foundered" ("C'est cette époque-ci qui a sombré!"), Rimbaud resolved to return to this ancient wisdom, as he said in the *Saison en enfer*: "Je croyais à tous les enchantements."

Actually the pioneer of this group of seer poets, Gérard de Nerval, was also the most purely visionary of them all, the one who lived most intimately with the world of dreams and who perceived most clearly the subtle fusion of the visible and invisible. It is the constant intrusion of the marvelous into everyday life which makes Aurélia a work of sheer enchantment. Those glimpses into the unknown, for which Baudelaire and Rimbaud must struggle, suffer, and revolt, seem only to be taken quite for granted by Nerval, as if nothing could be more natural: ". . . je ne pouvais douter de ce que j'avais vu si distinctement," he says, after having had the vision of his double. Undoubtedly his malady, like the deafness of Beethoven or the blindness of Milton, actually aided him in his quest in that it gave him a freer access to the unconscious.

Instead of his own past or childhood, Nerval seems to dream of his ancestral past. One is tempted to think that he did so because he attained a deeper level of the unconscious than Baudelaire or Rimbaud. *Aurélia* contains three such visions in which the poet encounters or becomes aware of the presence within himself of his dead relatives. In one dream he descends to a mysterious city which he discovers to be peopled with faces which greatly resemble his own. "Il me semblait que mes pieds s'enfonçaient dans les couches successives des édifices de différents âges," he says. At the gate of this underground city he is met by an old man dressed in white, who threatens him with a weapon to keep him from entering. When he finally gains admittance all the people gather around him eagerly asking him whether or not there is a God. Spontaneously, he replies "Yes," delighted with his own new inner certitude. In a second vision of his ancestors Nerval finds himself at banquet table with a large group of persons whom he again recognizes as his dead relatives. Many of them are dressed in ancient costumes and wear powdered wigs. One of them, who seems particularly lively and interested in him, turns out to be his dead uncle with whom he had lived as a child: "Notre passé et notre avenir sont solidaires. Nous vivons dans notre race, et notre race vit en nous," his uncle tells him.

In this way, Nerval holds, all individual existence is linked from within, the ego to the non-ego, the interior to the exterior, forming a chain of immanent consciousness. "Je crus comprendre qu'il existait entre le monde externe et le monde interne un lien," he writes after having had the vision of his ancestors. Furthermore, earthly events are charged with meaning since they are linked to an invisible world:

"Mais, selon ma pensée, les événements terrestres étaient liés à ceux du monde invisible." As a result of all this Nerval feels great happiness at his discovery of this new identity with nature and the material world, which he had not perceived before. "Comment, me disais-je, ai-je pu exister si longtemps hors de la nature et sans m'identifier à elle? Tout vit, tout agit, tout se correspond. . . ." As a Germanist, the translator of *Faust* at the age of eighteen, Nerval is probably thinking here of the opening pages of Novalis' *Die Lehrlinge zu Saïs*. In this statement of the doctrine of correspondences, as well as in many other respects, Nerval reveals his spiritual relationship to Baudelaire and Rimbaud. Just as Baudelaire refers at the beginning of *Les Fleurs du mal* to the magic of Hermes Trismegistus, so Nerval evokes the magic of the Cabala: "Mon rôle me semblait être de rétablir l'harmonie universelle par l'art cabalistique et de chercher une solution en évoquant les forces occultes des diverses religions." Like Orpheus, the seer poet thus initiates others into the mysteries and deciphers of the hieroglyphic symbols of Nature.

This same realization of the linked existence of man with nature gives rise to one of Rimbaud's most joyous lines: "J'ai tendu des cordes de clocher à clocher; des guirlandes de fenêtre à fenêtre; des chaines d'or d'étoile à étoile, et je danse."[8] His feeling of union with Nature becomes erotic in the poem "Aube": "J'ai embrassé l'aube d'été."[9] When his disillusionment set in, this former "alchemist of the Word" admitted in the *Saison en enfer* his occult interests: "Je croyais à tous les enchantements," he confesses, believing he had acquired supernatural powers. What was the nature of these so-called powers which all three of these poets seemed bent upon acquiring? Apparently the highest compliment to pay a poet was to call him a *voyant*; Baudelaire applies the term to Gautier in *L'Art romantique* and defines it there as the capacity to perceive correspondence and universal symbolism. Gautier returns the compliment by calling Baudelaire also a *voyant*. "Il possède aussi le don de *correspondance*, pour employer le même idiome mystique, c'est-à-dire qu'il sait découvrir par une intuition secrète des rapports invisibles à d'autres et rapprocher ainsi, par des analogies inattendues que seul le *voyant* peut saisir, les objets les plus éloignés et les plus opposés en apparence. Tout vrai poète est doué de cette qualité plus ou moins dévelopée, qui est l'essence même de son art."[10]

A contradiction presents itself at the very outset in Baudelaire's attitude toward the feeling of identity with nature. On the one hand he attaches great importance to the Swedenborgian doctrine of correspondence, yet in many passages he expresses his loathing of nature: "La Nature est laide," "ce culte niais de la nature," he says, and in two longer passages: "J'ai même toujours pensé qu'il y avait dans *la nature* florissante et rajeunie quelque chose d'affligeant, de dur, de cruel, un je ne sais quoi qui frise l'impudence."[11] In a letter to Fernand Desnoyers he writes: "Vous me demandez des vers sur la nature. . . . Mais vous savez bien que je suis incapable de m'attendrir sur les végétaux."[12] Under hashish, however, Baudelaire expresses an altogether different opinion, since he then has a direct experience of identity with nature: ". . . La personnalité disparaît et l'objectivité, qui est le propre des poètes panthéistes, se développé en vous si anormalement que la contemplation des objets extérieurs vous fait oublier votre propre existence, et que vous vous confondez bientôt avec eux."[13]

Finally Baudelaire even writes eloquently, as he said he could not about his perception of identity with the vegetable world. Upon seeing a tree, he says: "Vous prêtez d'abord à l'arbre vos passions, votre désir ou votre mélancolie, ses gémissements et ses oscillations deviennent les vôtres, et bientôt vous êtes l'arbre."[14] From these passages in *Les Paradis artificiels* it would seem safe to conclude that Baudelaire's conscious waking psyche makes fun of the idea of identity with the objects of the material world. This feeling of identity with nature is not, however, the "objective" experience which he thinks it is, but a subjective one.

What exactly did the seer poets mean by all the mysticism about a primitive language of nature, a mysterious alphabet which only seer poets were able to decipher and what did they hope to achieve? The answer to these questions may perhaps be found most clearly expressed by an occult writer of considerable renown, Eliphas Lévi (l'abbé Constant). According to him (and other occultists like Court de Gébelin and Fourier), all modern languages "fell" from an original universal language. Although no living language could be identified with this primitive language, its key has been preserved and handed down in the tarot cards. Eliphas Lévi hailed this discovery of the tarot cards as the key to the wisdom of the ancient world, and described this key which had been lost for centuries and which was recently discovered:

> Or, cette clavicule ou petite clef, qu'on croyait perdue depuls des siècles, nous l'avons retrouvée, et nous avons pu ouvrir tous les tombeaux de l'ancien monde, faire parler les morts, revoir dans toute leur splendeur les monuments du passé, comprendre les énigmes de tous le sphinx et pénétrer dans tous les sanctuaires. L'usage de cette clef, chez les anciens, n'était permis qu'aux seuls grands prêtres, et on n'en confiait pas même le secret à l'élite des initiés. Or, voici ce que c'était que cette clef; C'était un alphabet hiéroglyphique et numéral exprimant par des caractères et par des nombres une série d'idées universelles et absolues. . . .[15]

Only Martinists and Rosicrucians possess and have kept intact the true tarot, Lévi insists. Such knowledge was supposed to give the seer or *mage* power over the forces of nature and so Rimbaud says: "Je ferai de l'or, des remèdes."[16]

The reader should perhaps not leave these regions of the marvelous without noting two of the seer poets' most extraordinary experiences: the encounter with the "double" and the union with the pairs of opposites. Since Nerval is more explicit about his encounter with the "double" we should examine his passages on this subject first:

> Mais quel était done cet Esprit qui était moi et en dehors de moi?
> Etait-ce le Double des légendes, ou de frère mystique que les
> Orientaux appellent Ferouer?. . . . Une idée terrible me vint:
> "L'homme est double," me dis-je.[17]
> Il y a en tout homme un spectateur et un acteur, celui qui
> parle et celui que répond. Les Orientaux ont vu là deux
> ennemis: le bon et le mauvais génie. Suis-je bon?
> Suis-je mauvais? me disais-je.
> En tout cas, l'autre m'est hostile.[18]

These passages from *Aurélia* shed light upon one of the very cryptic poems of Rimbaud's *Illuminations*, "Conte." In the form of a simple kind of fairy tale or fable the poet narrates the inner drama which took place in the spring of 1871 at the time of the composition of the *Voyant* letters. The destructive prince of this symbolic fable is of course the poet himself as he was during his rebellious phase, dissatisfied not only with his personal life, but also with the world at large; the prince in the poem, like the poet, has dreams of changing society. In order to bring about these changes he launches upon a program of unlimited violence and destruction, doubtless in the belief that the old order of things must be destroyed before the new one can be established. But the prince's orgy of destruction changes nothing really; no one even takes notice of the evil he has done. Then one evening he has an extraordinary encounter with a Genie of ineffable, even inadmissible, beauty. Near the end of the poem Rimbaud says: "Le Prince était le Génie. Le Génie était le Prince." In other words the Prince (the poet) has met his "double." It is always at moments of great spiritual crisis that one encounters the "double" and for Rimbaud this was the time of his discovery of the phenomenon of voyance. When he says in the poem that the prince and the Genie "s'anéantirent . . . dans la santé essentielle" he is referring to the fact that when his destructive self, the *voyou*, meets his seer-self, the *voyant*, the latter brings a healthy end to the former. The Genie disappears, as they do in fairy tales, and the vision of the "double" is not one which lingers; such encounters are always brief. The connection between the fable and the cryptic last line of the poem, "La musique savante manque à notre désir," is not at first glance apparent, but what Rimbaud must have meant by it is that to express such an event as the one related here he prefers the simple form of a fable like this one to the more complex poetic genres.

Although Baudelaire's perception of the double is less mysterious and visionary than Nerval's and Rimbaud's, he nevertheless expresses several times his own sense of the "other" within him. "Qui parmi nous n'est pas un *homo duplex*?" he asks.[19] In the Baudelairean aesthetic the poet magician must succeed by his "sorcellerie évocatoire" in fusing these two selves, "sujet et objet, magnétiseur et somnambule" in order to produce "pure art."[20]

In their hashish visions the seer poets achieved a marked climax which they have all described in similar terms. After a period of hallucinations Baudelaire says that he reached a state of extraordinary beatitude in which he had a realization of his divinity: "Cet état nouveau est ce que les Orientaux appellent le *kief* . . . c'est une béatitude calme et immobile, une résignation glorieuse. Despuis longtemps vous n'êtes plus votre maître, mais vous ne vous en affligez plus."[21] Similarly, Nerval felt that he had been able to achieve "une communication avec le monde des esprits" and that he had "devenu semblable à un dieu et que j'avais le pouvoir de guérir . . . quelques malades."[22] Like Baudelaire, Nerval realizes that ". . . il existait entre le monde externe et le monde interne un lien" and that earthly events coincide with those in the supernatural world.[23]

The climax of Rimbaud's hashish visions is recorded in the poem "L'Eternité," which has all the profound simplicity of one of Blake's *Songs of Innocence*. Just as the Genie or the double was a creature in whom the pairs of opposites were reconciled, so eternity in this poem is a state of bliss in which the opposites exist in equilibrium. Because of the cryptic nature of the poem we should examine it closely.

L'Eternité

Elle est retrouvée.
Quoi?—L'Eternité
C'est la mer allée
Avec le soleil.

Ame sentinelle,
Murmurons l'aveu
De la nuit si nulle
Et du jour en feu.

Des humains suffrages,
Des communs élans
Là tu te dégages
Et voles selon.

Puisque de vous seules,
Braises de satin,
Le Devoir s'exhale
Sans qu'on dise: enfin.

Là pas d'espérance,
Nul orietur.
Science avec patience,
Le supplice est sûr.

Elle est retrouvée
Quoi?—L'Eternité.
C'est la mer allée
Avec le soleil.[24]

It will be noted that most of the stanzas of this poem contain two words in sharp contrast: 1. *la mer, le soleil* (fire and water); 2. *la nuit, le jour* (light and darkness); 3. and 4. *élans, Devoir* (opposite spiritual states); 5. *science, espérance* (knowledge and contingency); 6. *la mer, le soleil.* In a second version of the same poem later cited by Rimbaud in the *Saison en enfer*, one notes the substitution of the word *mêlée* for *allée*, suggesting more clearly the dissolution of the most extreme opposites, fire and water, as the climax of the experience.

Now the idea of eternity as a union of sun and sea, or fire and water—the masculine and feminine principles in occult thought—is a well-known alchemical symbol according to John Read in his study of alchemy entitled *Prelude to Chemistry*. The *prima materia* of the philosopher's stone, which was supposed to cure all diseases and turn the baser metals into gold, was symbolized by "firey water." Read cites the following Latin verse under an alchemical drawing of 1625: "Fire and flowing water are contrary to one another; happy thou if thou canst unite them: let it suffice thee to know this."[25] Read concludes that the philosopher's stone represented a union of the masculine and feminine principles: "Thus both the preparation of the stone and its application as a transmuting agent could be regarded . . . as essentially the union of the masculine and feminine principles."[26] These two passages confirm the psychologist Jung's statement concerning alchemy, that "the real subject of Hermetic philosophy is the *conjunctio oppositorum*," and doubtless led him to examine the meanings of alchemical symbols.[27] He compares these with dreams, which he says are also concerned with the reconciliation of opposites. "The symbols which rise up out of the unconscious in dreams point to a reconciliation of opposites and the images of the goal represent their successful reconciliation."

But what is the importance or the spiritual significance of the reconciliation of opposites in terms of human experience? Readers of the *Bhagavad-Gita* will doubtless be reminded that the ideal of saintliness upheld in that book was the freeing of the individual from the "pairs of opposites." Jung saw in alchemy a symbolic representation of the integration process. Because of his extreme youth and more primitive sense of unity with Nature, Rimbaud felt particularly sensitive to the dichotomies which underlie the very foundations of Western thought —Nature and Spirit, mind and body, good and evil—and which are being challenged in many philosophical circles today. Clearly the poems of Baudelaire, Rimbaud, and Nerval reflect the basic human urge for unity, for achieving wholeness, when the contents of the unconscious have been made conscious.

Notes

1. Edouard Schuré, *Les Grands Initiés* (Librairie Perrin, 1953), p. 259. For a fuller discussion of the subject of this essay see my study, *The Orphic Vision* (Lincoln, Nebraska, 1964).
2. Plotinus, *The Enneads*, trans. Stephen Mackenna and B. S. Page (London, 1930), Bk. VI, pp. 9–10.
3. Charles Pierre Baudelaire, *Les Paradis artificiels suivis des Journaux intimes* (Paris, 1947), p. 158.
4. Ibid.
5. Gérard de Nerval, *Aurélia* (Bordeaux, 1950), p. 82; my italics.
6. Carl Gustav Jung, *The Integration of Personality*, trans. Stanley Dell (London, 1940), p. 67.

7. Thomas De Quincey, *The Confessions of an English Opium Eater* (London, 1952), p. 235. See also *Les Paradis artificiels*, p. 189.
8. Arthur Rimbaud, *Oeuvres complètes*, Edition de la Pléiade (Paris, 1946), p. 235.
9. Ibid., p. 186.
10. Théophile Gautier, *Souvenirs romantiques* (Paris, 1929), pp. 300–301.
11. Charles Pierre Baudelaire, *Curiosités esthétiques*, *Oeuvres complètes*, Editions J. Crépet (Paris, 1947), I, p. 322.
12. Charles Pierre Baudelaire, *Correspondance*, *Oeuvres complètes*, Editions J. Crépet (Paris, 1947), I, p. 385.
13. Baudelaire, *Les Paradis artificiels*, p. 77.
14. Ibid.
15. Eliphas Lévi, *Dogme et rituel de la haute magie*, Editions Niclaus (Paris, 1947), vol. 2, pp. 332–333.
16. Rimbaud, *Oeuvres*, p. 213.
17. Nerval, *Aurélia*, p. 103.
18. Ibid.
19. Charles Baudelaire, "Critiques litteraires III," *L'Art romantique*, Editions d'art (Genève, 1945), p. 397.
20. Baudelaire, *Les Paradis artificiels*, p. 228.
21. Ibid., pp. 83–84.
22. Nerval, pp. 120, 133.
23. Ibid., pp. 184, 103.
24. Rimbaud, p. 132.
25. John Read, *Prelude to Chemistry* (New York, 1937), p. 275.
26. Ibid., pp. 131–133.
27. Carl Gustav Jung, *Psychology and Religion*, *Collected Works*, Bollingen Series (New York, 1955), p. 454.

A. C. Brench and Peter Young

MYSTICISM AND MODERN WEST AFRICAN WRITING

I

FRENCH-SPEAKING AFRICA IS BOTH POLITICALLY AND GEOGRAPHICALLY different from English-speaking Africa. In the first instance, the French policy of assimilation is entirely different from the British methods of indirect rule. Secondly, whereas the French colonial empire stretched from the Mediterranean to the Equator, the British possessions were, especially in West Africa, islands in this Francophonie. The homogenous nature of the French possessions made a centralized form of government and education possible. One could say that this part of the French Empire stretched from the Pas de Calais to the Congo, and the administrative center of Afrique Occidentale Française, Dakar, is still essentially a provincial French city. Not only was there a unified educational system, but more important, those students found suitable for further education followed exactly similar paths—according to their talents. It is not strange, therefore, to find that all of the early writers were in Paris and had passed through the schools or had been inhabitants of Dakar. This centralization, together with the French educational system and its emphasis on Cartesian logic, created a group of students who were all influenced by the same forces and were also closely knit, working and thinking together and collaborating in such ventures as *La Revue du Monde noir* and *L'Etudiant noir*. We can expect then, and do in fact find, a much greater homogeny among these students and a rather more coherent and abstracted approach to the problems facing them than among the English-speaking students, who come from varied backgrounds. African writing in French first appeared in quantity in the 1930s from expatriate students in France studying in various fields from French literature to veterinary science. Initially they nearly all produced poetry, the outstanding exception being Birago Diop whose short stories were acclaimed by Senghor as expressing "la vraie pensée nègre." This writing is the first expression of what later was called "négritude."

Two major themes dominated this early poetry and continued to dominate nearly all the literature published until independence: protest and nostalgia. The poets protested against their own assimilation and the rape of Africa with the concomitant exploitation of Africans in Africa. They were nostalgic for their homeland and for pre-colonial Africa, where the African lived his own life on his own land with his own gods.

Before discussing this poetry it is necessary to understand the writers themselves. They are all the product of the French educational system in the colonies, which differed very little from that obtaining in the "mother" country. The result of this education was normally to produce "black" Frenchmen. This was frequently the case in the nineteenth century and early decades of the twentieth. However, awakening political consciousness, resulting from the students' contact with the flourishing Communist Party and the radical surrealists made the students aware, for the first time, that they were being assimilated and thereby losing their own cultural inheritance. Another equally important and possibly more formative influence was that of the Negro-Americans who were frequent visitors to France in the late twenties and thirties. These writers, seeking a way out of their own cultural desert in the United States, were turning to Africa and African cultures as a possible source of inspiration and also as a foundation for their own culture. George McKay, Countee Cullen, and many others made contact with these young students and without any doubt contributed to their awareness of the alienation they suffered and the value of their own culture. These three influences, then, were responsible for the students' realization that they were being culturally disinherited. While they reacted against this, at the same time they also had to acquire the skills necessary for their country's survival in the twentieth century. Therefore they were caught in a dilemma from which it was extremely difficult to escape. Cheik Hamidou Kane summarizes this predicament:

> Il arrive que nous soyons capturés au bout de notre itinéraire, vaincus par notre aventure même. Il nous apparaît soudain que, tout au long de notre cheminement, nous n'avons cessé de nous métamorphoser, et que nous voilà devenus autres. Quelquefois, la métamorphose ne s'achève

même pas, elle nous installe dans l'hybride et nous y laisse. Alors, nous nous cachons, remplis de honte.[1]

Volo nolo, these students in France had to change, to become different from those Africans who stayed at home and continued to live in their villages, and even from those who lived in the towns. Equally, the public for their writings was limited to elite groups in the same position as themselves—colonials receiving higher education in France—and a minority of negrophile intellectuals. They were also at the mercy of French publishing houses whose main concern is profitability, as in any other business, and who were not therefore very favorably impressed by the writings of a small minority group with little appeal to the general public. With one or two exceptions, such as *Les Editions Latines*, publication of the African writers' work did not increase until the establishment of *Présence africaine* in 1947.

One obvious example of the changes which took place in these students is that, apart from a large majority of Muslims, most of them were converts to Christianity or to one or another brand of socialistic materialism, retaining to a greater or lesser degree residual traditional beliefs. They are then a product peculiar to this moment in history: both the standard bearers of Africa in the twentieth century and also alienated from it. They know that Africa has to change yet at the same time they idealize its past. They themselves have to evolve away from their own culture, and yet they wish to retain its purity. Their quest is for identity in a society which is meaningful to them as Africans.

Some, such as Birago Diop and Camara Laye, use creative writing as a means of retaining contact with their past life. Diop in his *Contes d'Amadou Koumba* (1947) recaptures his past by retelling the stories of his griot, Amadou Koumba, which show the same universal values found in folk tales throughout the world. Diop transcribes them into a written language which retains all the verve and verbal dexterity of the original oral tale. His characters are essentially African, but they are also universal archetypes. Laye's *L'Enfant noir* (1953) recounts his childhood in a village in Guinea. It too has this universal theme which he treats as sensitively as Diop does his folktales. And again, the child and his family are essentially African, as well as representing the universal members of a happy and united family. Others, including Senghor himself, explore the whole range of problems facing Africans, both those in Europe and those living under the colonial regime in Africa. Others still, such as D. T. Niane in *Sounjata* and Paul Hazoumé in *Doguicimi* (1935), recreated the pre-colonial past of Africa by recounting traditional legends of long-dead heroes whose magical and mysterious powers have been lost. They portray the heroic period of African history, implying that the present is not a true representation of Africa's potential and that, to be great, Africa has to rediscover this past glory and live up to it. This same theme is also found in Senghor's dramatic poem "Chaka" in which the Zulu leader is shown as one of the last bastions of the black peoples against European intrusion.[2]

Later writers, especially those published in the fifties, protest—mainly in their novels—against oppression by the colonial regime. Novelists such as Mongo Beti and Ferdinand Oyono both inveigh against this oppression and also satirize the Africans for accepting it and letting their lives become empty of meaning. All of them, therefore, in one way or another are concerned with the problem of finding an identity either for themselves or for Africans in general.

Together with this search for identity the writers are also seeking a means of recreating an ideal Africa. We see this in the nostalgic poems of Senghor:

> *Je ne sais* quel temps c'était, je confonds toujours l'enfance et l'Eden
> Comme je mêle la Mort et la Vie—un pont de douceur les relie.
> Or je revenais de Fa'oye, m'étant abreuvé à la tombe solennelle
> Comme les lamatins s'abreuvent à la fontaine de Simal.
> Or je revenais de Fa'oye, et l'horreur était au zénith
> Et c'était l'heure où l'on voit les Esprits, quand la lumière est transparente
> Et il fallait s'écarter des sentiers, pour éviter leur main fraternelle et mortelle.
> L'âme d'un village battait à l'horizon. Etait-ce des vivants ou des Morts?[3]

The same theme is found in Bernard Dadié's poem 'Ode à l'Afrique':

> J'accorderai mon luth pour égrener dans le soir
> tes litanies, au fil des heures quiètes.
> J'apprêterai mes doigts pour moduler sur la cora des griots habiles
> Au long des sentes et des méandres
> Les chansons des preux morts
> L'arc au point.[4]

This nostalgia is in sharp contrast to the mood of despair which overwhelms these writers when they consider the plight of Africa under the colonial regime. The most bitter attacks on the colonists are found both in these early poets and in the works of the later novelists already mentioned. Ferdinand Oyono's *Une Vie de Boy* (1956) and *Le Vieux Nègre et la Médaille* (1956) attack both the abuses of the colonists and the inertia of the "average" African. In both novels he is concerned with describing the white man's duplicity and upbraiding the Africans for ever trying to collaborate with these intruders. Both Tunde Joseph and Meka, the heroes of the two novels, attempt to reconcile Europe and Africa. Tunde, the "boy," and Meka, the old negro, learn from their mistakes, but for the former it is too late. Again it is Senghor who summarizes the situation:

> Seigneur Dieu, pardonne à l'Europe blanche!
> Il est vrai, Seigneur, que pendant quatre siècles de lumières,
> elle a jeté la bave et les abois de ses molosses sur mes terres
> Et les chrétiens, abjurant ta lumière et la mansuétude de
> Ton coeur
> Ont éclairé leurs bivouacs avec mes parchemins, torturé mes
> talbés, déporté mes docteurs et mes maîtres-de-science.
> Leur poudre a croulé dans l'éclair la fierté des tatas et des
> collines. . . .[5]

From this it is possible to see that these writers feel not only a sense of physical exile but also, and more important, spiritual exile and even spiritual isolation from their past, cut off as they are both in time and space and forced to become different from other Africans. The Africa of the past is an ideal which they are seeking and can never find. Jean-Marie Medza, the hero of Mongo Beti's *Mission Terminée* (1957), sets out on an endless quest for his ideal, with his bosom friend Zambo, at the end of the novel. He is disillustioned by the chicanery and pettiness of the villagers of Kala where he is staying, and he also realizes that the "city" education which he has acquired in the Europeans' school will no more fit him for life than the tawdry values accepted by his uncle, Zambo's father, and the other villagers.

Jean-Marie Medza's quest is not, however, simply a quest for an ideal society in which to live; it is also a search for himself. This is the second problem facing these African intellectuals caught, as it has so often been said, between two worlds. There is in the first place an assertion of the beauty of being black.

Je vous remercie mon Dieu de m'avoir créé noir,
D'avoir fait de moi
la somme de toutes les douleurs,
mis sur ma tête,
Le Monde.
J'ai la livrée du Centaure
Et je porte le monde depuis le premier matin.
Le blanc est une couleur de circonstance
Le noir la couleur de tous les jours
Et je porte le Monde depuis le premier soir.[6]

Yet, at the same time, this attribute is also disadvantageous, not only because the Europeans despise those of darker pigmentation, but also because the individual cannot find the totality of his personality in this "blackness."

Il me faut le cacher au plus intime de mes veines
L'Ancêtre à la peau d'orage sillonnée d'éclairs
  et de foudre
Mon animal gardien, il me le faut cacher
Que je ne rompe le barrage des scandales.
Il est mon sang fidèle qui requiert fidélité
Protégeant mon orgueil nu contre
Moi-même et la superbe des races heureuses. . . .[7]

The most poignant development of this loss of personality is found in C. H. Kane's *Aventure ambiguë*. The hero, Samba Diallo, is sent by his tribe, the Diallobé, to "apprendre à vaincre sans avoir raison," that is to say, to learn the ways of the Europeans. He fails and is partially assimilated by Europe yet remains partially true to his old faith. He finally chooses death as the only means of resolving the ambiguity of his existence.

It can now be seen that this literature has as its basis a dual objective: first, the recreation of a proud and virile Africa, and second, the integrity of the individual. Together these principles show that the writers are seeking, in Sartrian terminology, the integration of "l'être dans le monde," not only in the physical and rational sense but also, and more especially, in the spiritual sense. It cannot be said, however, that they want to sublimate their individual personality in this greater whole, rather do they wish to find their own totality within it, being an active part of it. It can therefore be seen that the conception of the mystical is very different from that which is given at the end of *Le Regard du Roi* (1954). Camara Laye's second novel ends with the hero, Clarence, being absorbed totally into the "God-King." The novel is a description of his search for this Ideal; gradually his whole personality is transformed until, at the end, he is ready to lose himself in the King, renouncing entirely his original personality and being content to accept that which the King will offer him. This concept, which is close to that of Christian mystics, is entirely different from that postulated by other African writers. They are creating an ideal and wish to be active parts of it. It is a question not only of sublimating themselves in Africa but also of being themselves this Africa. The ideal and its creator cannot live independently of each other.

II

A case similar to this could be maintained for the literature in English of West Africa, but there are certain important distinctions to be made. The first of these undoubtedly concerns the lack of an exact parallel to the French-speaking colonial experience of assimilation. The policy of indirect rule had its own perversions of traditional life which are in their way no less far-reaching than those of assimilation, but it is clear that, though very little less culturally dispossessing in its total effect on the modern African intellectual, the policy in the English-speaking countries nonetheless allowed a certain maintenance of traditional culture away from the centers of power. The literary results of this fundamental difference have been several, and the duality of the division, reflected in the opposition of the traditional to the "Westernized" culture, can also be detected in the writer's creative exploration of his cosmic experience.

Perhaps the first forcible comparison to strike the student of West African literature in English and French is the relatively less overt tone of protest. In accepting this distinction, one should not be misled into supposing that Anglophone and Francophone writers differ at root in their attitudes towards their Africanness. It was just such a misunderstanding on the part of the critics that led to the long and at times futile argument concerning the misinterpretation of Soyinka's "négritude" versus "tigritude" statements. It is in many ways a pity that the verbal facility of Soyinka's contrast should have brought about an unfortunate, as well as largely erronous, confrontation of the two literatures. But far more influential on recent critical thought about African literature has been the consolidation of the idea that the two literatures are in literary-historical terms fully congruent. This normal approach has been further validated by the fact that in the twentieth century the most vocal and influential expressions of Africanness at an early date were those of the black French-speaking writers such as Césaire and Senghor. The general acceptance of the common literary-historical origins of the literatures in French and in English in West Africa arises from the powerful feelings of solidarity of black people everywhere, but it must also be seen—and this is emphasized by a conviction on the part of the African and the European intellectual alike—that the roots of African literature are mainly to be found in the twentieth century. In the one case the critical error is emotionally justifiable, and in the other it is at its worst a suppressed expression of European patronage, willing to accept recent change but not the dignity of literary evolution. Whatever may be felt about this view of the reasons behind the conjugation of the literary histories of the two literatures, it is essential to seek the origins of the thought expressed in Anglophone literature in earlier times than is possible for the Francophone.

It has been suggested that in the literature of English-speaking West Africa the attempt to integrate into the cosmic ideal has expressed itself in two ways: the "traditional," in which the conception of the ideal has been according to the precepts of indigenous philosophy and conceptions of the universe, and the "dispossessed," in which the reaction against the cultural and spiritual dispossession of colonialism has resolved itself in the creation of an ideal Africanness in the most passionate way, "Felt in the blood, and felt along the heart." As is to be expected, since the writers of contemporary Africa are predominantly those whose experience involves the confrontation of the African and the Western, the "mysticism of dispossession" is by far the most common of the two spiritual quests.

For English-speaking West Africa the beginning of the quest is first detected in the nineteenth century with the cultural rediscovery made possible by the missionary linguists, notably those Africans like Bishop Crowther, who found themselves most deeply and personally affected. A very good case indeed could be made for detecting the rise of this spirit in the eighteenth century with the work of writers such as Equiano. One work in French should be mentioned, Baron Roger's *Fables Sénégalaises* (1828), in which the Wolof oral tradition was rendered into French verse, but in this case we can point to no more than a promise of the future, since the work remained a literary curiosity. The cultural rediscovery in Anglophone West Africa found expression in a number of ways: in the *History of Sierra Leone* (1868) of A. B. C. Sibthorpe, in C. C. Reindorf's *History of the Gold Coast and Asante* (1895), as well as in the thought of such men as Bishop James "Holy" Johnson. But it is in the work of the Ghanaian Casely Hayford that the statement began to break free of the early demands of the pamphlet into creative expression. In *Ethiopia Unbound* (1911), the statement of the theme of African spiritual and cultural integrity is integral. In the following statement there is a clear indication of the way in which the truly African as yet depended for its expression on the legacy of European cultural dispossession of the African. The Biblical tone is intentional.

> In the self-same era a god descended upon earth to teach the Ethiopians anew the *way* of *life*. He came not in thunder, or with a great sound, but in the garb of a humble teacher, a John the Baptist among his brethren, preaching racial and national salvation. From land to land, and from shore to shore, his message was the self-same one, which, interpreted in the language of Christ, was: *What shall it profit a race if it shall gain the whole world and lose its own soul?*[8]

The same spirit expressed through protest survives today. It is alive in the following poem by J. P. Clark, crying out in defiant anger and frustration at European dispossession of Africa's independent creativity.

Still a song shall arise
In my heart! Out of this pit
Of ash and dust they trampled it
A flame shall arise
Like leaves on tree, tip on tip
To burn on every lip.
Yam tuber too late for prize
Or price will, buried piecemeal,
At fall of flood rise again whole,
Turn out a hundred fold.
But enough, oh enough!
  For how can pestle
Sound in mortar a song
When Babylon of old
As yet unbroken in odd tongue
Poured on a bush of flaming gold
  Derision and dung?[9]

But it is out of the natural companion of protest, the definition and assessment of the ideal of Africanness, that the greatest hope of literary freedom arises. This too has had its simple expressions and, perhaps because it must of necessity follow the vital statement of protest, its possibilities have not as yet been explored beyond the statement, into the depths of personal spiritual evaluation. For the most part the statement of the ideal has been direct; and if it has been vaguely defined, it has not been vaguely felt. It is this mystical sublimation with the spirit of Africa that provides the central episode for the allegorically named Adam Questus in the West Indian writer Ronald Dathorne's *Scholar Man* (1964). In another way it finds expression in political clothing in William Conton's very uneven novel, *The African* (1960), when Kisimi Kamara contemplates the significance of an improbably large diamond given him as a keepsake. Here too, in the midst of intense personal feeling, the colonial disorientation is to be detected in the colonial view of Africa as a 'sleeping giant' waiting to be roused rather than as a world already intensely, spiritually, alive.

> In it I see hidden the glorious flame of Africa's spirit, the richness of her wealth, and the sharp edge of her energy. It has become for me the penetrating star of African freedom, a light by which to rouse a sleeping giant.[10]

The theme of the modern African's relationship to the African ideal has, then, taken many forms. It has been an integral part of almost as many philosophies as there are African novels, changing and adapting, like all religion, according to the themes and arguments of the moment. This lack of definition has been due in part to the normal processes of the attempt to relate the self to the conception of the ultimate whole; partly, too, it has had to wait for the passing of protest to the establishment of unstated, and essentially unstatable, premises, the transition of the literature from the passionate beginning through the slogan to the final confrontation with the problem presented by the need to explore, perhaps individually to adapt or reject, the very motivation of the quest. In this respect at least, the African writer's predicament is little different from that of all others who seek to create in their image of the truth. The agony of this indeterminacy has been nowhere better expressed in the literature than in the work of Soyinka. The spirit of Africa, for such it is though not so smugly labeled, moves as elusively as its definition in the mind of the modern African throughout his work. It is, for example, subtly suggested by some of the women in his work: in Segi of *Kongi's Harvest*, more lightly in Sidi of *The Lion and the Jewel*, and again in Simi of *The Interpreters* (1965), whose mystery and magnetism draws Egbo as his nature draws him to the heritage he has rejected, though "he knew and despised the age that sought to mutilate his beginnings." But it is in *The Interpreters*, the very title and theme of which is the interpretation of the nature of modern Africanness through the lives of modern Africans, that one comes closest to a careful exploration of the mysticism of dispossession. Africanness is the vision of the past that taunts Egbo, the fatal attraction of Simi, the frenzy of Sekoni and his sculpture 'The Wrestler' in which the American Joe Golder recognized the object of his quest and offered to buy it. Africa is all these things and many more, as vast and unresolvable as the changing canvas of Kola's Pantheon, of which Kola says in words which might no less be applied to the whole exploration of modern African experience:

> 'It requires only the bridge, or the ladder between heaven and earth. A rope or chain. The link, that is all. After fifteen months all that is left is the link. . . .'[11]

Attempts to examine man's relation to the ideal in traditional terms are rare in the literature for reasons apparent and inherent in the West African intellectual's necessary confrontation of the traditional and the modern. Perhaps the most interesting attempt of the kind is to be seen in Chinua Achebe's *Arrow of God* (1964), in which the common theme of culture conflict in the opposition of traditional society in Umuaro to white domination runs parallel to the theme concerning the rivalry between Ezeulu, Chief Priest of Ulu, the deity of Umuaro, and certain factions within Umuaro. The main observation of interest here is that of the nature of the deity Ulu, for though in terms of Umuaro he is the Supreme Being, he did not create Umuaro but was created by it, the deified abstraction of the organic spirit of the clan. Part of the irony of Ezeulu's failure, mercifully unknown to him in the refuge of his final madness, is that he drastically misinterprets the nature of Ulu whom he serves. For Ezeulu, Ulu is omnipotence, for does not his Chief Priest set the life of the clan by controlling the vitally important spiritual events such as the New Yam Festival? But Ulu *is* the clan, and as Umuaro changes so does Ulu; as the crack appears in the unity of the clan so does it appear in Ulu's omnipotence and in Ezeulu's uncomprehending mind. In this centering of the ultimate in man and in the spirit of man's life-preserving social organism, as seen by Achebe, the one fundamental difference is to be detected between the Western and the African mystical orientation.

This dual literary refocusing, in the mysticism, of both "tradition" and "dispossession" on man offers the clearest distinction from western ideas of mysticism. For the African writer the mystical ideal—existing as it does in protest, in personal reassessment in relation to ideals of Africanness, or in quite different terms, for Achebe at least, in the organic living force of traditional African society—centers on man and on his interpretation of himself rather than on sublimation with the mystical ideal. In one sense, West African literature in English may be said to have replaced the processes of mysticism with the profound possibilities of humanism.

III

Though there are clearly important differences between the literatures in English and those in French in West Africa, they are united in the object of exploring the nature of the ideal of Africanness and in attempting to establish the individual's relationship to it. This, it has been suggested, is in no usual sense describable as mysticism, though—in so far as it involves a spiritual quest and ideal—it can be seen as closely akin to the mystic's progress.

It is in contemplating the implications of this point that the enormity of the price the African writer has had to pay for the colonial experience begins to reveal itself fully. The colonial years, indeed all the centuries of careful European argument for African inferiority, following the great cultural rediscovery of the late nineteenth century could result in nothing other than protest and its companion, a reassessment of Africanness. In seeking to re-establish the nature of his relationship with Africanness, itself a concept concomitant with protest, the African writer's attention has been distracted from the possibilities of mysticism in purely African terms. And the possibilities of mysticism, in a sense much more intimate because much less outwardly directed into self-justification, certainly exist, as Father Tempels has so clearly shown.[12]

It would not be going too far to insist, and this can only be fully realizable when a happier future removes the need for protest, that the future of the literature of West Africa in European languages rests on the passing of protest. There are certainly ways in which the insistent note of protest, notably in Francophone writing, explicable and necessary though it remains, would threaten to induce a form of literary immobility, which is too high a price for any people to pay.

However, there are signs that the dilemma is not beyond resolution.

For just as Achebe's superbly craftsmanlike and sensitive examination of the theme of tradition and change might be said to have pointed to Soyinka's *The Interpreters* as being in almost logical sequence, so might *The Interpreters*, in its acute perception of the nature of modern African experience, be said to have pointed the way to a literature in the most profound way the product of an African ontology and cosmology. The realization of this promise is inseparable from the future literary and spiritual independence of the African writer.

Notes

1. C. H. Kane, *L'Aventure ambiguë* (Paris: Julliard, 1961), p. 133.
2. L. S. Senghor, "Chaka," in *L. S. Senghor, Poètes d'aujourd'hui* (Paris: P. Seghers, 1961).
3. L. S. Senghor, "Je ne sais en quel temps," in *Poètes d'aujourd'hui.*
4. B. B. Dadié, "Ode à l'Afrique," in *La Ronde des Jours* (Paris: P. Seghers, 1956).
5. Dadié, "Prière de paix II," in *La Ronde des Jours.*
6. Dadié, "Je vous remercie mon Dieu," in *La Ronde des Jours.*
7. Senghor, "Le Totem," in *Poètes d'aujourd'hui*, p. 125.
8. Casely Hayford, *Ethiopia Unbound* (London: C. M. Phillips, 1911), p. 160.
9. John Pepper Clark, *Poems* (Ibudan, Nigeria: Mbari Publications, 1962), p. 3.
10. William Farquhar Conton, *The African* (Boston: Little, Brown, 1960), p. 36.
11. Wole Soyinka, *The Interpreters* (London: A. Deutsch, 1965), p. 225.
12. Placied Tempels, *Bantu Philosophy*, trans. by Colin King from *La philosophie bantoue*, the French version by A. Rubbens of Franciscus Tempels' original work (Paris, Présence africaine, 1959), pp. 33 ff.

Charles T. Davis

THE HEAVENLY VOICE OF THE BLACK AMERICAN

BLACK PEOPLE AS A GROUP RECEIVE CREDIT FOR OCCUPYING BOTH ENDS of a spectrum that reflects the relationship between man and God. Some critical Americans consider blacks to be especially resistant to religious instruction, and they point to the continued strength of "nature" in Negroes, when "nature" is defined as a life without the restraints of a civilized society. These critics point, with a certain Puritanical pleasure, to the reputation for uninhibited consumption of alcohol, easy love, fighting, and stealing—in short, the elements that make up the stereotype of "Black Sambo" that survives still in the minds of a few unreconstructed Southern politicians. More Americans think that blacks are peculiarly receptive to divine influence, and they invariably cite as evidence to support this claim characteristic themes found in the Negro spirituals: the intense yearning for a spiritual home to replace a material one and the desire to merge with God in an effort to erase the memory of misery and unhappiness on earth.

Though we are not concerned here with the "natural" voice of American Negroes, we should note that the Sambo stereotype was strongly supported by a form of popular art, the minstrel show, that flourished in America in the nineteenth and early twentieth centuries and was exploited, to a lesser extent, by the writers of dialect poems and tales. What the American black is really like, then, has been thoroughly corrupted by an artistic tradition that had, finally, little concern for accuracy of representation. We wonder if the black man's reputation for possessing an affinity for things mystical is based similarly on such a precarious foundation.

Close inspection of the claim suggests that it is the Negro spiritual that is usually cited as supporting the black man's possession of the "heavenly voice." There is no doubt that those "black and unknown bards"[1] who created the spirituals were touched by a mystical fever of some kind, but can we attribute to their descendants, in uncounted generations, the same mystical powers with which the creators were endowed? We should be naïve if we did, and once again art has intervened. Mystical illumination should not be confused with the satisfaction, no matter how pious, of participating in an artistic performance, the singing of the spirituals. Art, high in the case of the spiritual, or low when we think of Mr. Bones and Sambo, taints both claims.

What amounts to a stand-off should discourage the making of sweeping generalizations of any kind about racial characteristics. Though we offer no new rash claims, we must say that most people concerned with the problem rarely consider the best evidence for attributing to the black man the extraordinary experience of communicating directly with divinity. We have heard much about the Negro spirituals; W.E.B. DuBois,[2] James Weldon Johnson,[3] and Alain Locke[4] have written eloquently about the haunting beauty of these songs, so intensely emotional and so otherworldly. We have heard less of an art form closely linked to the spiritual, the folk sermon. The sermon resembles the spiritual in coming from the same kind of religious experience. That is to say, it is the product of the black man's effort to assimilate and to adapt Christian ideas, an effort that folklorist Bruce Rosenberg dates as far back as the Second Great Awakening in 1800, if not before.[5] The sermon resembles the spiritual in not being entirely the property of black people. There are white spirituals and, of course, white folk sermons, but we hear more about black achievement in these areas possibly for the reason that for many years America has had a higher proportion of illiterate blacks than illiterate whites, or possibly because black accomplishments carry more emotional power and display more imaginative strength.

If we compare the folk sermon and the spiritual as instruments useful in conveying a sense of communication with God, we must insist that the folk sermon is far purer and far more efficient. The spiritual was sung commonly by a congregation or a group, repeating, with widely varying understanding and feeling, words that were remembered. Very seldom do we have the act of creation occurring in conjunction with the singing. Despite the most spontaneous and sincere of performances, we must admit to ourselves that ultimate credit must go to those "black and unknown bards" about whom we know so little. Not so with the folk sermon. In this art form the preacher quite literally begins with the assumption that he *is* the voice of God. "Is" is not quite correct, perhaps; "becomes" is better because the preacher gradually works himself toward an ultimate identification with God. That moment occurs when the black spokesman chants in a strong and rhythmical cadence the words that God has given, possibly, while leaning backward from the pulpit, with eyes closed, veins bulging in his forehead, and sweat streaming from every pore. The black performer, if asked to repeat what he has said at this moment, may be at a loss to reconstruct the chain of phrases that have come pouring from his mouth, made sacred for the short period just passed.

What is being described is by no means a dead art, to be reconstructed from documents or the memories of aged ministers, but one that lives still, in store-front churches in the ghettoes of American cities, in the tents of camp-meetings held on the outskirts of cities or in the country, and on the radio, at stations to be found usually at the extreme ends of the dial spectrum at those frequencies where the folk sermon must compete with country music and advertisements for patent medicines. It is possible, then, for a well-trained critic with a strong background in the tools and the methods of folklore to describe the art form with some precision by using contemporary models. And Professor Bruce Rosenberg has done so in *The Art of the American Folk Preacher*. He provides a shape for the authentic folk sermon that is suggestive in many ways. What has been looked at largely as an emotional or spiritual experience becomes an identifiable art form subject to analysis and comparison. Immediately invited, of course, is the chance to examine the artistic reproductions of the sermons—that is to say, the approximations constructed by literary artists—in light of an authentic model. *God's Trombones*[6] by James Weldon Johnson is a collection of poems that imitate the structure of the folk sermon and convey something, as a consequence, of the authority of the original form. One step removed from such a comparison is the critical exploration of the use of the art form of the sermon in another, perhaps more familiar, literary structure —the novel. James Baldwin, once a child-evangelist himself, does just this in *Go Tell It on the Mountain*,[7] giving to the sermon a flexibility and dimension undreamed of by the often illiterate or semi-literate black exhorter, who would claim that he was simply about God's work.

Now to describe the form. The first characteristic established by Professor Rosenberg's analysis is rhythm,[8] already alluded to when we spoke of the increased regularity in the phrasing of the preacher as he approached his climax. Indeed, Rosenberg has insisted that a rhythmical pattern transcends words in importance, that is to say, words as an expression of ideas or concepts. A significant part of the training of a neophyte in the art, often a child incapable of grasping much else, would be listening to and responding to an overall rhythmical pattern.[9] Customarily the beginning of a folk sermon would be prosaic, building on a reference to a text or to a situation that has led to the preoccupation with a particular theme. Then the preacher moves through a set of what may be called trial sequences toward increased regularity in phrasing. At the moment of climax we observe that the prosaic syntax and the imagery appropriate to mundane discussion give way, under extraordinary emotional pressure, to the verbal devices of a chanted poem, characterized by a strong beat, and to an imagery made luminous or symbolic by what the speaker takes to be providential intrusion. Then, at the conclusion, the preacher returns to the world of ordinary mortals in supplying a message that might be carried like a handkerchief from the church door.

Rosenberg's sample sermons display a number of easily identifiable devices. Nothing is more marked than the repetition in diction and syntax. We find parallel clusters in which the same phrase occurs or the same or similar grammatical constructions.[10] Then there are the repeated formula phrases, important in the structure of early epics in revealing ties to an oral tradition, which may record breaks in the development of the preacher's thought or represent direct appeals to the congregation.[11]

It is the formula phrase that suggests an important additional characteristic of the art form. We are reminded that the role of the congregation is not passive. Correctly and efficiently exhorted, the congregation responds in formula phrases of its own: "Preach it, brother," or "Yes, Lord," possibly. The reaction of the audience ideally takes the emotional pattern of the preacher's sermon. When the exhorter's chant becomes most regular and most insistent, the members of the congregation reach the climax of their excitement. As the folk preacher feels afterwards that God has spoken directly through him, those exhorted feel afterwards that God has spoken directly to them.

The congregation makes an additional contribution that is somewhat more difficult to define; it concerns the matter of continuity or, to be more accurate, the sense of continuity. A folk sermon may lack elements that provide connection and coherence in other forms. The epic, with oral origins too, would be a case in point; here narrative provides much of what is necessary for continuity. But there is no reason to expect a coherent narrative in a sermon. Story elements may appear, but they tend to demonstrate and to illustrate other points and not to be sufficient in themselves. What is lacking in narrative is seldom balanced by logic. Indeed, it is difficult to avoid the conclusion that much of what passes for continuity comes from the congregation itself, the reaction to the preacher's rhetoric. Continuity may exist when the congregation feels that the rhythmical pattern, or the larger emotional design to which that pattern is related, is fulfilled. This is overstatement, no doubt, for certainly imagery, references to bits of narrative (if not the sense of a developing tale), and repeated allusions to the problem or to the theme supply more concrete evidences of planned organization. But it is not overstatement by much. Baldwin, among the literary artists manipulating the form, realizes most thoroughly the great contribution of the audience, and the structure of *Go Tell It on the Mountain* reflects this fact.

The language and the imagery of the folk sermon derive, in part, from the Bible. Only in part. Perhaps a more significant contribution comes from the infusion of matter from ordinary life. Striking effects are the consequence of this rude juxtaposition of the familiar religious phrase and the homely illustration or elaboration. This point is seen clearly in a sequence, recorded by Rosenberg, of a sermon "The Twenty-Third Psalm," recited by Rev. Rubin Lacy on May 5, 1968, in Corcoran, California:

David in his old age
Can say the Lord is my shepherd
I shall not want
Devil kept on runnin' after David
They run him so tired
Sometime he was hungry
He had to eat the short bread
He didn't have time to go to the store
He had to eat the bread
That the trees issued
God from Zion (11. 103–113)[12]

As we know, Johnson modeled *God's Trombones* after the folk sermons. Though he has caught with accuracy the spirit of the black preacher, we note some differences. While the tone of Johnson's preacher is undoubtedly the same as that of an authentic black exhorter, it has, at the beginning of a sermon, more authority, the kind of strength reserved for a folk preacher nearer the middle of his sermon. Johnson eliminates the prosaic frame, the commencement and the conclusion, containing matter closest to the mundane world of the congregation. Though the pattern of growing intensity remains, the speaker in one of

Johnson's *Trombones* has not far to go. The moment of great excitement is recorded in the same old way—in more regular metrics and with an overwhelming amount of repetition in the phrasing. Johnson's preacher cries out in the sermon entitled "The Crucifixion" at the moment that the nail pierces the flesh of the hanging savior:

On Calvary, on Calvary,
They crucified my Jesus.
They nailed him to the cruel tree
And the hammer!
The hammer!
The hammer!
Rang through Jerusalem's streets
The hammer!
The hammer!
The hammer!
Rang through Jerusalem's streets.[13]

We discover formula phrases in Johnson's sermon, terms that represent stops in the development of the preacher's thought or permit time for recovery and redirection and, above all, appeal directly to the assembled congregation. Lacy's "God from Zion" has a counterpart in Johnson's "The Prodigal Son." There "Young man—/ Young man—" serves the same function; we watch helplessly as the wayward youth slips ever more deeply into the sinful ways of Babylon. The marvelous juxtaposition of the conventionally religious phrase and the vulgar action or image, often providing raciness in the folk sermon, appears in Johnson's *Trombones* too, with something less than the vigor of the folk model:

And God stepped out on space
And he looked around and said
I'm lonely—
I'll make me a world.

And far as the eye of God could see
Darkness covered everything,
Blacker then a hundred midnights
Down in a cypress swamp.[14]

Though the narrative element has increased significance in the

Trombones, it does not pre-empt the function of the message, the plain, sometimes rude instruction to the assembled church members about what they should carry from the service. At the end of "The Crucifixion," Johnson's preacher says, "Oh, I tremble, yes, I tremble,/ It causes me to tremble, tremble,/ When I think how Jesus died."[15] Indeed, we are not to forget the awesome magnificence of Christ's sacrifice. The message has a particular poignancy here because it echoes the phrasing of the great Easter spiritual, "Were You There When They Crucified My Lord?" We are reminded of the fact that the folk sermon and the spiritual came from the same source.

It is in the attention to the congregation that we sense an important difference between the art sermon and the folk sermon. Though Johnson's preacher in the funeral sermon, "Go Down Death," addresses specific people in his audience, "Heart-broken husband," "Grief-stricken son," and "Left-lonesome daughter,"[16] he is generally less precise. Actually, what is often missing in the *Trombones* is the pressure of an involved congregation actively goading the preacher to attain a more accurate expression of God's Word. Some indication of how that pressure works can be seen in another of Rev. Rubin Lacy's sermons, this entitled "God's Ploughboy," delivered on May 19, 1968, in Tulare, California:

I'm wondering do ya hear me today
Somebody here
Soft-peddlin' the gospel
Tryin' to soothe somebody
Twistin' the Word of God
I'm here to tell ya today
Preach the Word
Preach the Word
Don't care who don't like it
I don't care who it hit
Ohh preach the Word
I don't care who don't like it
I don't care who get offended about it
Preach the word (11. 207–220)[17]

Moreover, Johnson in the art sermon seldom musters at the climactic moment the kind of raw power that the folk sermon has when it is successful. The repeated references to "The hammer," in "The Crucifixion," fail to move even a sophisticated reading audience as much as

Lacy's definition of the *Word* at a moment of great intensity in "God's Ploughboy":

Because the gospel
Is the saving salt
That serves the soul
Umm-hmm
Preach
Because the gospel
Is the power of God
Unto those of salvation
To everyone that believe
Ohh preach the Word
I'm glad God told me
A long time ago
To preach my Word
Ohh go eat
Therefore (11. 231–247)[18]

Perhaps one of the reasons why we are so impressed by Lacy's rhetoric is the fact that the preacher has come very far from "That's the text / You'll find it in Hebrew thirteen to seventeen / That's the text."[19] On the other hand, Johnson's preacher strikes an opening note in "The Crucifixion" just slightly below the intensity of his later description of the agony of Jesus:

Jesus, my gentle Jesus,
Walking in the dark of the Garden—
The Garden of Gethsemane,
Saying to the three disciples;
Sorrow is in my soul—
Even unto death[20]

We are never far from the rhythm of the folk sermon throughout Baldwin's *Go Tell It on the Mountain.* The structure of much of the novel is given over to "The Prayers of the Saints" (Part Two), in which the closest relatives of the young black hero, John, offer confessions or testimonials about their own lives. Gabriel, John's stepfather; Florence, Gabriel's sister; and Elizabeth, John's mother, encouraged by the exhortation of the preacher, move toward some sort of ultimate illumination, in much the way the folk preacher struggles with the empty and misleading forms of the world to achieve a perfect statement of the Word. Baldwin is not content with correspondences so general. There are folk sermons incorporated into the testimonial of Gabriel, the deposed preacher. He has been deposed because he had found God's service no shield protecting him from the sins of lust and pride. As part of his recollection of the great turning points of his life, Gabriel recalls sermons of his own, often in their entirety, because they relate closely to and illuminate the action he is on the point of taking. When he is deciding to marry Deborah, the holy fool, the black girl who has been cruelly raped by whites and who has survived to remind the world of its corruption, Gabriel preaches eloquently on the wages of sin.[21] When he is attempting futilely to resist the physical attractions of Esther, after his marriage to Deborah, Gabriel retells the story, in the second book of Samuel, of young Ahimaaz who ran too soon to bring the tidings of battle to King David. Gabriel appeals to the flippant and careless Esther to commit herself to God, by commenting on Ahimaaz's words: "I saw a great tumult but I know not what it was."[22] Gabriel thinks that the statement applies to Esther's situation and in his pride and ignorance does not see that it applies with even more compelling force to himself, to his struggle to ignore or to master the seething sexuality rising within him.

Gabriel's sermon, delivered at the time he was brooding over Deborah's virtues of the spirit and inadequacies of the body, has a structure that is typical of the folk sermon. We see in Baldwin's description of the beginning of Gabriel's sermon a statement that would characterize accurately the first minutes of most folk sermons:

> He did not begin with a "shout" song, or with a fiery testimony; but in a dry, matter-of-fact voice, which trembled only a little, asked them [the congregation assembled for the Twenty-Four Elders Revival Meeting] to look with him at the sixth chapter of Isaiah, and the fifth verse.[23]

As Gabriel warms to his task, we hear the repeated phrase and the chant of the prose poem, with an insistent and inescapable beat:

> Let us remember that we are born in sin, in sin did our mothers conceive us—sin reigns in all our members, sin is the foul heart's natural liquid, sin looks out of the eye, amen, and leads to lust, sin is in the hearing of the ear, and leads to folly, sin sits on the tongue, and leads to murder. Yes! Sin is the only heritage of the natural man, sin bequeathed us by our natural father, that fallen Adam, whose apple sickens and will sicken all generations living, and generations yet unborn![24]

Gabriel's rhetoric lacks the rude juxtapositions of the vulgar and the conventional that enliven Lacy's sermons and occasionally touch the rolling periods of Johnson's preacher in the *Trombones*. Gabriel's sermons resemble Johnson's in avoiding dialect, seldom exhibiting even the colloquial nuances that give a special quality to the *Trombones*. We remember with pleasure the grammatical lapse in "Go Down Death": "But they didn't make no sound."[25] No liberties of this sort exist in the diction of Baldwin's preacher; Gabriel's language is much too close to that of the Old Testament to allow for anything approaching verbal humor. Instead we stagger from the buffeting of a flood of Biblical references and from the cosmic sweep of Gabriel's leaping imagination. Gabriel lives in two worlds—three, if we count the country of memory: the South of his youth and young manhood. But the two worlds that are present at the time of telling of the tale is Harlem of the 1930's, in the area of Lenox Avenue and 135th Street, and the valleys and the mountains of Israel, the timeless world of the Old Testament.

There is much evidence of Baldwin's shrewdness in the use of the congregation while the sermon develops. Gabriel, for example, receives assistance from an unidentified woman shortly after he has begun his eloquent condemnation of sin: " 'Yes!' cried a woman. 'Tell it!' "[26] And another sympathetic voice cries out shortly afterwards: "Amen! You preach it, boy!"[27] A close reading of the sermon reveals a certain order to these outbursts. As Gabriel approaches his climax, the voices of the inspired intruders tend to be identified. "Oh, yes . . . bless our God forever!"[28] is shouted by one of the elders, one of the twenty-four whom Gabriel, in terms of his professional reputation, wishes to impress most. But it is the cry of "Praise Him!" from Deborah,[29] at the high point of the excitement, that more than anything else convinces Gabriel of his success, for Deborah's approval—acceptance by the holy fool—is the key to the door that leads to high spiritual eminence. She has access to divine authority by right of having experienced ultimate violation. Her shout comes just before Gabriel's most sweeping pronouncement, when with the voice of God's anointed Gabriel says:

> Woe is me, for when God struck the sinner, the sinner's eyes were opened, and he saw himself in all his foulness naked before God's glory. Woe is me! For the moment of salvation is a blinding light, cracking down into the heart from Heaven—Heaven so high, and the sinner so low. *Woe is me*! For unless God raised the sinner, he would never rise again![30]

Gabriel speaks as if he had borrowed the voice of God, and we receive confirmation of this fact from a congregation that has responded with complete sympathy to the divine surge of Gabriel's rhetoric. "Yes, Lord!" shouts a voice, again unidentified, "I was there!"[31] And so have we all been, in intimate touch with divinity.

The most brilliant section technically of *Go Tell It on the Mountain* grows from Baldwin's sensitivity to the reaction of the congregation. This is the third and last part, "The Threshing-Floor," which records John's experience of conversion. The sense of the outside world, of what is happening actually in the Church of the Fire Baptized, is not very clear because we are entirely absorbed with John's inner struggle. There is, without a doubt, a sermon being preached just as John's agony begins. What it is we do not know, though it plainly serves as an exhortation to sinners to join the band of the faithful. John hears an unidentified voice, possibly the voice of the preacher, the cry of conscience, or the appeal in simplified form that comes out of his whole experience. Whatever it is, it is insistent:

> He wanted to obey the voice, which was the only voice that spoke to him; he tried to assure the voice that he would do his best to rise; he would only lie here a moment, after his dreadful fall, and catch his breath. It was at this moment, precisely, that he found he could not rise; something had happened to his arms, his legs, his feet—ah, something had happened to John.[32]

Other voices we hear in the background just before the vision of the Lord occurs. Again we have no identifications. Possibly, these are the words of people who assist the preacher on the occasion of a conversion, but what precedes their statements is invariably some sort of sermon appealing to the sinner to accept Christ. John hears one voice emerge from the background urging, "Yes . . . go through, Go through."[33] Another advises, "Call on Him. Call on Him."[34] Yet another queries, "*Have you been to the river*?"[35] Then comes a more disturbing inquiry, "*Sinner, do you love my Lord*?"[36] These voices linger in his mind and mix with the flood of memories that involve his relationship with his step-father, more pleasant recollections of his friend Elisha, of his mother and his aunt, and the sounds of the cosmos, from the roaring of the fires of Hell to the softer echoes of the moving feet of the saints in Heaven.

What occurs, at last, is a breakthrough of the kind that we discover in a folk sermon. There the preacher assumes God's voice, but here, on the threshing-floor with John, who has heard the divine summons, the experience of transcendence makes use of sight rather than sound. Earlier, we recall, at the climax of Gabriel's sermon on sin, one of the deeply moved auditors cried, "I was there."[37] And Baldwin records John's exciting moment in similar fashion:

> Then John saw the Lord—for a moment only; and the darkness for a moment only, was filled with a light he could not bear. Then, in a moment, he was set free; his tears sprang as from a fountain; his heart, like a fountain of water, burst. Then he cried; "Oh, blessed Jesus! Oh, Lord Jesus! Take me through!"[38]

God's voice does, and no writer of fiction has used that voice more skillfully than Baldwin has. He reproduces the art form of the folk sermon and explores its effects. He is both preacher and congregation, God and sinner, and he uses as a background—as a church, in effect—Harlem, the rural South, and the land of the Old Testament. Though part of the power that is generated in *Go Tell It on the Mountain* comes from Baldwin's own artistry, much of it has a source more widely shared, with James Weldon Johnson and with every black preacher who deplores modern ways and succeeds in making the old form work on Sundays. Surely, much of Baldwin's force in the novel rests upon the expectations that we have of the form of the folk sermon itself, the instrument that comes as close as humanly possible to offering black people the gift of the "heavenly voice."

Notes

1. James Weldon Johnson, "O Black and Unknown Bards," *American Negro Poetry*, ed. Arna Bontemps (New York: Hill and Wang, 1968), p. 1. The first lines read:
   O black and unknown bards of long ago,
   How came your lips to touch the sacred fire?
2. In "Of Our Spiritual Strivings," *The Souls of Black Folk* (Greenwich, Conn.: Fawcett Publications, 1961), p. 22.
3. See "O Black and Unknown Bards" and *The Book of American Negro Spirituals*, ed. J. Weldon and Rosamund Johnson (New York: The Viking Press, 1925).
4. Alain Locke, "The Negro Spirituals," *The New Negro, an Interpretation*, ed. A. Locke (New York: Arno Press and the New York Times, 1968), pp. 199–213.
5. Bruce Rosenberg, *The Art of the American Folk Preacher* (New York: Oxford University Press, 1970), pp. 14–16.
6. James Weldon Johnson, *God's Trombones: Seven Negro Sermons in Verse* (New York: The Viking Press, 1961).

7. James Baldwin, *Go Tell It on the Mountain* (New York: Dell Publishing Co., 1968).
8. Rosenberg, p. 76.
9. Ibid.
10. Rosenberg, pp. 49–51.
11. Ibid., pp. 54–56.
12. Ibid., p. 148.
13. Johnson, *Trombones*, pp. 41–42.
14. "The Creation," in Johnson, *Trombones*, p. 17.
15. Ibid., p. 43.
16. Ibid., p. 27.
17. Rosenberg, p. 184.
18. Ibid., pp. 184–185.
19. Ibid., p. 182.
20. Johnson, *Trombones*, p. 39.
21. Baldwin, pp. 102–105.
22. Ibid., p. 119.
23. Ibid., p. 102.
24. Ibid., p. 103.
25. Johnson, *Trombones*, p. 28.
26. Baldwin, p. 103.
27. Ibid.
28. Baldwin, p. 104.
29. Ibid., p. 105.
30. Ibid.
31. Ibid.
32. Baldwin, p. 194.
33. Ibid., p. 202.
34. Ibid.
35. Ibid., p. 203.
36. Ibid., p. 204.
37. Ibid., p. 105.
38. Ibid., p. 204.

Wilson Harris

HISTORY, FABLE, AND MYTH IN THE CARIBBEAN AND THE GUIANAS

THERE ARE TWO KINDS OF MYTHS RELATED TO AFRICA IN THE CARIBBEAN and the Guianas. One kind seems fairly direct; the other has clearly undergone metamorphosis. In fact even the direct kind of myth has suffered a "sea change" of some proportions. In an original sense, therefore, these myths, which reflect a link with Africa in the Caribbean, are also part of a native West Indian imagination and therefore stand —in some important ways, I feel—in curious *rapport* with vestiges of Amerindian fable* and legend.

Let us start with a myth stemming from Africa which has undergone metamorphosis; the one which I have in mind is called *limbo*. The *limbo* dance is a well-known feature in the carnival life of the West Indies today though it is still subject to intellectual censorship, as I shall explain as I go along in this paper. The *limbo* dancer moves under a bar which is gradually lowered until a mere slit of space, it seems, remains through which with spreadeagled limbs he passes like a spider.

The limbo was born, it is said, on the slave ships of the Middle Passage: there was so little space that the slaves contorted themselves into human spiders. Limbo therefore, in a curious way, as Edward Brathwaite, the Barbadian-born poet, has pointed out, is related to *anancy* or spider fables.

But there is something else in the *limbo-anancy* syndrome which is overlooked, as far as I am aware, and that is the curious dislocation caused by the chain of miles, reflected in the dance, so that a retracing of the Middle Passage from Africa to the Americas and the West Indies is not to be equated with a uniform sum. Not only has the journey from the Old World to the New varied with each century and each method of transport, but the journey needs to be reactivated in the imagination as a *limbo* perspective when one dwells on the Middle Passage: a *limbo* gateway between Africa and the Caribbean.

In fact here, I feel, we begin to put our finger on something which is close to the inner universality of Caribbean man. Those waves of

* Fable and myth are employed as variables of the imagination in this essay.

migration which have hit the shores of the Americas—North, Central, and South—century after century have at various times possessed the stamp of the spider metamorphosis both in the refugee flying from Europe and in the indentured East Indian and Chinese from Asia.

It is noteworthy in this context that C. L. R. James, in *Mariners, Renegades and Castaways*,[1] has adopted as his epigraph a famous passage from Herman Melville which runs:

> If, then, to meanest mariners, and renegades and castaways, I shall hereafter ascribe high qualities, though dark; weave round them tragic graces; if even the most mournful, perchance the most abase, among them all, shall at times lift himself to the exalted mounts; if I shall touch that workman's arm with some ethereal light; if I shall spread a rainbow over his disastrous set of sun; then against all mortal critics bear me out in it, thou just Spirit of Equality, which hast spread one royal mantle of humanity over all my kind!

The limbo then reflects a certain kind of gateway or threshold to a new world and the dislocation of a chain of miles. It is—in some ways—the archetypal sea change stemming from Old Worlds, and it is legitimate, I feel, to pun on *limbo* as a kind of shared phantom *limb* which has become a subconscious variable in West Indian theater. The emergence of formal West Indian theater was preceded, I suggest, by that phantom limb which manifested itself on Boxing Day after Christmas when the ban on the "rowdy" bands (as they were called) was lifted for the festive season.

I recall performances I witnessed as a boy in Georgetown, British Guiana, in the early 1930s. Some of the performers danced on high stilts like elongated limbs while others performed spreadeagled on the ground. In this way the limbo spider and the stilted pole of the gods were related to the drums as the grassroots and branches of lightning to the sound of thunder.

Sometimes it was an atavistic spectacle, and it is well known that these bands were suspected by the law of subversive political stratagems. But clearly the dance had no political or propaganda motives, though, as with any folk manifestation, it could be manipulated by demagogues. It has taken us a couple of generations to begin—just *begin*—to perceive in this phenomenon an activation of subconscious and sleeping resources in the phantom limb of the dismembered slave and god, an activation which possesses a nucleus of great promise, of a new, far-reaching poetic synthesis.

For the limbo—one cannot emphasize this too much—is not the

total recall of an African past, since that African past in terms of tribal sovereignty or sovereignties was modified or traumatically eclipsed with the Middle Passage and with the generations of change that followed. Limbo was rather the renascence of a new corpus of sensibility that could translate and accommodate African and other legacies within a new architecture of cultures. For example, the theme of the phantom limb—the reassembly of a dismembered man or god—possesses archetypal resonances that embrace Egyptian Osiris, the resurrected Christ, and the many-armed Siva of India.

In this context it is interesting to note that the limbo—which emerged as a novel reassembly out of the stigmata of the Middle Passage—is related to Haitian *vodun* in the sense that Haitian *vodun* (though possessing a direct link with African *vodun* which I shall describe later on) also seeks to accommodate new Catholic features in its constitution of the muse.

It is my view—a deeply considered one—that this ground of accommodation, this art of creative coexistence, pointing away from apartheid and ghetto fixations, is of the utmost importance and *native* to the Caribbean, perhaps to the Americas as a whole. It is still, in most respects, a latent syndrome, and we need to look not only at limbo or vodun but at Amerindian horizons as well—shamanistic and rainmaking vestiges and the dancing bush baby legends of the extinct Caribs which began to haunt them as they crouched over their campfires under the Spanish yoke.

Insufficient attention has been paid to such phenomena and the original native capacity these implied as omens of rebirth. Many historians have been intent on indicting the Old World of Europe by exposing a uniform pattern of imperialism in the New World of the Americas. Thus they conscripted the West Indies into a mere adjunct of imperialism and overlooked a subtle and far-reaching renascence. In a sense therefore the new historian—though his stance is an admirable one in debunking imperialism—has ironically extended and reinforced old colonial prejudices which censored the limbo imagination as a 'rowdy' manifestation and overlooked the complex metaphorical gateway it constituted in *rapport* with Amerindian omen.

In this work I do not intend to explore the Amerindian gateways between cultures which began obscurely and painfully to witness (long before limbo or vodun or the Middle Passage) to a native suffering community steeped in caveats of conquest, but I feel it necessary to indicate that these gateways exist as part of an original West Indian architecture which it is still possible to create if we look deep into the rubble of the past, and that these Amerindian features enhance the limbo assembly with which we are now engaged: the spider syndrome and the phantom limb of the gods arising in Negro fable and legend.

I use the word "architecture" because I believe this is a valid approach to a gateway society as well as to a community which is involved in an original reconstitution or re-creation of variables of myth and legend in the wake of stages of conquest.

First of all the limbo dance becomes the human gateway which dislocates—and therefore begins to free itself from—a uniform chain of miles across the Atlantic. This dislocation or interior space serves therefore as a corrective to a uniform cloak or documentary stasis of imperialism. The journey across the Atlantic for the forebears of West Indian man involved a new kind of space, inarticulate as this new "spatial" character was at the time, and not simply as an unbroken schedule of miles in a log book. Once we perceive this inner corrective to historical documentary and protest literature, which sees the West Indies as utterly deprived, or gutted by exploitation, we begin to participate in the genuine possibilities of original change in a people severely disadvantaged, it is true, at a certain point in time.

The limbo dance therefore implies, I believe, a profound art of compensation which seeks to replay a dismemberment of tribes (Note again the high stilted legs of some of the performers and the spider-anancy masks of others running close to the ground) and to invoke at the same time a curious psychic reassembly of the parts of the dead god or gods. And that reassembly, which issued from a state of cramp to articulate a new growth and to point to the necessity for a new kind of drama, novel, and poem, is a creative phenomenon of the first importance in the imagination of a people violated by economic fates.

One cannot over-emphasize, I believe, how original this phenomenon was, so original that it aroused both incomprehension and suspicion in the intellectual and legal administrations of the land (I am thinking in particular of the first half of the twentieth century though one can, needless to say, go much farther back). What is bitterly ironic, as I have already indicated, is that present-day historians in the second half of the twentieth century, as militant and critical of imperialism as they are, have fallen victim, in another sense, to the very imperialism they appear to denounce. They have no criteria for arts of originality springing out of an age of limbo, and the history they write is without an inner time. This historical refusal to *see*—which consolidates the incomprehension of the past—is the unwitting irony of the so-called new emancipated writer, and Gerald Moore in his new book, *The Chosen Tongue*,[2] (published by Longmans in 1969) brings it into sharp focus when he states—

> Both M. G. Smith, the Jamaican anthropologist, and V. S. Naipaul appear to believe that the West Indies possess no genuine inner cohesion whatever and no internal source of power. Having no common interests to cement them, the inhabitants of the area can be held together only by external force. Professor Elsa Goveia reaches an opposite but equally depressing conclusion. She argues that the West Indies had one integrating factor historically, and this has been "the acceptance of the inferiority of the Negroes to the whites."

In this context it is illuminating to recall that Froude, the famous historian of the nineteenth century, was doing on behalf of imperialism what many contemporary historians are doing in a protest against imperialism. He also set out to demonstrate that the West Indies had no creative potential. His view sprang from the arrogance of the nineteenth-century civilized European, whereas theirs would appear to spring from what Martin Carter, the Guyanese poet, calls the "self-contempt" of the exploited, formerly indentured or enslaved West Indian. Such a dead-end of history, in which nineteenth-century imperialist and twentieth-century anti-imperialist come into agreement, is material for a theatre of the absurd. J. J. Thomas, a Trinidad-born essayist, set out to rebut Froude's contentions, and his book (first published in 1889), has since been reprinted.[3]

However, the dilemma remains. I believe that the limbo imagination of the folk involved a crucial inner re-creative response to the violations of slavery, indenture, and conquest, and needed its critical or historical correlative, its critical or historical advocacy. This was not forthcoming since the historical instruments of the past clustered around an act of censorship and the suspicion of folk-obscurity as well as originality, and that inbuilt arrogance or suspicion continues to motivate a certain order of critical writing in the West Indies today.

Capitalism and Slavery, a brilliant and impressive formal thesis of research, was written by Eric Williams when he was at Oxford. Williams is now Prime Minister of Trinidad, and his book would seem to be the model that British West Indian historians have elected. But I must draw to your attention something which, I believe, confirms my view of the inbuilt censor in West Indian historical convention. Professor Elsa Goveia regards Dr. Williams as "the most influential writer on West Indian history to emerge from the West Indies during the present century." Yet in an article entitled "New Shibboleths for Old" she says of his recent work:

> In spite of all Dr. Williams's protestations about the need for cultivating a West Indian inspiration, in spite even of his own authorship of a *History of the People of Trinidad and Tobago*, can the reader be expected to draw any other conclusion than that a West Indian subject-matter is somehow worthless? Dr. Williams cannot have it both ways. If he ignores or devalues writers because they write about the West Indies rather than about other subjects, then he is perpetuating the very attitudes of mind which have in the past led to the neglect of West Indian studies which he himself constantly condemns. The combination of omissions and hasty dogmatism which mars his present book will not remedy the unhappy conditions which have for so long retarded the development of our understanding of "the unique antecedents of the people of the West Indies."[4]

This, I fear, is lamentably true. Until the gap is visualized, understood, and begins to close, the West Indian historian and anthropologist will continue to reinforce a high-level psychological censorship of the creative imagination and to consolidate a foreboding about the risks involved in every free election of spirits.

As such the very institutions of the day will become increasingly rigged by fear and misgiving, and political deterioration is the inevitable corollary. And this indicates to me that in the absence of a historical correlative to the arts of the dispossessed, some kind of new critical writing in depth needs to emerge to bridge the gap between history and art. Denis Williams stated the dilemma very effectively in *Image and Idea in the Arts of Guyana*:

> Yet the first fact of the Caribbean situation is the fact of miscegenation, of mongrelism. What are the cultural implications of this mongrel condition? It is important to have experienced the homogeneity, richness, the integrity of the racially thoroughbred cultures of the Old World in order properly to take the force of this question. It is important if only as a means of discriminating between our condition and theirs, of assessing the nature and status of our mongrel culture when contrasted with the cultures of the thoroughbred, of realising the nature and function of the ancestor as he determines our cultural destiny. For we are all shaped by our past; the imperatives of a contemporary culture are predominantly those of a relationship to this past. Yet in the Caribbean and in Guyana we think and behave as though we have no past, no history, no culture. And where we do come to take notice of our history it is often in the light of biases adopted from one thoroughbred culture or another, of the Old

> World. We permit ourselves the luxury, for one thing, of racial dialectics in our interpretation of Caribbean and Guyanese history and culture. In the light of what we are this is a destructive thing to do, since at best it perpetuates what we might call a filialistic dependence on the cultures of our several racial origins, while simultaneously inhibiting us from facing up to the facts of what we uniquely are.[5]

I would now like to resume the earlier thread of my argument in the dance of the folk—the human limbo or gateway of the gods—which was disregarded by or incomprehensible to an intellectual, legal, and historical convention. I had begun to point out that, first of all, the limbo dance becomes the human gateway which dislocates (and therefore begins to free itself from) a uniform chain of miles. In this context I also suggested that the gateway complex is also the psychic assembly or reassembly of the muse of a people. This brings me now to my second point about limbo, that it shares its phantom limb with Haitian vodun across an English-French divide of Caribbean cultures. This is a matter of great interest, I believe, because Haitian vodun is more directly descended from African myth, and yet, like the limbo which is a metamorphosis or new spatial character born of the Middle Passage, it is also intent on a curious reassembly of the god or gods. Therefore I ask myself, is vodun a necessary continuation of a matrix of associations which had not fulfilled itself in the Old World of Africa? If so, that fulfillment would be in itself not an imitation of the past—much as it is indebted to the past—but a new and daring creative conception in itself.

If Haitian vodun is a creative continuation or fulfillment of African vodun, one must ask oneself where the similarities and differences lie. The basic feature they hold in common is the "possession trance"—trance features, I may add, which are not the case with limbo.

Pierre Verger, in an essay appearing in *Spirit Mediumship and Society in Africa*, writes:

> Possession trances occur regularly among the Nago-Yoruba and Fon people of Dahomey during rites for *orisha* and *vodun*. . . . They are the culmination of an elaborate ritual sequence. Seen from the participant's point of view, such trances are the reincarnations of family deities in the bodies of their descendants—reincarnations which have taken place in response to the offerings, prayers, and wishes of their worshippers.[6]

In a footnote to his essay he defines *orisha* and *vodun* as

> the general names given by the Yoruba and Dahomean people respectively

to the deities worshipped by them. They are generally considered to be the very remote ancestors who dealt during their lifetime with some force of nature, and who can still do so on behalf of their worshippers.[7]

Pierre Verger has been speaking here of African vodun. I would like now to give my definition of Haitian vodun which appears in *Tradition, the Writer and Society*, as this will help me to unravel certain similarities and differences in African and Haitian vodun and to look back afresh at the significance of the human limbo gateway.

Haitian *vodun* or voodoo is a highly condensed feature of inspiration and hallucination within which "space" itself becomes the sole expression and recollection of the dance—as if "space" is the character of the dance—since the celebrants themselves are soon turned into "objects"—into an architecture of movement like "deathless" flesh, wood or stone. And such deathless flesh, wood or stone (symbolic of the dance of creation) subsists—in the very protean reality of space—on its own losses (symbolic decapitation of wood, symbolic truncation of stone) so that the very void of sensation in which the dancer begins to move, like an authentic spectre or structure of fiction, makes him or her insensible to all conventional props of habit and responsive only to a grain of frailty or light support.

Remember at the outset the dancer regards himself or herself as one in full command of two legs, a pair of arms, until, possessed by the muse of contraction, he or she dances into a posture wherein one leg is drawn up into the womb of space. He stands like a rising pole upheld by earth and sky or like a tree which walks in its shadow or like a one-legged bird which joins itself to its sleeping reflection in a pool. All conventional memory is erased and yet in this trance of overlapping spheres of reflection a primordial or deeper function of memory begins to exercise itself within the bloodstream of space.

Haitian *vodun* is one of the surviving primitive dances of sacrifice, which, in courting a subconscious community, *sees* its own performance in literal terms—that is, with and through the eyes of "space": with and through the sculpture of sleeping things which the dancer himself actually expresses and becomes. For in fact the dancer moves in a trance and the interior mode of the drama is exteriorized into a medium inseparable from his trance and invocation. He is a dramatic agent of subconsciousness. The life from within and the life from without now truly overlap. That is the intention of the dance, the riddle of the dancer.

The importance which resides in all this, I suggest, is remarkable. For if the trance were a purely subjective thing—without action or movement—some would label it fantasy. But since it exteriorizes itself, it becomes an intense drama of images in space, which may assume elastic limbs and proportions or shrink into a dense current of reflection on the floor. For

> what emerges are the relics of a primordial fiction where the images of space are *seen* as in an abstract painting. That such a drama has indeed a close bearing on the language of fiction, on the language of art, seems to me incontestable. The community the writer shares with the primordial dancer is, as it were, the complementary halves of a broken stage. For the territory upon which the poet visualizes a drama of consciousness is a slow revelation or unravelling of obscurity—revelation or illumination within oneself; whereas the territory of the dancer remains actually obscure to him within his trance whatever revelation or illumination his limbs may articulate in their involuntary theme. The "vision" of the poet (when one comprehends it from the opposite pole of "dance") possesses a "spatial" logic or "convertible" property of the imagination. Herein lies the essential humility of a certain kind of self-consciousness within which occurs the partial erasure, if nothing more, of the habitual boundaries of prejudice.[8]

I have quoted rather extensively here from my previous essay because I think this may help us to see, in *rapport* with Pierre Verger's definition of African vodun, that while the trance similarity is clear, the functions have begun to differ. Haitian vodun—like West Indian and Guianese-Brazilian limbo—may well point to sleeping possibilities of drama and horizons of poetry, epic and novel, sculpture and painting, in short to a language of variables in art which would have a profoundly evolutionary cultural and philosophical significance for Caribbean man. Such new resources (if I may diverge for a brief moment and speak as someone whose chosen tongue is English) are not foreign to English poetry except in the sense that these may be closer to the "metaphysical poets" —to a range and potency of association in which nothing is ultimately alien—of which Eliot speaks in his famous essay on the "dissociation of sensibility."

Such a variable emphasis is outside the boundaries of intention in African vodun, which is a conservative medium or cloak of ancestors. The gulf therefore between an inbuilt uniform censor and the imagination of a new art which exists in the British West Indies, in particular, is absent in Africa. African vodun is a school of ancestors: it is very conservative. Something of this conservative focus remains very strongly in Haitian vodun, but there is an absorption of new elements which breaks the tribal monolith of the past and reassembles an intertribal or cross-cultural community of families.

The term *loa*, for example, which means *spirit* or *deity*, is of Bantu origin, not Yoruba or Dahomean—the tribal homes, some say, of vodun. Furthermore, Harold Courlander, "Vodoun in Haitian Culture," writes:

> The various cults encompassed by the term Vodoun in its larger sense are not easy to set down diagramatically because of different degrees of blending and absorption in different regions of Haiti. Had the old cults or "nations" remained independent of one another, as they probably were in early days, they probably would have included the following: Arada (Dahomey or Fon), Anago (Yoruba), Mahi, Ibo, Kanga, Congo (including Moundongue, Solongo, Bumba, etc., or these elements also might have maintained independence), and Pétro (a cult in the African pattern that appears to have originated in Haiti). In certain parts of Haiti one still finds Ibo, Congo, and Nago cults that have resisted absorption, but this pattern does not hold for most of the country. . . . There has been intrusion of Catholic practices and doctrine into Vodoun. Many of the *loa* are identified with Catholic saints.[9]

Elsewhere Courlander writes: "Vodoun has perhaps the same meaning to some Haitian leaders as astrology to some leaders in India."[10]

All in all, while it is true that the role of Haitian vodun (or Vodoun) is part of a prophetic and esoteric perspective in the Haitian body politic, the strict collective traditional sanction which belongs to Africa has varied in a manner comparable in some degree to the cleavage we have noted between history and art in the British West Indies.

I could not help noting the following passage in Courlander's essay:

> The question of Vodoun's influence in politics in earlier days is blurred or distorted for a variety of reasons. European writers sometimes were unaware of Vodoun as a genuine religious pattern common to the entire nation, and, as we have noted, frequently delighted in depicting the superstitious character of the people. Haitian historians of the past were sensitive to the charge that the country was overrun with pagan rites, and they largely avoided mention of Vodoun. Little on the subject is likely to be found in government archives for much the same reason.[11]

It is my assumption, in the light of all the foregoing, that a certain *rapport* exists between Haitian vodun and West Indian limbo which suggests an epic potential or syndrome of variables. That epic potential, I believe, may supply the nerve-end of authority which is lacking at the moment in the conventional stance of history.

But we need to examine this with the greatest care in order to assess and appreciate the risks involved.

In the first place the limbo imagination of the West Indies possesses no formal or collective sanction as in an old tribal world. Therefore the gateway complex between cultures implies a new catholic unpredictable threshold which places a far greater emphasis on the integrity of the individual imagination. And it is here that we see, beyond a shadow of doubt, the necessity for the uncommitted artist of conscience whose evolution out of the folk as a poet, novelist, or painter is a symbol of risk, a symbol of inner integrity. With African vodun, as we have seen, the integrity of the tribal person was one with a system which was conservative and traditional. There was no breath of subversion, no cleavage in the collective. History and art were one medium.

With the Guianese-West Indian limbo that cleavage is a fact, and the rise of the imaginative arts has occurred in the face of long-held intellectual and legal suspicion. Therefore the rise of the poet or artist incurs a gamble of the soul which is symbolized in the West Indian trickster (the spider or anancy configuration). It is this element of tricksterdom that creates an individual and personal *risk* absolutely foreign to the conventional sanction of an old tribal world: a risk which identifies the artist with the submerged authority of dispossessed peoples but requires of him, in the same token, alchemic resources to conceal, as well as elaborate, a far-reaching order of the imagination which, being suspect, could draw down upon him a crushing burden of censorship in economic or political terms. He stands therefore at the heart of both the lie of community and the truth of community. And it is, I believe, in this trickster gateway—this gamble of the soul—that there emerges the hope for a profoundly compassionate society committed to freedom within a creative scale.

I would like to re-emphasize the roles of "epic" and "trickster." The epic of the limbo holds out a range of variables—variables of community in the cross-cultural tie of dispossessed tribes or families, variables of art in a consciousness of links between poetry and drama, image and novel, architecture and sculpture and painting—which need to be explored in the Caribbean complex situation of apparent "historylessness." And furthermore, in the Americas as a whole, it would seem to me that the apparent void of history which haunts the black man may never be compensated until an act of imagination opens gateways between civilizations, between technological and spiritual apprehensions, between racial possessions and dispossessions, in the way the *Aeneid* may stand symbolically as one of the first epics of migration and resettlement beyond the pale of an ancient world. Limbo and vodun are variables of an underworld imagination—variables of phantom *limb* and *void*, and a nucleus of stratagems in which *limb* is a legitimate pun on *limbo*, and *void* on *vodun*.

The trickster of limbo holds out a caveat we must reckon with in our present unstable situation. It is the caveat of conscience and points to the necessity for a free imagination which is at risk on behalf of a truth that is no longer given in the collective medium of the tribe. The emergence of individual works of art is consistent with—and the inevitable corollary of—an evolution of the folk limbo into symbols of inner cunning and authority which reflect a long duress of the imagination.

Notes

1. C. L. R. James, *Mariners, Renegades and Castaways* (New York, 1953). Epigraph in cover of paperback.
2. Gerald Moore, *The Chosen Tongue: English Writing in the Tropical World* (London, 1969), p.67.
3. J. J. Thomas, *Froudacity*, ed. John La Rose, intro. by C. L. R. James (London, 1969).
4. Elsa Goveia, "New Shibboleths for Old," *New Beacon Reviews*, coll. 1 (London, 1968), p.33.
5. Dennis Williams, *Image and Idea in the Art of Guyana*, The Edgar Mittelholzer Memorial Lectures, second series (Guyana: Ministry of Information, 1969), p.7.
6. *Spirit Mediumship and Society in Africa*, ed. J. Beattie and J. Middleton (London, 1969), p.50.
7. Ibid., p.65.
8. Wilson Harris, *Tradition, the Writer and Society* (London, 1967), pp.50–52.
9. Harold Courlander, "Vodoun in Haitian Culture," in *Religion and Politics in Haiti*, ed. H. Courlander and R. Bastien (Washington, D. C., 1966), p.15.
10. Ibid., pp.18–19.
11. Ibid., p.19.

Désirée Hirst

SYMBOLISM AND THE CHANGING CLIMATE IN THOUGHT: A PROBLEM IN LITERARY CRITICISM

THE FORMAL STUDY OF THE HISTORY OF IDEAS IS NEW, RELATIVELY speaking, and its impact on literary criticism is still limited. Its arrival has occasioned great nervousness on the part of some more old-fashioned orthodox *littérateurs*. One observes how various protective devices immediately come into play; the danger of literature being treated as material for propaganda, to uphold some theological position, some political creed, is instantly stressed, of course. The absurdity of "symbolizing" every concept of a poet; and the fact that the criteria of judgment upon a work of art are never purely ideological is strongly insisted upon. The real motives behind this unease are rather less than respectable, however. Regrettably, one is, quite simply, laziness. The mastery of the great mythological and symbolic systems which artists have always drawn upon is a difficult and exacting discipline. And while it is not necessary that all critics should subject themselves to such a discipline, they must take very seriously, at least, the work of those critics who *have* done so; realizing that a complete, or even accurate, estimation of the meaning and value of any one work of art—let alone the *oeuvre* of any particular creative artist—can never be arrived at without this minimum effort. So, while we do not all have to become Freudian specialists, sensible speculation on twentieth-century writing is not possible without at least a nodding acquaintance with the great psychiatrist's system. And a fairly thorough grasp of one or more major systems of ideas is an enormous help, surely, to any critic's method of operation.

As a start, perhaps it might be useful to look at the traditional situation of the informed reader. Early in this century, or, at least, at the end of the nineteenth, a classical education was still the vogue and most educated men—we have to remember that educated women, to whom our century owes so much, had not yet made much of an impact—were brought up on some form of Christianity, or Judaism, in the West. A pretty exhaustive—in some cases, an extremely rigorous—knowledge of the Bible was common. Certain epic poems, embodying a huge amount of mythological, speculative, and often definitely mystical material, were widely familiar. Homer, Virgil, Dante, the Italian romantic epic poets, Spenser, Milton, Goethe, Wordsworth, for example, apart from the great dramatists, were often well known to members of the English-speaking educated public. These might be equipped with considerable technical theological knowledge. Such classics as *Moby Dick* and *Ulysses* in the novel form are the fruits of this accepted learning. Pundits like Eliot and Pound have meantime explored further afield, equipping themselves with Eastern wisdom, among other kinds. But in this they were only following the example of their medieval and Renaissance predecessors, of the disciples of the Enlightenment and their successors of the Romantic Movement. Almost without conscious realization such men had absorbed an enormous mass of background knowledge then; and, in addition, they were acquainted with that mythology which passes for the history of nations.

A problem of peculiar complexity has arisen in the modern period, with increasing secularization and changes in educational method. We have lost touch with many of our roots. At the same time a vast flood of new knowledge has been made available to us. For the first moment in history the accumulated tradition of all branches of the human race is at our disposal should we wish to consult this deposit. And the past few decades especially have seen an enormous improvement in our understanding of the true nature of the Renaissance; partly through the excellent work of the scholars of the Warburg Institute in London. Some of the misconceptions dating from the "Enlightenment" have also been cleared up, and a more sane estimation of the medieval period in Europe has been arrived at—together with a better grasp of the Alexandrian Greek era—so that, while much ground which was previously held has to be laboriously recovered, a new perspective is also open to us.

Obviously in this strange situation the role of the historian of ideas is peculiarly vital. The work of "pure" critics—if one might use the phrase—cannot go forward with any real success unless this truth is recognized. (Whether such "pure" critics really do exist is another question altogether.) Two points must be strongly grasped. First, an aware reader will normally bring to bear on any book a mass of influences and ideas of which he himself may be only dimly aware. If the work of literature concerned should draw upon the traditions with which he is familiar, he will consider the author "lucid" and his work "self-evident." If, on the other hand, he encounters symbolism from traditions he is not for any reason acquainted with, he will think the work "obscure" and "esoteric." This should be obvious, but few critics admit to such simple truths. The second, and more complex, issue is the question of the motives animating the artists and writers themselves. The concept of "art for art's sake" is very new, and there may be reason to believe it is very artificial. Most art has been produced for truth's sake, or as an act of worship. Our greater understanding of pre-history and of anthropology enables us now to see how narrow was the nineteenth-century position adopted by Walter Pater or Matthew Arnold, itself the result of the odd agnosticism of the day. Yet many critics are still working on these Victorian premises, without always knowing it. They do not sufficiently accept the clear evidence that artists rarely go to the trouble of evolving their works unless they are caught up in the consideration of matters serious in themselves, more often than not concerned with the very meaning of life, and connected at every point with the values and pressures within the society that has thrown up these creative spirits. Whether he be in revolt against these values, arising as they do out of the tradition of generations, or in harmony with them, any artist is deeply affected by them. And unless he possesses the key to the code of these values the appreciator of art may find himself baffled by the art itself. Again, this should not need to be put into so many words, but it is a measure of the state of confusion within criticism that it must be. Until all these issues are properly weighed and the work of art placed in its true perspective, any assessment of why it is successful as such, in what way it gives pleasure, and to which human faculties cannot even begin to be made.

In a brief article on William Blake's aesthetics, I have already suggested that his attitude was close to that of the prophets of the Old Testament.[1] Neither Isaiah nor Ezekiel, nor for that matter the author of the Book of Revelations, necessarily considered himself a poet or literary artist. All these would have been amazed to be judged by the kind of criteria that were applied to Goethe, Byron, Wordsworth, or Shakespeare in the nineteenth century. These were men burning with the love of truth—as, I suspect, were Goethe, Byron, Wordsworth, and Shakespeare—and simply concerned to express this truth as accurately and as pungently as possible. In the process of doing so they produced what we call works of art. The impulses of any artist surely spring from the human desire to praise perfection, to define that perfection as precisely as is within human powers, and to rage against all that destroys it and mars that state of continuous awareness of life and the celebration of it which we all, through some ancestral memory of a lost paradise, feel to be our birthright. This is very much within the realm of piety—in the widest sense of the word. It is a kind of devotion. There is something fundamentally religious about it, even as expressed within the most secular and materialist situation, so that possibly William Blake's violent affirmations on the subject are not so cranky, so wide of the mark, as may appear. Blake considered the state of nations to depend on their reverence for art, and he thought of art as prayer. Sterile moralizing, the division of things into the right and proper and the wrong and thoroughly reprehensible, disgusted him, and he constantly strove for unity—wholeness of being—after the example of the mystics. (And indeed plainly the hallmark of high art is that every conceivable element is drawn into it, digested as it were, so that the trivial, the terrible, and the revolting are transmuted and become glorious.) With these convictions in mind, we see that the arresting aphorisms with which Blake, in his print engraved about 1820, surrounded the design of the Laocoön group of statuary (the famous original, showing the priest of Apollo and his sons in the grip of the avenging serpent, is of course in the Vatican, but he was no doubt working from the plaster cast in the Royal Academy of Art) present a consistent and impressive case. No doubt, too, when working on this print Blake had in mind Gotthold Lessing's *Lakoon*, his pioneer study on the limitations of poetry and the plastic arts which had caused such a stir in 1766.

With these considerations in mind, it becomes possible to make sense of strange statements like the following:

> If Morality were Christianity, Socrates was the Saviour.
>
> Art Degraded, Imagination Denied, War Governed the Nations.
>
> Spiritual War: Israel deliver'd from Egypt, is Art deliver'd from Nature & Imitation.
>
> A Poet, a Painter, a Musician, an Architect: the Man or Woman who is not one of these is not a Christian. . . .
>
> Prayer is the Study of Art.
> Praise is the Practise of Art. . . .

> All that we See is Vision, from Generated Organs gone as soon as come, Permanent in the Imagination, Consider'd as Nothing by the Natural Man.
>
> Art can never exist without Naked Beauty displayed. . . .
>
> The Old & New Testaments are the Great Code of Art. . . .
>
> All is not Sin that Satan calls so: all the Loves & Graces of Eternity.

Of course the views expressed in these cryptic affirmations are those of a mind at the same time caught up in a series of reactions from current fashions of thought and behaviour, and also asserting a complex philosophy based on the Bible reinterpreted through Neo-Platonic eyes. A hatred of hypocritical moralism, coy prudery, worldliness, the cult of money and violence, the emphasis on outward appearances coexists with a belief in the world of archetypal ideas, in Man's duty to echo the divine creativity through the imagination which is the dwelling place in the human psyche of these ideas, and in a very Lutheran concept of the "Natural" Fallen Man; fallen from his heavenly birth, from that "Perfection of an holy angelic Nature," which William Law, the great eighteenth-century exponent of the system of the Lutheran mystic, Jacob Boehme, describes in his *Spirit of Prayer*.[2] English Behmenism was a formidable influence for at least two centuries, as I have tried to demonstrate in my own study, *Hidden Riches: Traditional Symbolism from the Renaissance to Blake*.[3] John Beer's *Coleridge the Visionary*[4] reveals the extent to which Samuel Taylor Coleridge was affected by it, and Blake acknowledged his debt, together with that to Paracelsus, in the outline of his spiritual autobiography in verse, which he included in a letter of September 12th 1800, to his friend, the sculptor John Flaxman. Both Paracelsus and "Behmen" are likewise hailed in Plate 22 of *The Marriage of Heaven and Hell*.

This mixture of plain Lutheran Protestantism—reverence for the Bible with all its revelations of a creator God acting within history as Providence and drawing it to an Apocalyptical conclusion—with a not so plain Behmenism and a Neo-Platonic concept of emanation must at first sight be very confusing. Rather, as Law puts it, ". . . the essences of our souls can never cease to be because they never begun to be, and nothing can live eternally but that which hath lived from all Eternity."[5] Or, as another aphorism from *The Laocoön* has it: "What can be Created Can be Destroyed." It is confusing, especially since, at the same time, an almost Godwinian passion for the free, natural, and spontaneous—an artist's dedication to the Human Form Divine—is combined with a detestation of Realism—a preference for the inner idea over the outward form of an object. The sentiments of *The Laocoön*, stating succinctly the theories which informed years of Blake's practice in art and poetry, are really incomprehensible unless the reader acquires some knowledge of the currents of thought affecting him, the complexes of symbolism with which he was dealing, and accepts his own principle that "Without Contraries is no progression," a principle that makes more sense, again, when the repercussions of Nicholas of Cusa's doctrine of the "Co-incidentia Oppositorum" are considered.

The Cabbalistic concept of the Balance, symbolized by the opposite pillars of Rigor and Mercy joined by the central pillar of Mediation, also had a great impact on European thought from the Renaissance onwards. This side of Rigor, the Dark Fire World of Boehme, where the flames of wrath not only punish but provide the fuel for creative energy, seems to me the inspiration not only for Blake's satire, *The Marriage of Heaven and Hell*, with its exultation in "the fires of Hell," where the poet walks "delighted with the enjoyments of Genius, which to Angels look like torment and insanity," but also for "The Tyger" lyric out of *The Songs of Experience*, whose archetypal beast is ". . . burning bright / In the forests of the night." Though Kathleen Raine rightly emphasizes, in her recent monumental work, *Blake and Tradition*,[6] the literally sinister associations of the Tyger with the Gnostic Demiurge, springing from the influence on Blake of *The Divine Pymander of Hermes Mercurius Trismegistus* in John Everard's translation of 1650. (In *Hidden Riches* I have also explained why I myself suspect that the difficult image in this poem, of the stars throwing down their spears, cannot be fully understood without recourse to the Christian Cabbalist Robert Fludd's treatment of "The Severe Attributes of God," which "do rain into the starry world, influences of a contrary nature"; since there is evidence that Blake drew on the 1659 English translation of Fludd's *Mosaicall Philosophy* and on his symbolism in general.[7])

The violent collision of opposite meanings and influences—the holding together of concepts which appear impossible of harmonization, yet so often do have some subterranean connection—characteristic of William Blake's artistic method, reveals in its own way, no doubt, the grand endeavour of all artists to express the inexpressible, the ineffable, and to overcome that dilemma posed by the Taoist sage Lao Tzu, that

Those who know do not talk
And talkers do not know.

The literature of the English seventeenth century, indeed, bears many traces of a mystical peacefulness and nostalgia for the Eternal very close in atmosphere to that of the *Tao Te Ching*. Something of this may be discerned in Andrew Marvell's lyrics; in the strongly Neo-Platonic tension between Matter and Spirit. The same quality appears in Henry Vaughan's poems and in his brother's Hermetic prose. Henry Vaughan's "Night" is one of those rare works in literature written in praise of darkness and silence. Such passionate lines as:

> Dear Night! this world's defeat;
> The stop to busie fools; care's check and curb;
> The day of Spirits; my souls calm retreat
> Which none disturb!
> Christ's progress, and his prayer time;
> The hours to which high Heaven doth chime. . . .

and the longing for "the deep but dazzling darkness" that is in God, and for days "Calm and unhaunted as is thy dark tent," surely come from a soul familiar with the Dark Night of the Spirit, at home in the Cloud of Unknowing. While Thomas Vaughan's description, in his *Aula Lucis*, of the body when first inhabited by the spirit as a castle of crystal that grows muddied and dim as it becomes affected by the influences of this material world, has rightly been taken by Kathleen Raine as the key to Blake's very puzzling lyric "The Crystal Cabinet," clearly a poem on the subject of Generation.

> The Maiden caught me in the Wild,
> Where I was dancing merrily;
> She put me into her Cabinet
> And Lock'd me up with a golden Key.
>
> This Cabinet is form'd of Gold
> And Pearl & Chrystal shining bright,
> And within it opens into a World
> And a little lovely Moony Night. . . .

Interestingly, the Vaughan passage describes the opposite process from that of Marvell's "On a Drop of Dew," for there the drop, "trembling lest it grow impure" on the surface of the rose, is breathed back into the heavens. But Thomas Vaughan shows how, when light first enters matter,

> it is a glorious transparent room, a crystal castle, and he lives like a familiar in diamonds. He hath the liberty to look out at the windows but this continues not long . . . for at last the earth grows over him, out of the water, so that he is quite shut up in darkness. . . .[8]

Not only the increasingly admired Thomas Vaughan, but more obscure figures like Joseph Glanvill in his *Vanity of Dogmatizing* (1661), were moved to supple and soaring prose by themes not unlike Marvell's: the concept, for instance, of those exceptional persons, those noble spirits that occasionally move among mankind.

> . . . those Mercurial souls, which were only lent the Earth to shew the world their folly in admiring it; possess delights, which as it were antedate Immortality . . . The Sun and Stars, are not the worlds *Eyes*, but these. . . . These out-travel theirs, and skipping into *Vortexes* beyond their light and Influence . . . with an easie twinkle of an Intellectual Eye look into the Centre, which is obscured from the upper Luminaries. This is somewhat like the *Image* of *Omnipresence*: And what the Hermetical *Philosophy* saith of *God*, is in a sense verifiable of the thus *ennobled soul, That its Centre is everywhere, but its circumference no where.*

Naturally it is hardly necessary to stress that this tradition of Christian Platonism can be found affecting English authors much earlier than the seventeenth century. It is not only Donne and the Metaphysicals, Daniel and Shakespeare, but Spenser, above all, who bears its traces.[9] And during the medieval period the whole group of English Mystics from Richard Rolle to Father Augustine Baker, which has been so ably studied by Fr. Conrad Pepler,[10] were deeply colored by the values presented by the Neo-Platonist mystical theologian known as "Dionysius the Areopagite"; in particular this is true of the author of *The Cloud of Unknowing*. (Although one must emphasize the strong orthodox allegiance of these writers to the Incarnational aspects of Christianity. They never veered so far in the direction of Angelism as the Cambridge Platonist Philosophers sometimes did—Boehme himself, and the Hermeticists, and certainly William Law.) And associated with these medieval mystics in England is William Langland, whose *Vision of Piers Plowman* expresses at once an indignant radicalism and a truly visionary spirituality, one close in tone, in many ways, to the prophetic outbursts of William Blake's later poems.

But the eighteenth century in England was not so far removed from this mental climate as has been imagined. Not only were there the many groups, usually centered round William Law in some way, which really continued to live within the atmosphere of the previous age (several chapters of *Hidden Riches* deal with this phenomenon),[11] but the tenor of the time was in fact very different from the stereotyped notion of eighteenth-century life that has commonly prevailed. And this is now gradually being realized.

A recent article by Paul Fussell, "The New Irony & the Augustans"[12] dismisses the picture of ". . . a well-lighted (if not particularly clean) place accessible through a little social history and a handful of easy epithets like *moderate*, *rational*, and *unenthusiastic*." Reminding us of the strange quality of the classics of the period. "How frantic, how wry and offbeat, and in a way how mad, the great works are: *A Tale of a Tub*, the *Dunciad*, *Tristram Shandy*, *A Song to David*, *The Marriage of Heaven and Hell*, even *An Account of the life of Richard Savage*. . . ." And, in point of fact, Blake's own work provides a complete index of all the various preoccupations and intellectual fashions, all the cults of the day: from the scientific rationalist materialism he detested and the Christian Platonism towards which he turned; the use of Neo-Platonic myth and idea which was likewise borrowed by Coleridge and Shelley; Swedenborgianism; material from the Antiquarian Revival like the ballad form, renewed medievalism, Norse and Celtic literature; a new, artificial kind of Druidism; the Atlantis craze; a revived Astrology; the mass of oriental mythology, including translations of Eastern Scriptures contained in contemporary compendiums and in the publications of members of the East India Company; even the Methodist Movement and the stirrings of Anglo-Catholic High Church aspirations. In his designs and paintings the Neo-Classicism of regency dress and furniture, the "pure Greek line" used by Flaxman in his statuary and Josiah Wedgwood in his pottery is reflected. It is all there. No one could have mirrored his age more faithfully, yet this is the artist and poet so lately considered out of tune with his time, a freak. Certainly here is one whose contact with the past, and with the timeless, put him ahead of his time, and whose genius baffled all but other geniuses and a few discerning spirits in his own day. But that is another matter.

Yet in the succeeding period, after the Romantic Age was past, the Idealist tradition, which from Plotinus and St. Augustine has so often been associated with mystical intimations of different kinds, persisted and encountered new fortunes. It changed, and some of its underlying weaknesses were exposed. An overemphasis on spirituality as against the wholeness of Man led to various Manichean and Gnostic manifestations, to magic and the vulgarity of Spiritualism. This in its turn was a pointer to the increasing agnosticism of the day, the decline in

Christian faith, and to the secularism that provoked a thirst for substitute religions. The kind of occultism which lies behind W. B. Yeats' poetic system—closely related though it is to Blake's own and natural in one of Blake's early editors—reflects all these shifts. His work shows none of that piety that shines through the poetry of the Metaphysicals or the moving Neo-Platonic prose of Thomas Traherne or of William Law. Instead we have a mind interested in many of the same Oriental, Hermetic, and Celtic cults as Blake, but the mind of a mage, formed in the school of Madame Blavatsky and the Order of the Golden Dawn, concerned more with exercises said to have been handed down from the Rosicrucians than with any kind of devotion. On the other hand, Blake's Biblical illustrations, his designs for the poet Edward Young's *Night Thoughts*, and long passages of his later prophetic poetry are strongly Christocentric; there is almost a sentimentalization of the Saviour.

The nature of this shift can best be observed perhaps in the work of Christopher Walton, a student of William Law who gathered a mass of material designed for the use of some future hypothetical biographer of "the Celebrated Divine and Theosopher," which in 1854 he published himself.[13] Much of this consists of the papers Law had collected, often other men's manuscripts which he had copied out in his own hand, and of his correspondence with his disciples, along with accounts of various circumstances in all their careers. Amongst other things a very real understanding of the Behmenist system is shown, together with some appreciation of the nature of mysticism and of the mainstream of the literature on the subject in Europe. There is considerable grasp of the religious situation within the eighteenth century, an intelligent treatment of Quietism, and acquaintance with the encounters of various revivalist groups with the Quakers in Britain. And, since Walton was a Methodist from Worsley in Lancashire who settled in London as silk mercer in 1830 and later started a flourishing goldsmith's business in Ludgate Street, he was familiar with the inner history of Wesleyanism. But in 1856 *A Guide to the Peculiar Sciential and Experimental Knowledge*, which was considered necessary for any would-be biographer of William Law, was published and inserted into copies of Walton's book, though there has been speculation that it might be by another hand. At any rate, what are we to make of the exhortation to "examine some works treating of high Boodhist, Sivic and other Oriental, *Druidic*, etc., religions . . . likewise . . . the real *purificative* arts or rites and inductive physical and mental training of the ancient vestal pythonesses, sibyls, priestesses etc. etc."? *Popular Experimental Transcendentalism* or *Animal*

Magnetism with its subsequent Inductions" must be investigated, apparently, and "along therewith" the demand is that the biographer should "Witness some Really Good Cases of Magical Sleep or Trance, with Lucid Clairvoyance."[14] All this would have horrified the High Church Anglican theologian it was supposed to be concerned with, but it does indicate the changing climate of the time. As does the alchemic study of Mary Anne Atwood (Mrs. South), *Suggested Inquiry into the Hermetic Mystery* . . . of 1850.

Nevertheless this mixture of learning with sensationalism, of appetite for spiritual power with aspiration, cannot be dismissed contemptuously. It represents a degeneration, certainly, but also betrays the impact of modern science, of the current interaction with the East, and of determined attempts to rediscover an important part of cultural history which was in danger of being lost. If science could transmute matter in all manner of extraordinary ways, could not some super-science, by means of an understanding of rhythms, manipulate Nature through mental force alone, affect even the psyche itself, and bring about a self-induced exaltation of the spirit? Such a view of life was very attractive to figures like Yeats, whose imaginations were filled with godlike and heroic forms from the ancient epics and who had no very strong impulse towards worship. And modern Yeats scholars have demonstrated beyond doubt that his magical preoccupations and his peculiar variation of the Neo-Platonic tradition have to be taken seriously for an understanding of his poetry and prose. It is even possible, after all, that Yeats' exceptional wizardry over words and over the rhythms of verse owes a good deal to the very strenuous discipline he underwent during the years of his association with the Order of the Golden Dawn. (Much material on the G.D. has been preserved by a former member, Gerald Yorke, and a history of the order has now been undertaken for the Warburg Institute by Ellis Paul Howe. Only Israel Regardie's scarce work, *The History of the Golden Dawn* [Chicago, 1936], has been available up till now. And in addition a survey of secret societies from the nineties to the present by Francis King, Ritual Magic in England [London, 1970], published. Charles Williams' poetry and fiction bear the unmistakable marks of his period as a member of the order.[15] The complex story of this "underground movement" is a vital part of the background to twentieth-century literature.) The whole field, in any case, of Yeats' debt to MacGregor Mathers, the translator of *The Kabbalah Unveiled* (London, 1887), to the work of G. R. S. Mead, and to Harold Bayley's *The Lost Language of Symbolism* (London, 1912), as well as to Thomas Taylor, the eighteenth-century Platonist, to

Swedenborg, to Blake himself, and to Mme. Blavatsky, has been ably charted by F. A. C. Wilson in his *W. B. Yeats and Tradition* (London, 1958) and *Yeats' Iconography* (London, 1960). And Kathleen Raine has investigated Yeats' use of the Tarot cards in a paper given to the International Yeats Summer school at Sligo (now being published, with illustrations from Yeats' own pack, by the Dolmen Press, Dublin).

When considering Yeats' poetry one has to note, naturally, his encounter with the Catholic student of mysticism, Baron von Hugel, which is reflected in stanza VIII of his "Vacillation," where he specifically, though regretfully, admits that he cannot accept the Christian way.

> Must we part, Von Hugel, though much alike. . . .
> Homer is my example and his unchristened heart.
> The lion and the honeycomb, what has Scripture said?
> So get you gone, Von Hugel, though with blessings
> on your head.

Yet a few of his poems do betray an outlook very close to the mystical concept of stripping the mind of images, the ego of all its possessiveness and pride. The last is reflected in the mysterious "The Four Ages of Man," from "Supernatural Songs," and especially, paradoxically, in the fifth song "Rihb considers Christian Love Insufficient," where the force of hatred, defined as a broom, a sort of besom that can clear the soul, performs this function.

> Then my delivered soul herself shall learn
> A darker knowledge and in hatred turn
> From every thought of God mankind has had.
> Thought is a garment and the soul's a bride
> That cannot in that trash and tinsel hide:
> Hatred of God may bring the soul to God.

In such great poems as "Sailing to Byzantium" and "The Delphic Oracle upon Plotinus" Yeats puts forward the kind of Neo-Platonic picture of the Eternal World which had so impressed the Renaissance mind and caused Cambridge Platonists like Henry More and Ralph Cudworth to be convinced that the doctrines of Plotinus, Porphyry, and Iamblichus might be harmonized with Christian truth. Could not the sentiments of the following supplication perhaps be mistaken for those of some medieval devotee of the age when the influence of the pseudo-Dionysius was paramount?

O sages standing in God's holy fire
As in the gold mosaic of a wall,
Come from the holy fire, perne in a gyre
And be the singing masters of my soul. . . .

Yet Yeats is possibly more interested in traveling strenuously towards Byzantium than in really arriving there. Kathleen Raine, again, in another paper, "Yeats and Platonism"[16] given at Sligo and since published in *The Dublin Magazine*, has stressed that the pull of the sense world, with its cruel but exhilarating clashes, was very strong for him always. "That dolphin-torn, that gong-tormented sea" remained his natural element in many ways, and his sympathy with heroic combat and aristocratic pride of leadership made him adopt an activist stance which belongs more to the ethos of the magician than of the mystic. Few critics seem to have noted the presence of this activist element in both Blake's and Yeats' thought. The Fourfold Condition of "Eden" is in Blake's universe the place of "The Great Wars of Eternity, in fury of Poetic Inspiration" (*Milton*, Plate 30). He exalts to an extraordinary degree, the creative clash, though rejecting physical warfare which is a perversion of this "Fountain of the River of Life" to "bitter Death . . . & corroding Hell." Here is an artist's, or perhaps a prophet's, heaven rather than a timeless state of perfect *being* as such. The implications of this strange phenomenon are surely in some way connected with shifts taking place in the European value consciousness?

But so far I have been considering one line in the history of ideas and its effects on literature: the purely Idealist Tradition, coming through from the Renaissance, indeed arriving at that era through the Middle Ages out of the ferment of the Alexandrian period and consisting in fact of a complex of related ideologies—the Neo-Platonic philosophical doctrine, alchemical lore, the tradition of Jewish mysticism, the Kabbalah, as it was taken into Christian thought, and influences from the Hermetic teachings of a work like *The Divine Pymander*, with the repercussions of all this on the interpretation of the Bible by later Christian thinkers like Jacob Boehme, the Cambridge Platonists and William Law. An understanding of this Idealist strand in European thought is particularly important, since it throws so much extra light on authors from the medieval Christian mystics to the great Renaissance and Romantic poets, as well as on more modern writers drawing upon an even more widely syncretic background of ideas. Its effects on the symbolism of European visual art has been brilliantly treated, for instance, by Edgar Wind, in works like his *Pagan Mysteries in the*

Renaissance (London and New Haven, 1958, reprinted in 1960 and 1967). But then, quite apart from all this, odd mystical and spiritual associations are to be found in the work of writers who would never normally be connected with any such tradition. Who could be more of an undenominational Humanist than Bernard Shaw, for example? Yet he struck up an unexpected and profound friendship with a Benedictine Abbess, Dame Laurentia McLachlan, whose convent he used to visit regularly while attending the Malvern Festival. There was a rift in this friendship after the publication of his *Black Girl in Search of God*, since this apparently agnostic book offended the abbess. But after a while it was suggested by one of the nuns that Shaw might have been engaged in demonstrating something like that mystical rejection of limited human conceptions of the divine, which is the proper subject of apophatic theology, and which we have just been Yeats concerned with in his "darker knowledge" which turns "from every thought of God mankind has had." This was a revelation to the abbess—and indeed the idea may not have been so far from the truth—and, when Shaw made the mistake of confusing the descriptions of her career issued to celebrate her jubilee as a nun with obituary notices and wrote an appreciative letter about her to the convent, she was very glad to resume the relationship. The whole story appears in her biography and provides a curious sidelight on the character of a notable twentieth-century man of letters.[17]

To quote one or two other instances which could be followed up: the Talmudic nature of the dialectic in Franz Kafka's novels is fairly obvious and more attention should surely be paid to the effects of his very close relationship in his last years with the daughter of a Polish rabbi of Chassidic background. Then, strangely but precisely, there are mystical overtones, too, in the work of the novelist Virginia Woolf, daughter of the prominent agnostic literary critic, Sir Leslie Stephen, and wife of the publisher and politician, Leonard Woolf, whose views on life always seem to have been strictly sceptical. She herself clearly regarded religion as a superstition that the cultivated intelligence must necessarily reject, and there is nothing in her life like Katherine Mansfield's turning towards the occultist doctrines of Gurdjieff and Ouspenski as a substitute for more conventional devotion. Yet what are we to make of such a passage as this from her *Writer's Diary* (published after her death, London, 1953), describing the summers she spent at their country home, Monks House at Rodmell, Sussex?

> Often down here I have entered into a sanctuary; a nunnery; had a

> religious retreat; of great agony once; and always some terror; so afraid one is of loneliness; of seeing to the bottom of the vessel. That is one of the experiences I have had some Augusts; and got then to a consciousness of what I call "reality": a thing I see before me: something abstract; but residing in the downs or sky; besides which nothing matters; in which I shall rest and continue to exist.

This "great agony" is linked with "that vision I had, the unhappy summer—or three weeks at Rodmell, after finishing the *Lighthouse*," and the vision itself, formed the inspiration of her next novel, *The Waves*.

> One sees a fin passing far out. What images can I reach to convey what I mean? Really there is none, I think. The interesting thing is that in all my feeling and thinking I have never come up against this before.

And when she had finished *The Waves*, which ends with the famous challenge, the defiance uttered to Death, in February 1931, she wrote exultantly: "I have netted that fin in the waste of water which appeared to me over the marshes out of my window at Rodmell when I was coming to an end of *To the Lighthouse*." This aspect of her was sensed by the poet Stephen Spender, who as a young man knew Virginia Woolf and her husband. In his autobiography, *World Within World* (London, 1951), Spender notes how even her political perceptions reveal an all too close contact with that abyss which perhaps only faith can transform to beneficence. Describing their after-dinner talk he observes:

> Leonard and Virginia were among the very few people in England who had a profound understanding of the state of the world in the 1930's; Leonard, because he was a political thinker and historian with an almost fatalistic understanding of the consequences of actions. So that when, in 1934, I asked him whether he thought there would be a war he replied: "Yes, of course. Because when nations enter into an armaments race, as they are doing at present, no other end is possible. The arms have to be used before they become completely out of date." Virginia also had a profound political insight, because the imaginative power which she shows in her novels, although it is concentrated often on small things—the light on the branches of the tree, a mark upon a whitewashed wall—nevertheless held at bay vast waters, madness, wars, destructive forces.

Indeed it seems impossible to consider Virginia Woolf as a phenomenon in the literary scene of this century, let alone to investigate the possible causes of the madness which overcame her several times in her life, or of her final tragic suicide by drowning, without taking into account the collision between the mystical intimations she received and the practical scepticism, the ironic detachment from anything that could be called belief by which she was surrounded and which she intellectually affirmed.[18]

Even, then, in discussing the most apparently secular kinds of literature, the ideologies, feelings of need, the inner experiences of authors have to be taken into account and their situation within the mental and spiritual climate of thought charted. When the problem arises of those authors whose talent seems to desert them because they have become "preachers" instead of artists—figures like Tolstoi, for example, or even D. H. Lawrence—is it enough to say they have become too preoccupied with abstract ideas, too arid and fanatical? Is there not also some dishonesty in their thought and their feelings which is blocking the achievement of real art—some fixation, some effort to force truth into a mould consistent with a formula, a system which they have arrived at as a solution to their problems but which ends by obstructing their real progress into self realization? One so often has the impression in these cases of a man trying to shout down some disturbing voice within himself. Where there is an extraordinary humanity as well as the fervour of artistry, as in the poet Chaucer, surely there is an author who has learnt to listen, to express accurately all that his awareness brings to his discriminating attention. Then why do the voices of the great prophets from the remote past,—Isaiah or Jeremiah, perhaps—ring true, although the speakers were obviously extremists, literally fanatics, while other merely irritate and annoy and weary? A surprising combination of utter conviction and humility, a genuine self knowledge, might be suggested as the answer. Whatever answer to this baffling question is raised, the problem is one that emphatically demands exploration. As I insisted earlier, critics of literature here could profitably scrutinize motives, both conscious and unconscious, and regard artists, too, as sometimes being possessed by, and expressing, the great imaginative impulses that move mankind within each particular age. This traditional attitude is not so outworn or old-fashioned as may have appeared in the early days of the "New Criticism." There must always be a kind of wholeness preserved; not only the work of art as an isolated object is to be observed, although one can always learn more of better ways to so observe. For nothing and no one is really isolated and nothing makes sense outside its context. Sometimes to stand outside a specific time or tradition is the only way to realize how much we take for granted within what we know well. What we bring to the appreciation of art must be acutely perceived before that appreciation can become fully active.

Notes

1. Désirée Hirst, "On the Aesthetics of Prophetic Art," *The British Journal of Aesthetics*, July, 1964.
2. William Law, *The Spirit of Prayer Or The Soul Rising out of the Vanity of Time, Into the Riches of Eternity* (London, 1750), pp. 82–83.
3. Désirée Hirst, *Hidden Riches: Traditional Symbolism from the Renaissance to Blake* (London, 1964).
4. John Beer, *Coleridge the Visionary* (London, 1959).
5. William Law, *An Appeal to all that Doubt or Disbelieve the Truths of the Gospel* (London, 1742), p. 10.
6. Kathleen Raine, *Blake and Tradition* (London and New Jersey, 1969), vol. 2, chap. 16.
7. For example, the image in the Preludium to *Europe: A Prophecy*, "My roots are brandish'd in the heavens, my fruits in earth beneath," seems to be inspired by the diagram of the inverted sephirotic tree in Fludd's *Philosophia Sacra & . . . Metereologica Cosmica* (Frankfurt, 1626), Tom. II, *Tractatus secundus*, p. 157.
8. Raine, *Blake and Tradition*, vol. 1, p. 274
9. See, for example, Alastair Fowler, *Spenser and the Numbers of Time* (London, 1964).
10. Conrad Pepler, O. P., *The English Religious Heritage* (London, 1958).
11. Hirst, *Hidden Riches*, "The Turn of the Century," "William Law and 18th Century England," "The Swedenborgian Movement," "The Late Eighteenth Century."
12. Paul Fussel, "The New Irony and the Augustans," *Encounter*, June, 1970.
13. Christopher Walton, *Notes to and Materials For An Adequate Biography of the Celebrated Divine and Theosopher, William Law* (London, 1854).
14. Christopher Walton, *A Guide to the peculiar sciential and experimental knowledge of theology needful to compose an adequate biography of the . . . Christian philosopher, William Law* (London, 1856), p. xx.
15. Charles Williams, *Talliessin Through Logres* (London, 1938 and 1969), *The Region of the Summer Stars* (London, 1944 and 1969), *Descent into Hell* (London, 1937 and 1949), *The Greater Trumps* (London, 1932 and 1954), and *Witchcraft* (London, 1941).
16. Raine, "Yeats and Platonism," in *The Dublin Magazine*, Spring, 1968.
17. *In a Great Tradition*, tribute to Dame Laurentia McLachlin, by the Benedictines of Stanbrook Abbey (London, 1959).
18. I have attempted to consider this topic in a broadcast on the B. B. C. Third Programme, "The Vision of Virginia Woolf," May 18, 1970.

Reinhold Merkelbach

ENCHAINED GODS

TWO HYMNS OF EARLY GREEK LITERATURE RELATED HOW THE GODDESS Hera was enchained: one was supposedly a Homeric poem, the other was by Alcaeus. Wilamowitz and others have reconstructed the myth as follows: when Zeus had born from his head his glorious child, Athena, Hera was jealous and wished to bear a like child, without the collaboration of Zeus. And so she did; she bore a son, Hephaistos, but his legs were crippled. The mother was so angry about this that she seized him by the leg and flung him down from Olympus to the earth. Thetis took up the child tenderly and nursed him. He grew up to be an ingenious smith and produced wonderful works of art.

Hephaistos then wanted to take revenge on his mother for shutting him out of Olympus. He built a magnificent throne, to which he added invisible fetters, and sent it into Olympus, supposedly as a gift in honor of his mother. Hera was enchanted and sat down upon the throne, and when the fetters closed upon her, she was held fast; no one was able to set her free. The gods held counsel and deliberated: they decided to ask Hephaistos to come and free his mother. But the smith was sulky and recalcitrant: they had not wanted him in Olympus before, and now he had no inclination to come there. But if the gods would promise him Aphrodite as a wife, he would perhaps be disposed to come.

Ares, the other son of Hera, sure that he could easily compel Hephaistos by force, volunteered to fetch his brother, but Hephaistos hurled torches and fireballs at him. Ares saw no chance for the close combat for which he was equipped. The long-range missiles of Hephaistos frightened him, and he ran away.

The situation was difficult. There was, indeed, one other possibility: it was likely that Dionysus would be able to help, but he was the son of Semele, Zeus' mistress and the hated rival of Hera. Until now Hera had been able to prevent Dionysus from being recognized as a full god and numbered among the true Olympians. But now the embarrassment of the queen of gods was so great, and the shackles cut so painfully into her delicate flesh, that she was ready to make concessions. Dionysus demanded to be officially recognized as one of the twelve Olympian gods, in recompense for his service to Hera. Hera agreed, and Dionysus departed with a retinue of wild satyrs and extravagant maenads. Sheer force, such as Ares had used, was now out of the question; instead, Dionysus gave wine to Hephaistos. After a short while the smith became as obedient and tractable as a child. When he was fully intoxicated, the satyrs lifted him upon a donkey and led him in a triumphal procession up to Olympus.

This scene is represented on many vase paintings: one satyr plays upon the flute, another holds the drunken Hephaistos to keep him from falling, and the other satyrs dance and play with the maenads. It is a merry Dionysiac procession, a *komos*. A vase from Spina shows Dionysus and the satyrs on Olympus.[1] Hera is still bound to her throne, unable to move. Merry satyrs populate the illustrious Olympus, and Dionysus, master of the situation, majestically reclines upon a couch. He succeeded in making Hephaistos liberate his mother, and the story ended happily with the wedding-festival of Hephaistos and Aphrodite. Whether this was a hymn to Hephaistos or to Dionysus, may be disputed. Wilamowitz thought of a hymn to Hephaistos; Bruno Snell, in his discussion of the poem of Alcaeus, of a hymn to Dionysus. I feel strongly that the whole context is Dionysiac.

This gay myth raises some far-reaching questions. First, is there a relation between this myth and comedy? Secondly, is this myth connected with Greek ritual? And thirdly, there have been Greek statues of enchained gods; is there a relation between these statues and our myth? I shall touch on the first two questions briefly, but the third I want to explore in this paper.

It is quite evident that the procession of Dionysus, Hephaistos, and the satyrs and maenads up to Olympus is a prototype of comedy. There was a play by the Sicilian poet Epicharmus *The Komastai* ("the revellers") *or Hephaistos*. A vase painting from lower Italy shows a scene from the Comedy of Phlyakes (something like swollen dancers, padded phallic actors).[2] In the center of a scaffolding, Hera is seated upon the throne; before her two phlyakes are fighting. Their names are Enyalios and Daedalus: Enyalios is an epithet of Ares; Daedalus is a mythical smith, like Hephaistos. That the statues of Daedalus had to be enchained is often heard; otherwise they would have run away. Our Homeric hymn surely deserves a place of honour in the prehistory of comedy.

The relation of the myth to fire rituals is apparent. Hephaistos is the god of fire: in many rituals new fire is brought to the temple every year: here, the fire god is brought to Olympus. The myth seems to be the counterpart of a corresponding ritual.

More important is the connection of the myth with ceremonies of initiation. Hera seated upon the throne and surrounded by satyrs strongly reminds one of the Corybantic initiation, where the candidate for initiation was seated upon a throne, and the Corybantes danced furiously around him. Plato speaks of this initiation as of something well known, and Pindar wrote poems for such ceremonies. Of course, the candidate for this initiation was a boy, while Hera was an Olympian goddess. But what happened to men in these rituals had usually happened to the gods themselves in Greek mythology. While fettering and liberating were parts of many initiation ceremonies, there were also many corresponding myths, for example, of Dionysus enchained and liberated.

There have been statues of enchained gods throughout Greece, and the statue of Hera of Samos was one of the most famous among them. Thus the goddess was shackled in myth, and her image in reality—this leads us to the strange phenomenon of gods enchained. The problem has been thoroughly investigated by the late Karl Meuli from Basel, my teacher and friend, and in the remarks that follow, I shall be drawing heavily on his researches.[3]

If people fettered their gods, they may have done so for several reasons. First, because the god was the dispenser of all good things, men wanted to keep him right at their side. Then too, because the god was dangerous and hateful, men wanted to keep him from doing mischief. Or possibly both of these reasons may have been operating: the god was powerful and dangerous at the same time, and men wanted to have him present—but under strict control, as various examples of these varieties of enchained gods demonstrate. First, as the dispenser of all good things, Tyche, the goddess of the good fortune of a city, might be enchained. When Constantine the Great founded his new capital at the Bosphorus, he fettered Tyche to his new city; he had a statue of Tyche carved, to which a chain was attached. It was consecrated after a conjuration of the planetary gods and fastened to a cross by a clasp. The cross was carried by two statues, one the emperor himself, and the other his mother Helena. The statues were erected facing the east in a building in the middle of the town, in the Milion, then the bolt of the clasp was fastened and the key was buried beneath the pedestal of the statuary group. Thus Constantine ensured that Tyche would forever remain in the new city: that in every war the city would be victorious, and that there would always be plenty of food.

Secondly, gods were enchained because they were hateful and odious, as was especially the case of the gods of War and Death. The fettering of Ares and Aphrodite in the *Odyssey* is a kind of sequel to the fettering of Hera. The union of Hephaistos and Aphrodite was ill-starred, as might have been expected. Ares and Aphrodite committed adultery, but the cunning Hephaistos succeeded in fettering both of them, to the great satisfaction of the gods. This lay of the *Odyssey* might be regarded simply as an amusing story, but again there is a ritual background, for there are other traditions of the enchaining of Ares, as he was a god whom the Greeks detested. In an episode of the fifth book of the *Iliad*, Otos and Ephialtes imprison Ares in a huge jar (κέραμος); he is released only after a whole year. There was a shackled statue of Ares in the city of Syedra in eastern Pamphylia.[4] The inhabitants suffered severely from the Ares of the neighbouring Cilician pirates. At the request of the oracle of the Clarian Apollo, the citizens of Syedra erected a group of statues in the middle of the town: Ares held in chains by Hermes and convicted by the goddess of Justice, Dike.

The Etruscans even enchained the god of death. On some of their funerary monuments, the god of Death, with a wolf's head, is emerging from a huge jar (Figure 1). He has seized a young man and is about to drag him into the jar as a victim. Behind the young man stands an angel of death, tied up crosswise. But Death will not be able to take another, since the wolf is enchained by a collar, and a valiant young man strikes at him. So Death will be compelled to disappear again, until his next eruption from his prison, the jar or *orca* (we may probably call him Orcus).

So much for the second sort of enchained gods. The third and most important kind is that of gods benign and dangerous at the same time. The complexity of the phenomenon shows that we are dealing with a very old religious concept, for things reaching back into prehistoric times are never simple, but always complex. Notions which in our opinion are quite unrelated may have been almost united, to the men of the stone age.

The powerful fettered gods are always liberated, for a certain amount of time. The liberation took place on the day of the great festival of the god. The statue was unbound, taken out of the temple and conducted in a great procession through the city; sometimes it was ceremonially bathed. When the statue was carried through the streets, it was often accompanied by a parade of masks; indeed, these archaic fettered gods almost always seem to be gods of mask-festivals (for example, Dionysus, Kronos, Artemis). Great dancing festivals were often connected with these masquerades. Not only was the god liberated from his chains, but on his feast day men, too, were liberated from their usual restraints.

Let us now return to the fettering of Hera. In one of the most important centers of her worship, on the island of Samos, the statue of Hera was enchained. Numerous coins of the island from Roman times prove this, showing the goddess in fetters. Her arms are stretched out sideways; from her hands fillets and chains hang down to the ground and are fastened on the pedestal of the statue. But not only are Hera's hands bound, her body also is tied up crosswise, as a fragment of a clay-figurine from the temple precinct of Hera in Samos also shows.[5] Upon her head she bears a *polos*, a high headpiece. Upon an archaic wood carving from Samos,[6] representing the wedding of Zeus and Hera, Zeus lifts the garment of his bride to grasp her bosom. Before Zeus had liberated her, Hera was tied crosswise, and her arm is still caught inside the robe. While Zeus moves about freely, Hera resembles a column. The impression of a column is increased by the fact that the robe touches the ground and hides her feet. Enchained gods of archaic times were usually tree gods, gods of the pillar or the column. The famous statue of Cheramyes in the Louvre shows that the goddess was really taken to be a column: Hera seems to grow out of the earth like a tree; only her toes peep out from the robe.

In the cult legend of Hera of Samos, the goddess is put into fetters—Athenaeus quotes the story from Menodotus, a local historian of Samos. In ancient times, so the story goes, when besides the Greeks many Carians still lived on the island of Samos, there was a priestess of Hera by the name of Admete (the virgin). Once, Tyrrhenian pirates came across the sea and stole the archaic wooden image of the goddess, called βρέτας, "the piece of wood" (German *Brett*). The door of the temple was open, and the robbery was easy. The pirates carried the statue into their boat and set sail, but they were not able to move the ship an inch. They became frightened, deposited the image on the shore, put sacrificial cakes before the goddess, and ran away.

In the morning, Admete the priestess announced that the statue had disappeared, and a search was begun. The Carians found the statue by the shore. Simple-minded as they were, they thought the goddess had run away by herself, so they stood her against the trunk of a willow (λύγος) and bound her with willow branches. Then Admete came, unbound the statue, washed it, brought it back to the temple, and fastened it to the pedestal to prevent it from running away again.

In remembrance of this, Menodotus goes on, the Samians celebrated every year the festival of the Tonaia (from τόνος, "rope," with reference to the fettering). They took the wooden image of Hera to the shore, bathed it, and regaled it with sacrificial cakes. The Samians then banqueted and feasted in the open air and crowned their heads with willow branches.

It is clear that Menodotus' story is an aetiological legend of the Samian festival. The Samian priestess of Hera was called *Εὐαγγελίς*, "announcer of joyful tidings." On the day of the feast, the door of the temple was opened, the enchained statue untied and brought to the shore. It was enacted that the goddess had run away. The Samians who banqueted and feasted in the open air regaled her with sacrificial cakes. She was then bathed, on the shore or in a bath-tub; in the temple precinct of Hera of Samos, a big tub has been excavated. The statue was then chained again, put upon the pedestal, and brought back into the temple.

In Greece and Asia Minor, there were a number of enchained gods. Plato mentions the statues of Daedalus that were so accomplished they could move by themselves. Therefore, they had to be bound, to prevent them from running away. The Hellenistic scholar Polemo, who gathered many inscriptions, related that Dionysus was enchained on the island of Chios, so too the seated statue of Artemis in the city of Erythrai, and that everywhere there are stories about images of gods who are not willing to stay in their place, but wander elsewhere.

We possess an overwhelming array of examples and testimonies about gods in fetters, both in mythology and in cult. These have been collected by Meuli, and I could not possibly present them all here; I shall only mention Kronos, Prometheus, Dionysus, Hermes, the Carian Zeus, Iupiter Optimus Maximus Heliopolitanus, and Osiris and Isis. I shall discuss at some length a few of the varieties of Artemis: Artemis Orthia Lygodesma of Sparta, Artemis of the Ephesians, and Artemis of the walnut tree, Karyatis.

Artemis Orthia of Sparta was called Lygodesma—"fettered by willow branches." The British School at Athens has excavated her sanctuary: the finds were extraordinarily rich and have thrown a surprisingly favourable light on archaic Sparta. Artemis Orthia was a tree goddess and, at the same time, the mistress of a great and ecstatic mask and dance festival. During the excavations, many leaden figurines of masked dancers were found. The character of the dance festival may perhaps be inferred from the myth. According to it, Theseus kidnapped Helen while she was dancing with her playmates. Connected with these dance and mask festivals are often, throughout the world, processions of young men who go around begging for food. If people do not give voluntarily, the young men feel entitled to steal whatever they choose. There is evidently a relation between this custom and the famous ceremony at the festival of Orthia, in which Spartan boys had to steal cheese. A fragment of the poet Alcman describes the gods celebrating on the mountain peaks. Artemis prepares for them a huge cheese, made of the milk of lionesses, in a big bucket. This has rightly been related to the cheese ceremony at the festival of Orthia. However, the statue of Orthia was very dangerous: the two men who had found it, Astrabakos and Alopekos, were driven mad just by looking at it.

From many carvings and clay figurines we know what Artemis Orthia, fettered in willow branches, looked like.[7] In archaic carvings, Artemis is just a pillar, tied up horizontally, with a human head. The goddess often has wings and holds in her hands birds, snakes and wild beasts, lions and stags. A treetop springs from her head, for she is herself a tree. She always resembles a column, for there are often horizontal and vertical stripes upon her garment. On the vase of Clitias of Athens, Artemis, with a stag and a lion beside her hand, appears as mistress of the beasts.[8] She is winged, that is to say, she is also mistress of the birds, which is quite natural for a tree goddess. She stands upright like a pillar, and her garment has a chess board design.

The great Artemis of the Ephesians was a very similar goddess. On the coins of Roman times she is represented as a pillar. A high *pólos* (headpiece) indicates that the goddess is turning into a tree. Her hands are extended and fastened to the pedestal by chains. Upon one plate, the chains turn into fillets;[9] in other representations, Artemis carries chandeliers or torches in her hands. On a figurine in the Bologna Museum, the body of the goddess is tied like a mummy.

Several archaic statuettes have been found. It is impossible to discern whether the goddess or her priestess is represented in these statuettes, and we are not entitled to draw such a distinction. First there is a statuette, from whose head a high pillar, a tree, is growing; a bird sits right on the top.[10] Another figurine (Figure 2) shows Artemis as the goddess of destiny, with a bird and a distaff in her hands. The figurine has the appearance of a column; her headgear might be called a capital (the Greek words for capital are ἐπίκρανον or κεφαλίς, "headgear"). The body of the goddess is tied up crosswise, as if she were caught in a net, and she is fettered.

A third statuette (Figure 3) shows the goddess in a stiff and rigid attitude; her hands lie close to the body; a garment encloses the whole figure. One might call this a fetter garment. The vestment of the Ephesian goddess had a special name: κλείς, "lock," since in this dress the goddess was locked up. Cassandra wears such a robe in Euripides' Trojan Women. She had been the bride of Apollo; when she is doomed to become the slave and concubine of Agamemnon, she has to take off the fetter garment and the holy fillets of the god.

Of course, one may say: the hands of the statuettes lie close to the body because the wood, ivory, and bone carvers were not yet able to carve moving figures. This is certainly true. But in history and religion one explanation never excludes others: these figures look like columns because the art of woodcarving was only in its infancy, and because the goddess was really a pillar or a tree, and also because she was enchained.

We know of another statue of Artemis of Ephesus from Roman imperial times, which is preserved in many copies (Figure 4). She is still a pillar or a tree. The later statues show much more clearly than the archaic ones that she is the mistress of nature; to the early Greeks this was a matter of course, but to the people of the Empire, the power of the goddess had to be explained in detail by the many attributes of the statue. The goddess has many breasts, which nourish men and animals. At the same time, the breasts may be considered as so many eggs, grapes, nuts, or acorns. Artemis gave to man everything that grows and thrives in nature, especially the fruits of trees and the forest. On some squares of her body, one sees the bee; Artemis gave honey to man. Her priests were called king-bees (ἐσσῆνες), her priestesses bees (μέλισσαι). The bees dwell in the tree and fly to and from the tree, as do the priests and priestesses of the goddess. Archaic pieces of adornment from Rhodes show Artemis herself as a bee with a human head.

The seasons of the year are figured on the necklace of the goddess. Attached to her body are the heads (the *protomai*) of all the animals: when the hunter killed an animal, he dedicated the skull and the bones to Artemis. The goddess would vivify them again, for she was always the renewer of life. In the cycle of the seasons, the tree loses its leaves; the trunk alone remains with the naked boughs, a mere skeleton, but in the spring the tree blossoms again and puts forth new leaves. Artemis who gives new leaves to the tree will also give flesh to the bones of animals and men and revivify them.

This goddess is chained not only by the hands, as we see on the coins, but also across the body; for the squares on the body have been produced by tying her crosswise; even the breasts seem to come forth from a diagonal fettering. Horizontal and vertical folds are often seen on the back of the statues too. These folds are vestiges of the ancient fettering, now stylized and transformed, just as the chains connecting the hands with the pedestal have been replaced by fillets, chandeliers, or torches.

As we have seen, the enchained gods are very often tree gods at the same time. Tree gods, of course, are also a very complex and archaic phenomenon. It may perhaps be said that the tree god must have been one of the earliest religious conceptions of mankind. In the time of hunters and gatherers, when Demeter had not yet given man the crops, the tree was not merely a symbol of ceasing and renewed life: almost everything gathered by the women came from the tree, almost everything hunted by the men lived in the forest. One is probably right to conjecture that many religious festivals of the earliest men took place under holy trees or were processions with holy trees. It is not surprising, therefore, that the gods enchained—the gods of parades and festivals, of masquerades and dances—are almost always tree gods.

That these chained gods coincided with tree gods may be observed in many examples from Asia Minor. Over one hundred tree goddesses in fetters are attested in this area. In the Ankara museum, there is a Cybele from Phrygia, wearing a tall headpiece[12] (it may be called a capital, for the goddess is clearly a pillar). Her head touches the lintel, and it would probably be quite correct to say that she is the support of the house. She wears a veil and, as a tree goddess, she holds a bird in her hand. The vertical and horizontal folds of her garment remind one of the fettering. In the case of another Cybele,[13] very similar, the garment falls in vertical folds, which may suggest the grooves of a column. The goddess Eleuthera from Myra, in Lycia, is encircled by a fetter-garment. She was called Artemis Eleuthera by the Greeks. A well-known coin from the British Museum shows how Eleuthera appears from the tree (Figure 5). A Hellenized variation of this goddess is Artemis Kindyas, who was worshipped in Bargylia in Caria (Figure 6). She rises from the earth like a tree, with her arms crossed and hidden away beneath a fetter-garment; additionally, the body of the goddess is tied up. She looks at the spectator with a friendly smile, and yet her look is enigmatic.

Artemis Karyatis, in Greece, was the goddess of the walnut tree. It was thought that in her honor the bucolic processions had been instituted. *Karyatis* is the epithet of Artemis of Karyai in Laconia, the name of a bee priestess (*μέλισσαί*) and of a dance in honour of Artemis. The dancing girls themselves were called *karyatids*; the well-known female-figured column is also a Caryatid. How could it happen that the same word signified on the one hand a tree goddess—goddess of the pillar and the column—and on the other hand dancing girls? Columns and dancing girls seem to be things so different that a modern onlooker would probably say at first: "This one thing here is a decorated pillar; and that other thing there is the name of a special dance or of dancing girls; it is mere chance that the words denoting these different things are the same." However, sheer coincidence it cannot be; for the famous Acanthus column at Delphi shows three dancing girls who have come forth from the pillar and are now dancing around it.

Let us look more closely at the *Karyatids*. While they are dancing, they carry baskets upon their heads, they are *κανηφόροι*, "carriers of the basket." The basket is often called *kalathos*, and accordingly there is a special dance called *Kalathiskos*. When the Caryatids are supporting pillars, the *kalathos* has the function of a capital. The broadening of the upper end is characteristic of the pillar. If a tree is used as a supporting pillar, it is cut at the top above a fork, so that it will easily support a cross-beam. From the viewpoint of a mason, there is a purpose in the basket (the *kalathos*) of the Caryatids. At the same time, the Greeks of early times associated the Caryatids with dancing. One Caryatid from the treasure house of the Siphnians at Delphi wears on her head a stone *kalathos* on which a dancing scene is represented. The correlation between the female-figured pillars wearing the *kalathos* and the dancing girls with the *kalathos* is evident. We may, I think, say that the Caryatids, the spirits of the tree, are fettered during the whole year; but once a year, at the festival of the goddess, they are set free; they take the shape of human *karyatids* and step forth from the tree or column. Unself-consciously, they dance an ecstatic yet measured dance. The same explanation may be applied to the bearers of the basket, the *kanephoroi*. A vase from Spina shows among several moving figures a *kanephoros*, who might be called a walking column.[14] The girls, who played the role of a basket-bearer, had to learn special steps appropriate to a walking column.

I have mentioned that the *Karyatids* were connected with the origin of the bucolic processions; another aetiological tradition derives bucolic processions from the worship of Artemis Phakelitis in Sicily. This goddess was also fettered, for Orestes had brought her image, wrapped in a bundle (*φάκελος*), from Tauris. At Tyndaris in Sicily he bathed the statue in the river and consecrated it. At the end of the year, the bucolic processions took place, and the goddess gave prosperity to the cattle.

A third tradition says that the bucolic parades originated in the worship of Artemis Lyaia of Syracuse. These varieties of the goddess Artemis are essentially all alike. Artemis Lyaia, the liberator, must herself have been enchained. She untied herself once a year and liberated men from sorrow and misfortune, from civil war and illness. In the great procession Artemis went through the city of Syracuse in the shape of the basket bearer (*kanephoros*), surrounded by wild animals, among them a lioness. Presumably we have to imagine that many people wearing animals' masks accompanied the goddess—at least it is reported that many participants of the procession wore stag masks. The masked went around begging and collecting; they derided and reprimanded, just like the Dionysiac masks of Attic comedy: probably there was but little difference between this procession and a Dionysiac *komos*. At the end of the procession, they blessed the people and the city; they scattered all kinds of seeds (a *panspermia*) and gave benedictions for the prosperity of the cattle, of the crops, and of the people. They brought along with them, as they said, good luck and good health. Their song has been transmitted to us and runs: "Receive good Luck, receive good Health; we bring them from the Goddess, as she has ordered us":

> *δέξαι τὰν ἀγαθὰν τύχαν,*
> *δέξαι τὰν ὑγίειαν,*
> *ἃν φέρομες παρὰ τᾶς θεοῦ,*
> *ἇι κελήσατο τήνα.*

The gods I have presented here offer a manifold and rather confusing picture. Yet we may try to characterize them by some general remarks. The fettered gods were also always gods of liberation. They were themselves released for a certain time, on the days of the great festivals. Then processions went round, and the image of the god was taken out of the temple and bathed in the sea or in a river. The processions were often accompanied by various masks, and usually there were great dancing festivals. During these festivals, a strange atmosphere prevailed, a mixture of delight and shuddering, a sentiment of bliss blended with a distinct consciousness of the fragility of everything human. Very often it was the souls of deceased ancestors that came back in the masks. From these mask festivals tragedy and comedy alike were derived.

The gods enchained were always very powerful and able to bring man good fortune in every respect. But at the same time they were also very dangerous. It was, perhaps, advisable to enchain them, and to release them only on the day of the festival. Who knows what these gods would contrive if they were not kept under strict control?

At the same time, most of these enchained gods were also tree gods. I have suggested that the connection between gods enchained and tree gods may be related to the fact that the tree god seems to be a very ancient religious idea. This is, of course, an approximation only; much more could be said about this topic. If we follow the hints which lie in the word *Caryatid* itself, we should quickly find ourselves discussing the beginnings of temple building and of great stone sculpture. I do not want to expatiate so far; I only want to emphasize that this experience is typical. Ancient phenomena are always of a Protean nature, and we shall never succeed in isolating them. I shall, by way of conclusion, try to explain why this is so.

The notions of early man were never of an abstract nature; they were always in touch with things visible—I should almost say, they leaned upon things visible. Their notions were intimately connected with holy trees, waters, stones, and ceremonies of cult. Many old myths did not originate as stories, but were enacted. At that time, men thought in pictures, in perceptions. There was no translation of these pictures into abstract conceptions. Whoever wished to express his mind or his feelings laid down his meaning in words related to material things, in visible rituals, or in gestures and actions, in which material things were used. Man projected what he felt into outward objects. The hearer and the onlooker, on the other hand, understood the meaning immediately from an unsophisticated language, from gestures and actions, and from objects. For him also, the meaning lay in the things themselves; he did not translate what he saw into abstract conceptions. In this way of thinking, profound insight and mistaken inference rub shoulders.

For this reason, the conceptions and thoughts of early men seem to us strangely vague and fluctuating. For if one's thoughts are supported by material things and visible ceremonies as if on crutches, it can easily happen that the ceremonies and the appearance of things remain the same, while the conceptions connected with them change. Thus, many different conceptions were connected with a tree god. To one man, the tree represented the cycle of life and death. To another, the tree god was primarily the donor of the fruits and the master of the animals of the forest. To a third, the tree god was most important as a holy pillar, which alone was able to support the sheltering roof of a house.

These archaic conceptions are disturbing and confusing. We need patience and must cling to this one premise, that nothing can be archaic unless it could be seen by human eyes. The investigator will regularly meet with phenomena in which things are closely connected and overlap, which seem to be totally different to us, who think in abstract categories. When we have hit upon connections we would not have dreamt of, but which are full of meaning within the train of thought of the ancient world, it is very likely that we have caught sight of an archaic phenomenon, an object the investigation of which will repay every effort.

Fig. 1 Etruscan Funerary Monument, Museum of Perugia; courtesy of J. Thimme.

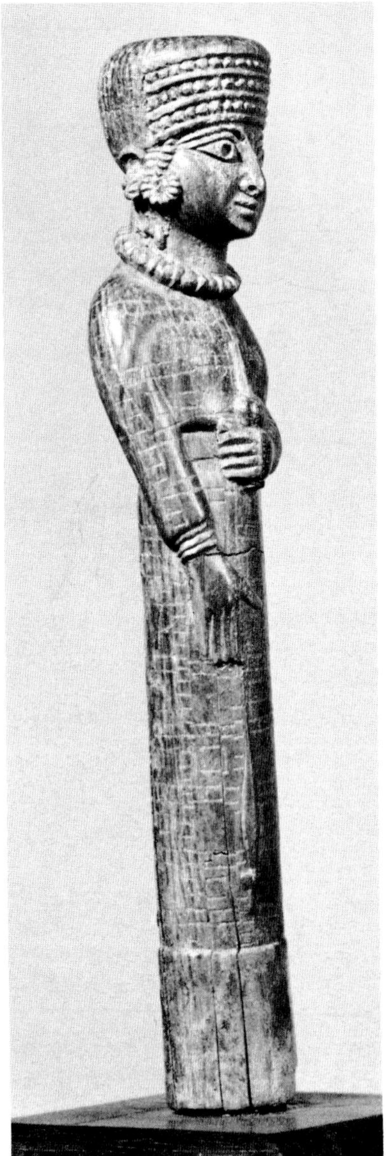

Fig. 2 Artemis of Ephesus with bird and distaff. Photo by Hirmer.
Fig. 3 Artemis of Ephesus in fetter garment. Photo by Hirmer.

Fig. 4 Artemis of Ephesus. Photo by Alinari.

Fig. 5 Artemis Eleuthera from Myra in Lycia appears from a tree. Coin in the British Museum.
Fig. 6 Artemis Kindyas from Bargylia; courtesy of Ines Jucker.

Notes

1. Nereo Alfieri and Paolo Enrico Arias, *Spina* (Munich, 1958), plates 110–11.
2. Margarete Bieber, *The History of the Greek and Roman Theater* (Princeton, 1961), p. 133, fig. 485.
3. A detailed account of Karl Meuli's researches is given in his *Gesammelte Schriften* (Basel, 1972).
4. Louis Robert, *Documents de l'Asie Mineure Méridionade* (Paris-Genève, 1966), pp. 91–100.
5. Ernst Buschor, *Athenische Mitteilungen*, 55 (Stuttgart, 1930), p. 2.
6. Karl Schefold, *Frühgriechische Sagenbilder* (Munich, 1964), plate 39.
7. See Richard M. Dawkins, ed. *The Sanctuary of Artemis Orthia at Sparta* (London, 1929).
8. Schefold, *Frühgriechische Sagenbilder*, plate 49.
9. Hermann Thiersch, *Artemis Ephesia* (Berlin, 1935), Abhandl. der Gesellschaft der Wissenschaften zu Göttingen, phil.-hist. Klasse, 3 Folge, nr. 12, fig. 55.
10. Ekrem Akurgal, *Die Kunst Anatoliens* (Berlin, 1961), p. 206, fig. 169.
11. A. Thiersch, *Artemis Ephesia*, fig. 20.
12. Akurgal, *Die Kunst Anatoliens*, fig. 60.
13. Akurgal, p. 98, fig. 62.
14. Alfieri and Arias, *Spina*, plates 85, 87.

Pierre Ponsoye

ASPECTS OF TRISTAN ESOTERISM

Amors qui totes choses vaint.
Berne *Folie Tristan*, 72

WHILE IT IS POSSIBLE THAT THE WORLD'S LITERATURE CONTAINS LOVE stories as beautiful as that of Tristan and Isolt, there is, no doubt, scarcely one which, apart from entertaining the foolish, harbors for the astonishment of the wise such a lofty and puzzling secret. Thanks to the admirable work of reconstruction and critique accomplished by medievalists since early in this century, chiefly in the footsteps of Joseph Bédier, the great story is well known today, at least in its main episodes: the deprived and exiled childhood of the orphan Tristan, the crossing to Cornwall, the quest for Isolt, the fatal hour of the love potion, the subsequent long ordeal of despair and joy culminating in the flight to the Wood of Morrois and ending in separation and death. A potion brewed in secret and drunk in error suddenly binds together two creatures not promised to each other, yet whose confrontation had been decided and induced from afar by the interplay of predestination and prowess: binds them with a bond stronger than will, honor, or plighted troth, guides them persistently toward one another despite every obstacle of prior claim or peril, by every means of courage, ruse, or "madness," and of which death alone will eventually fulfill and reveal the mysterious essence.

Such is the basic and unchanging plot-outline that minute comparisons of texts have permitted us to reconstruct from fragmentary poems as well as secondary versions of which some are abridged and some divergent. Those who proceed no farther will undoubtedly have a good summary of the legend and the spirit informing it, but they would be a long way from suspecting the immensity of Tristan matter and the wealth of symbolic currents crisscrossing within it in multiple and profound harmonies.

Seigneurs, cest conte est mult divers: "My lords, this tale is told in many ways," observed Thomas of Britain long ago, "so I shall keep to one version in my rhymes, saying as much as is needed and passing over the remainder"; thus he admitted the existence of several oral or written traditions.[1] This is not to imply that such diversity applies to the Tristan motif alone; the Celtic corpus offers many examples of it. But in this case the diversity presents such special characteristics that we are forced to regard it as a major trait without equivalent in all medieval literature apart from the Grail cycle. It does not derive from the individual imagination of the storytellers, nor from the prolonged popularity accorded by successive epochs to a theme of unusual richness. Assuming this was a factor, then it can only have been in matters of form and episode, or in the "courtly" coloration of certain versions; for above and beyond all differences of inspiration, form, or language, and despite the dispersion of texts in time and space, that other major trait emerges: the integrity of the basic symbolic theme, in its structure, rhythm, and finality.

Another characteristic is the resurgence in secondary versions of archaic elements unknown to the primary texts, and the new exploitation of symbolic motifs neglected or differently treated by them. And, finally, a still further trait is the association of the different works with a number of distinct schools: in some cases their authors expressly acknowledge their allegiance (for example, Gottfried von Strassburg to Thomas of Britain, and Thomas to the enigmatic Bréri), while elsewhere different characteristics of form or content testify to their derivation from one or many antecedent works. These differences, although not nearly as marked as those distinguishing the branches of the Grail legend, are sufficient to enable scholars to trace at least two principal and independent offspring: one known as the "common version," with Eilhart von Oberge, Béroul, the prose romance, and the Berne *Folie*; the other as the "courtly version," with Thomas, Gottfried, and the Oxford *Folie*. It is with these primary versions that such secondary versions as the following are more or less directly associated: the Norse (Brother Robert's *Saga*), German (Henrich von Freyberg, Ulrich von Türheim, German prose romance), English (*Sir Tristrem*), Italian (*Tavola Ritonda*), Spanish, Russian, and so on; not to mention a number of short episodic French poems such as the *Lai du Chèvrefeuille* by Marie de France, the *Donnez des Amants*, the *Roman de la Poire*, and the *Roman de l'Escouffle*, all of which spanned nearly two centuries and the whole of Christendom, with various additions and interpretations but with no rupture or perversion of the original symbolic theme.

How are we to explain this phenomenon of unity in diversity, freedom in fidelity? The great French medievalist Joseph Bédier has supplied the beginnings of a reply to this enigma. Painstakingly and assiduously he drew up two tables on the basis of the known texts: one a table of concordance, the other of divergence, and from these he was able to conclude as follows:

> . . . as a foundation to all the extant poetic tradition of the Tristan legend we find, not semicoherent compilations, but a true poem, composed during a lofty epoch, as early as the twelfth century, by a man of genius. It is not a formless vulgate but already one of those superior organisms of which all parts are synergistically bound together in such a way that all suffer from the smallest violation to any one of them.[1]

To this "superior organism" he gave the name of "archetype" to denote its synthetic character, both as to the Celtic elements integrated into its economy and to the various works of which it was the common source—unknown but necessary.

The results of Bédier's research have never been attacked in principle by succeeding medievalists, but his concept of the "archetype" has not always been accepted without reservation. Later research, notably that of G. Schoepperle and J. Loth, has shown the importance of parallel narratives and symbolic precedents; and Loth believed in particular that "the Britons of Wales had not the least need to be schooled by French storytellers or to appropriate French models in order to be able to compose romances that were equally spun out and at least equally orderly in structure."[2] Some researchers have even rejected all idea of an "archetype," as witness for example Pauphilet:

> J. Bédier believed he could recognize forty essential episodes which in his view formed the substance of the legend and were attributable to a single creator. Surely the extreme arbitrariness of this choice and the *petitio principii* it assumes must be obvious to all? For it is the knowledge of the legend's ultimate unity that prompts us to regard a given episode as essential because of its link with the rest. Yet at another stage of the narrative possibly twenty episodes might have sufficed. . . . Let us therefore renounce our pursuit of the chimera of the proto-poem.[3]

To this we may reply that Bédier's conclusions are the fruit, not of a *petitio principii*, but of a simple induction imposed by strict analysis of the texts, of which the comparison, whether we like it or not, compels us to acknowledge a common source. What *is* arbitrary is the gratuitous assumption that there may be "another stage of the narrative [where] twenty episodes might have sufficed," in view of the fact that we have before us a basic "scenario" of which the law of progression and the significance of the whole demand precisely that sequence of key-episodes enumerated by Bédier and found to be woven into the fabric of every known version. Actually, Pauphilet's objection is due mainly to his consideration of the tale's external dramatization at the expense of its deeper significance, thus, implicitly, joining the supporters of the theory of "lais" or of the compiling of partial and heterogeneous narratives. Whereas in fact, as Bédier clearly saw, it is this deeper significance which commands the tale's structural unity and the conditions for its cyclic development and which, above all, imposes the certainty of a unity of source.[4]

On the other hand, if it is certain, as Loth says, that the Britons of Wales, Cornwall, or Ireland were capable of composing poems just as orderly in structure, and that the matrix of the "matter" is Celtic and penetrated by archaic elements, the legend as presented in the Continental works nonetheless differs radically from the insular tales or narratives in its feudal framework, social environment, moral judgments, and, above all, in a fact on which commentators have laid little emphasis but which is nevertheless cardinal: the *transformation of the symbolism into* something much less mythical and much more obviously initiatory while still retaining the traces of its origins. Thus the insular tales are dominated by the presence of the Other World, inhabited by shadowy or supernatural entities, crowded with magical objects or taboos. There is nothing of all this in the French romances: the Other World no longer exists except as a memory in the symbolism of combat and quest, in which we have to search out the vestige or the correspondence (perilous land, crossing of the waters); where hostile forces have been humanized (the Morholt, the dwarf Frocin), or reduced to a classic type (dragon); where the magic element has been polarized in the philter or in poisoned swords; taboos have disappeared or been transformed (substitution of the philter for the *geis*,[5] according to certain commentators). Numerous ancient elements have been abandoned or persist only vestigially (e.g., the association of Tristan with the Boar, or of Mark with the Horse). Others have been the object of a new association (e.g., the name Drystan or Dröstan occurring in *The Mabinogion*, later Tristan, and acquiring thenceforward the meaning derived from its Latin etymology *tristis*—as a mark of his unhappy destiny). Also of note is the probable insertion of classical motifs (white and black sails) or Oriental ones (the sword between the lovers).

All this might be considered incidental, to be explained by mere changes in epoch or outlook, if we failed to observe what is actually a conscious conversion of the very substance of the legend with a view to constructing a highly organized theme, original in its finality, movement, and successive ordeals, by comparison with the rare extant fragments of the insular Tristan legend, with its typical initiatory characteristics (the theme of a gifted and deprived childhood, opposition between prowess and adversity, themes of liberating combats, ordeals, the quest, and so forth), where Fate has been substituted for taboos and shadowy forces, and where the heroes' magic powers and supernatural gifts or allies have been replaced by divine favor, prowess, and the "will of the heart" (Gottfried).

The result was a work of decantation, clarification, and above all symbolic synthesis, presenting the Tristan matter in the form of *materia preparata*, to use the alchemists' term. In reality, this matter would not have given birth to such a flowering—so diverse yet at the same time so profoundly unitary—had it not been *intellectually pure*.

Still, and here is the point, the work cannot be that of a "poet," however inspired, in the literary sense of the word, for it is not of an imaginative, reflective, or lyrical order: it is of an intellectual order. In fact it presupposes a profound knowledge of the nature and essence of symbols, that is, of intelligible truths, a true symbol being only the revelation of a principle, or a principle in action. If it was imposed with such authority, it is because this authority was the most infallible we know: that of the intellect, or true metaphysical cognition.

This is precisely where we find the key to the problem of Tristan and, incidentally, of all traditional literature of a symbolic nature, beginning of course with the sacred Scriptures. Those who are unaware of or refuse to acknowledge the real nature—indeed, the existence—of the intellect restrict themselves solely to the sphere of the mind, that is, to individual reflection, reason, and imagination, depriving themselves of the direct intuition of the Truth. The Truth being in itself universal and eternal, the mind can never, on its own, attain it except by the reflective process, whence the words *reflection* and *speculation* to denote its own activity. Only the intellect—the Aristotelian νοῦς—can apprehend it with a direct and immediate grasp. Truth and intellect are then, in the words of St. Thomas, "one in the act," *they form a single entity*.[6] And the symbol is the meeting-point offered to the intellect for this "joint act" with the intelligible Truth. For this reason the science of symbols and metaphysical cognition are one and the same thing.

Hence to recognize the intellectual nature of the mysterious source of Tristan is to recognize its suprahuman quality. His authority is not that of some arbitrary man or group of men through whom it finds expression, but that of the wisdom and instruction they have been charged with transmitting. In other words, it stems from the tradition of which they have been the witnesses at a given moment but which is eternal in essence inasmuch as it is inherent in the principles themselves. This tradition is therefore only a determination of the necessary and universal one Tradition in which divine wisdom has manifested itself since the birth of mankind, in the varying forms—prophetic or sapiential, ex- or esoteric—which it has donned in order to respond to the differing needs of mankind throughout the diverse cycles of its history.

If, therefore, Bédier judged correctly in qualifying as an "archetype" the unknown source of the multiple offspring of Tristan poems, those limits of literary exegesis to which he confined himself did not permit him to grasp the full scope of this conclusion, nor, moreover, to perceive that the concept of "archetype" is contradictory to that of a fixed text, a particular poem, composed by a particular poet.

In light of the above remarks, the most logical concept appears to be one of a framework of instruction established by an esoteric intellectual *foyer*—that is, an initiatory organization, a framework that may be thought of as a symbolic and doctrinal sketch, accurate enough to serve as guide for the storytellers to whom it is entrusted, luminous enough to claim their adherence, yet sufficiently stripped to allow free rein to their capacity for poetic interpretation.

This concept is, in our view, the only one capable of satisfying the different aspects of the problematics inherent in the Tristan sources. In particular it may be said that, if the works of the third or fourth generation remained fundamentally faithful to the original theme, it is because this theme comprised a secret instruction of self-imposed authority, and that to betray that instruction would have been to lose Tristan; there is a "truth" of Tristan just as there is a "truth" of the Grail.[7]

If, like the Grail narrators, by "truth" we understand a mystery, a principle of spiritual realization, how can there be a "truth" of Tristan? Are we not confronted here by what Albert Pauphilet called "the very type of doomed loves"? Even if the lovers may be excused because they drank the philter accidentally, are we not still dealing with a passionate enslavement, that is, the very opposite of spiritual liberation? Would not the "truth" of Tristan be, in fact, the perfect example of the spiritual disaster to be expected when "reason is made subject to desire"?[8]

This conclusion would certainly appear to be based on common sense. And yet "true lovers," those whom Gottfried calls "noble hearts," know that Tristan and Isolt are mysteriously "saved." The deep fascination of the tale consists in this deliberate ambiguity, in this constant test of intelligence and of faith in the superior essence of love; and it is important, if we are not to be thus led astray, to search for an infallible criterion of discernment. Such a criterion does exist: the divine protection of the lovers, manifested from beginning to end. Contrary to the claims of some, reference to God is no affectation; it occurs at each critical moment, and always to the heroes' advantage, leaving no doubt as to the intention attributed to God vis-à-vis the heroes: they are of the elect, not of the damned. For example, when the lovers are surprised asleep: "Mais, merci dieu, bien demorèrent/Quand il endormis les trouverent"[9] When their rendezvous was observed: "Dex me fist parler prémeraine."[10] When they were surprised by Mark in the forest: "Mais Deus aveit uvré pur vus/Quant trovat l'espee entre nus";[11] the hermit Ogrin: "Quant Dex vos en ot merci fait."[12] By contrast, it is the lovers' enemies whom God disgraces, *although all they do is tell the truth.* And He grants Tristan's prayer when the latter asks Him to ensure the blow intended for them (Béroul, ll. 4468 ff.).

Many such examples could be found among the various narrators. The lovers are so certain of this divine support that they count on it even after being surprised *in flagrante delicto*:

> Mais en Deu tant fort se fiot
> Que bien savoit et bien quidoit,
> S'a escondit peüst venir,
> Nus n'en osast armes saisir
> Encontre lui, lever ne prendre:
> Bien se quidoit par chanp defendre.[13]

This confidence is justified: at the time of the trial by the hot iron, Isolt, before swearing the oath, conceives the idea of being carried across a ford by a disguised Tristan so that she can swear she has never been touched by any man save Mark and that person. And God acquiesces in this fraud: her hand is not burned.

These last two episodes have greatly puzzled commentators. As for the first, some have believed—in defiance of the text—that in claiming judgment by arms Tristan was trusting not in God but in his athletic prowess. As for the trial by the hot iron, some have been reduced to assuming—still in defiance of the letter and spirit of the tale—that it signified a parody aimed at discrediting an outmoded judiciary procedure!

Those who have committed these errors of interpretation have failed to realize that this contradiction between wrongdoing and divine justification is part and parcel of the very fabric of the story, inseparable from its meaning. Without it we might still have a beautiful love story, but we would cease to have Tristan and Isolt and their mysterious election. The truth is that the tale *willed* this rational, moral, and theological impasse. It willed it so as to force the reader either to conclude that God can tell a lie as well as actually cloak sin, or, by an act of abnegation and prostration of the intelligence, to admit that He can do all things, against all morality and all reason, and that, beyond good and evil, His Pleasure, however disconcerting and contradictory it may seem, is invariably the expression of His marvelous and infinite Justice. For the reader this may perhaps open the door of intellective contemplation, of *excessus mentis*, where opposites are reconciled in the higher unity of intelligible Light.

This episode of judgment by the hot iron contains another teaching, conveyed by Gottfried von Strassburg in a passage as celebrated as it is misunderstood:

In Gotes namen grief si'z an
und truog ez, daz si niht verbran.
dâ wart wol geoffenbaeret
und al der werlt bewaeret,
daz der vil tugenthafts Krist

wintschaffen alse ein ermel ist:
er füeget unde suochet an,
dâ man'z an in gesuochen kan,
alsô gefüege und alse wol,
als er von allem rehte sol.

er'st allen herzen bereit,
ze durnähte und ze trügeheit.
ist ez ernest, ist ez spil,
er ist ie, swie man wil.[14]

This is the dubious theology that seems to flow from the facts: since, despite the fraud, the hand is not burned, Christ, or the Word, is a pliant principle which, subject to certain forms being respected, can be bent by anyone for any purpose. But Gottfried is not that faulty a theologian. His true doctrine lies concealed in the subordinate clause *dâ man'z an in gesuochen kan*. The Word bends and seeks only for the one who seeks It and bends according to Its will, that is, conforms to It, in accordance with the esoteric interpretation of certain passages in the Gospels such as Luke VI, 40: "The disciple is not above his master: but everyone that is perfect shall be as his master," or, will not be distinct from his master. This is the doctrine of identification through cognition.

Seen from this perspective, the idea of having herself carried across the ford by Tristan is no more than a subterfuge: this innocent contact was necessary in order that the oath—already valid in spirit if the Queen's contact with Tristan had never been guilty—also be valid in the letter; and deceitful though it is on the human level, it is no less veracious before God, with the transcendent truth of this love. Hence the implied vice in the oath's ambiguity resides neither in God nor in Isolt: it is in the blindness of men, who judge according to appearances and their own nature rather than by the divine sign nonetheless visible in this marvel of love.

This marvel will not be understood by Mark until after the lovers' death, when he learns of their secret and of the miracle of the brier that has grown through their tomb. He will say then that, had he but known the story of the philter, he would have given Tristan his wife and his lands, thus belatedly recognizing not only their innocence but also, implicitly, his nephew's higher claim to each, because Tristan had triumphed in his quest for Isolt and liberated Cornwall by himself alone.

This interpretation is corroborated by the fact that it is on Mark, according to Gottfried and other narrators, that the dishonor of the situation falls: "And who is to blame for the life so bare of honour that Mark led with Isolde?—for, believe me, it would be very wrong of anyone to accuse Isolde of deception! Neither she nor Tristan deceived him. He saw it with his own eyes, and knew well enough, without seeing it, that she bore him no affection. . . ."[15] But the narrators, in thus deeming his union with Isolt to be *de facto* null and void, nevertheless do not question—any more than do the heroes themselves—the consecrated legitimacy of his claim as spouse and king. This union, too, is desired by God, and the entire tragedy lies in this conflict of two principles of legitimacy existing on different levels.

But the story tells us that Isolt was pure: if there had been the least trace in her of *profane* love for Tristan, her hand would have been burned.

This leads us to a consideration of the philter, the agent responsible for the unfolding of the adventure from the moment Isolt was won. The first thing we note is that, brewed but once, for but a single occasion, it is also unique in its property of indissoluble unification, which persists even beyond death, as witness the miracle of the brier. This links it to the Hindu *amrita* or "potion of immortality." But the latter is of a purely celestial nature, said to issue from the eye in Shiva's forehead, whereas the philter has a dual nature, both celestial and terrestrial, *yang* and *yin* (to use the Taoist terminology): *yang* through its unitive and enlightening function, *yin* through its passionate and compulsive power. This *yin* or substantial side is underlined by its vegetable origin (it is an "herbal wine") and the fact that it has been concocted by Isolt's mother. It also appears in its character of blind passion, able to act on any two partners, the ultimate choice of these being solely in the hands of Destiny.

This dual nature is conveyed by the ambivalence of its power, sometimes as an "elixir of life" and of happiness, sometimes and simultaneously as a "poison," an agent of destruction and death. From beginning to end of the adventure, the lovers never cease to experience that coincidence of bitterness and sweetness, of suffering and joy, of death and life, as of two forces apparently opposed but in reality complementary, bidden to find equilibrium in the fulfilment of their love and thus of their inmost selves: not by neutralizing but by reducing their polarity to the pure unity of their common Principle, where essence and substance, act and power, coincide, and which is in fact Beatitude.[16] In each of the two lovers this realization will be expressed by the blossoming of his or her own nature, which entails integration with its complement; thus perfect femininity comprises an aspect of activity or spiritual "virility," and perfect virility an aspect of passivity respecting the Principle—in other words, wisdom.

So we see that what has led up to the predestined drinking of the philter is a process of identifying cognition through reciprocal integration, which is the true reason for the indissolubility of this union. And if it has divine approval, this is because it is a correlate of the cognition of the Principle.

This dual force, essential and substantial, celestial and terrestrial, must not be thought of as acting in a uniform manner throughout time. It is only in perfect union that its two inverse and complementary determinations find their equilibrium in that state of blossoming and dynamic repose that constitutes Beatitude. In the very process of unification—assuming a normal development—the reciprocal play of these two forces with an eye to their future equilibrium is expressed by an alternating and balanced predominance of each, as in every process of manifestation. Such is the teaching of all traditional doctrines, and especially of the Taoist *yin-yang* theory, or of alchemy in terms of the dual nature and dual motion of ascension and "descension" of the Philosopher's Stone. This is the universal process of evolution and involution, birth and death, *aspir* and *expir*, diastole and systole, *solve* and *coagula*.[17]

With this fundamental concept we have the key to the destiny of Tristan and Isolt from the moment they drink the philter. Indeed, in every version (aside from a few variations in detail) their destiny unfolds in two series of tests culminating on the one hand in the life of hiding in the Wood of Morrois and on the other in death, when Tristan, wounded, despairing of Isolt's arrival, relinquishes his hold on life, and Isolt, arriving too late, in turn dies in a kiss on the body of her lover. These two phases correspond to the two modes, equally necessary, of the knowledge of love through life and through death; for, as Gottfried says at one point, each is the "life" and "death" of the other, so that each must be known by turns as such to the other. This links up with the traditional teaching according to which, just as each state of manifestation is the fact of a *solve* and a *coagula*, so each spiritual realization—that is, each passage to a higher state—implies an inverse process of *coagula* and *solve*, or of "fixation of the volatile" and "volatilization of the fixed," or, again, of the "embodiment of the spirit" and the "spiritualization of the body." This is the fundamental and mysterious process of all initiatory realization.

The life led by the lovers in the Morrois after their flight or banishment shows traits of the first of these phases: it is life in the fullness of union, at last without alarm or hindrance, where all things, even misery, are transfigured. Thus Béroul:

Aspre vie meinent et dure.
Tant s'entraiment de bon amour,
L'un por l'autre ne sent dolor.[18]

In Gottfried's more elaborate version this life is described with characteristics that situate it clearly in the center of the human, or adamic, state: the two lovers epitomizing in themselves, complementarily and in terms of the respective prototypes of Man and Woman, the two modalities, masculine and feminine, of the whole Man, "created male and female," the primordial androgyne or "true man" of several traditions. An allusion to the Round Table—the esoteric fixing of the

Center of the World in the Arthurian domain—shows that Gottfried was plainly conscious of the initiatory implications: "Their high feast was Love, who gilded all their joys; she brought them King Arthur's Round Table as homage and all its company a thousand times a day! What better food could they have for body or soul? Man was there with Woman, Woman there with Man. What else should they be needing? They had what they were meant to have, they had reached the goal of their desire."[19]

The crucial moment of this episode is when Mark surprises the lovers asleep with Tristan's sword between them. This is the moment when the tide of the story "slackens" and is about to turn. It represents, in fact, that state of repose and blissful resorption through the perfect balance of *yang* and *yin* in unity, where they "are fulfilled" in reciprocal complementation. The two-edged sword separating and uniting them expresses this mystery while concealing it: it bespeaks a distinctiveness without merging which is but that of their perfect complementarity, where their supernatural union finds reflection. The sword symbolizes the Axis of the World binding every state of Being to the divine Principle, the "middle way" of Taoism, the "vertical way" of Islamic esoterism, at the center of the human state where all complementaries unite, all oppositions are resolved, and where, through the "strait gate" of its unitive centralization, the human being can pass to the higher states. This "strait gate" corresponds to the center of the cross, of which the sword is a frequent image—primordial symbol of the hierarchy of the states of Being, of their expansion and their resorption starting from the various levels of the Axis of the World. In at least one of the Tristan versions, the *Tavola Ritonda*, this assimilation of the sword to the cross is more than hinted at: "sempre che Messer Tristano dormia, sempre tra lui ed Isotta si mettava la spada sua ignuda in segno di croce."[20]

This symbolism is further underlined by the ray of sunlight piercing the roof of the leafy shelter (or of the cave, according to the versions that follow Thomas), thus irradiating Isolt's face. It is easy to see in this the image of the divine beam, both of Light and Love, descending into the initiatory Cave or the Cave of the Heart. It is reflected in the feminine face because this face is, in this world, the mirror *par excellence* of transcendent Grace or Wisdom; and it will be remembered that the Welsh form of the name Isolt, "Essylt," is said to mean "spectacle" or "place of contemplation."[21] But it may be more precisely claimed that it is because of Isolt's "mercurial" function in the pair. In this connection Gottfried alludes to "two radiances blending their light," one emanating from the sunbeam, the other a property of Isolt's face. We can see in the latter the "animated mercury" of the Hermetists, the "ignited water" or "liquid fire," "inasmuch," says René Guénon, "as [this mercury] is subject to the action of sulphur," which "exert [its] dual nature and causes it to pass from power to the act."[22] As for the ray of sunlight, its epiphanic character is clearly marked by certain texts, for example the Berne *Folie Tristan*: "Li rai sur sa face luisoit/ Moult faisoit Deus ce qu'il vouloit"[23]

Mark had come to strike. But, confronted by these three signs—the naked sword, Isolt's shining face, and the chasteness of their attitude—his arm dropped. Narrators attribute this change to a variety of emotions: doubt, pity, returning tenderness, repugnance at killing the sleeping. But the dominating factor is the shock and his subsequent behavior, which conveys his confused intuition of the mystery, his respect for it but also his refusal to accept it. He substitutes his sword for Tristan's, removes the wedding ring from Isolt's finger, interposes his glove (or a tuft of grass) so that the sunbeam will not burn the Queen's face. And with that he leaves.

Jean Marx has rightly pointed out that these gestures, analogous to those of an investiture, represent a "taking of pledges," and that through them Mark reaffirms his rights as spouse and legitimate suzerain, symbolically restoring his nephew to a position of obedience and the Queen to his seisin.[24] We may add that with Tristan's sword, the same that had killed the Morholt, he is trying to appropriate for himself the heroic strength and potency it symbolizes, and that the interposition of the glove corresponds to a more or less conscious intention to block out the invisible Light. All these gestures, precisely because of their symbolic value, possess a certain intrinsic efficacy. The fact that they were possible, and even the fact that the pair could have been surprised, makes it clear that the lovers' spiritual realization is not complete or, at any rate, not definitive; that (to use a different terminology, for instance, the technical one of Islamic esoterism) the lovers' condition is *hâl* (temporary "state") rather than *maqâm* (permanent "station"). While it is true that they have reached the Center of the human state, they have nevertheless not passed beyond it, nor have they broken certain of its ties. They remain under the jurisdiction of their suzerain by divine right, or relapse into that state. This explains not only why they do not for a single instant dispute Mark's rights, but also why they feel themselves bound just as much by his "taking of pledges" as by his clemency, and suddenly become aware—this time suffering from the knowledge—of the negative counterpart of their bliss: their *condition* in this world, a condition of dishonor, destitution, and exile.

And this shock of awareness causes them to accept the return to the world, that is, to duality and separation.

The narrators have been clearly at a loss to explain in some plausible manner this reversal of attitude, although the basic symbolism of the tale requires it. The "common version" attributes it to a limited duration of the philter's potency (Béroul giving it three years, Eilhart four), and modern commentators have not failed to point out the difficulties and contradictions implicit in such a concept. In our opinion the solution is to be found in the dual nature, *yin-yang*, of the philter. Something does indeed abate in the Wood of Morrois: the predominance of one aspect— that of power, concentration, and passion, *yin*—to give way progressively to the predominance of another—that of essence and sublimation, *yang*—which will permit the rupture of everything this love still comprised in the way of individual attachments. This process is the "spiritualization of the body" succeeding the "embodiment of the spirit," to be consummated only by the death of one by the other.

The lovers have long been aware that this death is written into their destiny: "El buevre fust la nostre mort," says Tristan,[25] and Isolt, at the moment of parting: "For when I am orphaned of you, then I, your life, will have perished."[26]

The last part of the tale is merely the story of that long death of which separation and exile are only the premises, a story punctuated by returns, where Tristan, disguised as an old man, a merchant, a leper, a madman, manages to see his mistress again for brief moments that become more and more fugitive and precarious. The most typical episodes of this period are Tristan's marriage to Isolt of the White Hands and the episode of "madness." We will not dwell here on the question of the marriage, except to say that actually it was not a betrayal—the marriage was not consummated—but a solution of despair, since Isolt of the White Hands may be regarded as a substitute, or rather as an attenuated reflection of the radiant reality of which Isolt the Fair is the incarnation. Their situation may be likened to that of the *Dona Gentile* for Dante in relation to Beatrice in the *Vita Nuova*, with somewhat comparable initiatory significance.[27]

But let us pause for a moment at the episode of "madness." Because of Tristan's calculated boldness in his role of madman and the extreme lucidity he displays in it, it has long been interpreted as a straightforward simulation. However, there is one version, that of the prose romance, in which Tristan appears genuinely deranged. Jean Marx has very properly drawn our attention to this version, pointing out its analogies with the spell-induced madness of certain heroes in Irish tales, and likening it to Lancelot's madness, Perceval's loss of reason after his first failure at the Castle of the Grail, and Merlin's prophetic madness. He is inclined to think that the motif of the madness-stratagem presented in the short poems of both the Oxford and the Berne *Folie Tristan* is actually a derivation from the more ancient motif of genuine madness, "based on an interpretation of a literary nature."[28] This observation seems very accurate to us, with the reservation that it is not, in our view, a case of mere "literary" interpretation but of exampling that conversion of symbolism in a more directly initiatory sense, of which we spoke at the outset of this essay and which, we believe, is at the very basis of the formation of the Matter of Britain.

The vital point is that, before Mark and his court, Tristan disguises his appearance but not the truth. On the contrary, he reveals it, for the first time and concealing nothing, at the risk of his own life and Isolt's. He is driven to do so, not by the needs of his stratagem, which demands no sort of public disclosure whatever, but by a force superior to all prudence and all reason, and it is here in fact that his "madness" lies. This madness is an intoxication, as Tristan himself says: "Vers est, d'itel baivre sui ivre,/Dont je ne quid estre délivre,"[29] but a perfectly lucid and controlled intoxication that is the opposite of dementia: a higher state of consciousness through transcendence of self, in short, an exalted wisdom. And this wisdom hides beneath the mask of madness in order that the truth of the mystery with which it is filled may find its voice. In finding its voice this truth passes for incoherence and scandal, precisely because it is the truth.

This moment of truth is more than a judgment upon Mark and the world: it is also a test for Tristan, who would not have won this mortal wager had he not been able to deny himself totally, and for Isolt, called upon to recognize her lover, despite the most revolting appearances, by the mere ring of truth in his words. "Why this cruel game?" wonders Joseph Bédier à propos the scene where Tristan, alone with Isolt, far from revealing himself insists on having her recognize him in his madman's guise, that is, his madman's "state." This is the game of what Dante called the *intelletto d'Amore*, the pure intuition of the Love-Light that knows immediately in itself, by itself, and for itself alone. It is the game, not of Tristan with Isolt, but of Love with itself, in two creatures it has chosen so that they should live by it, and soon die by it.

When Tristan—wounded, falsely informed that the sail was black—believes Isolt will not come, he ceases to cling to life. Isolt, before she too dies, kissing her lover's lips, says: "Since love has been between you and me in life, well may it also be in death."[30] And by her death she shows that this does indeed mean: "Since love has been the principle of our life, it is also the principle of our death." Here again this operative ambivalence is enough to prove, metaphysically, its transcendence: just as the lovers' active adherence to this principle is enough to make of this final act not—as has sometimes been believed and as Dante apparently desired—the termination of a moral and spiritual disaster that would consign them to the infernal circle of carnal passion, but the bodily expression of their initiatory death which, in reality, is a joint victory over life and death because it is the active solution of the existential duality into its quintessential unity.

This triumph of Love over life and death is what the tale wishes to convey with the miracle of the brier.[31] And the chapel erected between their tombs serves to confirm the significance of this miracle and its potency. The chapel corresponds to that sword of old in the Morrois; it too is a *segno di croce.*

These two signs tell us that Tristan and Isolt, throughout their tribulations and despite their errors and faults, were in truth the chosen and faithful witnesses to that mystery of Man and Woman whom God made *one* in His image,[32] that is, the direct expression of His Reality and a sign of their supreme vocation. This is the mystery of the unconceivable Love in which divine Essence and Nature, the Spirit of God and His Wisdom, the beginning and end of universal manifestation, are united. This is the mystery actualized by Tristan and Isolt in the reconstitution, by their life and their death, of the prophetic couple, Adam and Eve, before the Fall. But in so doing they signified what this actualization presupposes: the full realization of the interior couple that all men by nature carry within them in germ-form and of which the well-balanced flowering is absolutely essential to all spiritual development, as is variously taught by all traditional doctrines.[33] However little we may know of universal symbolism—the true and inexhaustible language of these doctrines—it is not hard to see that the totality of the adventure is in fact conceived as consequent upon that internal or microcosmic interpretation. Thus the gifted child, orphaned and deprived, visibly represents the exiled initiatory germ at the heart of a nature he has to conquer, that is, to transform. The victory over the Morholt represents the emancipation of the soul in relation to inferior elementary forces (the *tamas* of the Hindus), while the victory over the dragon is the triumph of the that-self transcending the individual this-self. And as we have seen, the Tristan-Isolt pair represents not merely the spirit-soul pair, but also in a more general way the microcosmic determination of universal Essence and Substance, the sulphur and mercury of the alchemists, the True Man which reunites in himself the influence of Heaven and Earth, placing himself between them as Mediator.[34]

So we can see why Gottfried could say of them: "Their life, their death are our bread. Thus lives their life, thus lives their death. Thus they live still and yet are dead, and their death is the bread of the living."[35] And we can understand that passage in certain manuscripts of the prose romance: "C'est amors et plus qu'amors de Tristan et d'Iseut la roïne de Cornouaille.[36]

[*Translated from the French by Lelia Vennewitz*]

Notes

1. Joseph Bédier, *Le Roman de Tristan par Thomas, Poème du XIIe siècle*, (Paris, 1902–1905), v. II, p. 186.
2. Joseph Loth, *Les Mabinogion* (Paris, 1913), v. 1, p. 42.
3. Albert Pauphilet, *Le Legs du Moyen-Age* (Melun, 1950), p. 109.
4. The following conclusion of Jean Frappier on this point may be considered that of most scholars: "Nothing, in any case, enables us to consider as illegitimate or illusory the reconstitutions attempted by such critics as Golther and Bédier, comparing the preserved versions. Though unable to seize in its perfect continuity an unique archetype, they succeeded at least in finding out a framework, the machinery of which corresponds to a definite concept of the *Tristan*," *Vues sur les Conceptions courtoises dans les Littératures d'Oc et d'Oïl*, in *Cahiers de Civilisation médiévale*, Poitiers, April–June 1959, pp.151–152 (author's transl.).
5. "A *geis* is a sort of a charm; the perpetrator of it uses it to work his will upon the victim, and the victim must obey or suffer unfortunate consequences." From Sigmund Eisner, *The Tristan Legend: A Study in Sources* (Evanston, 1969), p. 102, n. 56.
6. St. Thomas, *Contra Gent.*, lib. II, LV: "Intelligibile est propria perfectio intellectus; unde intellectus in actu et intelligibile in actu sunt unum.
7. We could not enlarge on the sources, nature, and fate of this esoteric current without embarking on a number of hypotheses for the discussion of which this is not the place and in which, moreover, the Tristan problem is inseparable from the vaster one of the Matter of Britain. Some of these hypotheses have been alluded to in our *L'Islam et le Graal* (Paris, 1957). But we may note at least one interesting point to which A. T. Hatto has drawn attention in the Introduction to his English version of the *Tristan* of Gottfried von Strassburg (Baltimore, 1960, p. 16), i.e.,

the likening of the doctrine of Gottfried's *edelez herze* to that of Guido Guinizelli's *cuor gentile*. This similarity assumes its full importance when we recall that Dante considered the latter his "father" and the father of the *Fedeli d'Amore* (*Purgatorio*, XXVI, 97 ff.).

8. *Inferno*, V, 37. This thesis seems to possess the authority of Dante, who places Tristan in the second circle of Hell, that of the carnal sinners. But he is there in the company of such fabled characters as Paris, Achilles, Helen, and Dido. It is clear that Dante has only taken him here for one type of lover among others, considering the negative aspect permitted, generally speaking, by the dual sense of symbols and, more precisely, the apparent ambiguity of the character. To whom better than to Tristan and Isolt might be applied the admirable line he places in the mouth of the pathetic Francesca: "Amor condusse noi ad una morte . . ."? It seems impossible to believe that, if Dante really knew their legend, he would have failed to appreciate the real meaning of their love.
9. "But, thank God, well remained, when asleep they found them," Thomas, Cambridge ms., ll. 6–7.
10. "God made me speak first," Béroul, l. 352.
11. "But God had been working for you when [Mark] found the sword between us," Oxford, *Folie Tristan*, ll. 881–82.
12. "When God had shown mercy on you for that," Béroul, l. 2380.
13. But on God [Tristan] so strongly relied / That well he knew and well believed, / If he could come to justification, / No one would dare to take up arms / Against him, raise up nor seize; / He was confident he could well defend himself in the lists, Béroul, ll. 813 ff.
14. Gottfried, ll. 15735–48: "In the name of God she grasped it, carried it, and was not burned. Thus was made manifest and proved to all the world that Christ, in His great virtue, is pliable as a windblown sleeve. He bends and seeks, when one is capable of seeking Him, pliantly and well, as He is bound to do. He is ready [for] all hearts, whether in honest deeds or deceit. Be it earnest, be it play, He is ever as one would have him," author's translation of text in Wolfgang Golther, *Tristan und Isolde von Gottfried von Strassburg* (Berlin-Stuttgart: Deutsche National-Literatur, Verlag W. Spemann, s.a.), pp.15, 35–48. It is hardly necessary to stress the importance of the inaugural invocation, *In Gotes namen*, which solemnly consecrates the ritual nature of the ordeal and testifies that Isolt places her life and honor in God's hands.
15. Hatto, *Tristan*, p. 275.
16. Compare this with the Hindu doctrine of the coincidence of *sat* (being) and *chit* (consciousness) in *ananda* (beatitude).
17. See René Guénon, *La Grande Triade* (Paris, 1967), 2nd edit.
18. "Rough life they lead and hard. / They love one another with such good love (that) / No one for the other's sake feels any pain," Béroul, ll. 1364 ff.
19. Hatto, *Tristan*, p. 263.
20. "Whenever Sir Tristan slept, he always placed between himself and Isolt his naked sword in the sign of the cross," Polidori ed., p. 245 (translator's translation). On this symbolism see René Guénon, *Le Symbolisme de la Croix* (Paris, 1931), new edition, Collection "10/18," Union Générale d'Editions (Paris, 1970).
21. Cf. Francisque Michel, *Tristan, recueil de ce qui reste des poèmes relatifs à ses aventures*, (London and Paris, 1835), introduction, p. xlix.
22. René Guénon, *La Grande Triade*, p. 105.

23. "The beam was shining on her face. / Much was doing God what He willed," *Folie Tristan*, Berne, ll. 203–4.
24. Jean Marx, *Nouvelles Recherches sur la Littérature Arthurienne*, (Paris, 1965), pp. 289 ff.
25. "The drink was our death," Thomas, Douce Ms., l. 2495.
26. Hatto, *Tristan*, p. 282.
27. *Vita Nuova*, XXXV to XXXIX. In this connection we may note that the beauty of Gottfried's Isolt shares, with that of Beatrice, the unique virtue of *beautifying* those who approach it: "whoever looks Isolde in the eyes feels his heart and soul refined like gold in the white-hot flame; his life becomes a joy to live. Other women are neither eclipsed nor diminished by Isolde. . . . Her beauty makes others beautiful. . . ." Hatto, *Tristan*, p. 150; cf. *Vita Nuova*, XXVI, l. 11.
28. Jean Marx, "Quelques remarques sur un passage du Roman de Tristan en Prose et sur ses Analogies avec des récits celtiques," in *Annuaire de l'Ecole Pratique des Hautes-Etudes*, 1954–55 (Paris, 1954).
29. "It is true, from such a drink I am drunk, / That I believe I never will be set free from it," *Folie Tristan*, Oxford, l. 461.
30. In J. Bédier, *Roman de Tristan*, "Extraits des parties anciennes du Roman en prose."
31. Prose romance: "Out of Tristan's tomb there grew a fair brier, green and leafy, rising higher than the chapel; and the end of the brier reached down onto Isolt's tomb and entered it. . . . The king caused it to be cut down three times; on the morrow it was as beautiful and in the same state as before. This miracle was upon Tristan and upon Isolt," translator's translation of the text in J. Bédier, *Roman de Tristan*, and Pierre Champion, *Le Roman de Tristan et Iseut* (Paris, 1958), p. 169. In the *Saga* the brier is replaced by two oak trees "or other trees"; in the *Tavola Ritonda* by a vine; in Eilhart, by a vine and a brier that cannot be separated and that draw their strength from the potency of the potion, *daz machte des trankes kraft*.
32. Genesis 1: 27; 2: 24.
33. As we have seen, this germ is the *yin-yang* in an enveloping state, or the Philosopher's Stone of the Hermetists. It is also the "immortal kernel," or *luz*, of the Hebrew tradition; or again, *hiranyagarbha*, the Hindu "golden embryo," the spiritual germ enveloped in the *brahmânda* or the "egg of the world" (called *pinda* in its microcosmic determination). This germ identifies with the primordial *avatâra*, the Hindu equivalent of the *Adam Kadmon* or "primordial androgyne." For all these matters we refer the reader to the works of René Guénon, especially *L'Homme et son Devenir selon le Vedânta* (Paris, 1947), ch. XIII and XIX, and *Symboles fondamentaux de la Science sacrée* (Paris, 1962).
34. Cf. René Guénon, *La Grande Triade*, ch. 14. From this perspective, we may add that Mark and Tristan, like the two Isolts, are nothing else than two states of the same being. Cf. Fulcanelli, *Le mystère des cathédrales* (Paris, 1957), p. 134–5 (author's translation): "In fact, uncle and nephew, chemically speaking, are but one thing, of same genus and from same origin. . . . Moreover, let us remark that the queen is spouse to the old man and to the young hero all together, in order to maintain the hermetic tradition which shows in the king, queen and lover the Great-Work's mineral triad."
35. Trans. A. T. Hatto, *Tristan*, p. 44.
36. "It is love and more than love, Tristan's and Cornwall queen Iseut's love," in E. Loeseth, *Le Tristan et le Palamède des manuscrits français du British Museum, étude critique* (Christiania, 1905), p. 23.

Annemarie Schimmel

THE INFLUENCE OF SUFISM ON INDO-MUSLIM POETRY

IN THE GRAND PRAISE-POEM TO GOD WITH WHICH THE INDO-MUSLIM Ghālib (d. 1869)[1] opens his collection of Persian poetry, and which describes the different manifestations of the Divine in contrasting symbols, he calls God—among many other descriptions—Him "Who has kept the lovers in the station of gibbet and rope. . . ." Lovers have to suffer, to undergo martyrdom, if they really deserve this epithet. Modern Urdu poetry in both India and Pakistan has used this expression, *dār u rasan,* "gibbet and rope," in many progressive poems, and it became a commonplace to design the lover no longer as a man absorbed in the abysses of Divine Love and willing to be killed by the defenders of religious law, but rather as the man who strives for the realization of his political and social ideals: the progressive, the socialist, the representative of the oppressed classes or races who would gladly seal his message with jail or death, as so many Indian nationalists have done.

This seems to me one of the most striking examples of the transformation of a purely mystical idea into a secular theme. For Ghālib did not invent this symbol of "gibbet and rope"; he himself relied upon a centuries-old tradition which goes back to the hero of Muslim mysticism, Ḥusain ibn Manṣūr al-Ḥallāj, executed—with gibbet and rope—in 922 in Bagdad, allegedly because of his theopathic utterance *anā'l-Ḥaqq,* "I am the Creative Truth," which became the war-cry for generations of later mystics against dry orthodoxy. He was, however, put to death because of a combination, difficult to disentangle, of political, social, and religious charges brought against him.[2]

In order to understand Ḥallāj's outstanding position, and, on the whole, the impact Islamic mysticism has exerted for more than a millenium upon the thought of many a writer and most of the poets from Istanbul to India, a short glance at the history of the mystical movement in Islam seems necessary.

Sufism—so called after the woolen (*ṣūf*) garment which the early ascetics of Islam used to wear—has been explained as an amalgamation of different foreign influences on Islam: Neoplatonic or Christian, Gnostic or Indian, Buddhist or Iranian.[3] In fact, all of these currents have, in later periods, influenced Sufism to a certain extent; but the roots of this movement are found, as L. Massignon has pointed out, in the meditation on the Qur'ān, the uncreated word of God, and the imitation of the Prophet Muhammad. The first generations after Muhammad, who should be rather called ascetics, stressed night-prayer and renunciation—no doubt as a reaction against the growing wealth and luxury in the expanding Islamic empire. They were well aware of the dangers of worldly life, an attitude which led in the following decades to an overstressing of the concept of *tawakkul*, "trust in God," which eventually did not allow any active participation in worldly affairs. On the other hand, the woman saint Rābi'a al-'Adawīya (d. 801 in Basra) introduced the theme of pure and disinterested love into the puritan atmosphere of early asceticism, and taught that man should love God, without hope for Paradise or fear of Hell. This idea of love was developed later in most delicate details, but formed also a stumbling block for the orthodox theologians who considered obedience the only possible form of man's relation to God. Love, and mutual love, between Lord and servant seemed to them impossible.

However, the mystics continued along this line: the ninth century produced the figure of Bāyezīd Bisṭāmī in Khorassan (d. 874) who seems to have been involved in the "negative" way to union with God —a man of towering loneliness whose unitive cry "Glory be to Me" was, in later times, often mentioned with Ḥallāj's *anā'l-Ḥaqq*. And we see the great devotee of Iran, Yaḥyā ibn Mu'ādh (d. 871) with his touching prayers for forgiveness, as well as the many-sided figure of the Nubian Dhū'n-Nūn (d. 859) in Egypt, who is credited with having brought into relief the doctrine of *ma'rifa*, intuitive knowledge of the heart, and whose prayers abound in descriptions of God's beauty and grandeur as praised by everything created. There are the different members of the "school of Bagdad": the sober Muḥāsibī (d. 857) with his meticulous and scrupulous system of merciless psychological control of the "self"; the "lover" Sumnūn; the enthusiastic Nūrī, who set the first great example of true mystic brotherhood by his offering to undergo capital punishment for the sake of his co-Sufis; and, above all, the figure of Junaid (d. 910), prudent and wise—wise enough to discuss the central problem of mysticism only in letters full of allusions. This is the problem of how to fulfil the first and uppermost commandment of Islam, the *tauḥīd* (to declare that God is One), not merely by words but by an existential act of the worshiper. This problem has been discussed and formulated by almost every mystic, and explanations range from a pure act of attaining to complete surrender and perfect union of will with that the Divine Lord, to the idea of love-union, and eventually to an all-embracing feeling which no longer says "There is no god but God," but rather "There is no existent but God," thus reducing the relation Creator-created to the relation of the two aspects of one single Reality which permeates everything and remains still *absconditus*, being immanent and transcendent at the same time.

Ḥallāj—influenced by Sahl Tustarī, who taught that the faithful one is bound to constant repentance, and by Junaid—had traveled through many countries, from India to Turkestan, and was well aware of his outstanding and peculiar position in the Muslim community. His word *anā'l-Ḥaqq* is the expression of one who feels that in the rare moments of ecstasy the Uncreated Divine Spirit speaks through the medium of the created human spirit, thus making man his living witness. His theory of the two natures in God brought him into dangerous proximity to Christian ideas. His poetry and prose are of great beauty, of touching purity, sometimes tinged with symbols of alchemy and kabbalistic wisdom; they reflect the constant tension between the wish for union and its obstacle which is called "I" and which can be razed only through death. That is why he danced in his chains when he was led to the place of his martyrdom. . . .

With Ḥallāj ends the first formative period of Sufism, and his death almost coincides with the end of the glory of the Abbasid caliphate, a time during which Greek science and philosophy had been translated into Arabic, Islamic law had been formed, the traditions of the Prophet been codified, in short, a time during which the whole fabric of Islamic culture as it was known in the West for centuries had been woven together.

In Sufism a period of systematization follows; pious mystics try to reconcile Sufism with orthodoxy and, like Ghazzālī, shape the classical picture of Sufism which became widely accepted.

Other possibilities inherent in Sufism developed in divergent directions. The mystical leader, formerly only a venerable personality, became the *shaikh*, the *pīr*; to obey him is the absolute duty of the disciple —the expression of *perinde ac cadaver* has been used in these circles. Saintworship, theoretically elaborated already by al-Ḥakīm at-Tirmidhī (d. ca. 897) became a living force that attracted the broad masses. In the course of the twelfth and thirteenth centuries mystical fraternities were founded which still bear the names of their founders: the Qādirīya ('Abdul Qādir al-Gīlānī, d. 1166) and the Rifā'īya; the

Suhrawardīya and the Chishtīya whose members mostly worked in India; the Mevlevīya (Whirling Dervishes) and the rustic order of the Bektāshī in Turkey. Others followed. These orders, uniting their followers in a certain ritual, and offering spiritual guidance, were extremely helpful in the dissemination of mystical thought, and even more, it was they who brought Islam into the remotest corners of the borderlands, whether in India, or Africa. The simple faith, love of God and the neighbor, and the emotional aspect of mystical life, like the use of music and poetry, attracted millions of people who would never have listened to the dry expositions of classical theologians or to the logic of the learned doctors of Islamic law.[4]

And, what is more important, in those centuries there grew a mystical poetry, especially in the Persian area, which was to influence almost the whole land between Istanbul and Delhi, and even farther. The early Arabic mystics had expressed their feelings in poetical forms, but it was left to the Persian genius to develop a poetry of extraordinary beauty, be it lyrical or didactic. We still do not know exactly how far the mystical quatrains which are ascribed to Abū Sa'īd ibn Abī'l-Khair (d. 1049) are really his own—there is strong doubt whether they were written by him at all—but they reflect the simple feelings which were prevalent among the mystics of those days. The short form of the *rabā'ī* lent itself perfectly to an aphoristic expression and could easily be memorized. That many of these verses could be ascribed to different authors does not diminish their importance as lovely witnesses to mystical ideas.

On the other hand, the mystical *mathnawī* was elaborated: the didactic poem with rhyming couplets was used, in this capacity, for the first time by Sanā'ī of Ghazna (d. ca. 1131). He invented that loosely knit fabric of associative ideas, where one story leads to a moral maxim, one word in that adage again to a new story, and so forth until we reach, after long digressions—which may be lovely and entertaining, but sometimes also boring—the original story once more. This art was elaborated by Farīduddīn 'Aṭṭār (d. 1220) whose "Manṭiq uṭ-ṭair" ("The Discourse of the Birds") has gained world-wide fame. His other mystical *mathnawīs* are likewise worth reading and meditating upon, and so are his lyrics and his "Biographies of the Saints" which have given the classical form—to return to our first subject—to the picture of the martyr-mystic Ḥallāj.[5] And after 'Aṭṭār comes Jalāluddīn Rūmī (d. 1273) who, hailing from Balkh, settled down in Konya in Central Anatolia; his love for the wandering dervish Shamsaddīn of Tabriz inspired his lyrical poems which he wrote as if they contained his beloved's works—under Shams' name—and which contain almost 30,000 verses of extremely intense feeling; then followed his immense didactical *Mathnawī* that came into existence through the "reflections" of Shams in his later mystical friends.[6] His love found its most spectacular expression in the mystical whirling dance that forms the main ritual in the Mevlevi order, which was organized by his son.

The fact that Rūmī could identify himself so much with the mystical beloved who appeared to him in human form is due to the development of the theories of mystical love which were brought forth in the fascinating accounts of some Persian mystics—of Aḥmad Ghazzālī, the brother of the great theoretician of Sufism, and of his disciple, 'Ainul Quḍāt Hamadhānī, who had to pay with his life for his "heretical" ideas in 1132, just as the young Suhrawardī Maqtūl, the founder of the Illuminationist school, who was executed by the Syrian authorities in 1191. A special role is played by Rūzbihān Baqlī (d. 1209), the visionary and lover who commented upon Ḥallāj's enigmatic sayings and preserved them for posterity. The beloved who is shown in these theories is cruel, not caring for the lover, and is as beautiful and fascinating as he is tremendous (the two aspects of God: *jamāl*, beauty, and *jalāl*, power), but the lover is happy with his fate, obedient, longing for pain and more pain. Once Rābi 'a had said that "Love means to remain at the door of the beloved even if one is sent away," but none of the later mystics would subscribe to this view. Love means to undergo every humiliation provided the beloved wishes it, and whatever he chooses is not only considered good but is received in perfect happiness. Affliction, pain, wounds, death—these are the signs of His love. To indulge in suffering—that is the sign of the lover because he knows that God tries him this way, and the greater the affliction the happier he feels. If Western readers are shocked by some examples of Persian and Urdu poetry because the lover gladly makes his head a ball for the polo mallet of his beloved, they should know that the classical theories of mystical love are concealed behind these and similar metaphors. The poets could go back to the Qur'ānic story (Sūra 7: 171) that when God asked the hitherto uncreated children of Adam, "Am I not your Lord?" they answered in preeternity, "Yes, *balā*." But *balā* means also "affliction," and thus mankind has accepted God's rule and His will to shower afflictions upon those whom He specially loves: "The Prophets, then the saints, and then the others, and then the others," as the Prophetic tradition goes. And Iblīs, Satan—sent away by God because of his refusal to prostrate himself before Adam—becomes the prototype of the true lover of God who has only one object of worship, God Himself, and suffers gladly when God drives him away only "if Thou lookest at me when Thou punishest me."[7]

The idea of the suffering lover is one of the salient features of Indo-Muslim poetry, and we may add that the whole complex of the cruel beloved and the suffering lover is found in all fields of poetry: we may interpret this Beloved as God Himself, as the cruel mistress, as the coy young unbearded boy (in whose beauty many would see a reflection of Divine Beauty according to an alleged saying of the Prophet), as the faithless courtesan, or even as the worldly ruler whose whims were to be accepted without complaint. Thus mystical love-theory and political and social practice are interwoven very closely.

The same is true for the whole poetical mode of expression which is nourished mostly from Qur'ānic expressions and symbols taken from Qur'ānic figures, so that a religious stream flows through the whole imagery of Persian, Turkish, and Urdu poetry even when it speaks of the most worldly things. The Qur'ānic vocabulary is used in strangely profane settings: comparing the face of the beloved to the Holy book, or the beautiful wine in the bottle to Joseph in prison, or the wish to meet the beloved to the desire of Moses to behold God (in either case the answer is *lan tarānī*, "You will not behold me!"), and tens of thousands of other instances.

Let us turn once more to the thirteenth century, the time when the greatest systematic thinker of Islamic mysticism, the Spanish-born Ibn ʿArabī (d. 1240), wrote his voluminous works which formed the foundation and compendium of what has been called Islamic monism, or pantheism—the theory of *waḥdat al-wujūd*, the unity of existence. His philosophy was spread over the Islamic world in a short time and was poetically rendered by many mystics, and thus integrated into popular feeling, covering almost every utterance of the earlier mystics, and interpreting them exclusively according to Ibn ʿArabī's theories.[8]

The two great mystical writers of the thirteenth century, Jalāluddīn Rūmī and Ibn ʿArabī, are the key figures for the development in the following centuries and, to a certain extent, down to our day. One should not forget that, thanks to Ibn ʿArabī's systematization, the veneration of the Prophet, already popular—and theoretically explained in the works of both mystics and orthodox theologians—gained an even more important place in Islamic thought. The Prophet becomes the Perfect Man par excellence, and, as such, an almost half-mythical being who looms large in the religious feelings of his community as the intercessor at doomsday, the mediator between man and God. As such he is reflected in innumerable pious songs in every Islamic language. Only in the last eighty years has a historical approach to his personality been explored in the Islamic countries, beginning in India.

India was partly under Muslim influence from 711, when the Arabs conquered the valley of Sind up to Multan and founded a number of religious centers in the lower Indus valley. The names of scholars in many fields who belong to this area are well-known to Arabists. In the later ninth century, Multan was taken by the Ismailis, a branch of the Shia movement, which may have brought some heterodox elements into Islam in Sind. It is strange enough that Ḥallāj wandered through just that part of India in 905; and still today his name is well known to every villager there: for in the thousand years following his execution, he has been converted into a symbol of suffering love or of the sad fate of those "who openly tell the secret of the King" and have to suffer death at the hands of the orthodox, who are in their turn likewise slaves of the One King—the slaves who have to maintain law and order. It is touching to listen to simple Sindhi singers who praise in beautiful melodies the burning and consuming love of Manṣūr, The Victorious One, as he is often called by his father's name, and a single glance at the large corpus of folk literature in this area shows that there are thousands of allusions to him and to his fate, and that almost everybody who was ready to offer his life for the sake of freedom and love, considered himself a successor of Manṣūr. This feeling is echoed in many verses and in many stories throughout the country.[9]

But this influence is not limited to Sind. We find almost the same expressions in the folk poetry of the Panjab and in Pashto, for the northwestern part of India came under Muslim rule about the year 1000. This rule then expanded toward Bengal around 1300, and to the south at approximately the same period, until the largest part of India was under Muslim rule by the late sixteenth century.

The literatures of Muslim India are composed in a wide variety of languages.[10] First of all, the Arabs brought with them their native tongue, which soon became the vehicle of learned expression in the Indus valley and remained so in all parts of the country which later came under Muslim rule. As the language of the Qur'ān, it was the language to use for commenting upon the Holy Book, for writing on traditions of the Prophet, for expounding the doctrines of Muslim law, and likewise for the *'aqliyāt*, the philosophical sciences, like logic and metaphysics. It was only for a certain time in the Deccan that Arabic was used more as a literary language; in the sixteenth century the rulers of Golconda attracted Arab scholars and literati. Poems patterned on the classical Arabic style, as well as some interesting records of travels and biographical notes, were written in Qur'anic language. Its importance as the theological language has remained unchallenged until the present—to such an extent that some ardent Pakistani Muslims even wanted the language of the Qur'ānic revelation to become the state language of Pakistan.[11]

When Maḥmūd of Ghazna conquered Northwest India at the beginning of the second millenium A.D., he brought both Persian and Turkish elements into the country, and Persian, having reached a first apex in the Shāhnāme of Firdōsī, was to remain the official language of the Muslim courts, and the language of literature in general, till 1835, when the British replaced it by English. Not only the Muslims but everyone who had to deal with them learned Persian, and a number of Hindu writers and poets in this language are known to us. These poets used without difficulty the classical vocabulary of Persian poetry—and that means, to a large extent, of Sufism.

Turkish was spoken by the military forces in India, who were mostly recruited from among Central Asian Turks; and century after century, new groups of Turkish-speaking people came down to the fertile plains from the Central Asian highlands. As a literary vehicle, however, Turkish was used for the first time by the Mughal emperor Bābur, who wrote his famous *Memoirs* in Chagatay Turk—a work which bears in every line the stamp of an unusual personality: warrior, statesman, poet, and mystic in one.[12] Other members of his court, and of smaller courts (e.g., in Sind) followed his example, and even in the eighteenth century Turkish was spoken, and partly written, in many families, Turkish descent being considered most noble. This attitude is, in the nineteenth and twentieth centuries, somehow reflected in the deep interest of Indian Muslims in the fate of the Ottoman Empire and in Turkish politics.

Urdu, having sprung from Indian roots but strongly mixed with Persian and some Turkish elements, grew as a literary language in the Deccan, and Maulvī 'Abdul Ḥaqq has shown that due especially to the influence of the Sufis in the southern provinces, Urdu—first in its Dakhni variety—developed into a literary language. In 1700 on it was adopted, along with Persian, in the North too; and after a short time poets of first rank wrote in this language instead of Persian. It soon was made capable of expressing the finest nuances in poetry, and has played a decisive role in the literary activities of the nineteenth and twentieth centuries.[13]

As to the regional languages of Muslim India, one must take into consideration Pashto—spoken in the North Western Frontier and the adjacent Afghan provinces—an Indo-Iranian language of difficult grammar, which produced, however, interesting examples of mystical and profane poetry, though only little prose.[14] Further there is Balochi, again Indo-Iranian, with an almost unrecorded folk literature which shows interesting traces of popular Sufism.[15] The language of the Panjab, which has been used for mystical expressions since the middle ages and which has become the literary language of the Sikh community, has—on the Muslim side and in more recent form—produced a number of excellent popular poets, all of them mystics, mostly in the seventeenth and eighteenth centuries.[16] The same holds true for Sindhi. Perhaps the richest among the West Pakistani languages, it is grammatically complicated, and contains an immense treasure of folk poetry and popular legends. Some of the finest mystical verses ever written in the world of Islam, as well as, in our days, quite a number of good short stories are written in Sindhi.[17]

Bengali has likewise been influenced for centuries by the Muslim tradition, since the country was under Muslim rule and has still a very dense Muslim population. Bengali folk poetry shows traces from Rūmī's *Mathnawī*, which has been read there by Muslim and Brahman since the fourteenth century, as well as antecedents from the common Islamic stock of legend and tales. It was only in the nineteenth century, thanks to the Hindu revivalist movement and the activities of men like Ram Mohan Roy and later through the influence of Tagore, that Bengali became more closely associated with Hinduism in the Western mind; but since the 1920s, new impetus has been given to Muslim poetry too, and after partition some of the finest Pakistani short stories have been produced by Bengali Muslims.[18]

This is the linguistic situation—to mention only the important traditions and leaving out languages like Kashmīrī (which, however, contains many a legend of Muslim saints, like 'Aṭṭār's famous story of Shaikh Ṣan'ān who became a swineherd out of love for a Christian lady). South Indian languages, likewise, have only occasionally been used by Muslim writers and can be neglected in this study.

It will be clear from the foregoing that the language which attracts our interest first is Persian, and under its influence Urdu. Persian had a fixed terminology and fixed poetical expressions when it came to India, and already the first poets who wrote in Lahore during the later eleventh century—Abū'l-Faraj Rūnī and Mas'ūd ibn Sa'd Salmān—used the language with all its intricacies. But one of the most influential works was Hujwīrī's *Kashf al-Mahjūb* (written around 1050 in Lahore), the first treatise on mystical problems composed in Persian.[19] Its author's tomb is still a place of pilgrimage, and the impact of his book on his contemporaries and on later generations must have been great. He, too, composed a book on Hallāj (which is unfortunately lost) that may have helped in shaping the general attitude towards this mystic.

The thirteenth century was the high time of Persian literature in India not less than in Iran proper, and it was likewise the high time of mysticism from Anatolia and Egypt to Delhi. Members of the great fraternities settled down in India: Bahā'uddīn Zakariya from the Suhrawardī order went to Multan, and was followed by the ardent lover Fakhruddīn 'Irāqī (d. 1289), who is considered one of the best mystical poets in Persian; his illuminating "Flashes" of mystical wisdom have been commented upon in India many times. The strange Lāl Shahbāz took residence in Sehwan, which has been the center of a not very orthodox Sufism; he, too, composed verses which are, like those of 'Irāqī, still recited in the country. Mu'īnaddīn Chishtī chose Ajmer, in the heart of hostile Rajputana, for his residence; from there the Chishtī order branched out north and south. It should not be forgotten that the founder of the so-called slave-dynasty of Delhi, Quṭbaddīn Aibek, was a great admirer of the saint Quṭbaddīn Bakhtiyār Kākī, whose tomb is still a place of pilgrimage.[20] In the Panjab, his disciple Farīdaddīn Ganj-i Shakar (d. 1265) preached and practiced the sincere devotion of the Chishtī order,[21] and his foremost disciple, Niẓāmuddīn Auliyā (d. 1325) took over the spiritual reign of Delhi.

More than any other country, it seems, India was a good soil for mystics. Faithful disciples surrounded the masters, the rulers often were interested in their company, and, what is more important for us here, the disciples recorded the words and deeds of the *shaikh* very carefully, asking him later for correction and approval. Thus, instead of scattered information such as that about earlier mystics, we have detailed accounts of almost all the great saints of Muslim India from the thirteenth century on. However, the literary genre of *malfūẓāt*, "sayings," is not only important because of the mystical teachings contained in these works, but also because of the many sidelights which are shed, through stories and anecdotes, on political and social conditions in certain years and certain places. More than the official historiography, the *malfūẓāt* give an unbiassed picture of life in medieval India, and now and then we find in them a poignant social criticism.[22]

At times, the *shaikhs*, or *pīrs*, would gather their disciples around them and, especially in the Chishtī order, would indulge with them in music. Music and dance have been a controversial subject for the mystical writers, and some of the orders strictly forbid both of them as unislamic, while others permit them. In such meetings the *shaikh* would recite verses, or a singer would be asked to do so, and these verses—sometimes purely mystical but mostly using the vocabulary of profane love—would be repeated by the auditorium, and would become in a short time part of everyday speech, and thus tinge the outlook of the people. We cannot stress enough the fact that in the Muslim countries (especially in the Persian-influenced areas) poetry is the language that conveys what really matters, and that the oral transmission in meetings and *mushāʿiras* makes a good verse spread like fire through the town or the country. A modern poet like Iqbal did not choose in vain the medium of poetry to make his philosophical and theological ideas on Islamic revival known to the public—he is the true successor of the mystics whose songs of divine love brought people into ecstasy, or were repeated over and over again as consolation during the visitations of fate. Men like Niẓāmuddīn Auliyā have deeply influenced the attitude towards life of the average Indian Muslim. Niẓāmuddīn was especially fortunate, since a close friendship related him with the leading poet of his age, or rather, one of the best Persian poets, Amīr Khosrau, a man of Turkish stock, who is by far the most prolific writer in lyrics, epics, and belles-lettres, and is endowed with an almost incredible talent for wordplays, puns, and elegant style. To be sure, it is not easy to detect much of Muslim India's mystical wisdom in Amīr Khosrau's verses, and yet a closer look shows how masterfully he has interwoven his apparently worldly poetry with all the concepts that medieval Sufism had developed. His odes in honor of the Prophet of Islam, or those composed for his mystical preceptor, are touching examples of true devotion.[23] Khosrau's younger contemporary, Ḥasan Dihlawī, does not carry the playfulness of expression to such an extent; he is sincere and deep, and each of his lines could easily be memorized, teaching the simple lesson of unconditioned love for the Eternal Beauty.

In the Deccan it was Gīsūdarāz (d. 1422) who first introduced mystical poetry, and he is also credited with having composed the first treatise on an Islamic subject in early Dakhni Urdu. His commentaries on Ibn ʿArabī's *Futūḥāt al-makkīya* and on ʿAinul Quḍāt Hamadhānī's *tamhīdāt* show the direction Sufism was to take in India.

We know from the curricula of medieval Indian schools that a number of important books on Sufism were treated in higher education, and it is only natural that copies of many more books should have come to the Subcontinent with the scholars and the pious who had performed their pilgrimage to Mecca and had met there kindred spirits from all over the Muslim world. We know that the *Mathnawī* of Jalāluddīn Rūmī was known in India shortly after his death; this compendium of mystical teachings in which we can find everything, from lofty pantheism to simple teachings of orthodox Islam has been read and reread in almost every Muslim home in India, since it transforms every thought in the light of divine love. Commentary upon commentary was written for it from the Middle Ages down to the nineteenth century, and the authorities do not hesitate to prefer some of the Indian commentaries to all the rest. Translations into the different regional languages were made, even in our days: we have the *Mathnawī* in Panjabi verses and in Sindhi poetry, part translations in Pashto, and several versified translations in Urdu. Thus the great work became available to everybody (and even the stern Emperor Aurangzeb, enemy of the mystics in general, was moved to tears whenever the *Mathnawī* was recited to him). And even more, the simple meter of this didactic poem has been used hundreds of times in poems which deal with philosophical or mystical problems: the last examples are the *mathnawīs* of Iqbal, *Asrār-i Khūdī* and *Rumūz-i Bekhūdī*, as well as *Jāvīdnāme*, which were written, as Iqbal explicitly states, under the direct influence of Rūmī who is depicted, in the last mentioned work, as the spirit leading the poet through the spheres into the presence of God Almighty.[24]

Rūmī was, no doubt, interpreted by the earlier mystics and poets completely in the light of Ibn 'Arabī's *waḥdat al-wujūd*, the "existential monism," and it is easy to detect traces of this as well as of any other theory in the 26,000 verses of his *Mathnawī*. Iqbal, who had looked at the work from this viewpoint when he wrote his thesis in Munich in 1907, later discovered the dynamic character of Rūmī's teaching, and thus formed a very modern image of him. During the centuries, many stories from the *Mathnawī* have been remodeled by other poets, and many sayings from this work, as well as from his lyrics, have been incorporated into the daily speech of the Indian Muslims. An interesting example is that of the Sindhī mystic, Shāh 'Abdul Latīf Bhitā'ī (d. 1752), who has in his famous *Risālō*—the most touching work of Sindhi poetry—often alluded to Rūmī's sayings, and has even translated them verbally into Sindhī.[25] To put together quotations from the Qur'ān, the Prophetic traditions, the *Mathnawī*, and Shāh 'Abdul Latīf's *Risālō* was not unusual with later Sindhi mystics. And this is not surprising: according to numerous stories whose veracity we need not doubt, there were three books which a mystical leader would definitely possess, namely the Qur'ān, the *Mathnawī*, and the *Dīwān* of Ḥāfiẓ (who, of course, was interpreted mystically). That is why almost everybody was acquainted with Rūmī's verses, and it is impossible to enumerate, for instance, the many allusions to the first lines of the *Mathnawī*, the "Song of the Reed," in profane Persian, Urdu, and related poetry: the poet who praises the power of his reed pen may speak of "throwing fire into the reed bed" (thus combining two allusions from the above-mentioned poem), or may compare his pen to the miraculous reed which sings the touching melody of longing, when he tells his longing for his beloved, or for the kindness of the mighty ruler. A great poet could be called, like the Panjabi Bullhē Shāh (d. 1758), "the Rūmī of Panjab," just as Iqbal earned the honorific title "Rūmī of his age."

But besides the open and hidden influence of Rūmī, that of other Persian mystics should not be forgotten. It seems that the works of Farīduddīn 'Aṭṭār were brought to India very early, for the "Biographies of the Saints" as written by him have influenced the popular imagination much more than other—though more trustworthy—biographical notes on the early Sufis. To take again our model case, Ḥallāj, we find that the Indo-Muslim poets have described his life and fate almost exclusively in terms taken verbally from 'Aṭṭār, and have even gone so far as to see in 'Aṭṭār himself one of the martyrs of love, like Ḥallāj or like Shams-i Tabrīz, Jalāluddīn Rūmī's mystical beloved.[26] Likewise, 'Aṭṭār's "Discourse of the Birds" has furnished Persian and Indo-Muslim poetry with a large number of symbols: the soul-bird, although used from oldest times in its different manifestations for poetical purposes, has been described so aptly in 'Aṭṭār's poem that the poets, when using any bird symbol, would refer—knowingly or not—to his definitions of its peculiarities; the sugar-chewing parrot who is fond of the mirror; the nightingale; enamored by the rose, and so on. His story of Shaikh Ṣan'ān, taken from the same work, has already been mentioned, and still today Ṣan'ān, the mystic who undergoes deprivations and undertakes an apparently unworthy and blameworthy task out of love, is a well-known symbolic figure, not only in religious but also in profane literature; and the expression that he gave away the *tasbīh*, the rosary, in exchange for the *zunnār*, the infidels' girdle, or Brahman's thread, has become one of the favorite commonplaces of almost all Indo-Muslim poets.

The basic themes, as contained in 'Aṭṭār and Rūmī, have been elaborated in India by poets and mystics alike; then, in the sixteenth century, the new influx of Persian poetry strengthened the already existent mystical preferences. Though it would be almost impossible to classify poets like 'Urfī (d. 1595) or Kalīm, the great masters of the "Indian style," as true mystics, their verses are so filled with the classical vocabulary of Sufism that we can by no means discard it.

> Come, oh love, and make me despised by the world, for to hear a few good counsels from non-suffering people is my wish . . .

This line of 'Urfī touches a number of mystical experiences, like suffering in divine love and gladly accepting, even craving for, this suffering; the poet wants to become an outcast, a *malāmātī*, opposed to the "establishment," the guardians of law and order who do not know what love means and always try to counsel the lover. It was because of these implications that this ephemeral poetry appealed to those who heard it, because it evoked an atmosphere which was familiar to them from their very childhood and might or might not interpret it in a mystical sense.

From the late fourteenth century the Qādirīya order became prominent in the Western part of the Subcontinent, and folk poetry there is deeply tinged by veneration for 'Abdul Qādir Gīlānī; his representatives even found their way to the Mughal court where the heir-apparent Dārā Shikōh and his sister became affiliated with the Qādirīya.[27] To Dārā—executed by his brother Aurangzeb in 1659—we owe both mystical poetry and prose, and a Persian translation of the Upanishads which, in turn, was translated into Latin by Anquetil Duperron in 1801 and influenced German idealistic philosophy much more than it fostered an understanding between Hindus and Muslims in seventeenth-century India.

Even the stern school of Naqshbandī mysticism, which reached India in the later days of Akbar and whose representatives fought relentlessly against the emotional stress and the overbearing pantheistic currents in Indo-Muslim thought (which were, of course, strengthened by Akbar's interest in a unification of religious expressions, and his attitude towards the Hindus)—even these Naqshbandī mystics influenced literature to a large extent. The name of the first great poet in Urdu is connected with members of this order: was it not Shāh Gulshan, the Naqshbandī master of Delhi, who was responsible for Walī's coming to Delhi—Walī, who had been the leading figure of Dakhni Urdu poetry?[28] And while Shāh Gulshan never took to writing in Urdu, the son of his beloved disciple 'Andalīb, Mīr Dard (d. 1785), became the first great mystical poet in Urdu. Though his output in Persian poetry and prose is far greater than that in Urdu, his Urdu *Dīwān* is considered rightly one of the finest works in this language: a rare combination of deep thought, intense feeling, and unpretentious expressions; his poetry may be compared perhaps to some of the best poems of his younger German contemporary, Matthias Claudius. His charmingly simple verses can be enjoyed even today, more than many later and more sophisticated poems in Urdu.

I personally think that we can likewise establish a kind of spiritual chain which leads not only from Bedil (d. 1721), whose poetry and prose shows an extremely intellectual approach to mystical ideas, and a most complicated style, but also from the Naqshbandī Sufi Nāṣir ʿAlī Sirhindī—perhaps via Mīr Dard—to Ghālib, who has used in his Urdu *Dīwān* a number of expressions which get their full meaning only when interpreted in the light of the mystical tradition. Even though we do not classify Ghālib among the mystics proper, there is no doubt that he would not have been able to convey his feelings, or rather to make his ideas understandable, unless he had used the traditional imagery of the Sufi poets. A line like this:

> Do not be stingy today with wine because of tomorrow
> for that would express a bad opinion about the cupbearer of the heavenly fountain. . . .

can be interpreted as pure Sufism: "tomorrow" always means, in this context, the Day of Judgment; the cupbearer of the Kauthar, the fountain in Paradise, is the Prophet Muḥammad or, more frequently in the language of Shiite writers—like Ghālib—ʿAlī ibn Abī Ṭālib, Muḥammad's cousin and son-in-law. The poet is sure that his sin—of drinking wine during his lifetime—will be forgiven at Doomsday through the intercession of the Prophet, who will not leave a member of his community in Hell. Ghālib's touching hymns and sighs to the Prophet and to ʿAlī, the Shia *imām*, show that he was probably much more of a mystic than most of his modern admirers would like to admit. Did he not say:

> We mean "coquettery" and "ogling"; but in speech, our aim
> Is not fulfilled without saying "dagger" and "scimitar."
> How much one may speak about the vision of God,
> It is impossible without saying "wine" and "goblet."

And why should he *not* be deeply obliged to the tradition of Sufism?

We saw that Persian poetry in India carried within itself the whole tradition of mystical experience and mystical metaphors, and we may repeat that not only the role of Shāh Gulshan as mediator of Urdu poetry is remarkable, but that Urdu itself, as we mentioned, owes its existence as a literary language largely to the efforts of the mystics. It was they who, in the different centers of their activities—the Panjab, Bijapur, Golconda—wanted to explain the mysteries of divine love and divine grace to the people who flocked around them and who understood neither Arabic, the language of the Qur'ān and of the lawyer divines, nor Persian, the language of poetry and historiography. Thus the mystical leaders had to recur to the vernacular, even if they sometimes thought it necessary to start their book with an excuse for using the popular idiom, but "one should not look at the outward form but to the inner meaning", as Mīrānjī (d. 1496) explains. They composed little songs for their followers, songs which condensed their teachings and which might also be used in musical assemblies. Then would follow the composition of small treatises in the vernacular, mostly rhymed so that they were easy to memorize, and eventually larger books, like *mathnawīs* and, later, prose works. Thus, the language was prepared for adapting itself to higher poetry of non-mystical content. That is how we should see the development of early Dakhni Urdu literature and the other regional languages. It should be remembered that the mystics in every civilization have played a most important role in the development of language—suffice it to mention Mechtild von Magdeburg and her fellow-mystics, or Meister Eckhard in medieval Germany, or Italian mystics of the same time, or Yūnus Emre in Turkey (d. 1321) —thanks to whose genius Turkish almost suddenly flourished into a beautiful poetical language—or, in our Indian environment, the works of the mystics in Sind, the Northwestern Frontier, and Panjab. And it should be recalled that the earliest Sufis in the Arab countries likewise contributed a great deal to the refinement of the Arabic language.[29]

We may see almost the same features in the Pashto-speaking area. Although there are rumors about the existence of a very old Pashto literary tradition, it is not completely clear when Pashto literature in the true sense starts. If we believe Professor Ḥabībī and the *Pata Khazāna*, Pashto poetry has been uttered by many a pious warrior in the first centuries of Muslim rule; but the first reliable sources do not go farther back than the early Mughal period, when Pīr-i Raushan founded his mystical group, fighting against the Mughals, and Akhund Darvāza (d. 1638) composed his works to refute Pīr-i Raushan's "heretic" ideas. Pashto literature culminates a few decades later in the fascinating figure of Khushḥāl Khān Khatak (d. 1689), the warrior poet, whose work shows a blending of religious, even mystical, elements with most worldly affairs.[30] In Khushḥāl we see one of the best examples of a true Muslim in whose veins the joy of life and the trusting resignation to God's will pulse simultaneously. He, the tribal leader—after bitter experiences with his grim enemy, the Mughal emperor Aurangzeb—left to the Pathans a most impressive heritage of poetry in every field. Though some of his family members and other eighteenth-century poets have elaborated exclusively the mystical ideas of classical Persian heritage and translated them into their mother tongue, Khushḥāl Khān too is deeply influenced by the Sufi tradition. For instance, in his *Rubā'īyat*, where he expresses joy and grief in touching, sometimes poignant, verses and teaches morality according to both the code of honor of the Pathans and the Islamic tradition, he sometimes reaches unexpected heights of vision and acknowledges the last wisdom to those who "see through the light of God" and no longer count outward manifestations of wisdom or intelligence. However, his is not the high-soaring mysticism of many of his contemporaries but that kind of practical piety which had been taught by Ghazzālī and by moderate members of the Suhrawardī order. Other Pashto poets write exactly in the strain of the classical tradition of Rūmī, 'Irāqī, and Jāmī, and have adapted the imagery of Sufism to the language of the Pathans.[31]

The situation is slightly different in the Panjab and in Sind. In both provinces contact with the Indian religious tradition proper had been very strong for centuries, and a mystical feeling was, so to say, more "in the air." The first great centers of Sufism in thirteenth-century India were mostly located in these areas, and it was from here that a large number of Hindus were converted to Islam, the mystical and humanistic aspect of which appealed to them and gave them a new freedom as well as a new relation to a personal God. It is quite possible, and has been maintained by some scholars with good reason, that the development of *bhakti* piety in Hinduism is due, at least partly, to the activities of the Muslim mystics who infused into Hinduism a new attitude of love and personal relationship between God and the soul. On the other hand, it is certainly due to Hindu influences that the mystical poetry in Sind and in the Panjab shows some trends which are almost unknown in Arabic and Persian mystical expression. The most important one is the revaluation of women. Arabic classical mystical poetry, most beautifully expressed in the poems of Ibn 'Arabī and his contemporary Ibn al-Fāriḍ (d. 1235), uses the feminine form when speaking of the Divine Beloved; love mysticism was wrapped in the garment of pre-Islamic Arabic poetry—the poet longs for his mistress and wanders in the desert, following her traces.[32] Persian poetry has inherited from the Arabs the story of Majnūn, the "demented one," who seeks his beloved Lailā in the desert, talks with the gazelles, and at last finds himself united spiritually with her. Further there is the semi-historical story of Khosrau, his beloved Shīrīn, and the stone-cutter Farhād who hopes to win Shīrīn by unceasing and intense labor and is, eventually, cheated by King Khosrau. In both cases the object of love is feminine. And even though allusions to these two stories are frequent in Persian and related poetry, one should not forget that in *ghazal*, lyrical poetry, it is almost impossible to define whether the object of love and adoration is masculine or feminine (there is no gender in Persian and Turkish). Faithful to the tradition of Sufism we shall mostly think of the graceful adolescent who has been considered, by many Sufis, a manifestation, or reflection, of divine beauty. Thus, the feminine element is excluded to a large extent from Persian lyrical poetry, which has been, for centuries, the vehicle through which mysticism was made known among the masses. Even Potiphar's wife in her love for Joseph is not as popular with Persian poets as Joseph himself, the manifestation of absolute beauty.

In Sind and the Panjab, however, the poets return to the classical legends and tales of the Indus valley, and refine them into touching symbols of human spiritual experiences. "Our soul is the tragic heroine Hir,", says the greatest exponent of Panjabi poetry, Wārith Shāh (d. 1789);[33] and the story of *Hīr Ranjhā* in the Panjab, the romances of *Sohnī Mehanwal* and *Sassuī Punhūn* in Sind (and partly in the Panjab) are the best examples of this approach. To be sure, already one of the first Urdu poets, Shāh 'Alī Muḥammad Jīv Jān (d. 1515) of Gujerat, had symbolized the soul as bride; but this tradition is not so common in later Urdu which accepted more and more Persian imagery.

Especially illuminating in this respect is Shāh 'Abdul Latīf, the unsurpassed master of Sindhi mystical poetry, deeply influenced by Jalāluddīn Rūmī. He has elaborated old folk tales in such a way that even today everyone will be able to recite his version.[34] There is Sassuī, the girl adopted by a washer family who grows into a lady of famous beauty; the prince of Kachch falls in love with her and stays with her until his family, one night, makes the couple drunk and drags him away. Sassuī, in despair, tries to follow the traces of the camels, but dies in the desert. In the hands of the Sindhi poets, headed by Shāh 'Abdul Laṭīf, this becomes a parable of the soul, lost in this world, united for a short time with her Divine Beloved, but in the sleep of heedlessness—

a typical concept from the Persian tradition—she loses him and has to undergo terrible experiences in the desert until she feels that he lives in her, notwithstanding nearness and distance, and she is eventually united with him in death. There is Sohnī who swims every night to the island in the Indus where her beloved grazes his cattle, until one night her sister-in-law replaces the earthen jar, which she uses as a float, with an unbaked jar so that she drowns in the flood. And there is Maruī, the simple girl who has been carried away to Umarkot by the ruler; she longs for her home and can not be seduced by any worldly temptation. Blackening her face and neglecting all outward signs of beauty she waits faithfully until the prince sends her home to her beloved: the soul, fallen into the tempting snare of worldly affairs, but patiently waiting for the moment of return to the meadows of eternal bliss. Many other female characters are found in Shāh 'Abdul Laṭīf's work: the softhearted fishermaid Nūrī who wins the king's heart by her sweetness and obedience; the proud Līlā who looses her husband because of her greed for wealth; and many unnamed women, like the wife of the seafarer who expects the boat of her husband to return from Ceylon, full of spices; or the lonely wife who sits in the reed hut at the riverside, imploring forgiveness from her husband who will take her back after a time of penitence, and many others.

In no part of the Islamic world has the soul been so completely identified with women. No doubt the Indian legends of Krishna, worshiped and longed for by the *gopis*, may be at work in this tradition, and mystical Sikh literature in the Adi Granth likewise praises the soul in terms taken from the ideal faithful wife who suffers everything from her beloved husband and never turns away from him.[35] The Sindhi heroines, however, are more forceful than all the other representatives of the soul, and we may go back to Rābiʿa, the first mystic to introduce the concept of disinterested love into Sufism, to find a real model for these female characters.

The picture drawn by Shāh 'Abdul Laṭīf on the basis of simple folk tales was repeated and elaborated in the two following centuries, and even in modern Sindhi short stories and in progressive poetry we will definitely find allusions to these heroines of mystical love, and to their death in the search for the Beloved who is, just as in the Persian tradition, both the Beautiful and the Powerful, even the Cruel.

In the Sindhi tradition we have to mention one more name, that of Sachal Sarmast (d. 1826), who wrote in Sindhi, Siraiki (the northern dialect), Persian, and sometimes in Urdu. His Sindhi and Siraiki poetry has a great intensity of feeling. Whereas Shāh 'Abdul Laṭīf conceals his ideas behind the veil of traditional symbols, Sachal Sarmast—"the intoxicated"—speaks out with whatever is in his heart. The great martyrs of Islamic mysticism are his heroes, and Sohnī and Sassuī are placed together with Manṣūr Ḥallāj, Shaikh Ṣan'ān, 'Aṭṭār, and Sarmad, the mystical poet from Dārā Shikōh's court (executed in 1661). He sings the glory of the unity of all things, and eventually sees God in everything, true to the mystical tradition of 'Irāqī and Jāmī: "He is both Manṣūr and the judge who condemns him, He is the Qur'ān and He is the Veda, He is Abū Ḥanīfa [the great Muslim jurist, d. 767] and He is Hanuman.[36]

Verses like these have often induced the reader of Sindhi and Panjabi poetry to believe that here Islam is only an outward shell, and that the whole corpus of mystical poetry in these areas has been formed by adopting Hindu ideas and feelings. We certainly admit that an exchange of thought has taken place and that during the sixteenth and seventeenth centuries some attempts were made to reconcile Islam and Hinduism on the basis of an all-embracing pantheism or monism. The example of Prince Dārā Shikōh is typical of this movement. In provinces like Sind we find the phenomenon that Hindus not infrequently became disciples of a Muslim mystical leader, even without formally embracing Islam. They have sometimes written poetry precisely in the strain of the Muslim mystics, just as the Persian-writing Hindus at the court of Delhi used the traditional material of Persian poetry. They have even written poems in honor of the Prophet of Islam.[37] That a Hindu teacher wrote the first historical biography of Muḥammad in Sindhi in the beginning of our century is no doubt due to the influences of these mystical contacts. It was also the Hindu literati who first commented upon the mystical literature of both Sind and the Panjab and who, quite naturally, tended to explain everything in terms of Hindu mysticism. Poems like Shāh 'Abdul Laṭīf's *Sur Ramkālī*—where the yogis are described in a terminology taken totally from the Qur'ān—were good starting points for these scholars.[38]

However, one aspect should be emphasized again and again in defense of the Islamic character of this literature: the veneration of Muḥammad both in the court poetry and in the folk poetry of these regions, a veneration which makes the literature unmistakably Islamic.

The person of the Prophet became a center of veneration during the first generations of Islam. His behavior, *sunna*, was imitated, and soon his virtues were described and exaggerated. Around 900 A.D. a complete Muḥammad mysticism had been developed, and the Prophet, who did not want to be anything but "a slave to whom was revealed," became the Perfect Man, the mediator between God and man, and rose to almost cosmic heights. His birthday was celebrated, and upon this occasions thousands of lovely poems have been written in the lands of Islam.[39] Each and every collection of poetical works would contain at least one praise-poem to the Prophet, immediately after the opening praise- poem to God—both being of course, strongly mystically tinged. The history of this devotional literature has yet to be written, and here the influence of Sufism on folk poetry is especially worth studying.

Again, Sindhi gives perhaps the best example of this kind of poetry. Not only did the great theologians set out to write long, rhymed stories about the miracles of the Prophet (they rhyme for ease of memorization, but are really anything but poetry), but also school children would learn stories about the miraculous birth and the deeds of Muḥammad, and would have recourse to him as the Intercessor at Doomsday. In a population that is largely illiterate, the influence of these pious and occasionally very beautiful stories on the formation of the mind is incredibly great; thus the Prophet became more and more of a mythological figure over the centuries. His name and often also the names of members of his family were mentioned in folk songs for every occasion; not only were there special short mystical poems called *maulūd* (birthday poems) for him but all the different forms of praise, prayer, petition, and ballads about his miracles are found in Sindhi folklore. At weddings, at a child's birth, in every moment of life, the consoling figure of the Prophet, the Beloved of God, was with the people. A similar love of the Prophet is visible also in Balochi folk poetry, and everywhere in Muslim countries. The same Shāh 'Abdul Laṭīf, who praised the yogis in Qur'ānic terms, wrote what is perhaps the most attractive compendium of mystical thought on the Prophet: in his *Sur Sārang* he describes how the whole world longs for rain and how happy everyone is when the clouds eventually send down signs of divine mercy to quicken the dead earth. Then suddenly he turns to a praise of the Prophet. This is quite logical for anyone used to the symbolism of Islamic mysticism: rain is called "a sign of Divine Mercy," so much so that Anatolian villagers may just say *raḥmet*, "mercy," when they mean rain. Muḥammad, too, has been sent by God "as mercy for the worlds", *raḥmatan lil'ālamīn* (Sura 21:107). Thus to equate his power, which gives life to the spiritually dead, with the summer rain is perfectly justified. Just like a rain cloud the merciful power of Muḥammad extends from Istanbul to India (thus the Sindhi poet); and the comparison was also well known in Urdu and related poetry: Ghālib has called his *mathnawī* in honor of the Prophet "The pearl-bearing cloud," and in one of his Urdu verses he speaks of the cloud of mercy which comes along the sky, and the blisters of its feet which have grown on the long way, turn into pearl-like precious rain drops. (Are we not reminded of the description of the Buddha as a rain cloud in the early Mahāyāna texts?)

The lullabies of village mothers in Pakistan contain words of praise for the Prophet, or his praise can be expressed in the form of a lullaby, or as a *barāmāh*, a poem which enumerates the twelve months of the year and tells what the beloved, or the poet, does during each month. The form is Indian and was used in Persian poetry for the first time by Mas'ūd ibn Sa'd Salmān of Lahore in the late eleventh century. Sindhi, Panjabi, Urdu, Bengali, and rarely Pashto poets have used this form, alternating between the months of the Indian, or Persian, year, and those of the Muslim year, which gave them an opportunity to think of the different events connected with Islamic history: the death of the Prophet's grandson Ḥusain in Kerbela in Muḥarram; the Prophet's birthday in the third month; the birthday, one month later, of 'Abdul Q̣ādir al-Gīlānī, founder of the popular Q̣ādirīya order; the ascension of the Prophet to Heaven; the night of mid-Sha'bān, *shab-i barāt*, when sins are forgiven and destiny is fixed again; the fast in Ramaḍān and the wonders of the *lailat al-qadr*, as described by the mystics; and in the last month, the pilgrimage to Mecca where the poet, faithful to the mystical tradition, wants to see himself offered as a sacrifice in honor of God, or wants to rub his forehead at the threshold of his Beloved, the mausoleum of Muḥammad in Madina. Similar thoughts have been expressed in the *sīḥarfī*, the Golden Alphabet, which is common to all the literatures of Muslim India, and in which the concepts of Sufism, the different stations and stages of the mystical path, have often been explained by the author.

Since for many centuries poetry was practically the only vehicle for influencing the illiterate masses—who have had and still have an incredibly good memory for verse—the importance of these poems can not be overrated. Poetry was the daily bread for millions of people who formed their whole Weltbild according to the picture presented to them by the poets, and the poets—even when they functioned also as news agents in the rural districts—were mostly under the influence of Sufism in one form or another. The population thus imbibed the virtues of mysticism: true love of God, intense hope for the helpful hand of the Prophet, steadfast faith in the mystical leader "who plants the jasmine-plant 'Allāh' into the heart" (Sulṭān Bāhū, d. 1691). They learnt willingness to suffer and even to offer their lives, to accept gladly the afflictions which the Divine Beloved would shower upon them. They sometimes heard the echo of that saying alleged to be of the Prophet: "Mankind are asleep, and when they die, they awake," often repeated by poets of the Subcontinent as this by Mir Dard:

> Woe, ignorant, at the time of death it will be proved:
> A dream was, whatever we have seen, and what we
> had heard, a tale. . . .

And they might listen to the description of human life as a footprint in the desert, soon forgotten. Perhaps this attitude of outward passivity (through strong spiritual aspirations) as reflected in poetry, was the only way to survive in the turmoil of political events in India, as well as in the poverty-stricken villages of faraway Upper Sind or Balochistan.

It may be asked why we concentrate to such an extent upon the literatures of the provinces instead of going back to the mainstream of Persian and Urdu literature, or devoting more time to narrative or epic literature. As for narrative literature, we can mention only a number of romantic, quasi-historical, or completely fanciful epics which were composed both in Persian and, then, in Dakhni and Urdu: here there is little influence from Sufism, and the influence is even less in the new kind of prose literature which came into existence in nineteenth-century Urdu. However, it seems indicative of the general mode of thought that the first successful Urdu story was *Bāgh o Bahār*, or the "Story of the Four Dervishes": the figure of the dervish, the mystic and religious mendicant, has become such a common feature in every kind of narrative literature that there is scarcely a story, fairy tale, or romance in which the wandering dervish, or his Hindu counterpart, the yogi, does not appear at some crucial point to contribute to the disentangling of the threads of the story.

Poetry never discarded the mystical expressions which had been an inherent part of its tradition. The attitude so typical of mysticism—to unite in speech two antithetical expressions and to show by these contrasting pairs either the dialectic movement in creation, or to admit that all the contrasts and opposites are again one in the Eternal One—has given to Persian and Urdu poetry one of its most common rhetorical devices. However, one should beware of interpreting these symbols too literally. Just as Ḥāfiẓ and his followers have often been decried as revolutionaries against the theologians, because they frequently used the contrast Molla-Sufi, or spoke of their preferring *kufr* (infidelity) to

Islam, Urdu poets (and those writing in the regional languages) have made use of these same expressions, even though they were pious Muslims in their daily life.

There is no doubt that both mystics and poets are somewhat outside the pale of orthodox Islam; already the Qur'ān contrasts the poets' vague and seducing words with the simple Prophetic call to God, and Muḥammad called profane poetry, which talked about such illicit things as wine and love, "the spittle of Satan." As to the Sufis, they have considered themselves by no means antagonists of Islam but rather the defenders of living faith, opposed only to the dry legalism of the jurist, and advocating the primacy of experience over tradition.

Since both poetry and mysticism thus stood in a certain contrast to orthodox legalism, and both were mostly concerned with expressing the experience of love, it is easy to understand why even in profane poetry almost every line contains an expression which cannot be evaluated correctly unless its "mystic" root is discovered. This oscillation between inner and outward meaning makes Persian and Urdu poetry so fascinating. A few examples:

> Flee from our ranks, when you are not a man of uproar:
> Someone who has not been killed, does not belong to our tribe.

This verse of Naẓīrī (d. 1612) alludes to death through the hands of the legalists, who kill him who proclaims love openly and thus leads to rebellion. The lines have in our time inspired Iqbal, who uses them for his theory of dynamic love, of martyrdom and resurrection to a higher life. Kal īm says:

> Who has reached [the goal], closes his lips from "How" and "Why"—
> When the way is finished, the caravan-bell becomes speechless.

The caravan-bell leads the wayfarer towards the goal (that is why Iqbal called one of his collections of poetry *Bāng-e Darā*, *Call of the Caravan-bell*); often even the heart of the traveler has been compared to the bell. But every sound and feeling ends in union; there is neither need for the bell, nor will the traveler ask for the waymarks. "Traveler" is, at the same time, the name for the mystic who proceeds on the mystical "path" (*ṭarīqa*), and who is unable to express his feelings once he has reached the Beloved. For the Muslim reader, the image may also recall the story of Majnūn, following the caravan of his beloved Lailā.

Walī, the great poet of southern Urdu (d. ca. 1707), again sings of worldly love in the terms of religious images:

> Who has made his place in the corner of your love—
> For him the torn reed-mat has become the throne of
> Solomon.

Solomon, the king and prophet with miraculous powers, possessed a throne which was borne by the wind; hence his throne has become a metaphor for everything precious. The reed-mat is the typical attribute of the dervish, and has been described, as such, by many a poet; the contrast of ruler and beggar, *Shāh u gadā*, has formed a topic of Islamic mystical and didactic literature for many centuries. In love, both of them are alike; the poor man then is superior even to the king and to the prophets of yore.

The poets long since had accepted the idea—expressed first by Rābiʿa and then by innumerable later mystics in different countries—that it is not Paradise which matters, and that the Houris and castles are nothing to be longed for. (They would even make a pun on the word *quṣūr*, which in Arabic means both "castles" and "shortcoming.") Their goal is the vision of the Beloved, or the never ending way into the fathomless depths of the Godhead, as Ghālib puts it in an unsurpassable way:

> If that is the garden of Riżwān [Paradise] which the ascetic
> has praised so much—
> It is only a rose-bouquet in the niche of forgetfulness of us
> who have lost ourselves. . . .

The "moth and candle" metaphor, first used by Ḥallāj in his *kitāb aṭ-ṭawāṣīn* for hinting at the secret of burning and being consummated in the light of divine glory, has become everyday speech with the poets who no longer even think of the mystical implications of this saying. And the contrast of rosary and *zunnār*, the "infidels' girdle"—probably used for the first time in a larger context by ʿAṭṭār—becomes, for them, no more than a playful way of showing how the black, that is, infidel, curl of the beloved has entangled them like a *zunnār*.

Ghālib is perhaps the last great exponent of this ambiguous style which makes the true rendering of Persian and Urdu poetry into a European language so difficult, if not almost impossible.

The poets following Ghālib in India aimed at a renewal of poetry and art and tried to go back to "nature," to a kind of purposive art as it was inspired by nineteenth-century English poetry. Yet they too are bound to use the expressions coined by the mystics, because only in this way could they appeal to a larger public. Akbar Allahābādī, the grim satirist (d. 1921), contrasted Darwin and Ḥallāj in his famous quatrain:

> Manṣūr said "I am God"—
> Darwin said "I am a monkey."
> My friend mockingly remarked:
> "Everybody speaks according to his understanding."

The proverb, found in Hāfiz' lyrics, is often used in discussing of mystical adepts.

The most splendid example of this continuous influence of mystical imagery on modern poetry is that of Iqbal, who fought relentlessly against the debilitating influence of poetry like that of Ḥāfiẓ; he, who attacked mysticism in the person of its forefather Plato, and thoroughly disliked any kind of pantheistic thought, still used the full vocabulary of the mystics of Islam. He wrote in a letter of 1918:

> By Persian Sufism the enchantment of the heart, beauty and glamour have appeared in literature, but in such a way that human nature is debased by it. In Islamic Sufism there appears power in the heart, and the effect of this power also shows itself in literature.

To be sure, Iqbal changes the meaning of some of the main concepts of Sufism, like that of Ḥallāj's *anā'l-Ḥaqq*, or the *baqā* (remaining in God), but his poetry is only intelligible if one knows the whole tradition behind it. He tries to go back through the thick crusts of pantheistic or monistic interpretations which had changed the person-to-person character of Islamic mysticism (just as similar crusts of commentaries and supercommentaries had hidden the dynamic character of classical Islam and its law); but after having lifted these veils he shows a deep understanding for the issues of early Sufism. His ideal is not *fanā* (annihilation), "which is more dangerous than the destruction of Bagdad" because it leads to the stagnation of intellectual life and moral quest. With this idea he is in agreement with some modern Western critics of later Sufism. "The Sufi has taken the wine of the Day of the Covenant as an excuse for doing nothing," he says in the *Żarb-i*

Kalīm; since the Qur'ānic verse, Sūra 7:171, was quoted not only for accepting every kind of affliction, or for willingly dying at the door of an unattainable beloved, but also for apologizing for the poet's fondness of liquors or other illicit pleasures. Iqbal prefers to see in early Sufism "purity of religious work," penetration of the divine commandments into the Ego. Ḥallāj (as reinterpreted by Massignon) is his model, trying to revive a spiritually dead community; Rūmī, the greatest mystical poet, becomes his mystical leader, comparable to Khiḍr, the saint of the travelers and wayfarers:

> It is time that I reopen the tavern of Rūmī:
> The shaikhs of the Ka'ba are lying drunk around
> the church—

Like Shaikh Ṣan'ān in 'Aṭṭār's story, the Muslim leaders in the twentieth century have become seduced by the charm of Western ways of life.

Iqbal admires the great saints of India, and expects spiritual enlightenment from their descendants; but he violently attacks pīrism, which keeps illiterate people in a state of complete dependency, with the mystical leader exploiting the ignorance of his poor followers. This image of the pīr—and of saint worship as diametrically opposed to the values of modern life and modern society—has also been, by the way, one of the more frequent subjects of modern short stories in Indo-Pakistan after partition: here is a point where, in the negative attitude towards mysticism, the social criticism of the progressive writers finds a most welcome outlet.

Iqbal has put his finger on several wounds of a society which has to live in the modern world and is still filled with medieval thought and feeling; but he is deeply indebted to the same mystical traditions in their classical form. A poem like the *Jāvīdnāme*, the account of his journey through the spheres in the company of Jalāluddīn Rūmī, bears in every line the stamp of the Sufi tradition which has described spiritual experiences under the symbol of an ascension since the days of Bāyezid Bisṭāmī. The use of the profession of faith *lā ilāha illā Allāh*, "There is no god but God," in this book is likewise revealing: both the Russian bolsheviks and the German philosopher Nietzsche are said to have remained in the *lā*, the "No," by negating the inherited systems of Capitalism or of Christianity, but neither of them has reached the stage of *illā*, of affirmation that there is a God, the Ruler of the Universe.[40] This way of using the basic formula of Islam is often found in earlier mystical tradition. Iqbal's meditations on the two levels of time, though influenced by Bergson, essentially go back to a favorite mystic expression, according to which the Prophet said: "I have a time with God to which even Gabriel who is pure spirit has no access"—the "Time without time," the moment when the mystic completely breaks off the "infidels' girdle" of created and therefore serial time—this central idea of Iqbal's is much closer to traditional Sufism, where many definitions of *waqt*, "time," or the moment of rapture, are found than in European systems of philosophy.

Examples could easily be multiplied; however, suffice it to show that even a reformer-poet like Iqbal, who seems at first to be an antagonist of "mysticism" (in the sense of unorthodox branches of Islam), is dependent upon this tradition much more than is visible from his use of the traditional symbols of Molla versus lover, Islam and *kufr*, and so on.

And in our day we still see that whole phrases of mystical expressions are used in poetry collections and in poems and that even the most progressive poet cannot help using some of them, though in a secularized manner. Even these progressive writers will probably feel a certain predilection for the mystical approach to religion rather than the orthodox interpretation, so that Ḥallāj and his *dār u rasan*, "gibbet and rope," have still a certain fascination for them. To prove this, however, a long and careful analysis of the vocabulary and style of modern writers in Urdu, both in India and Pakistan, and of writers in the regional languages would be necessary.[41]

Notes

Most of the literature used for this article is in Persian, Urdu, Sindhi, Pashto, Turkish, and other languages; we found it useful to include in the notes only those works which are available to the general reader in English, French, or German.

1. Mirzā Asadullāh Ghālib (1797–1869) is considered the greatest Indo-Muslim poet; he wrote both in Persian and Urdu. Cf. Ralph Russell and Khurshid ul Islam, *Ghalib, Life and Letters* (Cambridge, 1969). Unfortunately, no attempt at translating Ghālib's poetry into English has been successful.
2. Cf. L. Massignon, *La Passion d'al Hosayn ibn Mansour Al-Hallaj, martyr mystique de l'Islam* (Paris, 1922), 2 vols; A. Schimmel, *al-Halladsch, Märtyrer der Gottesliebe* (Cologne, 1969), with a large bibliography.
3. The best short introductions to Sufism are G. C. Anawati and L. Gardet, *Mystique Musulmane,* (Paris, 1961); R.A. Nicholson, *Studies in Islamic Mysticism* (Cambridge, 1923); and A. J. Arberry, *Sufism* (London, 1950).
4. Cf. Sir Thomas Arnold, *The Preaching of Islam* (London, 1913, Lahore, 1945).
5. Cf. Hellmut Ritter, *Das Meer der Secle* (Leiden, 1955).
6. Cf. R. A. Nicholson's (ed. and trans.) commentary on the *Mathnawī*, Gibb

Memorial Series (London, 1925–1940), 8 vols. Rūmī's first mystical beloved, Shamsuddīn, disappeared (probably murdered by jealous disciples of the master); in later years, Rūmī found new manifestations of the Divine Beloved in Salāḥuddīn Zarkūb and Ḥusāmuddīn Chelebī, who inspired the *Mathnawī* just as Shamsuddīn inspired most of his lyrics.

7. Cf. L. Massignon, *al-Ḥallāj, kitāb aṭ-ṭawāsīn* (Paris, 1913); Schimmel, *al-Halladsch*, pp. 81 ff.
8. About Ibn 'Arabī see A. Affifi, *The Mystical Philosophy of Muhyd'-Din Ibn al-'Arabi* (Cambridge, 1939); H. Corbin, *Creative Imagination in the Sufism of Ibn 'Arabi* (Princeton, 1969); S. H. Nasr, *Three Muslim Sages* (Cambridge, Mass., 1964).
9. Cf. Schimmel, *The Martyr-Mystic Hallaj in Sindhi Folkpoetry*, Numen IX, 3 (Leiden, 1962).
10. Cf. A. Bausani, *Storia delle letterature del Pakistan* (Milano, 1958); Aziz Ahmad, *An Intellectual History of Islam in India* (Edinburgh, 1969); A. Schimmel, *Pakistan. Ein Schloss mit tausend Toren* (Zürich, 1965). For a general survey of Muslim culture in the subcontinent, see I. H. Qureshi, *The Muslim Community of the Indo-Pakistan Subcontinent* (The Hague, 1962); M. Mujeeb, *The Indian Muslims* (Montreal, 1967); Aziz Ahmad, *Islam in Indian Environment* (Oxford, 1964).
11. Cf. Zubaid Ahmad, *India's contribution to Arabic Literature* (Lahore, 1967), and M. A. Mu'id Khan, *The Arabian Poets of Golconda* (Bombay, 1963).
12. Cf. H. Storey, ed. English translation by A. S. Beveridge, *Persian Literature* (London, 1927), vol. 7, pp. 529 ff., gives an account of the whole literature around the *Bāburnāme*; A. Schimmel, "Bābur Padishāh as a Poet," *Islamic Culture*, vol. 36, 1962.
13. There is no satisfactory history of Urdu Literature. Cf. Garcin de Tassy, *Histoire de la littérature Hindoui et Hindoustani* (Paris, 1870); R. Saksena, *A History of Urdu Literature* (Allahabad, 1927); E. G. Bailey, *History of Urdu Literature* (Calcutta, 1932), Muhammad Sadiq, *History of Urdu Literature* (Oxford, 1964).
14. Cf. O. Caroe, *The Pathans* (New York, 1958); H. G. Raverty, *Selections from the Poetry of the Afghans* (London, 1867).
15. Cf. M. Longworth Dames, *Popular Poetry of the Baloches* (London, 1907).
16. Mohan Singh, *A History of Panjabi Literature* (Lahore, 1933); L. Rama Krishna, *Panjabi Sufi Poets* (Oxford, 1938).
17. In the West, most of the pioneer work on Sindhi has been done by the German missionary Ernst Trumpp (d. 1885). Cf. Schimmel, *Ernst Trumpp. A brief account of his Life and Work* (Karachi, 1961). About Sindhi literature in general see Schimmel, "The Activities of the Sindhi Adabi Board," *World of Islam* (Leden, 1956), NS VI, pp. 3–4, and "Neue Veröffentlichungen zur Volkkunde von Sind," ibid., NS IX.
18. Enamul Haqq, *Muslim Bengali Literature* (Karachi, 1957).
19. Hujwīrī, *kashf al-mahjūb*, trans. R. A. Nicholson (London, 1911).
20. For the whole development, see the books mentioned in n. 10 and Yusuf Husain Khan, *L'Inde Mystique aux Moyens-Ages* (Paris, 1928); A. Ghani, *History of the Persian Language and Literature at the Mughal Court* (Allahabad, 1930), 3 vols.; J. Marek, "Persian Literature in India," in J. Rypka, ed., *History of Iranian Literature* (Dordrecht, 1968); and H. Sadarangani, *Persian Poets of Sind* (Karachi, 1957).
21. K. A. Nizami, *The Life and Times of Shaikh Farīd ud-Dīn Ganj-i Shakar* (Aligarh, 1955).
22. K. A. Nizami, *Some Aspects of Religion and Politics in India During the Thirteenth Century* (Delhi, 1961).

23. The only biography in English is that of Dr. Waheed Mirza, *Amīr Khosrau* (Calcutta, 1935).
24. Cf. Schimmel, *Gabriel's Wing. A Study into the Religious Ideas of Sir Muhammad Iqbal* (Leiden, 1963), with an extensive bibliography.
25. H. T. Sorley, *Shāh 'Abdul Laṭīf of Bhit* (Oxford, 1940; reprint ed., 1967).
26. Cf. Schimmel, "The Activities of the Sindhi Adabi Board."
27. K. R. Qanungo, *Dārā Shikoh* (Calcutta, 1952); B. J. Hasrat, *Dara Shikoh, Life and Work* (Vishwabharati, 1953); Yusuf Husain Khan, *L'Inde Mystique*; L. Massignon *Un essai de bloc islamo-Hindoue*, RMM LXIII, 1926; B. A. Hashmir, ed. and trans., "Sarmad," *Islamic Culture*, 1932–33.
28. Cf. Sadiq, *History of Urdu Literature*, ch. 4.
29. Cf. L. Massignon, *Essai sur les origines du lexique technique de la mystique musulmane* (Paris, 1954).
30. E. Howell and O. Caroe, *The Poems*, selected translations (Peshawar, 1963); D. N. Mackenzie, *Poems from the Divan of Khushal Khan Khattak* (London, 1965).
31. Cf. H. G. Raverty, *Poetry of the Afghans.*
32. Cf. Corbin, *Creative Imagination*, esp. pp. 157 f.
33. Cf. Mohan Singh, *History of Panjabi Literature.* The subject of Hir Ranjha has been dealt with also by Persian-writing poets of the Panjab and Sind.
34. Cf. Sorley, *'Abdul Laṭīf*, and Trumpp's edition of the *Risālō* (London, 1866).
35. Cf. Mohan Singh, *Mystik und Yoga der Sikh-Meister* (Zürich, 1967).
36. Cf. Schimmel, "The Activities of the Sindhi Adabi Board."
37. Cf. Schimmel, "Neue Veröffentlichungen zur Volkskunde von Sind," pp. 237 ff.; "Translations and Commentaries of the Qur'ān in Sindhi Language," *Oriens* XVI, 1963; "The Veneration of the Prophet Muhammad as Reflected in Sindhi Poetry," in *The Saviour God*, ed. S. G. F. Brandon (Manchester, 1963).
38. Cf. the review of J. Fück on L. Rama Krishna's *Panjabi Sufi Poets*, in Orientalische Literaturzeitung, vol. 43, 1940.
39. About the development of the veneration of the Prophet, see Tor Andrae, *Die Person Muhammads in Glauben und Lehre seiner Gemeinde* (Stockholm, 1917). See also Constance Padwick, *Muslim Devotions* (London, 1961).
40. Cf. Schimmel, *Gabriel's Wing*, about the use of the formula "There is no god but God," pp. 87 ff.
41. See the examples given by A. R. Barker in *A Reader of Modern Urdū Poetry* (Montreal, 1968).

Jo Sanders

ZEN BUDDHISM AND THE JAPANESE HAIKU

ZEN BUDDHISM, WHICH CAME FROM INDIA BY WAY OF CHINA TO JAPAN, has had a great influence on Japanese culture in general and Japanese art in particular. Suzuki points out that "the idea that the ultimate truth of life and of things generally is to be intuitively and not conceptually grasped is what Zen has contributed to the cultivation of artistic appreciation among the Japanese people."[1] At this very point we find the closest connection between Zen and haiku poetry, that is, in their intuitive rather than conceptual apprehension of life which is concentrated into one brief, yet atemporal moment. This is *satori* in Zen, or what Yasuda calls "the haiku moment,"[2] the aesthetic experience in haiku. Satori is enlightenment (similar to the concept *wu* in Chinese), a self-awakening, quite similar to the *unio mystica* of Christian mysticism. The haiku poet may also experience an enlightenment, which is seeing reality as it is, seeing "kono-mama" or "sono-mama" (similar to the Sanskrit *thatata*): the suchness, the is-ness of things, with no value judgments as to goodness, badness, or the comparative worth of objects, but accepting everything just as it is. A glimpse into the intrinsic nature of things is afforded by haiku, the seventeen syllable brevity of which allows us one swift image of the world *en soi*.

Haiku is a form of Japanese poetry which is generally characterized by three main elements: first, its form, usually consisting of seventeen syllables divided into the pattern 5–7–5; second, the use of a seasonal word or theme; and third, the restriction of the poem to one scene, experience, or image. The best haiku do not directly express emotions or ideas; a concrete picture is presented and its interpretation is left to the reader. As Otsuji indicates, "What is expressed in a haiku is a very small aspect of phenomena; yet what the poet experiences is the reality hidden behind what he expresses."[3]

Suzuki states that a haiku puts forward images reflecting intuitions. "These images are not figurative representations made use of by the poetic mind, but they directly point to original intuitions, indeed, they are intuitions themselves. When the latter are attained, the images become transparent and are immediate expressions of the experience. An intuition in itself, being too intimate, too personal, too immediate, cannot be communicated to others; to do this it calls up images by means of which it becomes transferable. But to those who have never had such an experience it is difficult, even impossible, to reach the fact itself merely through images, because in this case images are transformed into ideas or concepts, and the mind then attempts to give them an intellectual interpretation. Such an attempt altogether destroys the inner truth and beauty of haiku."[4]

The roots of haiku reach back to the very beginnings of Japanese poetry. Yasuda indicates that the characteristics typical of haiku: ellipsis, condensation, spontaneity, and nakedness of treatment, are already commonly found in the *katauta* form of poetry around 700 A.D. Related verse forms—sedoka, choka, and tanka—developed into the renga or linked verse, the opening stanza of which was called hokku and was written in the pattern 5–7–5. The hokku fulfilled a function similar to the use of the title in the West: it summarized the theme of the poem. From this hokku the haiku developed into an independent form as early as the fifteenth century.

The haiku has undergone very little change since its origin. The zenith of its evolution was undoubtedly reached in the seventeenth century with the poetry of Basho (d. 1694); since then there have been small peaks in the history of haiku, but the general trend in quality has been downward. In 1957 there were approximately fifty monthly haiku magazines being published in Japan and individual haiku appeared frequently in other periodicals. Henderson estimates that over a million new haiku are published each year, and innumerable others are written privately and enjoyed within a limited circle.[5] These figures would perhaps suggest a haiku renaissance today. There is indeed a renewed interest in haiku, but it must be emphasized that this does not necessarily indicate a spiritual renaissance; many haiku are written by poets who have never experienced satori.

In order to understand where satori is to be found in haiku, we must examine the concept of satori more closely. Unfortunately, the best one can do is hint at its innermost nature because, as in the *unio mystica* of Christian mysticism, one can work all around the essence of the experience verbally without really approaching the heart of the phenomenon. Blyth has referred to satori as a "spiritual orgasm";[6] Suzuki explains it as acquiring a new viewpoint for looking into the essence of things.[7] He tries to define satori by enumerating its most prominent characteristics, and it is striking how similar they are to the features of *unio mystica* reported by Christian mystics. These eight traits are:[8]

1. Irrationality. Satori is not attained by a logical process of ratiocination, and it cannot be explained coherently.
2. Intuitive insight. Another name for satori is *kensho*, which means "to see essence or nature." One perceives the essence of reality; objects become transparent. Satori is the knowledge of an individual object and also of reality which is at the back of it.
3. Authoritativeness. Because the satori experience is direct and personal it cannot be refuted by logic; it is sufficient unto itself.
4. Impersonal tone. Satori is a highly intellectual state, not an emotional one.
5. Feeling of exaltation. One feels a calmness and mild exaltation at the overcoming of the individual being.
6. Affirmation. This is not seeing things in a positive or negative view, but accepting them as they are.
7. Sense of the Beyond. The experience of satori extends beyond the personal level, although it never embraces the concept of a personal God as Western mysticism may do.
8. Momentariness. Satori usually comes abruptly and unexpectedly and is a very brief experience.

Although nearly everyone agrees with some of Suzuki's points, many experts would omit some of his characteristics and add some that he has not mentioned. A briefer listing of traits, yet one which is preferred by some, is the following:[9]

1. Illumination.
2. Thoughtlessness yet awareness. Non-distinction or *jijimuge* is the "unimpeded interdiffusion of all particulars."[10]
3. Elimination of dualism. There is no perceiver, no "perceived," no subject, no object. "The perceiving I is in one sense unaltered," explains Humphreys. "It still sees the morning paper that it knows so well, and the bus to the office remains unaltered, but the perceiver and the perceived have merged into one, and the two-ness of things has gone. The undifferentiated totality of things is, as it were, understood from inside."[11]
4. Stoppage of breathing.

Satori may be either a sudden or a gradual achievement. It may be totally unexpected or it may come after a series of steps or stages designed to lead one up to enlightenment, such as the koans provide. However, even using the gradual stages provided by meditation on the koans, satori comes abruptly and often when one least expects it. Also, there are various degrees of satori, depending on the depth of the experience.

To achieve satori is to overcome the dualistic way of thinking; it is to become conscious of the unconscious. Only the experience which evolves from a person's inner being can be truly his own. His innermost being opens up its deep secrets only when he has passed beyond the realm of conceptual thinking to the sphere of the unconscious, of *mushin*, no-mind, which means "going beyond the dualism of all forms of life and death, good and evil, being and non-being."[12] The mind is empty of thought, as Takuan (d. 1645) demonstrates in this poem:

> To think that I am not going
> To think of you any more
> Is still thinking of you.
> Let me then try not to think
> That I am not going to think of you.[13]

In a state of mushin one may become egoless; the unconscious may go beyond a personal unconscious, or even a collective unconscious, to a sort of cosmic unconscious.[14] Hisamatsu calls satori "recognizing the real noumenon of a person, his original feature . . . [It is becoming] one who is unhinderedly free, released from all chains, one who recognizes himself truly, being no longer attached to the forms of matter and of spirit, one who faces the present world of existence and non-existence, life and death, good and evil, pro and con."[15]

Eugen Herrigel calls satori "jumping into a new dimension."[16] The first characteristic of the new way of seeing, he asserts, is "that all things are of equal importance in its sight. . . . They all seem to have acquired an absolute value." Haiku underscores the basic equality of all things when the body of a dead dog or a "horse pissing" near the poet's ear are not better or worse, no more or less important than Basho's frog or the cherry blossoms at Yoshino. Blyth correctly maintains that in haiku "man has no dignity, nature no majesty."[17] The truth of the universe is expressed in one small intuitive image. Let us look more closely at Basho's famous frog haiku:

The ancient pond.
A frog jumps in.
Plop!

This is not just a serene landscape interrupted by a frog plunging into the water. It is this, but it is also much more: it opened a new perspective of reality for Basho. A Christian would say that Basho saw God in a frog as frog. The sound of the water "was heard by Basho as filling the entire universe. Not only was the totality of the environment absorbed in the sound and vanished into it, but Basho himself was altogether effaced from his consciousness."[18] Basho ceased being the old Basho; he heard the plop of the frog in the water and was enlightened. He saw the suchness, the is-ness of things; he beheld the world with new eyes. Reality became transparent for him in this experience of satori. Basho was not unprepared for this, for he had attained *mushin*, the state of no-mind, having gone beyond consciousness to the cosmic unconscious. In the middle of his selflessness, the sound of the water cut across his tranquility and caused him to perceive reality from a new point of view.

Satori is impersonal in that the Self has been overcome and an unconscious level below the ego has been reached. Haiku, too, must be egoless. The poet must not project his philosophy, ideas, or purposes into the poem; he is merely the person giving expression to the intuition. An example of haiku which is rather poor because it speculates against speculation was written by Basho:

When the lightning flashes,
How admirable he who thinks not—
"Life is fleeting."

Humor is an essential element in Zen Buddhism and may also find a place in haiku, but wittiness certainly does not belong there. In haiku the poet must submerge himself in an object until its intrinsic nature becomes evident. Witty or speculative haiku come from without, not from within; they contain no Zen and certainly are never representative of a poet's satori. There cannot be such a thing as a haiku with a point; this device merely drags the poem down to the level of an epigram. Sokan's haiku does not succeed, in my opinion:

If to the moon
One puts a handle—what
A splendid fan!

In haiku, just as in the Christian *unio mystica* or the Buddhist satori, there is a central point of silence, a *sanctum silencium*, which can never be touched by words. That is why haiku merely points, suggests, indicates; it never explains. In haiku as in most good poetry, the half is better than the whole. Moritake (d. 1549) goes a bit too far in making an obvious comparison:

A morning-glory!
And so—today!—may seem
my own life-story.

The brevity of the haiku poem is by no means an accident. Kenneth Yasuda, Herbert Read, and Igarashi explain it as being the average length of the breath a person draws, and thus the length of the haiku is determined by the number of words one can utter in a normal breath. Yasuda calls this the duration of the state of "ah-ness."[19] That is, when one is moved by a scene, say the first spring crocus, the duration of one's wonder, as expressed by a drawn-out "ahhhhhhhhh," is the length of a breath. So too the experience works in haiku. This act of perception is explained by Read: "All art originates in an intuition, or vision. . . . This act of vision or intuition is, physically, a state of concentration or tension in the mind. . . . The words which express this vision are arranged or composed in a sequence or rhythm which is sustained until the mental state of tension in the poet is exhausted or released by this objective equivalence."[20] Blyth agrees with this interpretation of the length of haiku: "The philosophic significance of 5, 7, 5 in Japanese syllables, may be this. Seventeen such syllables are one emission of breath, one exhalation of soul. The division into three gives us the feeling of ascent, attainment and resolution of experience."[21]

Blyth, in his authoritative four-volume work on haiku, sums up the spirit of Zen Buddhism in Japanese haiku: "A haiku is the expression of a temporary enlightenment, in which we see into the life of things. . . . Each thing is preaching the law [Dharma] incessantly, but this law is not something different from the thing itself. Haiku is the revealing of this preaching by presenting us with the thing devoid of all our mental twisting and emotional discoloration; or rather it shows the thing as it exists at one and the same time outside and inside the mind, perfectly subjective, ourselves undivided from the object, the object in its original unity with ourselves. . . . It is a way in which the cold winter rain, the swallows of evening, even the very day in its hotness and the length of the night become truly alive, share in our humanity, speak their own silent and expressive language."[22]

Notes

1. D. Suzuki, *Zen and Japanese Culture* (New York, 1959), p. 218.
2. K. Yasuda, *The Japanese Haiku* (Rutland, Vermont, and Tokyo, 1957), p. 24.
3. Otsuji, *Otsuji Hairon-shu* (Tokyo, 1947), p. 131.
4. Suzuki, *Zen and Japanese Culture*, pp. 240–241.
5. H. Henderson, *An Introduction to Haiku* (Garden City, New York, 1958), pp. 1–2.
6. R. H. Blyth, *Zen in English Literature and Oriental Classics* (Tokyo, 1942), p. 176.
7. Suzuki, *Introduction to Zen Buddhism* (Kyoto, 1934), p. 127.
8. Suzuki, *The Essentials of Zen Buddhism* (New York, 1962), pp. 163–168.
9. C. C. Chang, *The Practice of Zen* (New York, 1959), pp. 152–3.
10. C. Humphreys, *Zen Buddhism* (London, 1949), p. 115.
11. Ibid., p. 116.
12. Suzuki, *Essentials*, p. 441.
13. Suzuki, *Zen and Japanese Culture*, p. 112.
14. Ibid., p. 110.
15. S. Hisamatsu, "Zen and the Various Acts," *Chicago Review*, vol. 12, no. 2, 1958.
16. E. Herrigel, *The Method of Zen* (New York, 1960), p. 46.
17. Blyth, *A History of Haiku* (Tokyo, 1964), vol. 1, p. 28.
18. Suzuki, *Zen and Japanese Culture*, p. 228.
19. Yasuda, p. 31.
20. H. Read, *Form in Modern Poetry* (London, 1953), pp. 44–45.
21. Blyth, *History of Haiku*, vol. 2, p. 350.
22. Blyth, *Haiku* (Tokyo, 1947–52), vol. 1, pp. 270–271.

Eisig Silberschlag

INTERPRETATIONS AND REINTERPRETATIONS OF ḤASIDISM IN HEBREW LITERATURE

ḤASIDISM IS A PARADOX: POPULAR IN APPEAL AND ESOTERIC IN DOCTRINE, communal in its emphasis on religious experience en masse and elitist in its cult of the chosen individual, the *Ẓaddiḳ*.[1] As a regenerative force in modern theology it has become an object of discussion among scholars and thinkers. Popular writers like Isaac Bashevis Singer forced literary critics to confrontations with a movement which has its roots in a millennial milieu of mystic visionarism and visionaries and which aimed at an inner transformation of man and an ultimate leap into the spiritual stratosphere—beyond the concerns of the merely human world. Small wonder it is that serious students of literature fall into the error of characterizing Ḥasidism as a "puritanic sect."[2] Others, aided and abetted by Martin Buber, the master-interpreter of Ḥasidism, draw far-fetched analogies between Zen and Ḥasidism, or the Sufis and Ḥasidism.

BIOGRAPHY OF THE WORD

The movement derives its name from the biblical word Ḥasid which means "pious" or "loyal." It denotes a person who practices *Ḥesed*—piety or loyalty.[3] While the noun and the adjective are common in the Bible, the verb appears there only three times.[4] The scarcity of the verbal root seems to imply that Ḥasidism involves the entire human being, not a sporadic action.

In Hellenistic times—especially in the period of the Maccabean revolt—a pious group of Ḥasidim seems to have existed.[5] They opposed idolatry and resented immorality, which they associated with Hellenism or Hellenization. They participated in the Maccabean revolt and in the conquest of Jerusalem by Judas Maccabeus in 165 B.C. But they eschewed political goals; they considered the preservation of pristine piety as their objective.

In talmudic times, roughly between the second century B.C. and the end of the fifth century A.D., the term Ḥasid was applied to some sages.[6] Hillel, who died at the dawn of our era, was eulogized as a humble man and a Ḥasid.[7] And he himself used the word in a famous saying: "and an ignorant man cannot be a Ḥasid. . . ."[8] A special type of Ḥasid is represented by Honi the Circle-Drawer—a Hebrew Rip van Winkle. Part sage and part miracle-man he practiced extreme piety in his personal life and had the power to solicit rain in prayer and be heeded. After a hibernating sleep of seventy years he rose to find a new generation with which he could not establish any rapport.[9] The term Ḥasid was also extended to Gentiles, and thus, in a characteristic gesture of generosity, the pious Gentiles were admitted to "a portion in the world to come."[10]

In talmudic times Ḥasid seemed to imply a good, law-abiding man who fulfilled his moral obligations, for he was often mentioned in one breath with "men of deeds,"[11] a loosely knit group of people who were held together by the intensity of their ethical beliefs, by extreme devotion, and by impeccable ways of life. There was also an early group of Ḥasidim who were especially addicted to prayer.[12] It was also in talmudic times that the abstract noun *Ḥasidism*[13] appeared with increased frequency as a desirable virtue or in connection with some sage: "the fear of sin leads to Ḥasidism and Ḥasidism leads to holiness of spirit."[14] In biblical times the Ḥasid was a pious or loyal person, in Hellenistic times a member of a conservative group who opposed Hellenism, and in Talmudic times the keeper of a privileged type of piety. In the Middle Ages a movement of piety was initiated by Samuel the Ḥasid and his son Judah of Ratisbon. That movement found its maturest expression in the *Book of Ḥasidim*,[15] which was written in Germany in the thirteenth century and was authored by Samuel the Pious, his son Judah, who was regarded as *the* author of the book, his pupils, and R. Elazar Rokeaḥ. The fifty years between the end of the twelfth century and the middle of the thirteenth were, of course, a time of cultural growth among the Jews of Spain, Provence, and Germany. It is the golden age of Tosafists, Jewish philosophy, and Jewish mysticism. It is also the great age of German Ḥasidism with its mystical overtones.[16]

The *Book of Ḥasidim* was held in high esteem as a manual of popular ethics in the form of parables, tales, and epigrams. It was unabashedly edifying; it was written for "God-fearing men . . . so that they will learn how to fear God."[17] And it was undoubtedly influenced by monasticism: mysticism, asceticism, saintliness, scholarliness—these were the virtues extolled by the book. Romantic love—a demonic passion, all-absorbing and all-destructive—was also a Christian influence.[18] In the *Book of Ḥasidim* intimacies between the sexes are not only discouraged, but even an innocent glance at a woman is to be shunned.[19] Such examples of sinful love fit the medieval author Andreas Capellanus who had probably written his tract, *The Art of Courtly Love*, in the twelfth century.[20] But they seem strange in a book like *The Book of Ḥasidim*, where a rigidly ethical tradition clashed with a romantic, almost hedonistic notion.

Around 1700 Judah Ḥasid Levi of Podolia preached the proximate advent of the Messiah in Poland. He represented a type of Ḥasidism in an era which was receptive to new visionary overtures. In 1666 Sabbatai Zevi was converted to Islam, and the most popular messianic movement among Jews ended in a fiasco. Judah Ḥasid Levi, perhaps a Sabbatian in secret, founded a movement of Ḥasidim which advocated repentance, ecstatic prayer, and emigration to the Holy Land. In 1699 and 1700 he organized about one thousand or fifteen hundred followers who settled under his leadership in Jerusalem. When the Messiah failed to arrive in 1706—the date of Sabbatai Zevi's reincarnation, exactly forty years after his conversion—many Ḥasidim became discouraged and returned to their previous homes; some fell under the spell of Christian missionaries and became Christians in the Holy Land. Yet the failure associated with R. Judah Ḥasid Levi's venture is such a redemptive failure that a serious historian, Professor Ben Zion Dinur, begins modern Jewish history with this immigration to Palestine rather than with the French Revolution.[21]

Despair, disappointment, and spiritual emptiness characterized the masses of Jewry in the beginning of the eighteenth century. The times were ripe again for a redemptive drive under charismatic leadership.

ḤASIDISM: ORIGINS AND CHARACTERISTICS

Major Trends in Jewish Mysticism, the seminal work of Gershom G. Scholem, concludes with a chapter on Ḥasidism, undeniably "the latest phase" of esoterism in an uninterrupted tradition of growth for more than two thousand years. In the first millennium Ḥasidism was cultivated by individuals and small coteries. By the beginning of the second millennium it gained ever wider acceptance until, as a mystic movement of national redemption, as Sabbatianism, it engulfed all Jewry during the second half of the seventeenth century. A hundred years later Ḥasidism dominated the religious experiences of Jewry in eastern Europe—and in eastern Europe only. Even in our own time, after two hundred years, it is still a major force in New York City and in many communities of Israel. And, through the transpositions of Martin Buber, it has vitalized contemporary Christian theology. It seems, therefore, just and fair to regard Ḥasidism not only as a latter-day development of Jewish mysticism (though some scholars have denied its mystic qualities)[22] but also as a fresh phase of nonrational theology in Judaism and, through Judaism, in Christianity.

In eastern Europe rabbinic learning had reached its apogee in the eighteenth century. The great compendia of Jewish law were thoroughly observed; the *Set Table*[23] of R. Joseph Karo (1488–1575) was covered with the so-called *Tablecloth*[24] of R. Moses Isserles (1530–1572) and became popular throughout eastern Europe. A brilliant assemblage of rabbinic stars in succeeding centuries has refined the law with hairsplitting argumentation which vied with the original analyses of the law in the Babylonian academies of Sura and Pumneditha. What Nathan Note Hanover said of Polish Jewry in his own time, remained true almost to the beginning of our century:

> Throughout the lands of Jewish dispersion there was nowhere as much learning as in Poland. Each community maintained talmudic academies, and the head of each academy was given an ample salary so that he could maintain his school without worry and so that the study of the Torah might be his sole occupation. . . . Each community maintained young men and provided for them a weekly allowance in order to study with the head of the academy. . . . There was scarcely a house in Poland where Torah was not studied. Either the head of the family was himself a scholar or his son or his son-in-law or one of the young men eating at his table. . . .[25]

Solomon Maimon (1754–1800), with greater insight and with less charity than Nathan Note Hanover, made the pregnant observation that . . .

> . . . the Jewish nation is . . . a perpetual aristocracy under the guise of a theocracy. The learned men who form the nobility in the nation, have

> been able, for many centuries, to maintain their position as the legislative body with so much authority among the common people, that they can do with them whatever they please.[26]

Within that context of theocratic and aristocratic nomism, Ḥasidism would not and could not flourish as an antinomian reaction against rabbinic learning. But, to a large extent, it was a rebellion of starved emotionalism against hyperintellectualism, folk wisdom against philosophical wisdom, intuitivism against rationalism, lightheartedness and joyfulness against seriousness and joylessness, inwardness instead of adherence to outer forms of religion. It continued to mythicize Judaism in the spirit of kabbalist antecedents. It became—to borrow a metaphor from physics—a new field of meaningful significance. The Jew rather than Judaism dominated the center which emanated and absorbed the holiness of living. In Leviticus 19:1 it had been written: "You shall be holy, for I, the Lord your God, am holy." The Ḥasidim converted the future of the biblical verse into the present tense.

On the sociological plane Ḥasidism was an uprising of the masses against the dominance of the supercilious scholar, the emergence of the *'Am ha-Arez*[27] against the *Talmid Ḥakam*.[28] Ultimately the *Talmid Ḥakam* was exchanged for the *Ẓaddiḳ*; the intellectual snob gave way to the charismatic leader. But the charismatic leader leads by virtue of mysticism and emotionalism rather than by logic and knowledge of the law. He is one of God's intimates, whose prayer, enthusiasm, and superhuman power reshape and restore spirituality to this world. He is not a recluse but a missionary to the masses and an intermediary between the deity and the people. He is even dragged down to depths of evil by the sinfulness of the masses—for they are the men of matter while he is the man of form—and his descent is a condition of his ascent.

The Ḥasidic rabbi is addressed by a Hebrew acronym which means *Our Lord, Our Teacher, Our Master*. This is not merely a change in nomenclature; it is a shift in emphasis. But it is wrong to regard the new title as an authoritarian sobriquet. It is more likely a bending of the divine to the human, a deization of the human rather than a humanization of the divine. There is here, perhaps, an approximation to Christianity and the reason for the fascination of Christianity with Ḥasidism via Buber's interpretation. The *Ẓaddiḳ* who is Lord, Teacher, and Master can be easily translated into a Christian figure.

That there were Ḥasidic individuals, perhaps even Ḥasidic groupings before Ḥasidism, is an established fact.[29] That they had connections with or that they were inheritors of Sabbatianism has been proven by Scholem.[30] Yet the man who is regarded as the founder of Ḥasidism reshaped Jewry. Meek, not excessively learned, optimistic: these were his outstanding qualities. A simple faith, a sunny temperament, a love for the common people—these traits led to popular leadership. Like Jesus and Mohammed he wrote nothing; but he talked with a conviction born of simple faith. Unlike Jesus and Mohammed he founded no religion: his brand of Judaism is traditional Judaism with slight modifications and ample changes in emphasis. Popularly he was known as Baal Shem Tov (1700–1760). And in Jewish mysticism Baal Shem or Baal Shem Tov is a man who possesses knowledge of the name or names of God and uses magical formulas, apotropaic terminology, or natural therapy for the cure of the sick.[31] Both he and his followers, however, employed folk cures in such a way that "after the usual method of the conjurer they sought to turn the attention of the spectator from these, and direct it to their Kabbalistic hocus-pocus."[32] For the environment —except for the scholarly elite—was permeated with superstition. (In his *Autobiography* Solomon Maimon tells the story about a cook who was cutting up a carp and preparing the fish for the Sabbath. "It seemed to him that the dead carp uttered a sound. This threw everybody into a panic. The rabbi was asked what should be done with this dumb fish that had ventured to speak. Under the superstitious idea that the carp was possessed of a spirit, the rabbi enjoined that it should be wrapped in a linen cloth and buried with pomp.")[33] Latter leaders of Ḥasidism exploited the simplistic faith of the masses for their own benefit.

In primary Ḥasidic sources Baal Shem Tov appears as a man having many successive occupations—teacher's assistant, ritual slaughterer, cantor—until he finds his vocation. Seven years of solitude in the Carpathian mountains strengthen his resolve for leadership. His gregariousness—in the streets, in the market places—brings him recognition. Pipe in mouth, he converses with men and even women—against the explicit warning of the sages: ". . . and talk not much with Woman."[34] He settles in the Podolian town of Mezbizh (Międzyboż) and becomes the sage and saint of Mezbizh.

From the first important author of Ḥasidic lore, Jacob Joseph ha-Cohen of Polnoye, we learn about the founder's habits. Prayer looms large in the life of the Baal Shem Tov and his successors, for prayer with intensity and enthusiasm leads to a "divestiture of corporeality" (*Hitpashtut ha-Gashmiyḥut*). It was R. Nahman of Bratzlav who maintained that "the main vitality comes from prayer."[35] And it was said of Shneur Zalman of Liady that "privately he would pray in silence but in his public prayers he would shout for all the world to hear."[36] Other traits cultivated by the founder of Ḥasidism were *Hitlahavut* (enthusiasm), *Debekut* (adhesion to God), and *Kawwanah* (intensity of mystical intention or revival of "the ossified rites" in the beautiful phrase of Martin Buber).[37] These virtues—prayer, enthusiasm, adhesion to God, intensity of intention—led to true self-realization. An acute observer of early Ḥasidism, Solomon Maimon, noted that the "new sect" maintained these new principles: "elevation of the body through the intensity of prayer; devotion with exertion of all our powers, and annihilation of self before God;[38] satisfaction rather than restriction or suppression of bodily needs; cheerfulness which is a function of a genuine piety rather than fasts and vigils and constant study of the Talmud";[39] mass visits to the leaders, in order to enjoy community of spirit and be inspired by their holiness. Maimon maintained that the new sect spread because it advocated vitality and cheer instead of ascetic study; it tended to be fanatical and it propagated the love of the marvelous.[40]

Since much has been made of the gaiety of Ḥasidism, a caveat is in order. It was not a gaiety which celebrated the sensual outlook on life. It was not a gaiety which advocated insouciance. It was a gaiety which led to spiritual resuscitation.

The cardinal virtues of Ḥasidism center around the relation of the individual to God. They are based on naïve yet original interpretations of scripture. Yehudah Steinberg, who has experienced Ḥasidism in his native Russia, makes one of the Ḥasidim interpret the verse in Deuteronomy 34:10 ("Never again did there arise in Israel a prophet like Moses") thus: "People think that this is praise; in reality this is accusation. Woe to the *Ẓaddiḳ* who was not able to raise a man like him in his generation. As a matter of fact, this is not a *Ẓaddiḳ* at all; this is a eunuch."[41]

Baal Shem's grandson, Rabbi Baruch, told a story about his grandfather who was asked about the essence of service and replied characteristically: "I have come into this world to point another way"—away from asceticism and mortification of the body. And he continued: "Man should try to attain to three loves: the love of God, the love of Jewry, the love of Torah." This is new emphasis upon an old triad which has its root in the Zohar, the classic of the mystics.[42] The search for the three loves must be an individual concern: "We say God of Abraham, God of Isaac and God of Jacob; we do not say God of Abraham, Isaac and Jacob, so that you may be told: Isaac and Jacob did not rely on Abraham's tradition, but they themselves searched for the Divine."[43] But search alone is not sufficient: "Genuine religiosity is *doing*."[44] Searching and doing by individuals who share common beliefs create a true community of holiness.

What is novel in the Ḥasidic movement is its revivalist enthusiasm, its de-emphasis of learning, and its cult of personality. Its revivalist enthusiasm expressed itself in prayer which involved the body in dancing, in clapping hands, and in communal singing.[45] The de-emphasis of learning produced popular learning and literature: the folktale and the epigram, the parable and the legend. They relied on edifying tracts and commentaries of the Middle Ages, on mystical disquisitions, on Sabbatian sources and, possibly, on the illuminations of the Paduan scholar and poet, Moses Hayyim Luzzatto (1707–1746).[46] The cult of personality was the early strength and later the undoing of the movement. In the heyday of Ḥasidism, between the middle of the eighteenth century and the middle of the second decade in the nineteenth century, a procession of saintly personages appeared in eastern Europe: Dov Ber of Mezritch (1710–1772), Jacob Joseph ha-Cohen of Polnoye (c. 1710–c. 1782), Levi Isaac of Berdichev (1740–1809), Jacob Isaac of Lublin (1745–1815), Rabbi Naḥman of Bratzlav (1772–1810), Shneur Zalman of Liady (1747–1813). Some of these personages became the unwitting founders of Ḥasidic dynasties which deteriorated as they grew in power. Their princely ostentation, a costly trait, encouraged the worst obscurantism among the people.

The founder was believed to be on terms of intimacy with God; his special relationship with the Supreme Being granted him the power of miraculous therapy and special "rabbinic sight," *dem Rebben's Kuk* as it was expressed in the vernacular Yiddish. As a matter of fact, Jacob Isaac, the main protagonist of Buber's only novel, *For the Sake of Heaven*, is called The Seer because "when he was born, he had been able to see from world's end to world's end."[47] Moreover, he had the gift of seeing whether a man was good or evil. "He saw each soul's ultimate descent and root, whether it had once proceeded from the side of Cain or Abel. . . ."[48]

There are differences of attitude and emphasis among the groupings of Ḥasidism. Baal Shem Tov, Dov Ber of Mezritch and his pupils, Shneur Zalman of Liady, the founder of the Ḥabad movement, Rabbi Naḥman of Bratzlav and his disciples all differ in their mystic fervor and in their messianic de-emphasis. Most of them stress the redemption of the individual rather than the redemption of Israel. True, Menahem Mendel of Vitebsk and his followers settled in Israel in 1777, and Rabbi Naḥman of Bratzlav spent almost a year (1798–1799) in the Holy Land, but they are the exceptions which confirm the rule.

The best known splinter movement of Ḥasidism developed in Lithuania. It derives its name *Ḥabad* from an acronym of three intellectual concepts: *Ḥokmah* (wisdom), *Binah* (understanding), *Da'at* (knowledge).

Yet it is best described as emotionalism tinged with intellect rather than intellect tinged with emotion. For the founder of the movement, Shneur Zalman of Liady, the triad is a ladder of contemplation. The first rung, wisdom, brings to birth the idea that "all is in God." Understanding, the second rung, is meditation upon the idea that "all is in God." Knowledge, the third rung, is adhesion of the heart to its source in God. Wisdom is higher than understanding, and understanding higher than knowledge, but through understanding and knowledge man may repossess wisdom.[49] One can also say that "a man may feel intuitively that a certain opinion is correct without being able to put his reason into words. This is *Ḥokmaḥ*. When a man knows why he holds an opinion, when he can defend it in argument, he has attained *Binah*. *Daʿat* is neither intuitive knowledge [*Ḥokmah*] nor expository knowledge [*Binah*] but an attachment of the mind to the idea. *Daʿat* is only possible where a man has a deep concern for the subject."[50]

In the third chapter of *Tanya*, which became the Bible of the Ḥabad movement, Shneur Zalman of Liady presents an involved explanation of the triad: "the intellect includes wisdom, understanding and knowledge . . . the intellect . . . is called wisdom. . . . When one educes the potential into the actual, when one thinks in order to understand truly and profoundly: this is called understanding. . . . Knowledge is based on the verse: . . . and Adam knew Eve (Genesis 4:1). It implies attachment and union; it is the faculty which binds one's mind with a very firm and strong bond . . . to the . . . Infinite (*En Sof*).[51]

Wisdom, understanding, knowledge—these are the three components of the Jew's divine soul. His bestial or instinctual soul (*ha-Nefesh ha-Behemit*) is subject to change from evil to good; from good to evil. His divine soul is the source of such qualities as love and fear of God; his instinctual soul is the source of social ethics. The Jew's mission is to change his instinctual soul to goodness, to strive for the superiority of his divine soul.

The son of Shneur Zalman of Liady, Dov Ber of Lubavitch, wrote many tracts in Yiddish and Hebrew which are mainly Ḥasidic commentaries on the festivals, on biblical books, and the Zohar. One of them, a *Tract on Ecstasy*,[52] enumerated many types of ecstasy in an involuted style. And it is rather important to note that the so-called rational splinter of Hasidism stressed non-rational ecstasy:

> My whole aim from youth, on behalf of my beloved friends, who seek the words of the living God in truth, is for the light of eternal life to be fixed firmly in their soul to the full extent indeed. This is the matter of the

> revelation of the divine in their soul . . . the ecstasy of their soul. . . . The matter will be understood if it is prefaced by a well-known comment on the verse in Deuteronomy 4:4: "But you who cleave to the Lord your God are alive. . . ." Without cleaving they are not called living but dead. . . .[53]

Ḥabadism presents an ethical and mystical stance. To change from evil to good—that is the ethical obligation; from good to divine—that is the mystical endeavor. It was the mixture of exoteric and esoteric doctrine and practice which gained for the Ḥabad movement hundreds of thousands of adherents. Even their present headquarters in Brooklyn attract endless processions of visitors and disciples to their leader. They call themselves "Lubavicher Ḥasidim" because Duber (Dov Ber), the son of Shneur Zalman of Liady, settled in the town of Lubavich, in White Russia. His son-in-law, Menaḥem Mendel, adopted the name Schneorsohn which is, to this day, the distinguished family name of Ḥabad leaders. The adherents of the movement are also scattered in many communities of Israel. There is even an agricultural settlement, *Kefar Ḥabad*, which carries on a long-standing tradition of buttressing the moral stance with economic solidity, for it was the son of Rabbi Shneur Zalman of Liady who envisaged Jewish agricultural settlements in the Crimea.

Other Ḥasidic enclaves did not fare as well as Ḥabadism. They deteriorated after the first flush of Ḥasidism in the first five or six decades after the birth of the movement. Mystical intention (*Kawwanah*) was vulgarized by magic letter-manipulation (*Gammatria* and *Notariḳon*),[54] Ẓaddiḳism was corrupted by political manipulation. Leaders of Ḥasidism were often bribed by the state to drive their adherents into submission to political authority. They became easy targets of scorn for enlightened Jews and Christians.

SOURCES OF ḤASIDISM

The two hundred and thirty years of Ḥasidism can be divided into two periods: a short period of growth (c. 1750–c. 1815) and a long period of decline (1815 to the present).

Ḥasidism had to fight on two fronts almost from its inception: defensively against entrenched Judaism and offensively against reformist Enlightenment. The fight against entrenched Judaism reached its apogee in 1772 when a ban was pronounced upon Ḥasidism under the influence of Elijah of Vilna, the chief representative of rabbinical

Judaism. Ironically the great Gaon was called a Ḥasid, but his Ḥasidism was not identical with that of Baal Shem Tov; his piety consisted of strict adherence to rabbinic precepts, almost perpetual study which included the totality of traditional lore—even Kabbalah.

The fierce opposition against Ḥasidism by rabbinic Judaism continued into the nineteenth century but the ban and the persecutions and the burnings of Ḥasidic books fanned the zeal of the adherents; they emerged victorious in entire sections of eastern Europe: in Galicia, in the Ukraine, in Volhynia, in Podolia, and even in Lithuania, the bastion of rabbinism. The Oppositionists (*Mitnaggedim*) did not concede defeat. But they were quite powerless against the attractive suasions of the new movement.[55]

The first writers who transmitted stories about the Baal Shem Tov were his disciples or members of his family. Such a disciple was Jacob Joseph of Polnoye, the author of several works including the first printed work on Ḥasidism.[56] The grandson of the Baal Shem Tov, Moshe Hayyim Ephraim, was the author of the work *Camp-Flag of Ephraim*.[57] The homilies of Dov Ber of Mezritch were published after his death by his disciple Solomon of Lutzk,[58] and by another famous disciple, Levi Isaac of Berdichev.[59] The literary form of these books was the homiletic commentary on the Pentateuch, the *Haftarot*,[60] the Five Scrolls, and the Talmudic sayings. The chief books of Jacob Joseph of Polnoye used that form. They sometimes present sermons which combine knowledge, folklore, meditation, and original interpretation. A beautiful homily on the folly of sin is given in Jacob Joseph's commentary on "And this is the story. . . ." (Genesis 25:19 ff.). First, the biblical connection between folly and sin is established: we have done foolishly and we have sinned (Numbers 12:11). Then, with less justification, another biblical verse is adduced to buttress the contention (Isaiah 5:20). Then a Talmudic passage is brought to bear on the subject: a man does not transgress unless a spirit of folly enters into him (*Sotah* 81a). Then the author reverts to the original application of Scripture and Talmud and makes his point. There are three types of men: the straightforward, honest man who acts according to his intellect; the bestial man who is guided only by his will; and the median man who sees both good and evil, who is guided by either intellect or will and who makes decisions after inner struggles.[61]

The books of Dov Ber of Mezritch, Rabbi Elimelech of Lizensk, and Rabbi Levi Isaac of Berdichev are essentially homoletical tracts. Their comments on the Bible or the Talmud were oral; later they were committed to writing. Most Ḥasidic books imitated medieval genres:

edifying tracts, mystic and homiletic commentaries, or anthologies of epigrams by famous rabbis. Even the so-called new genre of Ḥasidic literature—the moral story—is hardly innovative: it is designed to preserve the sense of the miraculous, the intuitive wisdom of the Ẓaddiḳ, the moral stance. The Ḥasidic stories are derived from the founder, who loved the brief, incisive tale—almost a parable. They reach their apogee in Rabbi Naḥman of Bratzlav, the best and the profoundest of Ḥasidic storytellers. In spite of the seductive paraphrases of Buber and the fine English translation of Buber by Maurice Friedman, the immediacy and the simplicity of the original suffer serious losses in their impact on both the sophisticated and the unsophisticated reader.[62] Thus, for example, the title of "The Story of the Rabbi and his Only Son" is smoothed down to "The Rabbi and His Son." And a comparison of the first paragraph in a literal translation from Setzer's text with a translation of Buber's paraphrase by Friedman is a good measure of the distance from the original.[63]
In the original:

> There was once a rabbi. The rabbi had no children. Then he became the father of an only son. He brought him up and married him off. The son sat in the attic always and studied as is customary with rich people. He only studied and prayed all the time. Yet he felt he was missing something. But he did not know what was missing.[64]

In Friedman's translation of Buber's paraphrase the paragraph is expanded into two pages.

> There was once a rabbi who had dedicated his life to the Torah, applied all his mind to investigating it, and guarded the law with all his will so that it should be observed in the community even in the smallest detail. When a single son was born to him in his late years, this seemed to him a reward and an assent of God. It was as if, from above, a confirmation of his way of life had been allotted him, and he vowed to himself that all the days that remained to him he would see to it that his son, like him, penetrated the depths of the teaching and did not diverge a hair's breadth from the demand of the law. That his son, like him, should be an enemy of those enthusiasts who dared to join their rambling dreams to the primal and everlasting might of the Torah.
>
> The son grew up and became great in the wisdom of the holy books. He had a little room in his father's house where he used to sit, collecting all his senses in order to absorb himself in the mysteries of the scriptures. But his soul could not persevere over the books, and his glance did not stay on the endless surfaces of rigid letters, but again and again flew out over

yellow billows of corn to the dark streak of the distant fir woods. His soul flew thither with his glance and lulled itself in the silent air like a young bird. Yet he ever anew forced his eye and heart back into the narrow prison, for he wanted to know, and the knowledge was certainly in the books. But even though he held his head bent with both hands over the pages covered with signs, his soul still did not allow itself to be imprisoned. If it could not nourish itself on the abundance outside the window, then it looked within itself, as into an unknown and mysterious landscape.

Nevertheless, he grew strong in the knowledge of the teaching, although it was not from the maze of signs before him that his wisdom streamed; it was as if it came from within himself. At the same time, there grew in him that strength of being that is named holiness. Wisdom and holiness unite, however, in that incomprehensible transformation called "the rung of the lesser light," which appears from time to time in a single human soul and departs with it. But like one who imagined himself ignorant, although within himself he embraced the world, the son of the rabbi supposed that for the sake of the truth he must investigate the writings still further. As soon as he approached the books, however, he felt himself abandoned in a boundless void. So he returned ever again into the world of his inner vision. But in it, too, he did not find satisfaction.[65]

The reader has no choices; he has two texts of a story, an original steeped in simplicity and a paraphrase steeped in sophistication. And both have their seductive characteristics: one possesses the roughness of the folk-mind; the other the elegance of the esthete (but not in the pejorative sense). It speaks for the vitality of the Ḥasidic story—especially Naḥman of Bratzlav's story—that it can effect a modern reader in its original version and in sophisticated paraphrases.

A creative rephrasing of Ḥasidic stories has been attempted by numerous anthologists. None was done with greater ardor than by Jiri Langer (1894–1943). A native of Prague, he decided to experience Ḥasidism at its source. In 1913 he visited Belz in eastern Galicia which had been thoroughly Ḥasidified and which nourished the most sensitive interpreters of Ḥasidism: Agnon and Buber.[66] There he not only observed Ḥasidism; he lived it. And he penned a moving account of life in Belz—perhaps the best modern account of Ḥasidism in its native habitat.[67]

In nine chapters—or "gates" in medieval terminology—he has retold oral and written stories about the saints of Ḥasidism in their spiritualized world. But unlike Buber, the sophisticated and metaphysical spokesman of Ḥasidism, Langer moves his listener with an uncommon simplicity which flows from the source—from the contact with the saint of Belz and his followers.

OPPONENTS OF ḤASIDISM

Not only the orthodox, but also secularized scholars and writers opposed Ḥasidism and the Ḥasidim. One of their earliest observers and critics, Solomon Maimon, has castigated them from an "enlightened" point of view: their emotionalism leads them into excess; their vanity accounts for their belief that they are "organs of the Godhead"; they are apt to regard an impulse as a divine call. In short, they are ruled by passion instead of reason and knowledge.[68] Graetz, the historian, and Krochmal, the thinker, were also implacable foes of Ḥasidism. Graetz went far in his animosity: he called Ḥasidism "this odious excrescence of Judaism."[69] Krochmal, the gentle philosopher, called the Ḥasidim "the hypocritical sect . . . fumes from hard liquor confuse their brain and obfuscate their intellect. . . ."[70] Mapu intended his abortive novel, *The Visionaries*, as a critique of the period of Sabbatai Zevi—the source of Ḥasidism—in his view.[71] Joseph Perl, Isaac Erter, Isaac Bär Levinsohn, A. B. Gottlober, Abraham Mapu, Judah Leb Mieses, Peretz Smolenskin, and Mendele Moker Sefarim attacked Ḥasidim in word and deed. Judah Leb Mieses—and he was not the only one—played the role of an informer: he denounced the Ḥasidim to the Austrian authorities as near-heretics, "religious fanatics."[72] Even Ahad Ha'am remembered Ḥasidism with bitterness in his autobiography: "I was born . . . in the town of Skvira, in one of the darkest corners of Ḥasidic regions of Russia."[73] But already Isaac Bär Levinsohn (1788–1860), father of Hebrew Enlightenment in eastern Europe, poked fun at Ḥasidism: "these 'men of God' are everywhere but mere men can nowhere be found."[74] They despise general education; they are manipulators of Hebrew letters for purposes of general obfuscation; they love 'the bitter drop' and their religious enthusiasm is generated by alcohol; they are prone to lewdness; they are full of superstitions; they interpret Scripture willfully and foolishly; they are ultra-conservative; they fear the corrupting ways of large cities. And their leaders are venal liars and deceivers."[75]

The favorite weapon against Ḥasidism was irony, sarcasm, ridicule, and, above all, hyperbole. Two books of Joseph Perl, *Revealer of the Concealed* and *Examiner of the Ẓaddiḳ*,[76] ridicule mystifications of Ḥasidism with merciless venom. Written in the popular epistolary form, they chat away the substance of Ḥasidism with aphoristic abandon. The journey to the *Ẓaddiḳ* is a farce; with tongue in cheek Perl notes: "It is known that the whole of Judaism depends on the journey to the *Ẓaddiḳ*."[77] The fusion of eroticism and mysticism which is typical of many religions elicits the remark that "prayer is like intercourse."[78]

Elegance of style is a sin: "When someone writes in a pure style, he is regarded as a heretic. . . ."[79] Erudition is the preserve of the *Ẓaddiḳ*: "Sages are not erudite. The true Ẓaddiḳim are."[80] They are also rulers of the world: "the Ẓaddiḳim can force God, blessed be His name, to do what they will. They perform miracles with their holy words."[81] It is not too much to say that the adoration of the *Ẓaddiḳ* in a certain sense replaces the worship of God, hence a semblance of relic worship which is foreign to Judaism: the pipe of the Baal Shem Tov is endowed with special powers; it can put evil men to sleep and render them harmless.[82] In a hyperbolic gesture the Baal Shem Tov is endowed with greater powers than the Almighty. "And the Ẓaddiḳim in our generation are more important than the Holy One, blessed be He and the patriarchs and Moses our Master. . . ."[83] It goes without saying that the *Ẓaddiḳ* can see and not be seen.[84]

Special attention is given to Ḥasidic hagiography in Perl's *Revealer of the Concealed*. The book of legends about the founder of Ḥasidism, *Praises of Israel Baal Shem Tov*,[85] is castigated mercilessly: "I don't know who the author is and what the word Besht signifies: is it the name of a man or an angel? Sometimes it seems he is a man among men, eating and drinking and sleeping with his wife in one bed like a rustic . . . sometimes it seems to me that he is an angel conversing with angels, with the Messiah, with Elijah, with the dead."[86]

The Examiner of the Ẓaddiḳ, the sequel to the *Revealer of the Concealed*, indulges in similar though less vigorous satire. The didactic end of the book carries no conviction. The Ḥasidim are blamed for the pollution of faith and for the abandonment of the simple arts of the artisan as a means of economic survival.[87]

Isaac Erter (1791–1851) satirized Ḥasidism with subtle vigor. As a physician he was sensitive to the droll and crude therapy of the Ḥasidic rabbis: it consisted of an unholy mixture of incantations and folk remedies—and it was a very profitable business. Unlike Perl, Erter used self-mockery to drive home his disgust with the new sect. Like the rabbis, he maintained, he was in the business of healing. But they assumed superior airs and spoke about everything under the sun and understood nothing. Yet he, Erter, practiced medicine as successfully as they did: his dead were as dead as the individuals who had been in the healing custody of the rabbis. But there is a difference between him and them: "I go on foot, they rush in the street with horse and carriage."[88] Interestingly, Mendele Moker Sefarim also exposed the medical fakeries of the Ḥasidim in the novel *The Fathers and the Sons:* vile concoctions and magical incantations—these are the remedies given to the sick by the wonder-rabbis.

Metempsychosis and medicine are strange bedfellows; they lie side by side in Ḥasidic lore. Erter deprecates this union and xeposes the failure of therapy and the mystic fraud as they were practiced by unscrupulous Ḥasidim. Unlike Perl, again, he combined allegory, which was popular in the age of Enlightenment, with an imaginative stance which was rare among the addicts to Reason. In a chapter of his book, *A Watchman Unto the House of Israel*, he describes a vision: Ḥasidism and Wisdom appear to him in the guise of two ladies. The former seeks to convince him how easy it is to become her devotee and guide the people in her name: with a bit of cunning and folly "it is not difficult for a man to lead astray a straying people who seek miracles."[89] He is promised greatness and urged to imitate Israel Baal Shem Tov. But he is drawn to Wisdom, which is a quest for truth and a satisfaction of intellectual curiosity.

Somewhat later Gottlober disparaged the lechery of the Ḥasidim in fiction. In a story "Voice of Joy and Salvation in the Tents of Ẓaddiḳim" he ridicules a certain Ḥayyim Michal who serves God in fear and love, studies Ḥasidic lore all the days of his life, prays with enthusiasm, refrains from seeing any man or woman—except one young woman who visits him daily and asks him to intercede with a wonder-rabbi and crave his blessing for the curse of her childlessness. She is successful; she bears a son with a strange resemblance to Ḥayyim Michal.[90]

The most prolific writer in the age of Enlightenment, Peretz Smolenskin, mounted a relentless attack on Ḥasidism. The foe was the incarnation of multifaceted vice. Ignorance, lack of decorum, mystical obfuscation, miraculous fakery and false exaltation, thievery and bribery, lying and lewdness—this is the incomplete list of Ḥasidic transgressions. At best the Ḥasid is a carefree rascal:

> He will revel and sing, and whenever there is a celebration or a glass of wine, he is sure to be there . . . but you will not find him leading the life of a sensible man but rather that of a madman, without rhyme or reason.[91]

Smolenskin hurls his most venomous shafts at the *Ẓaddiḳ* and his holy machinations:

> . . . every eye was riveted on the door which the Ẓaddiḳ was about to enter . . . young and old they regarded him with awe, scarcely daring to look at him before he took his seat like the lord in judgment—ready to pardon penitents who had come to confess their sins and bare their sorrows before him. . . .[92]

In other passages of his novels Smolenskin ridicules the wonder-making powers of the Ẓaddiḳim, their ostentation and their pseudo erudition. The awesome respect of men and women for these individuals is a ludicrous farce in his view, an homage of the innocently ignorant to the consciously ignorant.

In Smolenskin the caricature of Ḥasidism reached its peak; and only fifty years later did the idealization of Ḥasidism find its greatest master in Agnon.

ADMIRERS OF ḤASIDISM

Hess in *Rome and Jerusalem* and Eliezer Zevi Zweifel (1815–1888) in *Peace on Israel*[93] heralded new attitudes. Hess, the former admirer of Marx, sympathized with the communal attitudes of the Ḥasidim; Zweifel lavished praise on the three Jews who conferred originality and even greatness on eighteenth-century Jewry: Mendelssohn, the Gaon of Vilna, and Baal Shem Tov.

These were lonely voices in the sixties and seventies of the previous century. Even Judah Leb Peretz (1851–1915),[94] who was to change Jewry's attitude toward Ḥasidism with his enticing stories, published as late as 1875 an anti-Ḥasidic poem, "Partnership," in the best tradition of the Enlightenment. He ridiculed the Ḥasidim's excessive enthusiasm in prayer, their addiction to alcohol, and their pursuit of miracles.[95] Later, in his memoirs, he remembered a Ḥasid who would down his brandy "in one gulp" but munch his cookie meditatively.[96]

It was not until 1894, when Peretz began to write his *Ḥasidic Tales*, that he effected a turning point in everyone's attitude toward Ḥasidism. This complete re-evaluation is one of the most curious phenomena in the development of the shifts in ideas and emphases in social and religious movements. The swift conquest of the field of psychology by psychoanalysis, the emphasis on intuition by the influential works of Henri Bergson, the refined techniques of anthropology—these fostered a new receptivity to the non-rationalist movement of Ḥasidism. The researches of Simon Dubrow and Samuel Abba Horodetzky into the historical backgrounds of Ḥasidism, the seductive paraphrases of Ḥasidic stories by Martin Buber and Micah Joseph Berdyczewski, the poetic tales of Judah Leb Peretz and the realistic tales of Judah Steinberg—all these savants and men of letters effected a new approach to Ḥasidism. It culminated in *The Bridal Canopy* by Samuel Joseph Agnon, who recreated the world of Ḥasidism with reverent piety.

The resuscitation of Ḥasidism was more than an act of romanticism on the part of some writers and scholars: it filled a deeply felt need for religious regeneration and it lacked the faddist overtones which characterized the introduction of Zen Buddhism into the West by non-Jewish authors. The rationalist bias of the enlightened had blinded them to the virtues of Ḥasidism. Since they had lost faith in religious regeneration from within, they had committed themselves to secular transformation from without. The opposite climate of opinion prevailed a hundred years after the initial attempts at discrediting Ḥasidism. The psychic void, left by the deterioration of religion, had to be filled by non-rational movements: intuitionism, mysticism, Jungian archetypes, and the whole angelology and demonology of men uncovered by psychoanalysis.

Peretz, who was anti-Ḥasidist initially, became the prime mover in the re-assessment of Ḥasidism. Like Janus he faced backward and forward. He began with an anti-Ḥasidic stance *à la* Erter, and he pioneered pro-Ḥasidism. From his deep interest in the folklore and imagination of simple people he fashioned a new trend in Hebrew literature: neo-Ḥasidism.

The short story "If Not Higher" is a perfect example of the new attitude toward Ḥasidism. The *Ẓaddiḳ* of Nemirov disappeared every morning in the period of penitence preceding the High Holidays. His adherents believed that he had flown to heaven to intercede for his people. But a skeptical Jew from Lithuania was determined to explode the myth. He stole into the *Ẓaddiḳ*'s room, hid under his bed, watched him rise and put on peasant's clothes, and followed him to the forest. There the skeptic saw him wielding the ax on a tree, bringing the wood to a sick Jewish woman, and lighting a fire for her. But the poor woman was worried: "How will I pay?" The rabbi answered reproachfully: "Fool, you are a poor, sick woman. I trust you this bit of wood. I have faith that you will pay. But you have a powerful God, a mighty God and you don't trust him. . . ."[97] The *Ẓaddiḳ*, in the guise of a peasant with the name of Vassil, managed to convince her that she can pay later and that he will trust her. That did it: the Lithuanian Jew when he heard the Ḥasidim say that the *Ẓaddiḳ* flew heavenward, added: "if not higher."

All the ingredients of this story would have been mercilessly satirized by a Perl or an Erter, by a Levinsohn or a Gottlober: the miracle-working rabbi, the unattended visit of the rabbi to a woman, the superstitious faith of the Ḥasidim in their rabbi. But the art of Peretz—slightly aided by the hush technique of a Maeterlinck and the mystifications of French symbolists who were in vogue at the end of the nineteenth century—reduced the allegedly superhuman miracle to a mere human situation. And by reducing it, by making it believable, he actually elevated it again into the metaphysical realm.

Nothing aroused the ire of the enlightened as much as the myth of metempsychosis. Erter castigated it mercilessly. But Peretz knew how to infuse a new vitality into the hoary myth. In his story "You Shall Not Covet," a saintly, learned, ascetic person was about to depart this life. But the neglected body refused to release his soul: "I have not lived at all. . . . And each organ struggled with the angel of death. The heart said: I have not felt anything yet. The eyes argued: we have not seen anything yet. The hands asked: what has been ours? The feet cried: where did we go?. . ." All the other limbs fought valiantly and bitterly. And the saintly person sighed the sigh of envy in his agony: "he envied those who died an easy death." And another transmigration was earned by the transgression against the commandment "you shall not covet."[98]

The saintly person became Reb Zanvele Purisover—rich, learned, hospitable to a fault. He befriended the stranger, even the deformed, even the hunchback. One such guest had argued with him a point of ritual law and seemed to win the argument. Reb Zanvele had to catch his breath outside the door. The wintry night, the fresh snow, the radiant sky: these cleared his mind and showed gaps in the guest's reasoning. He walked in ecstasy, crossed and recrossed the market place, left the street of the town and lost his way. After considerable wanderings he arrived at an inn, entered a room where half-drunk peasants toasted each other and kissed each other and wept with tenderness.

> And then Reb Zanvele who was a greater scholar than the Rabbi, a better singer than the cantor, a better reader of the Torah than the Lithuanian teacher, who had the most beautiful house, a woman of valor for a wife, the brightest children. . . . Reb Zanvele, the best counselor, the most honest arbiter, the most generous philanthropist . . . lost control of himself . . . and envied in his heart of hearts, each peasant who sat beside the warm hearth. . . . And a new series of transmigrations began for Reb Zanvele.[99]

The juxtaposition of wealth and want, intellectuality and ignorance, elegance and rudeness: Peretz achieved it in the final passage of the story "You Shall Not Covet." And he gave a poetic re-interpretation of the doctrine of metempsychosis, for in that story it is not a punishment for a life of crime; it is a correction, on a different life-plane, of one single blemish.

Peretz seems to have been fascinated by the idea of transmigration on another level. In the story "The Reincarnation of a Tune" he describes the nuances of notes, tunes, and melodies with the ear of a musician and the heart of a mystic. Few writers had the auditory sensitivity of a Peretz.

> Everything depends on *who* sings and *what* he sings. With the same bricks one can build a synagogue and a church, a palace or a prison. . . . With the same letters one can write the mysteries of the Torah and the biggest heresies. And with the same sounds one can ascend to the highest levels of enthusiasm and cleavage to God, but one can also descend to the deepest hell and wallow there like a worm in the mud.[100]

It is, perhaps, no accident that Peretz's highest sensitivity to melody appears in the story "The Kabbalists." For melody is a mystical experience in his view.

> There are tunes which must have words: this is a very low level. There is a higher level: a tune that sings itself, a tune without words, a pure tune.
>
> But that tune still needs a voice and lips through which it emerges. And lips are physical and the voice of the order of nobler physicality is still physical in essence.
>
> Or shall we say the voice is on the boundary line between the spiritual and the physical?
>
> At any rate, the tune that needs a voice, that depends on lips is not pure, not wholly pure, not truly spiritual.
>
> The true tune sings itself without a voice. It sings itself inside, in the heart, in the intestines.
>
> And this is the meaning of King David's words: All my bones shall say . . .[101] the tune must sing in the marrow of one's bones, there must the tune be, the highest praise for God blessed be He. This is not the tune of a creature of flesh and blood, this is not an artificial tune. This is part of the tune with which God has created the world, part of the soul which he poured into the world.[102]

One of Peretz' first Hebrew poems bears the title "Nageniel,"[103] angel of music. And his first Ḥasidic story, "Doctrine of Ḥasidism," begins with an econmium on the Rabbi of Nemirov, who would say that "the whole world is a song and dance before the Holy One blessed be He . . . the whole world is a song, we are all singers . . . each letter of Holy Writ is music, each soul is music. . . ."[104] This is romantic exaggeration, this is hyperbolism run amok; but this is empathetic understanding of Ḥasidism.

Peretz also pioneered in the domain of Ḥasidic drama. *The Golden Chain*, a play in three acts, first appeared in Hebrew under the title *Ruin of A Ẓaddiḳ's House.*[105] Later it was reworked in Yiddish as a complicated portrait of four generations of Ḥasidim who were given to an abundance of talk and a scarcity of action.

The Ḥasidic plays par excellence were written in our generation by Harry Sackler. Possessed of unique gifts—historical empathy and dramatic imagination—he recreated on a vast canvas both Cananite civilizations and early American civilization, both rabbinic and Ḥasidic Jewry. In essay, story, and play he attempted to fathom the eternal mystery of Judaism and reconstruct mystical personalities with a certain sobriety which distanced him from them. Like Buber he was fascinated by the personality of Rabbi Jacob Isaac, the Seer of Lublin. Unlike Buber who devoted a novel to the saintly man, Sackler chose a crucial episode in that life and fashioned it into a playlet in three scenes. The Seer was about to be married to a beautiful girl. But with innate psychological and parapsychologial powers of observation, with an incipient talent of penetrating sight, he noticed her captivating vivaciousness, which betrayed sexual experience, and he expressed it by implication: "This is my bride. But that other—that shadow. . . . There will be no wedding."[106] In spite of the bridegroom's unwillingness there was a wedding with unhappy consequences: divorce, the father's shame and rage, the prospective marriage with the young squire of the manor house. The bridegroom's master, aware of the penetrating sight of the Seer and its awesome possibilities, hoped that the children would not inherit "the terrible and ominous power." His parting words to the man who in turn would be master and saint: "You shall be the first and the last of your line. . . ."[107]

Sackler managed to impress dramatic delicacy and intensity on three scenes of extraordinary tension. The natural and the supernatural: they are also delicately balanced in an earlier playlet *Eastward*, a dramatization of events which force the young rabbi Naḥman of Bratzlav to undertake an arduous trip to the Holy Land. Three days of incessant rain had imposed gloom upon him and his surroundings. Why the flood when he had prayed for dew? The friend who is about to offer a simple explanation of natural phenomema is impatiently interrupted: there are no simple interpretations. Self-incarceration deepens the melancholy of the young saint. The seekers of advice and the sick in need of soothing promises have been turned away. Dialogue with a mysterious stranger points to a change of mood and a fateful decision. The wall that rises between him and his Maker indicates a journey to the Wailing Wall: "I have to direct my steps to the top of the mountain which rims the heart of the world."[108] And he leaves his family to the tender mercies of strangers because in reality "there are no strangers in the world."[109] It is incumbent upon him to fulfill the command which was given to Abraham: Go forth from your native land . . . (Genesis 12:1). And when it is pointed out to him that his grandfather, the Baal Shem Tov, had attempted the trip to the Holy Land unsuccessfully he parries the thrust of the objection with a witty phrase: "Grandfather had no grandfather like my grandfather."[110]

With the art of a watercolorist Sackler painted his gentle playlets on Ḥasidic themes. The more ambitious full length play, *Journey of the Ẓaddiḳ*,[111] is a study in contrasts: the spiritual and the workaday world clash in antithetical antiphony. The choice of a saintly heir by the Ẓaddiḳ, the struggle of the heir with his instinctual drives, the victory of the powers of holiness over the powers of defilement— these are dramatized with technical skill and a delicate irony. It is an artistic achievement of first rank, perhaps the best Ḥasidic drama of our generation.[112] But it could not compete in popularity with *The Dybbuk*[113] which was written by Solomon Zanvil Rapoport under the pseudonymn of S. Anski (1863–1920). Originally composed in Russian, it was translated into Yiddish by the author and brilliantly done in Hebrew by Ḥayyim Naḥman Bialik. It was first performed by the Vilna Ensemble in Yiddish in 1920 and by Habimah—the National Theater of Israel at the present time—in Moscow in 1922. The meagre plot—the exorcism of a *Dybbuk* from the body of a girl—is compensated by folklore in imaginative profusion. Brilliantly acted by both theatrical companies it became a classic in Europe and America. In the history of the theatre it marked the end of naturalism as represented by Stanislavsky and the beginning of expressionism as represented by Evgeny Vakhtangov.[114]

Peretz, Anski, and Berdyczewski were collectors of folklore, which enriched their creativity and pioneered new approaches to Ḥasidism. Though complicatedly interdependent they managed to preserve their independence in spite of mutual cross-fertilization. It is no mere accident that the very first article of Berdyczewski on Ḥasidism was entitled—like the first Ḥasidic story of Peretz—"Doctrine of Ḥasidism."[115] The influence was pervasive, both in the essays and in the stories of Berdyczewski. It led him back to Ḥasidism, for he grew up in a Ḥasidic environment, abandoned it, adopted Nietzscheanism and—via Nietzsche and Peretz—returned to Ḥasidism in nostalgic reverence.

Like Peretz he was enchanted by the Ḥasidic dance. And he used the identical phrase of the psalmist to express the intensity of bodily movements: "All my bones shall say . . . (Psalms 35:10) . . . These dances are great . . . poetry which does not come from joyous lips but speaks through movement."[116] Berdyczewski was also enamored of the Ḥasid's form of prayer: "His feet—they stand on the ground but his whole body rises and ascends above the heights of the clouds. . . ."[117]

Though not original in his objective evaluation of Ḥasidism, he stressed with admiration the triad of concepts which animated the movement: enthusiasm, cleavage to the divine, holiness of life. He welcomed the pioneering studies on Ḥasidism: Hillel Zeitlin's *The Methods and Currents of Ḥasidism*,[118] Abraham Kahane's and Samuel Abba Horodetzky's studies of the Baal Shem Tov. And he gave unstinting praise to the stories of Peretz and Steinberg when they first appeared at the turn of the century. His own Ḥasidic tales are stylized elaborations of such source material as *The Praises of the Baal Shem Tov* and *The Stories of Rabbi Naḥman*. They concentrate on legends about wonder-rabbis from the founder of the movement to the latter-day saints. It is rather strange for a disciple of Nietzsche to have been as fascinated by the miraculous and the supernatural as Berdyczewski was. In his tales, souls wander from world to world, Elijah visits mere mortals and changes the course of their lives. A good example is the story of the poor rabbi who studied assiduously and, by mere chance, noticed a great light in the crack of a wall. He rose, examined the hole, and found a jewel. That night Elijah appeared to him and told him that he could choose the jewel, which would make him rich or wisdom, which would illumine the world. He chose the latter course.[119]

Berdyczewski, the uneasy revolutionary in Hebrew literature, sympathized with Ḥasidism because it deviated from traditionalism. In his poetic craving for change in Jewish life—from fascination with the book to union with nature, from legalistic surfeit to mystic rapture—he seemed to find an ally in Ḥasidism.

Judah Steinberg (1863–1908) loved Ḥasidism for its own sake. In the beginning of the twentieth century he published Ḥasidic stories which lack the perceptive, lyrical, almost musical quality of a Peretz and the supernaturalism of a Berdyczewski. But they are permeated with naïveté and with realism. And, at times, they reflect the conflict of Ḥasidism with nationalism. Thus, for Zaydl the watchmaker, Zionism is a religious movement, a beginning of redemption. He pawns two watches to buy a share of the Colonial Bank, a Zionist institution, and keeps it in a special bag. He suffers from environmental obloquy: his faith in Zionism conflicts with the faith of his fellow-Ḥasidim who cannot condone association with "heretics" like Zionists.[120]

Steinberg is at his best when he integrates Ḥasidism with the orthodox environment as in his folk tale "The Two Brothers of Blessed Memory."[121] With mock precision he enumerates ranks of perfection among Ẓaddiḳim: some are the eyes of the people, the masters of the revealed tradition. Some are the mouth and the teeth of the people; they are the keepers of the keys of livelihood. And then there are those who are the heart of the people; there is no higher rank than theirs. On this hierarchical substrate Steinberg builds his story about two brothers, Rabbi Elimelech and Rabbi Zusya, who wander from place to place in order to reform evildoers—not by edifying sermons, but by taking, as it were, their sins upon themselves and forcing the sinner to repent. Thus, an adulterer would not be shamed by direct assault on his personality. But Rabbi Elimelech would say to his brother within the hearing of the adulterer: I have committed adultery. And Rabbi Zusya would answer with a question: When? Where? And then a recital of circumstances would follow, and Rabbi Zusya would rebuke his brother and admonish him to repent. But how to justify the lie? This is the mystery. Steinberg uses a similar method in the story "Saturday Night." First he announces an axiom: the best way of serving God is through joy; sorrow is the work of Satan; one has to avoid sadness or fight it. Then he proceeds to tell the story of Baal Shem Tov who arrived at this triple truth after many trials and tribulations.

In the early decades of this century several writers made ambitious attempts at literary transformations of Ḥasidism. They produced novels on Ḥasidic themes and personages. *Yeḥiel the Hagrite*[123] by Simon Halkin (1898—) is the work of a youthful writer whose hero strives after a living God. The protagonist may be a visitor of the Bohemian haunts in Greenwich Village; he may be unsettling the emotions of a few dreamy girls; he is rooted in Ḥasidic ancestry, in Ḥabadism. Perhaps he is guilty of a double flirtation—sexual and theological. In his reveries he oscillates between futility and frustration. But the paucity of action is not entirely compensated by the inner monologue of Yeḥiel Hero.

Yohanan Twersky (1900–1967) portrayed Ḥasidism on the basis of personal experience and historical studies. With the ease and nimbleness of a Maurois he concentrated on the piquant episode and the essential characteristic in four novels. In *The Inner Court* he depicted his own family background of the Ḥasidic townlet of Chernobil in the vicinity of Kiev; in *The Heart and the Sword* he chose as his theme Rabbi Naḥman of Bratzlav's pilgrimage to the Holy Land; in *From Darkness to Light* he painted the period of the Baal Shem Tov and the Gaon of Vilna; in *The Virgin of Ludmir*[124] he concentrated on the unique role of womanhood in the Ḥasidic movement. There was novelty in his method: he explored depth psychology and the addiction to psychologism which were fashionable in European and American literature a generation ago.

The novel *The Gaon and the Rabbi*[125] by Zalman Shneur is essentially a double Plutarchian portrait of great personages in the eighteenth century. The Gaon emerges as an ascetic and a recluse with an insatiable thirst for learning; but such a person is obviously not the stuff of a novel. And so, for plot and drama, Shneur concentrates on the Gaon's relentless fight against Ḥasidism, which leads to the banning of the sect and the burning of its books.

Rabbi Shneurson is an incarnation of peaceability, an amalgam of intellectual aspiration and emotional satisfaction. But his calm character serves as a point of polarization rather than a magnet of unity. There is no doubt about Shneur's sympathies: he loves Shneurson but he only admires the Gaon.

It is an unfortunate fact of modern Hebrew literature that even a writer of Shneur's stature did not produce an outstanding novel on Ḥasidism. It was Agnon who accomplished this task. Though he has built up a solid reputation in Hebrew literature and earned the Nobel Prize in 1966, the highest literary award and the first to be accorded to a Hebrew writer, he is essentially a *laudator temporis acti*, a praiser of the past. This is not a detriment—except in the eyes of those whose vision of the present is synonymous with the latest headlines. Those who see the present as a repository and refinement of the past will accept Agnon's vision of the past as a contemporaneous adventure.

With his unique gifts of reconstruction and transformation of the past he enshrined forever the bygone glory of Ḥasidism in a major novel, *The Bridal Canopy*, which was published in 1931 and which immediately recalled *Don Quixote*—another romantic recreation of a bygone past. Both novels presuppose a medieval way of looking at life: man is a wayfarer in a strange world, a *homo viator*. And both novels, *The Bridal Canopy* and *Don Quixote*, are stories about unrealistic, fantastic heroes in adventurous travels to nowhere. But unlike *Don Quixote*, whose mind is crammed with the romantic heroes of medieval knighthood and whose desire is to emulate or better them, Reb Yudel, the hero of *The Bridal Canopy*, is sated with biblical and talmudic and homiletical lore. And his desire is to equal the great saints and sages in piety. Like *Don Quixote* he has a goal: not to endanger his life in quest of the beautiful Dulcinea del Toboso, but to find three husbands for his three nubile daughters. Like Don Quixote Yudel has his Sancho Panza: note the Waggoner; whose two horses—not Rosinante, but Drawme and Wilrun—are straight from the Song of Songs.[127] And they indulge in beautiful dialogues:

> And Drawme said to Wilrun: Brother Wilrun, do you remember the times before the roads were put in order, when travelers never journeyed by night because of the perils, but betook themselves to the inn while it was still day, and the horses could rest in the stable and put their bones to right? But now that the roads are in order we have to travel day and night without a chance to gather strength and rest our limbs, so that the horse forgets he's a horse but dashes along like a crazy beast, excuse my mentioning them both in the same breath.
>
> Said Wilrun, Shut up and don't remind me of the early days. For Wilrun had known better times, being well brought up and eating and drinking and happy and glad, yet having now fallen so low as to be a yoked beast and a burdened steed. And so he was not fond of reminiscences. Like a young prince round whose neck was hung a fine jewel which he went and lost. So whenever he went out he would sink his chin on his chest so that nobody should notice the loss. And both Drawme and Wilrun turned their heads and sighed for the days of their youth which had fled and could not be caught afresh.[128]

Don Quixote is the epic of Spain, *The Bridal Canopy* is the epic of Ḥasidic Jewry—with sequels in the story "In the Heart of the Seas" and in many other tales.

No translation, not even the translation of I. M. Lask which was published in 1937 and republished in 1967, can do justice to this masterpiece. Its idiomatic language can be transposed, paraphrased or metamorphosed; but it cannot be translated. Not only the Hebrew style but also the idiom of Ḥasidic life in the early nineteenth century, reflected in the novel, does not lend itself to translation into English. For the novel depicts a life of dedication to Torah—the sum total of Jewish law and lore. It is a life of expectation: the Messiah, the future Redeemer of the world and the eliminator of the exile and all its attendant ills, is just around the corner.

The hero of the story, Reb Yudel, is not only an individual, he *is* the Jewish people. His name is a diminutive of Judah, the individual and then the tribe that gave Jews their name. His three marriageable daughters—Gittele, the good one; Blume, the flowering one; Pessele

(Bess, Elizabeth)—are the cause of his extensive journeys. For Yudel, spurred by the naggings of his wife Frummet, the pious one, sets out to find three bridegrooms for his daughters. (Marriage in those old days was not the business of the parties concerned: it was the business of their parents.) Add to this note the Waggoner and the two horses, who are very much part of the story, and you have the main *dramatis personae*. But the cast is inexhaustible. Almost any village or town on the list of Yudel's peregrinations enriches the cast. Like all good stories, *The Bridal Canopy* has a happy ending: the three daughters are married off to learned husbands; Reb Yudel and his wife live to see their children's children and, at the end of their days, they settle in the Holy Land.

The thread of Yudel's journey is a thin thread of narrative. Village follows village, story follows story. Yet the story within the larger context of the main plot develops the characters horizontally rather than vertically. Their virtues and vices, which are known almost from the very beginning, gain in width. And the stories within their main plot lead an independent and a dependent life. As a matter of fact some of them have been published separately as far back as 1920. In 1931 Agnon published his novel—really a second version—and in 1953 a third revised version. Like Yeats, his contemporary, Agnon has been revising endlessly.

But it would be unjust—and many of his critics are guilty of that injustice—to regard Agnon as the mere poet of Ḥasidism. He has devoted a considerable portion of his work to European and Palestinian Jewry in this century. And since this century is often regarded as the century of the alienated individual, much has been made of the alienated types that roam his novels and stories. It was but a step to bring in Kafka, that master of the theme of alienation and compare him with Agnon.

Nothing can be more unjust to both of them. They are worlds apart: Agnon's characters move in a landscape of love and compassion. And the Almighty's protective vigilance envelops them like a refreshing breeze of the summer. Kafka's characters are moved by uncertainty, accused without knowing the terms of their guilt, judged without comprehending the intent of justice. Agnon's is a deeply ethical landscape; Kafka's is an amoral landscape. Finally, Agnon as well as most of his characters live by the traditions of Judaism; Kafka and his characters are completely deracinated. That is, perhaps, Agnon's great worth for our generation: in a world of shaken values, he stands—together with his works—for the solid principles of moral regeneration. And these principles are not preached: they are lived by men and women who are raised to the level of esthetic experiences by the immortal art of Agnon.

ḤASIDISM IN HEBREW POETRY

It is a paradox: the poets of Ḥasidism were writers of fiction—Peretz and Agnon. The leading poets of the Hebrew Renaissance in the twentieth century, Bialik and Tschernichowsky, were almost untouched by Ḥasidism. And Shneur, the author of the *The Gaon and the Rabbi*, published one memorable poem on Rabbi Levi Isaac of Berdichev in 1942. Yet most contemporary Hebrew poets sympathized with Ḥasidism. It was a Hebrew poet in America, E. E. Lisitzky who discovered a Ḥasidic intensity in Negro prayers and spirituals.[129] This linkage, not sufficiently explored, opened a window on interesting resemblances in folk imagination and folk art. Another Hebrew poet, who wrote his most significant poetry in America, created a dramatic dialogue, "Ahijah and Israel," on a Ḥasidic theme. Ahijah the Shilonite, prophet in the days of Jeroboam I and teacher of Israel Baal Shem Tov according to legend, converses with his student in paradise. Our world is a dream; the upper world is garment:

> The soul clothes God, the world clothes the soul:
> The upper world with its myriads angels and saints
> And the lower world with earth, heaven and hosts. . . .
> If soul could see the infinite in splendor and in fullness,
> It could not last a minute. . . .[130]

This is a typical fragment of a typical poem by Regelson: philosophical yet poetical, spiritual yet close to the magnificence of our planet. It is true: Ḥasidism is mere pretext for the intellectual conceits of Regelson. But the pre-eminent triad of the poets in the twenties of our century—Gruenberg, Shlonsky, Lamdan—expressed Ḥasidism in soulsearching poetry. Rabbi Levi Isaac of Berdichẹv appears in Gruenberg's verse as "the dadaist in prayer shawl and phylacteries," a modernized saint whose life was a sacrament, whose love for his people was a passion, and whose homiletical work, *The Holiness of Levi*,[131] was an infinite longing for the Ineffable. Both Shneur and Gruenberg used the intercession of the saintly rabbi against the calamitous background of the holocaust. And both developed the cautious streak of rebellion in the rabbi's famous prayer into conditional defiance.

Gruenberg cultivated other saints of the Ḥasidic pantheon: the learned Rabbi Israel of Rizhin, the fiery Rabbi Uri of Strelisk, and the generous Rabbi Meirl of Premishlan. The first imparts "translucent repose" to the poet; the second instructs him in the thunderous voice; the third commands extreme poverty: he has never kept his meagre supply of money more than a day because he wanted no metal coin barrier between him and his Maker.[132]

Consciously and deliberately Gruenberg used Ḥasidic locutions to enrich the texture of his poetry. And he was one of the first poets of this century to demand of the Hebrew writer that he explore and exploit the untapped sources of linguistic treasures in the totality of Hebrew writings, in Bible and Talmud, in Midrash and Kabbalah, in the liturgy and in the devotional works of Ḥasidism.

The unbridled intensity which characterized Ḥasidic prayer and dance became a distinguishing feature of the unbridled line of Gruenberg which often reached sixteen syllables. Whitman, so unpopular at mid-century in English-speaking countries, became the patron saint of Gruenberg: "The Hebrew Walt Whitman"—that was the ecstatic call of poet to poet across the years and across language barriers. But "Ḥasidic Walt Whitman" might have been an equally good, if not better, battle cry. For Gruenberg characterized Whitman in Ḥasidic terms: "that singing bundle of flesh and blood who defies corporeality."[133]

Unlike Gruenberg, Lamdan glorified Ḥasidic dances with sophisticated self-consciousness, and that was his innovation: while the original Ḥasid danced with the abandonment of joy, the Lamdanic Ḥasid danced with the exultation of sorrow and despair. In "The Chain of Dances," the most popular segment of the most popular book of poetry in the twenties, *Massadah*,[134] there is a constant antithesization of fathers and sons, a confrontation across centuries. Fathers danced thus: one hand clasped the shoulder of a friend, another hand held the Torah; the burden of an entire people was borne with love. Sons dance thus: one hand joins the hand of a friend in a circle, the other hand clasps the woes of a generation. The poet forces a pattern of unity on the dances of different generations: in the Ḥasidic dance a feeling was created that the burden of an entire people was borne with love, in the contemporary dance a feeling is created that the dance is one great circle of sorrows. In other words, the forms of artistic expression change, the content of sorrow is a constant, unchanging value. Ḥasidic intensity remains; Ḥasidic joy has departed.

Shlonsky was the only popular poet of the twenties who was not deeply affected by Ḥasidism. Like Auden he was trapped by his own lingual virtuosity. And he made a lasting contribution to the development of the Hebrew language through his supple verse. But Ḥasidism was merely grist to his lingual mill; it became a force in the ballads of Samson Meltzer in the thirties—the most genuine and sensitive interpreter of Ḥasidism in verse. His storytelling talent converted Ḥasidic tales into genuine poetry. And a folklike imagination enabled him to create unforgettable vignettes of Ḥasidic life. Thus, in his "Dobush and the Baal Shem-Tov," to quote an example from his numerous ballads, the poet engineers a meeting between two folk heroes of the eighteenth century: the old Ukrainian robber, revered in legend and song, and the father of Ḥasidism. Toward the end of his days Dobush experiences a change of heart and seeks to save his soul from damnation. At the advice of Baal Shem Tov he abandons the axe and the gold, two symbols of his power, and looks into the waters of the Prutetz:

> Skies below us, skies above us in this land of limpid light.
> Waters of the Prutetz wander on and on in roving might.
>
> They meander like the days of one who is about to die.
> To the Prut the Prutetz flows—whither ebbs our
> life away?
>
> Life was given by our Maker, life goes back to Him
> again.
> Man is like the wave of water, all his deeds are vile and
> vain.
>
> Man is like the water-mirror, mirroring the will of God.
> Man does what He asks of him, what He commands
> with gentlest nod.[135]

The advice of Baal Shem Tov works: the river soothes the conscience of the robber. On his return to his hide-out Dobush scatters his treasures in the best tradition of the folk song. The homespun philosophy is almost biblical in its simplicity and devout humility. And it acquires its proper form and rhythm in the ballad which, as a poetic folk form, is eminently suited to the recital of feats of physical and spiritual valor.

Baal Shem and Dobush are antithetical types and the symbols of two different cultures. In "The Dance of Rabbi Zusya" Meltzer uses antithesis in the context of one culture. The ballad tells the story of two brothers, Rabbi Zusya and Rabbi Elimelech who go into voluntary exile in order to do penance and who stop at a country inn in the course of their journeys. At night a gang of drunkards arrives and pulls Rabbi Zusya out of his sleep and into the whirl of their wild dance. Rabbi Elimelech wakes up and sees a great light and hears "a song like a song of angels." Suddenly he realizes that his brother dances with heavenly visitors. He asks to be drawn into the charmed circle. The sound of the voice dispels the song, the dance, and the vision. Then, at the request of Rabbi Elimelech, the brothers exchange places for the night. But when the gang of drunkards returns, it draws again, with unmistakable certainty, Rabbi Zusya into the whirl of their wild dance. By that time Elimelech realizes that only his brother has been admitted to superhuman company.

And, at this point, the profundity of the parable is told so subtly that it almost escapes notice. Rabbi Elimelech wakes his brother without a trace of jealousy: twice he had been honored to participate in angelic song and dance. But the recipient of that heavenly bounty is totally unaware of his good fortune. Living in an esoteric state of exultation and illumination he is almost envious of the exoteric mind which perceives, by a special act of grace, what has become almost commonplace to his uncommon sense.[136]

It is of extraordinary interest that many ballads and verse stories of Meltzer are woven around the central personality in Ḥasidism: Baal Shem Tov. The poet's early years in the Galician townlet of Tlust which reverberated with legends of Baal Shem Tov's mother and his orphaned youth, of Baal Shem Tov's habits and customs, stimulated Meltzer's folklike imagination. Sometimes he is merely the poetic reporter of a Ḥasidic town. At his best he is the poetic interpreter of a movement which, for him, lost none of its pristine freshness. In his native town it was still possible to hear and see Elijah the prophet in the guise of a benevolent Ukrainian peasant who helped push Baal Shem Tov's wagon of provisions out of the mire. And by an interesting interposition, Baal Shem Tov himself appeared as a poor wanderer on the eve of a Seder and saved a Jewish family—and perhaps a Jewish community—from a slandering blood-libel.

As in Gruenberg's works, other great figures of Ḥasidism are also subjected to poetic interpretion in Meltzer's poetry: Rabbi Israel of Rizhin, who flees from the persecution of the Tsar and is accompanied by a heavenly orchestra on his way, the Rabbi of Chortkov with his luxurious court, and, of course, Rabbi Levi Isaac of Berdichev. But their light dims in the splendor of Baal Shem's simplicity, whose intense love of Jewry and whose popular brand of piety appeal to men who are unhappy in their heterodoxy and their sophisticated nihilism.

In his best ballads Meltzer achieves a feat of extraordinary quality: he has learned how to tell a folk tale in verse without debasing its inherent poetry. And he has revived the ancient art of the balladist which has become almost extinct in the chief European literatures and, until the twentieth century, never acquired a place of prominence in Hebrew literature. He utilized all the favorite tricks of the ballader with consummate skill: the repetition of individual verses, the refrain, the studied artlessness of rhyme, the faulty prosody, slang, and even current phrases of foreign origin. He has succeeded in translating into an art-medium his warm concern with the fate of the Jews and his romantic love for the Jewish townlet, its ethical pathos and its Ḥasidic traditions. S. Shalom, a contemporary mystical poet, also spent his childhood in a Ḥasidic environment and wove his experiences into his long autobiographical poem *On Ben Pele*. In short, musical chapters of two four-line stanzas he manages to allude to the main stations of suffering in his personal life. But he yearns for the Ḥasidic house into which he was born and for the devotional air which hovered over the workday, the Sabbath, and the holiday. His Ḥasidic mysticism is contemporary with the tragic elimination of masses of Jewry during the Second World War. Thus, in a moving ballad, a rabbi is about to be shot, together with his Ḥasidim, by a Nazi firing-squad. They dig their own grave, they are on the brink of ultimate despair. In the funereal silence the Rabbi asks for water in a loud voice. No one dares to do his bidding; only a humble tailor in chains runs to the spout and brings water for the rabbi who washes his hands and recites the Confessional. When the officer gives the fatal command, the Rabbi smiles: there is still a Jew who knows how to die a martyr's death and how to conquer evil with death.

The great holocaust inspired some Ḥasidic poems of Shalom but it did not overwhelm his poetry. Aaron Zeitlin, on the other hand, was moved like Gruenberg to devote a whole book to the disastrous tragedy of European Jewry. As a son of Hillel Zeitlin—a writer who loved Ḥasidism with ecstatic abandon and preached its virtues in supercharged prose—he was imbued with its spirit to such an extent that he could write:

> Every man is an Israel Baal Shem
> Hidden, cave-dwelling.
> There is a forest in the cave
> Like the cave of Israel in the Carpathians.
> Satan grew the forest.
> God grew Satan.[137]

Zeitlin could turn a word or a phrase into a delightful homily, as his Ḥasidic ancestors were wont to do. But in his predilection for mysticism he is closer to William Butler Yeats than to Shalom or any other contemporary figure in modern Hebrew literature. Like the Irish poet, he is fascinated by the mystery of this world while the soul of mystery seems to elude his rational mind. In the dying and undying twilight he finds allusions to "the unrevealed twilight of the heart," and in the twilight of the heart he seeks an allusion to the Ineffable. But it is difficult to ascertain whether the poet aims at the heart of mystery or simply mystifies a common experience. For the Jew, Zeitlin reserves a special rank in the hierarchy of the world: he is what Spinoza was, according to the German poet Novalis, a God-intoxicated man—in a word, a Ḥasid.

CONCLUSION

On the scientific, on the novelistic, on the dramatic, and on the poetic planes scholars and authors have reassessed their immediate spiritual heritage. Some have sought religious regeneration through Ḥasidism; some have looked at it with nostalgic regret. All believe in its mystic strength and potent message for our time. That is why Ḥasidism proved to be a valuable article of cultural export. Theological circles in England, America, and Germany found this exotic product of eastern Europe interesting, stimulating, and even fascinating.

Through the writings of Buber Ḥasidism has become a widespread cult, a poetic stance, a mystic energy. His influential *I and Thou* can be regarded as *the* Ḥasidic poem of the twentieth century, but its language must be characterized as ecstatic discourse in prose.[138] Though it makes frequent allusions to the Buddha and to Socrates, to Dante and to Goethe, it is permeated with the spirit of the Baal Shem Tov and Shneur Zalman of Liady, the Preacher of Mezritch and Rabbi Naḥman of Bratzlav.[139] For Buber, in an excellent epigram of self-evaluation, has maintained that he became a filter of Ḥasidism.[140] How much of a filter can best be seen in the passage on prayer which can be duplicated in many a Ḥasidic source:

> The man who prays pours himself out in unrestrained dependence, and knows that he has—in an incomprehensible way—an effect upon God, even though he obtains nothing from God; for when he no longer desires anything for himself, he sees the flame of his effect burning at its highest.[141]

The whole existentialist stance of the book—an elaboration of Ḥasidic ideas of confrontation between man and man, man and nature, God and man—has influenced theologians like Reinhold Niebuhr, art critics like Sir Herbert Read, and psychiatrists like Leslie H. Farber. The Lutheran pastor, Albrecht Goes, who rose to eminence in Germany after the Second World War, paid tribute to Buber's influence on three generations in Germany. And he maintained that *I and Thou* was as important to him and his contemporaries as bread.[142] It was indeed a seminal work—as seminal for religious transformation as the difficult *Tractatus Logico-Philosophicus* by Ludwig Wittgenstein for the development of logic, linguistics, and philosophy. Both books are difficult, almost obscure. *I and Thou* remains enigmatic even after the summation of the contents by the author:

> The "complete," the legitmately religious existence of man, does not stand in a continuity but in the genuine acceptance and mastery of discontinuity. It is the discontinuity of essentiality and inessentiality that I understand as that of the I-Thou relation and the I-It relation to all being.[143]

In *I and Thou* Buber formulated these relationships in ecstatic imprecision:

> I perceive something. I am sensible of something. I imagine something. I will something. I feel something. I think something. The life of human beings does not consist of all this and the like alone.
> This and the like together establish the realm of It.
> But the realm of Thou has a different basis. When Thou is spoken, the speaker has no thing for his object. . . . Thou has no bounds.[144]

This is what Franz Rosenzweig termed *das neue Denken*—the new mode of thinking—for it involved commitment and participation.

It is not an exaggerated claim: Ḥasidism—via Buber—has become a dominant influence in the intellectual history of the West. It provided, at times, ephemeral stimulation; it built a permanent base for spiritual regeneration.

Notes

1. *Ẓaddiḳ* means "just" or "righteous" in biblical Hebrew. In Ḥasidic lore he is a mediator between God and man, endowed with a special spirituality which enables him to see God when He is concealed from others. See *Toledot Ya'aḳov Yosef*, (Jerusalem, 1961–62), p. 23. The Zaddik influences life on and beyond our planet;

he is a miracle man and the embodiment of wisdom. Buber, who correctly equates Ẓaddiḳim with the righteous, adds that the term actualy means "those who stood the test" or "the proven." See his *Tales of the Ḥasidim* (New York, 1947), p. 1. This is a leap into bold hypothesism. For a detailed discussion of the qualities of the *Ẓaddiḳ* as reflected in the primary source of Ḥasidism—the writings of Rabbi Jacob Joseph of Polnoye—see Samuel H. Dresner, *The Ẓaddiḳ* (London, New York, and Toronto, 1960), chaps. 5–9. For the *Ẓaddiḳ* in the writings of Elimelech of Lizensk see Rivkah Shatz, "le-Mahuto Shel ha-Ẓaddiḳ ba-Ḥasidut," *Molad* 144–145 (1960), pp. 365–378.

2. See V. S. Pritchett's review of books by Singer and Wiesel in *The New York Review of Books* (May 7, 1970), p. 15.
3. This meaning s.v. *Ḥesed* (2) in Koehler and Baumgartner, *Hebräisches und Aramaisches Lexikon zum Alten Testament*, third edition, with the participation of Hartmann and Kutscher (Leiden, 1967), p. 323. It is a better English equivalent than the vague *lovingkindness* in the biblical translations. On recent studies of *Ḥesed*, see Gerald A. Larue in his preface to Nelson Glueck's study of *Ḥesed in the Bible*, trans. Alfred Gottschalk (Cincinnati, 1967), pp. 1–32. The study by Glueck first appeared in 1927 as a published doctoral dissertation under the title *Das Wort ḥesed im alttestamentlichen Sprachgebrauche als menschliche und göttliche gemeinschaftsgemässe Verhaltungsweise*. Buber equates Ḥasidim with "the devout or, more accurately, those who keep faith with the covenant"; see his *Tales of the Hasidim*, p. 2. The qualifying phrase "more acurately" is an unfounded assumption.
4. In a special unrelated meaning *revile*, the verbal root, appears in Proverbs 25:10; twice in identical meaning, "show yourself loyal," in 2 Samuel 22:26 and in Psalms 18:26.
5. In Greek: *Ἀϐιδαῖοι ἰ ϐυναγωγὴ Ἀϐιδίων* 1 Maccabees 2:42; 7:13; 2 Maccabees 14:6. Apparently the Greek had no equivalent term.
6. Y. Sotah 9:24, *et al.*
7. On Hillel as Ḥasid see Adolph Büchler, *Types of Palestinian-Jewish Piety From 70 B.C.E. to 70 C.E.* (London, 1922), pp. 15–22, 25–26. The book was reprinted by Ktav Publishing Company (New York, 1968).
8. Abot 2:6. The treatise Abot discusses the Ḥasid on numerous occasions. Thus 5:13—"He who says what is mine is yours and what is yours is yours is a *Ḥasid*." A few other interesting sayings concerning the *Ḥasid* are found in Abot, 5:14; 5:16; 5:17.
9. Ta'anit 23a.
10. *Tosefta*, Sanhedrin 13.
11. *Anshe Ma'aseh*, on the meaning of the term see Büchler, *Types of Piety*, pp. 83–87.
12. The designation *Ḥasidim Rishonim*. See Büchler, *Types of Piety*, pp. 106–108; on the dates of these early Ḥasidim, p. 78.
13. *Ḥasidut* in Hebrew.
14. Sotah 9:15.
15. *Sefer Ḥasidim*; a convenient and critical second edition by Jehuda Wistinetzki (Frankfurt, 1924). On the authorship see J. Freimann's introduction to *Sefer Ḥasidim*, pp. 13–14.
16. On the development of mysticism among German Ḥasidim, see the first chapter of Joseph Dan, *Torat ha-Sod Shel Ḥasidut Ashḳenaz* (Jerusalem, 1968), pp. 9–45.
17. *Sefer Ḥasidim*, sect. 1, p. 1.
18. The book is conscious of Christian influences: "In each city habits of Gentiles are imitated by habits of Jews. . . ." ibid., sect. 1301, p. 321.

19. Ibid., sect. 38, p. 39. See also Simon G. Kramer, *God and Man in the Sefer Ḥasidim* (New York, 1966), p. 94.
20. Translation by J. J. Parry (New York, 1941). The title in the original is *De Arte Honeste Amande*. Dr. Monford Harris regards the work of Capellanus as a possible source for the *Sefer Ḥasidim*. See his article, "Concept of Love in *Sepher Hassidim*" (*sic*!), *Jewish Quarterly Review*, vol. 50 (July, 1955), pp. 15–18.
21. See his *Israel and Diaspora* (Philadelphia, 1969), p. 90.
22. See Gershom G. Scholem, *Major Trends in Jewish Mysticism*, paperback edition (New York, 1967), p. 327.
23. *Shulḥan 'Aruk* in Hebrew; first edition (Venice, 1564). It is one of the most authoritative codes of religious practice among Jews.
24. *Mappah* in Hebrew, a series of additions and comments which appear in most editions of the *Shulḥan 'Aruk*.
25. For a different translation of the passage in *Yeven Meẓullah*, see Abraham J. Mesch, *Abyss of Despair* (New York, 1950), pp. 110–111.
26. See *The Autobiography of Solomon Maimon*, translated from the German with additions and notes by J. Clark Murray (London, 1954), p. 147.
27. Literally, "people of the land," rural population. In this sense it is used in the Bible, e.g., 2 Kings 24:14. In rabbinic literature it means *vulgarian, ignoramus*, or especially a person ignorant of Jewish law and lore; in this sense—and not in the Biblical sense—it is used today.
28. Literally, "disciple of the wise," it denotes a scholarly person, well versed in Jewish law; and it is used as the antithesis of *'Am ha-Areẓ*.
29. See, for instance, S. A. Horodetzky, ed., *Sefer Shibḥe ha-Besht* (Berlin, 1922), p. 25; also Maimon, *Autobiography* pp. 81–84.
30. Scholem, *Major Trends in Jewish Mysticism*, pp. 330–334. See also J. G. Weiss, "A Circle of Pneumatics in Pre-Ḥasidism," *The Journal of Jewish Studies*, vol. 8, 3–4 (1957), pp. 199–213.
31. Apotropaic terminology is attested in both the Gilgamesh Epic and the Bible. See Patrick D. Miller, "Apotropaic Imagery in Proverbs 6:20–22, *Journal of Near Eastern Studies*, vol. 29 (April, 1970), pp. 129–130.
32. Maimon, *Autobiography*, p. 170.
33. Ibid., p. 105.
34. Abot 1:5; the sages also stressed the connection between women and witchcraft, Abot 2:7.
35. *Sefer Likkute Maharan* (Ostraha, 1820–21), p. 11b.
36. Dobh Baer of Lubavitch, *Tract on Ecstasy*, trans. from the Hebrew with an introduction and notes by Louis Jacobs (London, 1963), p. 48.
37. Martin Buber, *On Judaism*, ed. Nahum N. Glatzer (New York, 1967), p. 92. See also J. G. Weiss, "The Kavvanoth of Prayer in Early Ḥasidism," *The Journal of Jewish Studies*, vol. 9, 3–4 (1958), pp. 163–192.
38. See Maimon, *Autobiography*, p. 166.
39. Ibid., p. 167. On joy in Ḥasidism see A. Shochat, "Al ha-Simḥah ba-Ḥasidut," *Ẓiyyon* vol. 16 (1950). pp. 30–43. The author rightly refers to the verse which was constantly on the lips of the Ḥasidim: "Worship God in joy" (Psalms 100:2). And he traces the development of worship through joy in the writings of Cordovero, Luria, and the moralistic literature of Jewry in the seventeenth century.
40. Maimon, p. 172.
41. Steinberg, *Kol Kitbe Yehudah Steinberg* (Odessa, 1912–13), vol. 4, p. 163.
42. There is a well-known adage; "The Holy One, blessed be He, the Law and Israel

are one." Though it does not appear in the Zohar, it is derived from that book, which maintains that there are three levels tied to one another: The Holy One, blessed be He, the Law and Israel. (Zohar 3:73). On the distinction between the two adages see Gershom G. Scholem, "Demuto ha-Historit Shel R. Yisrael Baal Shem Tov," *Molad* 144–145 (1960), p. 354. The article presents the best evaluation of the historical Baal Shem Tov, as distinguished from the imaginary person.

43. Quoted by Martin Buber, *On Judaism*, p. 81.
44. Ibid., p. 93.
45. Ḥasidic music, and Ḥasidic songs, and Ḥasidic melodies, with their multiple borrowings from Slav peoples, still await the labors of musicologists in combination with Jewish scholars.
46. It is possible that, even before their publication, the writings of Moses Hayyim Luzzatto influenced the mystical trends of Ḥasidism. See I. Tishbi, "Darke Hafazatam Shel Kitbe Kabbalah le-Ramḥal be-Polin u-be-Lita," *Kiryat Sefer*, vol. 45 (December, 1969), p. 154.
47. See Martin Buber, *For the Sake of Heaven*, trans. Ludwig Lewisohn (Philadelphia, 1945), p. 4.
48. Ibid., p. 5.
49. See the introduction by Jacobs to Dov Baer of Lubavitch, *Tract on Ecstasy*, p. 9.
50. Ibid., p. 37.
51. For a slightly different translation, see Nissen Mindel's version of *Tanya* (New York, 1965), pp. 31–33.
52. The term used by Dov Ber is *Hitpa'alut*. Another term for ecstasy corresponds to the Greek, etymology (ἔκστασις): *Hazazah mi-Meḥomo*. See *Tract on Ecstacsy*, p. 13.
53. Ibid., pp. 60–62.
54. *Gammatria* can be defined, among other connotations, as "the use of letters for their numerical value; homiletic interpretation based on the numerical value of letters." See Marcus Jastrow, *Dictionary*, s.v. The pseudoscience, perhaps of Ionian origin, was practiced by Jews since Hellenistic times. See the interesting remarks and recent bibliography on *Gammatria* in S. Gervitz's article "Abram's 318," *Israel Exploration Journal*, vol. 19 (Jerusalem, 1969), p. 110. *Notariḳon* is abbreviation, an acrostic method, a mere hint of a word. See Marcus Jastrow, *Dictionary*, s.v.
55. On the persecutions of Ḥasidism see Simon Dubnow, *Toledot ha-Ḥasidut* (Tel Aviv, 1930), pp. 107–169. Dubnow is still the best historian of Ḥasidism.
56. *Toledot Yaa 'ḳov Yosef.* (Koretz, 1779–80).
57. *Degel Maḥane Ephraim* (Koretz, 1810–11).
58. *Maggid Debarav le-Ya'aḳov* (Koretz, 1783–84).
59. *Or ha-Emet* (Husiatyn, 1898–99).
60. *Haftarot*, "Conclusions": portions of Prophets which are read in the synagogue after the pertinent sections of the week during the morning services on the Sabbath, holidays, the Ninth Day of Ab, and on fast days.
61. *Toledot Ya'aḳov Yosef* (Jerusalem, 1961–62), p. 71.
62. Most of the stories of Rabbi Naḥman of Bratzlav were transcribed by his amanuensis after they had been told to the disciples. How faithful are the transcriptions? One can only guess. Samuel H. Setzer has endeavored to establish a critical edition in his *Sippure Ma'asiyyot-Wunder Ma'asiyyot Fun Rabbi Naḥman Braslaver* (New York, 1929). The sayings and stories of R. Naḥman have been extensively anthologized. The personality of R. Naḥman is the subject of a playlet by Sackler

—see *infra*—and a poem by the author. See Eisig Silberschlag, *'Ale, 'Olam, be-Shir* (New York, 1946), pp. 82–85.
63. The distance would be better measured by a comparison of the Yiddish original and the German translation of Buber.
64. Setzer, p. 157.
65. Martin Buber, *The Tales of Rabbi Naḥman* (New York, 1956), pp. 49–51.
66. Agnon was born in eastern Galicia; Buber was educated there by his grandfather, Solomon Buber, a well-known scholar and editor of midrashic literature. Both in Galicia and Bukovina which, between 1775 and 1848, was a district of Galicia, Buber experienced Ḥasidism at its source. See Martin Buber, *Mein Weg zum Chassidismus* (Frankfurt am Main, 1918), pp. 10–13.
67. See the Introduction to Jiri Langer, *Nine Gates to the Chassidic* [sic!] *Mysteries*, trans. Stephen Jolly (New York, 1961), pp. 3–19.
68. See Maimon, *Autobiography*, p. 167.
69. "Der Chassidismus, dieser hässliche Auswuchs des Judenthums. . . ." See Graetz, *Geschichte der Juden*, vol. 11 (Leipzig, 1870), p. 592.
70. S. Rawidowicz, ed., *Kitbe R. Naḥman Krochmal* (Berlin, 1924), p. 416. A similar sobriquet, "the hypocrites" (*ha-Mithassedim*), was used by S. J. Rapoport. See Samuel Werses, "ha-Hasidut be-'Ene Sifrut ha-Haskalah," *Molad* 144–145 (1960), p. 382. On Rapoport's attitude toward Ḥasidism see also Isaac Barzilay, *Shlomo Yehudah Rapoport* [Shir] *And His Contemporaries* (Ramat Gan, 1969), p. 80.
71. On *The Visionaries—Ḥoze Ḥezyonot* in Hebrew—see especially J. Klausner, *Historiyyah Shel ha-Sifrut ha-'Ibrit ha-Ḥadashah*, vol. 3 (Jerusalem, 1938–39), pp. 390–392.
72. The German phrase is *Religionsschwärmer*. See J. Klausner, *Historiyyan*, vol. 2 (Jerusalem, 1936–37), p. 265.
73. Ahad Ha'am, *Kol Kitbe Ahad Ha'am*, Dvir edition (Jerusalem, 1949), p. 466.
74. Isaac Bär Levinsohn, *Yalḳut Ribal* (Warsaw, 1878), p. 31. "Men of God" were identified as Ḥasidim by Rabbi David Ḳimḥi, ibid., p. 85.
75. Ibid., pp. 149–151.
76. *Megalleh Temirin* in Hebrew, first published in Vienna in 1819; *Boḥen Ẓaddiḳ*, first published in Prague in 1838.
77. See Introduction to *Megalleh Temirin*, pp. 6a, 49a.
78. Ibid., p. 10a.
79. Ibid., p. 7a.
80. Ibid., p. 6a.
81. Ibid., p. 8b.
82. Ibid., p. 57a–57b.
83. Ibid., p. 62b.
84. Joseph Perl, *Boḥen Ẓaddiḳ*, pp. 19, 46.
85. In Hebrew, *Shibḥe ha-Besht*. "Besht" is an ancronym of Baal Shem Tov.
86. Joseph Perl, *Meggalleh Temirin*, p. 36b.
87. Joseph Perl, *Boḥen Ẓaddiḳ*, p. 116.
88. See Isaac Erter, *ha-Ẓofeh le-Bet Yisrael* (Tel Aviv, 1944–45), p. 57; the title is based on Ezekiel 3:17.
89. Ibid., p. 19.
90. Gottlober "*Kol Rinnah wi-Yeshuah be-Ohale Ẓaddiḳim*," in *ha-Shaḥar*, vol. 6 (Vienna, 1874–75), pp. 157–158.
91. The translation is Patterson's. See *The Hebrew Novel in Czarist Russia* (Edinburgh, 1964), p. 208.

92. Peretz Smolenskin, *Ha-Toeh be Darke ha-Ḥayyim*, vol. 3 (Vienna, 1880), p. 58. The translation differs somewhat from Patterson's version in his article "The Portrait of the Saddik in the Nineteenth Century Hebrew Novel," *Journal of Semetic Studies*, vol. 8 (1963), p. 172.
93. In Hebrew, *Shalom ʿAl Yisrael*. Even before Hess and Zweifel we meet with a rare instance of interest in Ḥasidic proverbs. The editor of *Kerem Ḥemed* quotes with approval six proverbs of the Maggid of Dubno. See Eisig Silberschlag, "Parapoetic Attitudes and Values in Early Nineteenth Century Hebrew Poetry," in *Studies in Nineteenth Century Jewish Intellectual History*, ed. Alexander Altmann (Cambridge, Mass., 1964), p. 137, n. 90. Jacob Samuel Byk (1784–1831), a well-known *Maskil*, also sympathized with Ḥasidism. See Isaac Barzilay, *Shlomo Yehudah Rapoport* (Ramat Gan, 1969), p. 76.
94. There is no doubt that Peretz was born in 1851, in spite of his official birth certificate which was deposited in the archives of the municipality of Zamość—the birthplace of Peretz—and which listed May 18, 1852, as his birthday. There was no precision in those days, either on the part of the parents or on the part of Russian officials. The jubilee of Peretz was celebrated in 1901. See N. Meisel, *Sefer Judah Leb Peretz* (Merhavyah, 1960), pp. 432–434.
95. See his poem "ha-Shutafut" in *ha-Shahar* (Vienna 1874–75), pp. 551–552.
96. See Isaac Leib Peretz, *My Memoirs*, trans. from the Yiddish by Fred Goldberg (New York, 1964), p. 75.
97. "If Not Higher," in *Peretz*, trans. and ed. Saul Liptzin, *Yivo Billingual Series* (New York, 1947), pp. 180–181. My translations differ from Liptzin's.
98. *Peretz*, p. 214.
99. Ibid., p. 222.
100. Ibid., p. 236.
101. Psalms 35 : 10.
102. *Peretz*, p. 226.
103. The poem appeared in the magazine *ha-Boḳer Or* (1875–76), under the editorship of Abraham Ber Gottlober.
104. See "Mishnat Ḥasidim" in *Kitbe J. L. Peretz*, vol. 3 (Tel Aviv, 1925), p. 69. Many critics of Peretz have noticed his sensitivity to music. See F. Lachower, *Toledot ha-Sifrut ha-ʿIbrit ha-Ḥadashah*, vol. 3 (Tel Aviv, 1946), pp. 55–58. R. Benjamin (Joshua Radler-Feldman) thought that "Peretz himself was reincarnation of a tune. He was music and musician." See R. Benjamin, *ʿAl ha-Gebulin* (Jerusalem, 1922), p. 227.
105. "Ḥurban Bet Ẓaddiḳ" in *Kitbe J. L. Peretz*, pp. 105–116.
106. Harry Sackler, *The Seer Looks At His Bride* (Boston, 1932), p. 12.
107. Ibid., p. 29.
108. "Kelape Mizraḥ" in Sackler, *Sefer ha-Maḥazot* (New York, 1943), p. 414.
109. Ibid.
110. Ibid., p. 416.
111. *Nesiʿat ha-Ẓaddiḳ* in Sackler, *Sefer ha-Maḥazot*, pp. 199–268.
112. Sackler has not achieved recognition on a scale commensurate with his talents. For an appreciation of his dramatic *oeuvre* see Eisig Silberschlag, "Zevi Sackler," *Biẓaron* (1944), pp. 252–254. Recently G. Shaked, *ha-Maḥazeh ha-ʿIbri ha-Histori bi-Teḳufat ha-Teḥiyyah-Noseim we-Ẓurot* (Jerusalem, 1970), pp. 148–150; 183–184; 218–221.
113. *Dybbuk* means "cleaver," usually the soul of a dead person that enters the body

of another. For a convenient English summary of the play see Mendel Kohansky, *The Hebrew Theater—Its First Fifty Years* (Jerusalem, 1969), pp. 34–36. For the theory of the *Ẓaddiḳ's* descent as a necessary condition of ascent, see the important article of Joseph Weiss, "Reshit Zemihatah Shel ha-Derek ha-Ḥasidit" in *Ẓiyyon*, vol. 16 (1950–51), pp. 82–88.

114. On Vakhtangov and his role in the production of *The Dybbuk* see Mendel Kohansky, *Hebrew Theater*, pp. 34–43.

115. In Hebrew, *Mishnat Ḥasidim*. See *Kol Maamare Micah Joseph Berdyczewski* (Tel Aviv, 1951–52), pp. 3–5. Under the original title "Mishnat Ḥasidim," it appeared in 1899. See Meisel, p. 379. Berdyczewski changed his favorable attitude to Peretz in later years. Ibid., pp. 383–386. On Peretz's attitude to Berdycḥewski see now Jeshurun Keshet (Koplewitz), *Micah Joseph Berdychewski (Ben-Gurion) Hayyav u-Poalo* (Jerusalem, 1958), pp. 90–92. It is interesting to learn from Immanuel Ben-Gurion, Berdyczewski's son, that in his teens his father wrote a tract under the title *Ḳorot ha-Ḥasidut we-Rodefehah*. It has not been preserved for posterity. Ibid., p. 281.

116. *Kol Maamare Micah Joseph Berdychzewski*, p. 6.

117. Ibid.

118. Zeitlin, *Ha-Ḥasidut le-Shitotehah we-li-Zeramehah* (Warsaw, 1909–10).

119. Micah Joseph Berdyczewski, *Zefunot we-Aggadot* (Tel Aviv, 1955–56), pp. 319–320.

120. *Kol Kitbe Yehudah Steinberg*, vol. 4, pp. 11–14.

121. Ibid., pp. 143–146. These two brothers are real personages, disciples of Dov Ber of Mezritch: Meshullam Zusya (Zishe in Yiddish) of Hanipol (Annopol), who died in 1800, and his younger brother Elimelek of Lizensk, who died in 1809. On the parables of the two brothers see Martin Buber, *Tales of the Hasidim—the Early Masters* (New York, 1947), pp. 235–264; also Jiri Langer, *Nine Gates*, pp. 115–137.

122. Ibid., pp. 150–154.

123. In Assyrian inscriptions the Hagrites are inhabitants of northeastern Arabia. They are mentioned several times in the Bible: see, for instance, 1 Chronicles 27:31. In modern Hebrew the word is connected with immigration. In both the ancient and the modern sense the Hagrite is a stranger, a foreigner.

124. The Hebrew titles of the novels are, respectively: *he-Haẓer ha-Penimit, ha-Lev we-ha-Ḥerev, Me-Ḥoshek le-Or, ha-Betulah mi-Ludmir*. They were published in a period of fifteen years—between 1949 and 1964.

125. In Hebrew, *Ha-Gaon we-ha-Rab*.

126. On the concept of man as wayfarer, see Gerhart B. Ladner, "Homo Viator: Medieval Ideas on Alienation and Order," *Speculum* vol. 42 (April, 1967), p. 256.

127. Song of Songs 1:5.

128. S. Agnon, *The Bridal Canopy*, trans. I. M. Lask (New York, 1937), pp. 110–111.

129. See E. E. Lisitzky, *be-Ohale Kush* (Jerusalem, 1953), p. 3.

130. See Abraham Regelson, *Ḥaḳukot Otiyetayik* (Tel Aviv, 1964), p. 220.

131. In Hebrew, *Kedushat Levi*; it first appeared in Slavita in 1797–98.

132. Uri Zevi Gruenberg, *Anacreon 'Al Ḳoteb ha-'Iẓabon* (Tel Aviv, 1928), p. 71.

133. Gruenberg, *Kelape Tishim we-Tishah* (Tel Aviv, 1928), p. 35.

134. The fortress which resisted the Romans after the fall of Jerusalem in 70 A.D., it symbolizes heroic resistance borne out of despair and hope; hence, the ardent interest in the archeological recovery of the fortress by Professor Yigael Yadin. See his beautiful volume *Masada* (New York, 1966).

135. Shimshon Meltzer, *Shirim u-Balladot,* third edition (Tel Aviv, 1953), p. 36.
136. On Rabbi Zusya and Rabbi Elimelech see n. 121.
137. Aaron Zeitlin, *Shirim u-Poemot* (Jerusalem, 1949), p. 108.
138. The translator has remarked that *I and Thou* is indeed a poem; see the introduction to Martin Buber, *I and Thou,* trans. by Ronald Rego Smith, second edition (New York, 1958), p. xi.
139. In recognition of his services to Ḥasidism and as a mark of personal friendship, Agnon dedicated seven paraphrases of Baal Shem Tov's stories to Buber; they appeared under the title *Sippurim Naim Shel R. Yisrael Baal Shem Tov, Molad* 144–145 (1960), pp. 357–364.
140. Paul Arthur Schilpp, ed., *The Philosophy of Martin Buber* (La Salle, Illinois, 1967), p. 731.
141. Martin Buber, *I and Thou,* pp. 82–83.
142. E. William Rollins and Harry Zohn, ed., *Men of Dialogue: Martin Buber and Albrecht Goes* (New York, 1969), pp. 204–205.
143. *The Philosophy of Martin Buber,* pp. 742–743.
144. Martin Buber, *I and Thou,* p. 4.

Joseph P. Strelka

MILAREPA AND THE POETRY OF TIBETAN YOGA

MILAREPA, "THE GREATEST POET-SAINT EVER TO APPEAR IN THE HISTORY of Buddhism" as he was called, is not yet well known in the Western World. The first and so far only complete translation of his famous *Hundred Thousand Songs* (*Mila-Grubum*) into a Western language, that of Garma C. C. Chang, is still quite recent.[1] It has, however, already been stated that Milarepa could be compared in some ways to a poet of the stature of Dante. He not only raised the Tibetan vernacular[2]—as the Italian writer raised the Florentine dialect—to a medium of the highest literary expression; he also put forth a universal view of life and religion comparable to that Dante presented in his *Commedia*. The collection of Milarepa's songs has therefore been called "an immense treasury of spiritual teachings, a repository of yogic instruction, a guide on the Bodhi-Path,"[3] and has been read as "the biography of a saint, a guide book for devotions, a manual of Buddhist Yoga, a volume of songs and poems, and even as a collection of Tibetan folklore and fairy tales,"[4] covering the "quintessential teachings of practical Buddhism."[5] As opposed to Dante's work, however, the story of Milarepa's descent into the hell of black magic, his ascent through purification by hardships (purgatory), and his initiation and the earthly heaven of Buddhahood is told in another book.[6] *The Hundred Thousand Songs of Milarepa* encompasses instead a manual of Tibetan Tantrism set in the form of songs surrounded by stories of the personal happenings and experiences of Milarepa.

Tibetan Tantrism is the power behind these songs and from it stem their great anagogic qualities. Tibetan Tantrism is based on the identicality of mind and prāna.[7] These dual or even antithetical forces are seen as one entity manifesting itself in two different forms or stages. There exist two principal paths in Tibetan Tantrism: one of them emphasizes taming the Prāna, which is called the "Yoga with Form" or the "Path of Skillfulness" or "Path of Means"; while the other, which is called the "Path of Liberation,"[8] emphasizes taming the mind. Milarepa practiced both methods; the former one is practiced through the profound path of the six Yogas of Naropa[9] and the latter through the path of Mahāmudrā.[10] As far as the mystical experience of the state of Mahāmudrā can be expressed in words, Milarepa did it in a most concise, compressed, and congenial way and by using the poetic form of songs, the aesthetic properties of which reach into the unconscious, he further stressed the need for surpassing the methods of rational knowledge and abstract teaching.

It is said that Milarepa, who lived from 1052–1135 A.D., had a fine voice and loved to sing even as a boy. Yogihood and Enlightenment made him sing more often and more joyfully than before. In the *Mila-Grubum* Milarepa answered all the questions and demands of his patrons and disciples with freely flowing poems or lyric songs, and the Tibetan people thought that their number came close to one hundred thousand, of which only a very limited number were written down and put into a certain order by "the Mad Yogi from gTsan."[11]

The "saint-troubadour" Milarepa sang about his own experiences and life, pointing repeatedly, either directly or indirectly, to his Yogi practices as the main source of poetic expression:

When I practice Mahāmudrā,
I rest myself in the intrinsic state,
Relaxingly without distraction or effort.
In the realm of Voidness,
I rest myself with Illumination.
In the realm of Blissfulness,
I rest myself in Awareness.
In the realm of Non-thought,
I rest myself with a naked mind.

In manifestations and activities,
I rest myself in Samādhi.
Meditating on the Mind-Essence in such a manner
Numerous understandings and convictions arise.
By Self-illumination all is accomplished without effort.
Looking no more for Enlightenment,
I am extremely happy.
Free from both hope and fear,

I feel very joyful.
Oh, what a pleasure it is to enjoy
Confusion when as Wisdom it appears![12]

Sometimes he gives an overall view of the basic ideas of his mystical realization in a few lines as when for example he sings:

All the manifestation, the Universe itself,
  is contained in the mind;
The nature of Mind is the realm of illumination
Which can neither be conceived nor touched.
These are the Key-points of the View.

Errant thoughts are liberated in the Dharmakāya;
The awareness, the illumination, is always blissful;
Meditate in a manner of non-doing and non-effort.
These are the Key-points of Practice.

In the action of naturalness
The Ten Virtues spontaneously grow;
All the Ten Vices are thus purified.
By corrections or remedies
The Illuminating Void is ne'er disturbed.
These are the Key-points of Action.

There is no Nirvāna to attain beyond;
There is no Samsāra here to renounce;
Truly to know the Self-mind
It is to be the Buddha Himself.
These are the Key-points of Accomplishment.

Reduce inwardly the Three Key-points to One.
This One is the Void Nature of Being,
Which only a wondrous Guru
Can clearly illustrate.[13]

The excellent British translator of a number of Milarepa's songs, Sir Humphrey Clarke, tried to show some of the songs' formal qualities by rearranging them in a strictly intrinsic way. He entitled, for example, one of his groups of songs "Allegory" and another one "The Function of Number."[14] From a broader viewpoint, however, one which takes into consideration the entire Tibetan Tantric background of these songs, the term "allegory" at least in its more precise and narrower meaning should perhaps be replaced by the term "symbolism." Of course, Milarepa has, as do most mystics, a tendency to use metaphors and to stretch them to parables; but even if they often look like real allegories in which the directly given image simply stands for an abstract thought and therefore can be decoded in a rational way, their Tantric background implies many different levels of comprehension and brings them therefore closer to quite complex and *multimeaningful* symbols. If Milarepa sings about the Prāna-Mind as a horse it seems to be a perfect allegory:

> "Listen to me, dear patron!
> A horse of Prāna-Mind have I;
> I adorn him with the silk scarf of Dhyāna.
> His skin is the magic Ensuing Dhyāna Stage,
> His saddle, illuminating Self-Awareness.
> My spurs are the Three Visualizations,
> His crupper the secret teaching of the Two Gates.
>
> His headstall is the Prāna of Vital-force;
> His forelock curl is Three-pointed Time.
> Tranquillity within is his adornment,
> Bodily movement is his rein,
> And ever-flowing inspiration is his bridle.
>
> He gallops wildly along the Spine's Central Path.
> He is a yogi's horse, this steed of mine.
> By riding him, one escapes Samsāra's mud,
> By following him one reaches the safe land of Bodhi.
>
> My dear patron, I have no need of your black horse.
> Go your way, young man, and look for pleasure![15]

After starting out at the naturalistic level of addressing the young man he met at Silver Spring he leaps to the highest mystic level of a synthesized paradox and then, instead of simply adding more single parts to a simple allegory out of lack of imagination as it is done quite often in bad political rhetoric, he shows different levels and different perspectives of the central metaphor in order to point out the entire complexity and difficulty of the experience as such.

"The pursuits of art, painting, sculpture, and poetry are not contrary to Buddhist philosophy. The painting monks of Tibet follow careful meditation before and during the painting of religious subjects. In the 'mandalas' [geometrical diagrams for meditation practices of a sacred circle and square: the dwelling place of deities], symbolism, magic and art are perfectly welded into one inseparable unit," wrote one critic. In spite of this insight into Tibetan sacral painting, which he only compares to the copying of the songs of Milarepa and not with their creation and phenomenological essence, the same critic called the songs "of a didactic order, *teaching and* telling of his experiences or chanting the basic tenets of Tibetan Buddhism."[16]

Milarepa's songs are not at all didactic in the actual meaning of the word but rather they are more akin to the kind of symbolism, magic, and art perfectly welded into one unity which characterises the mandalas. They may seem to be on the dry and didactic side for the average Western reader who looks at a printed English version, but such a reader usually misses many important elements. Besides the fact that Milarepa's poems are real songs in the original sense of all lyric and nondidactic poetry of world literature,[17] some of the aesthetic qualities are lost in the translation such as, for example, the poetic effect of breaking down a phrase and using each component word to begin a line.[18] The songs of Milarepa are poems arising out of a state of mystical experience and meditation and are also attempts to communicate something of its essence. They bear as little relation to didactic teaching as the Sutras, which are actually meditation manuals, do to the philosophical texts of Western abstract knowledge.

In the last analysis these songs do not express a specific philosophical or moral doctrine but rather the Mahāmudrā-experiences of a mystic. They thus have no rules at all and can hardly be comprehended as mere abstract terms or words. Milarepa himself states:

> In the practice of Mahāmudrā
> There is no room for thinking with a clinging mind.
> When Realization of the State-Beyond-Playwords arises
> There is no need to chant or keep the rules.[19]

Or as Garma C. C. Chang put it from a biographical viewpoint: "Unlike many religious leaders, who exerted themselves in various tasks for the creation of their new Orders, Milarepa never tried to build a temple, form a group, or set up an organization of any sort, but faithfully followed his Guru's injunctions by leading the life of a true mendicant yogi in the remote mountains, the life of a saint-troubadour, wandering from place to place to preach the holy Dharma through his songs."[20] There was no such Dharma in the sense of an orthodox system of metaphysics but there were only the mystical insights of the yogi himself. This means that the most important part of the magic and symbolism of these poems and their poetic charm is lost to the non-practitioner of Mahāmudrā. Even the number one hundred thousand occurs not by accident but has a deeper meaning in the light of the four times one hundred thousand fundamental preparatory practices of the Tantric Path. In other words, the songs of Milarepa are not only better explained, as far as their creation is concerned, by considering their mystical background and its anagogic qualities, but in fact they cannot truly be comprehended without a consideration of the background from which they derive part of their expressive power.

As a consequence of this unorthodox openness to everything, the personality of Milarepa as well as the expressions of his songs embraces practically all potential possibilities of the development of man. The result of this attitude is on the one hand the immense number of different aspects of the totality of life and on the other hand the complete avoidance of any rational, systematic channeling of his ideas. This becomes especially obvious in the story of Milarepa's challenge by logicians and theologians, which shows how unimportant to him the overcoming of the world by means of a system was. He put emphasis on entirely different qualities as far as the confrontation with the surrounding world, his fellow human beings, and all sentient beings was concerned. It was this attitude of non-obstruction, acceptance, and love which led to the paradoxical state in which the entirely spiritualized Yogi, saint and "superman," acted and reacted in a way which could not be more human and humane. The warm feelings and affection he had for his disciple Rechungpa, whom he treated like a son; the compassion he had for all sentient beings, for example his saintlike saving of a dying black sheep at the market of Nya Non; and last, the way of his conscious acceptance of the poison which killed him, shows him as a kind human being very much alive and not at all as a supranatural creature which has lost all connections with our world. There is a deep meaning—not only in one specific metaphoric sense—when he sings:

> I am a yogi who lives on a snow-mountain peak.
> With a healthy body I glorify the Mandala of the Whole.
> Cleansed of vanity from the Five Poisons,

I am not unhappy;
I feel nought but joy!

It is, however, understandable that one could have the impression of a tendency toward didactic literary forms, and this becomes especially clear if one compares the Mahāmudrā tradition and Milarepa's songs with the Zen tradition and its haikus.

Several similarities between Mahāmudrā and Zen have been pointed out: first of all their common tendency to stress the observation and cultivation of the Innate Mind and the fact that they require only a minimum of ritual and yogic preparations.[21] In addition, Milarepa has been compared with Hui-Neng because his life and his songs have given birth to a greater number of mystically enlightened beings than have any other Mahāyāna Buddhist Schools except the one of Hui-Neng, who was in a certain sense the founder of Zen. There is however a slight difference between the methods of Mahāmudrā and Zen. Mahāmudrā gives more explanations and works through a process of gradually raising, sustaining, expanding, and deepening the Yogi's realization of the Innate Buddha-Mind. In Mahāmudrā the Guru can transmit a first glimpse of realization in the Yogi's earlier stages. The Zen method, on the other hand, often leaves its student completely in darkness for a long period, in order at a certain moment to transmit to him a deeper state of enlightenment in a sudden burst of insight.

The difference between the adequate poetic forms, the haiku on one hand and Milarepa's songs on the other corresponds to the previous distinction; the haiku tries in an instant to grasp the adequate aesthetic correlative of a mystic intuition and direct experience. The songs of Milarepa are more explicit and therefore, especially for the average Westerner, easier to understand. As does the haiku poet, Milarepa also draws an impression of a section of nature, but then he goes on to show how this impression is transcended in the view of a mystic and then is reintegrated at a third stage as a powerful manifestation of Voidness:

Along the banks of the stream
And in the middle of the lake,
Cranes bend their necks, enjoy the scene,
  and are content.

On the branches of the trees, the wild birds sing;
When the wind blows gently, slow dances
  the weeping willow;

. . . .

From the top of the Resplendent Gem Rock,
I, the Yogi, see these things.
Observing them, I know that they are fleeting and
transient;
Contemplating them, I realize that comforts and
pleasures
Are merely mirages and water-reflections.

. . . .

Strange indeed are Samsāric phenomena!
Truly amusing are the dharmas in the Three Worlds,
Oh, what a wonder, what a marvel!
Void is their nature, yet everything is manifested.[22]

From these examples it should be clear how the relationship of literature with mystic or esoteric traditions can not only influence literature's anagogic qualities but can even find expression in the literary forms themselves, a fact which once again indicates that the higher mutual penetration of content and form in literature is in a profound sense correlative to the subject-object relationship within man's mind.

At least for Milarepa himself the unity of the living oral Mahāmudrā tradition, symbolized in his revered Guru, the realization of Buddhahood, and the creativity of lyric production was taken for granted. Therefore he says in the last song of the collection:

When my body has the Guru's blessing,
It can work many miracles
And many transformations.
When my mouth receives the Guru's
Blessing, it can sing lyric songs
And give Pith-Instructions.
When my mind receives the Guru's
blessing
It realizes and is the Buddha.[23]

In his opinion, meditation and poetry cannot be separated; they constitute but two different ways of practicing devotion, for the source of poetry lies in meditation:

Oh friends, let us try
firmly to practice our devotion.
Let us forget all worldly things,
For the next life preparing![24]

Notes

I should not have been able to write this paper without the help and assistance of Professor Garma C. C. Chang, to whom I should like to give my sincerest thanks.

1. *The Hundred Thousand Songs of Milarepa*, translated and annotated by Garma C. C. Chang, 2 vols. (New York, 1962). Parts of the work have been translated before but have never attracted appropriate general attention: Berthold Laufer, *Aus den Geschichten und Liedern des Milarepa* (Vienna, 1902); Sir Humphrey Clarke, *The Message of Milarepa* (London, 1958); Antoinette K. Gordon, *The Hundred Thousand Songs* (Rutland, Vermont, and Tokyo, 1961).
2. Cf. Peter Fingesten, introduction to *The Hundred Thousand Songs*, trans. Antoinette K. Gordon, p. 17.
3. Peter Gruber, in Foreword to *The Hundred Thousand Songs of Milarepa*, trans. Garma C. C. Chang, vol. 1, p. xi.
4. Garma C. C. Chang, trans., *The Hundred Thousand Songs of Milarepa*, vol. 2, p. 679.
5. Garma C. C. Chang, vol. 2, p. 682.
6. Jetsün-Kahbum, *Tibet's Great Yogi Milarepa*, ed. W. Y. Evans-Wentz (London, Oxford, and New York, 1969).
7. The Sanskrit term *prāna* is, even according to a translator of the rank of Garma C. C. Chang, "extremely difficult" to translate. It means air, energy, vital force, breathing, propensity—all of which constitute a unity in the doctrines of Yoga.
8. Cf. W. Y. Evans-Wentz, ed., *Tibetan Yoga and Secret Doctrines* (London Oxford. and New York, 1969), especially Books III and IV, pp. 155–276; and Garma C. C. Chang, trans. and ann., *Teachings of Tibetan Yoga* (New Hyde Park, New York, 1963).
9. Cf. Herbert V. Guenther, *The Life and Teachings of Nāropa* (Oxford, 1963).
10. Mahāmudrā is a Yogic practice which leads to the realization of the Dharmakāya or the Primordial Mind by meditating on Sūnyata (Voidness).
11. He was a disciple of Phag. Mo. Gru. Pa, who himself was a pupil of Milarepa's follower and chief disciple Gambopa. Cf. *The Hundred Thousand Songs of Milarepa*, trans. Garma C. C. Chang, vol. 2, p. 688.
12. Chang, vol. 2, p. 378.
13. Chang vol. 1, pp. 79–80.
14. Clark, *The Message of Milarepa*, pp. 46–65, 66–81.
15. Chang, vol. 1, p. 163.
16. Peter Fingesten, introduction to *The Hundred Thousand Songs* trans. Antoinette K. Gordon, pp. 18, 19; italics are mine.
17. Cf. appendix to *The Hundred Thousand Songs*, trans. Antoinette K. Gordon, pp. 107–112.
18. Cf. *The Hundred Thousand Songs of Milarepa*, trans. Garma C. C. Chang, vol. 2, pp. 360, 361. n. 5.
19. Chang, vol. 2, p. 457.
20. Ibid., p. 681.
21. Chang, *Teachings of Tibetan Yoga*, p. 14.

22. *The Hundred Thousand Songs of Milarepa,* trans. Garma C. C. Chang, vol. 1, pp. 64 f.
23. Chang, vol. 2, p. 671.
24. Ibid., p. 672.

Toshihiko Izutsu

THE ARCHETYPAL IMAGE OF CHAOS IN CHUANG TZŬ: THE PROBLEM OF THE MYTHOPOEIC LEVEL OF DISCOURSE

I

IN THE HISTORY OF CHINESE THOUGHT CHUANG TZŬ STANDS IN SHARP contrast to Confucius and the Confucian thinkers. Chuang Tzŭ is essentially a "seer" who tends to lose himself in the limitlessly vast metaphysical domain of Nothingness, who enjoys himself completely and nonchalantly in a transcendental realm of Being "beyond good and evil." Confucius and his followers are those who, by nature and on principle, keep to an austere ethical view of man and the world. What characterizes the Confucian school in the most remarkable way is its realistic and rationalistic mode of thinking, while Chuang Tzŭ's world view is based on a nonrealistic, nonrationalistic approach to thought, which we might call the "shamanistic" mode of thinking.

The visionary experiences of Chuang Tzŭ are most probably of a shamanistic origin, although, it is true, the philosophical world view as he actually presents it—in an extremely sophisticated form—may seem at first quite remote from the crude, primitive forms of ecstasy usually associated with the term *shamanism*. Shamanism is a universal spiritual phenomenon, observable in many different cultures throughout the history of the human race, and has not necessarily been confined to the "primitive" history of man. Quite the contrary, it appears in divergent forms at various levels of elaboration, furnishing a peculiar spiritual basis for a number of important aspects of human culture. And there is a certain respect in which we might quite reasonably consider the thought of Chuang Tzŭ as a very peculiar form of philosophical shamanism.[1]

As the shaman puts himself into the state of trance and goes beyond the limitations of time and space, he enters into a domain of archetypal images. In this atemporal and aspatial dimension of consciousness, the world in which we live transforms itself into something completely different from what we are normally accustomed to seeing. The familiar things we perceive around us cease to show their known faces. Leaving their natural mode of existence, they are all transformed into images, and at this trans-empirical level of appearance they form among themselves entirely new relationships; things thereby assume a symbolic significance.

Extraordinary images spring forth one after another out of the very depth of the shaman's ecstatic consciousness. One of the basic functions of the mind of the shaman is *mythopoiesis*: the images thus produced tend to establish among themselves an existential order of their own, which goes on developing in accordance with the basic patterns inherent in those images. The most natural concretization of such an experience is poetry; the fact, shamanistic visions are one of the historical sources of poetic creation.

What will occur when a great visionary of this nature happens to possess also the genius of a first-rate philosopher? If, in other words, he combines the unusual capacity for seeing archetypal visions and expressing them in a poetic form with the capacity of philosophizing on his own visions, analyzing on the basis of his ecstatic experiences the structure of the world, and searching for the hidden meaning of the existence of things, man, the world, and himself. Chuang Tzŭ was precisely such a man, a rare combination of visionary mysticism and rational thinking. Hence an acute interest is naturally aroused in us for the structural make-up of Chuang Tzŭ's philosophy.

II

In setting out to analyze Chuang Tzŭ's thought we must attach equal importance to the two aspects of his personality just mentioned—his visionary nature and his talent for logic—and try to understand the whole complex that is his personality from these two angles alternately. We must approach him first as a great visionary who happens to be endowed with an unusual capacity for logical and abstract thinking, and second as a most thoroughgoing rational thinker who is at the same time a visionary.

In being a visionary endowed with a logical power of thinking, he is distinguished from his contemporary Ch'ü Yüan, the great shaman-poet of the state of Ch'u, known through the celebrated *Elegies of Ch'u*. Ch'ü Yüan is a shaman who describes in an exuberance of symbolic imagery the visionary states through which his raptured soul gradually ascends to the heavenly domain of immortality and eternity. The ecstatic oblivion of ego in the midst of the primordial purity of Being, as described by Ch'ü Yüan and the other shaman-poet appearing in the *Elegies*—the author of *Yüan Yu*, "(Spiritual) Journey to a Far-off Country"—is substantially the same as that experienced by the Taoist sage in "sitting-in-oblivion," the process of which is admirably analyzed by Chuang Tzŭ himself. But in the poetic world of the *Elegies of Ch'u* there is no intellectual elaboration of the original experience. The ecstatic visions are only poetically reproduced. In Chuang Tzŭ, on the contrary, every archetypal image is made to carry on its back a philosophical meaning. And Chuang Tzŭ is ready at any moment to develop at the level of abstract rational thinking, the philosophical meanings carried by the images, as is well attested by his logical treatment of the absolute Nothingness in terms of a triple negation.[2]

In being a rational thinker who is at the same time a visionary, Chuang Tzŭ clearly differs from another famous contemporary, Hui Tzŭ, a brilliant dialectician of his time. In the limited field of logical and conceptual thinking, Hui Tzŭ was a good friend and the best rival of Chuang Tzŭ. Hui Tzŭ, however, finds no way out of the narrow confines of reason and logic; he can see nothing beyond the horizons of the empirical world. In the eyes of Chuang Tzŭ, who usually lives in what he calls the Wilderness-of-Limitlessly-Wide, Hui Tzŭ in this respect is but a "small" man.

III

Thus in Chuang Tzŭ as a thinker there are recognizable two different strata: (a) the stratum of logical thinking or philosophizing, and (b) the stratum of the spontaneous evolvement of imagery. If we approach the thought of Chuang Tzŭ from the particular viewpoint of (a), we may say that it is a result of his philosophical world view having evolved in the concrete form of symbolic imagery. But we can also reverse the order, approaching the matter from the viewpoint of (b), and say that Chuang Tzŭ's thought is the result of an intellectual refinement and theoretical development of the original visions that have been revealed to him as a visionary-mystic. In any case, these two strata are here inseparably intertwined with each other. And that precisely is the primary factor which determines the symbolic structure of Chuang Tzŭ's thought.

With a view to clarifying this particular point, let us take up the celebrated image of "butterfly" and analyze it in a preparatory way. Here is the passage:

> Once, I, Chuang Chou,[3] dreamt I was a butterfly. Flitting about freely to my heart's content, I was indeed a butterfly. Happy and exhilarated, I had no consciousness at all of being Chuang Chou.
>
> All of a sudden I woke up, and lo, I was unmistakably Chuang Chou. Did Chuang Chou dream he was a butterfly? Or did the butterfly dream he was Chuang Chou? I do not know for sure. There is, on the other hand, an undeniable difference between Chuang Chou and a butterfly!
>
> This situation is what I call the Transmutation of Things (*wu hua*).[4]

We clearly observe here a spontaneous evolvement of imagery. But it is not only that, for behind the charming story of the Dream of a Butterfly Chuang Tzŭ is developing one of his favorite metaphysical theses, the "chaotification" of all things. The truth of this observation is shown by his own concluding remark: "This situation is what I call the Transmutation of Things."

The Transmutation of Things or *wu hua*, is in fact one of the key terms of Chuang Tzŭ's philosophy. Briefly stated, the idea is as follows. In the world of so-called "reality," that is to say, in the ontological dimension of phenomenal appearance (corresponding to the empirical level of consciousness), things are clearly distinguished from one another. "There is an undeniable difference between Chuang Chou and a butterfly." A man cannot be a butterfly, nor can a butterfly ever be a man. But, Chuang Tzŭ argues, there is another ontological dimension (corresponding to a transcendental, nonempirical level of consciousness which is actualized in ecstatic experiences) in which everything loses its essential self-identity and in which, consequently, all things become "chaotified" into a state of metaphysical undifferentiation. This latter is what is called by Chuang Tzŭ the chaos (*hun tun*), the ontological state of the free interfusion of all things, which, according to Chuang Tzŭ himself, is best to be represented as a vast and limitless, atemporal and aspatial Space where all things freely merge into one another and thereby become merged into One.

This metaphysical thesis is succinctly and vividly presented through the image of Chuang Chou in a dream having been transformed into a butterfly. The "dream" evidently represents the nonempirical level of consciousness and the corresponding ontological state of the chaos, in which all essential distinctions between individual things (here symbolized by Chuang Chou and the butterfly) become blurred and ultimately lost in the "chaotic" oneness of the Absolute.

Did everything start here from the dream? Did Chuang Chou once actually see himself in a dream transformed into a butterfly and then reflect upon it in search of the philosophical meaning of his own dream experience? Or is it rather the case that he first established his philosophical thesis of the "chaotic" unity of all things and then expressed it in a metaphorical way? It would be hard to decide, but is it not necessary to do so. We must rather say that both factors were there from the very beginning, running parallel to each other. For the very structure of the mind of a man like Chuang Tzŭ is such that, from the moment he begins to think, it starts to function in a mythopoeic way.

IV

The point that has just been made comes out far more conspicuously in the famous myth of the Mysterious Bird, which we encounter at the very outset of the Book of Chuang Tzŭ. In this story, the same philosophical thesis of the Transmutation of Things is given a gorgeous mythopoeic presentation with particular reference to the transcendental dimension of consciousness which alone enables man to see the "chaotic" unity of all things as an actual fact of spiritual experience. The ontological situation that has been described in the preceding example through the modest symbol of a dream is now brought up to a cosmic grandeur; all the symbols used are "abnormally big."[5]

> In the dark mysterious Ocean of the North there once lived a Fish whose name was known as K'un. Its size was so huge that nobody knew how many thousand miles it really was.
>
> This Fish transmuted itself into a Bird whose name is now P'êng. The back of P'êng is so large that nobody knows how many thousand miles it really is.
>
> Now the Bird suddenly pulls itself together and flies off. Lo, its wings are like huge clouds hanging in the sky. Taking advantage of the [raging storms of wind which cause the] turbulence of the sea, the Bird intends to journey toward the dark mysterious Ocean of the South. The southern Ocean is the Lake of Heaven.
>
> In fact, in the Book entitled "Cosmic Harmony" (*Ch'i Hsieh*)[6] in which are recorded many extraordinary events and strange things, we find the following description of this Bird: "When P'êng sets off for the dark mysterious Ocean of the South, it begins by beating with its wings the surface of the water for three thousand miles. Then up it goes on a whirlwind to the height of ninety thousand miles. Then it goes on flying for six months before it rests."[7]

Up to this point, the description of the Bird P'eng has been so made as to indicate symbolically the enormous (that is, cosmic) size of the True Man, whose transcendental consciousness has become one with the very Ground of Being. Everything is inordinately big in this myth. The bird is huge; the whole situation in which it behaves is correspondingly big. This impression of hugeness mirrors the spiritual "bigness" of the True Man, who has transcended the pettiness of common sense and the triviality of ordinary worldly existence, who is now freely roaming in the Field of Nothingness. It goes without saying that this is not a description of the objective "bigness" of the True Man, but that it is rather a symbolic presentation of the inner sensation of infinite "bigness" which he feels in himself. His *felt* "bigness" is presented externally in the concrete image of a colossal bird, soaring far above the world of "small" experiences, at the height of ninety thousand miles.

This passage is immediately followed by another in which Chuang Tzŭ gives a masterly description of the impression the bird gets of the trivial things and events on our earth as the bird looks down from that vertiginous height. Unlike the heavenly region in which the bird is now flying, the world below is a "dirty" domain of worldliness and vulgarity. Yet, strangely enough, this "dirty" world of ours, when viewed from the sky, strikes the bird's eye as an infinitely beautiful blue expanse. Nothing could be a better symbol for the metaphysical chaos of all things than this image of the world of multiplicity as a single sheet of spotless blue.

> [Look at the world in which we are actually living. You will see everywhere nothing but] ground vapor stirring; dust and dirt flying about; the living beings blowing fetid breaths upon each other!
>
> The sky above on the contrary, is an immense expanse of dark blue. Is this azure the real color of the sky? Or does it look [so beautifully blue] because it is at such a distance from us?
>
> However this may be, the Bird now, looking down from the height, perceives [in the world below] nothing but a similar [immense expanse of deep blue].

The point I would like to make here concerning this myth of the bird is that it is not a mere imaginary fabrication. Yes, it *is* a myth, but it is not a myth which Chuang Tzŭ has artificially (or artistically) fabricated in order to make it symbolize a particular philosophical conviction of his own. The myth is too real, there is too much in it of subjective involvement, to be a symbol of that kind. In reading the myth we get an ineradicable impression that Chuang Tzŭ is trying to impart to us something which he himself is actually feeling, something which is actually occurring in his consciousness. It is no other than Chuang Tzŭ himself who, transmuted into the colossal bird, is soaring in the limitless azure expanse, far above the noise and bustle of the secular world. Remarkably enough, the same inner sensation of soaring in the sky is described by the shaman-poet of the *Yüan Yu* ("Journey to a Far-off Country"),[8] with the conspicuous difference, however, that the description there is made through a series of nakedly shamanistic images. It is interesting to observe in this connection that the first Chapter of the *Chuang Tzŭ*, in which the myth of the Mysterious Bird is found, is entitled *Hsiao Yao Yu*, that is, "Free Wandering," reminiscent of the ecstatic spiritual journey of the shaman.

What characterizes Chuang Tzŭ's myths in general and definitely distinguishes them from the narrative or lyrical poems of pure shamanism is the fact that in Chuang Tzŭ there is clearly observable, behind the creative and artistic process of evolving imagery, the process of philosophizing, with no discrepancy between the two processes. The two are in fact the single process of mythopoeic thinking.

V

The above observation would seem to justify the position I am going to take concerning the linguistic aspect of Chuang Tzŭ's thought: that the most characteristic trait of Chuang Tzŭ's use of language lies in the highest importance he attaches to what we might call the mythopoeic level of discourse. I propose to distinguish this level of discourse methodologically from what may be called the mythical (or mythological) level of discourse. Theoretical confusion between these two levels of discourse—precisely because they are so closely akin to each other, both historically and structurally—is liable to be highly detrimental to a correct understanding of Chuang Tzŭ's symbolism.

The mythical or mythological level of discourse may be characterized as a particular level of discourse at which words are used in such a way that they disclose all the prehistoric memories and associations that lie dormant in them. Fantastic images are thereby called forth out of the deepest recesses of the mind. The primordial images thus evoked from the forgotten past of humanity tend to conglomerate into a more or less coherent narrative form and bring into being the various myths. The shaman, considered in his linguistic aspect, is the man who is endowed with a special ability to conjure up primordial images of this sort out of the semantic storehouse of language. The myths of the so-called primitive peoples are mostly of this nature. When they are further worked out and brought to a higher degree of theoretical elaboration, they may lead to the birth of a cosmogony which may well be regarded as a philosophy of Being in its most primitive form.

What is striking, however, about the myths of this nature is that there is no real transcendence in them. There certainly is a *kind* of transcendence—the imaginary transcendence from the empirical order of things. In the inordinate exuberance of imagery the shaman feels himself to be in a world of realities that exist above and beyond the world of daily experiences. But from the point of view of a Chuang Tzŭ, this is not transcendence in the real sense of the term.

Real transcendence in Chuang Tzŭ's sense is attained only at what we would designate as the mythopoeic level of consciousness. Actually even a cursory glance at his "myths" would immediately convince us that he always and systematically uses language in such a dimension of consciousness. Hence the importance of the mythopoeic level of discourse, as distinguished from the mythical, for a correct analysis of Chuang Tzŭ's thought. The nature of the mythopoeic level of discourse has already been indicated earlier in the present paper in a preparatory way. It refers, in brief, to a peculiar use of language by which myths are created on the one hand, but by which, on the other, and exactly at the same time, philosophical thinking is evolved. It goes without saying that "Philosophy" in this context must be understood in the particular sense in which Chuang Tzŭ himself would understand it: as a thinking process naturally arising from the very existential experiences of the True Man, who has unified himself with the ultimate metaphysical chaos. The kind of "philosophy" which is contained in ordinary myths would, for a Chuang Tzŭ, be nothing more than the petty thinking of "men of lower grades."

VI

It will be evident that the peculiarity of the mythopoeic level of discourse demands from the reader or listener a peculiar way of understanding. In other words, the things and events that are described on the mythopoeic level of discourse would completely lose their meaning unless they were understood in terms of that very level of discourse. If one finds Chuang Tzŭ's words too "big," too bizarre and grotesque to be taken seriously,[9] it is simply because, instead of trying to understand them in their proper dimension, one tries consciously to bring them down to the ordinary level of discourse and interpret them there. It often happens that one, even being well aware that Chuang Tzŭ is using language in quite an unusual way, is still quite at a loss as to where one should properly locate his words. Here is an example:

> Far, far away on Sacred Mountain there lives a Holy Man. His skin is as white as ice or snow. His body is lithe, lissom and graceful as the body of a virgin. Not eating the five grains, but sucking only wind and drinking dew, he rides clouds and mist, drives flying dragons, and wanders about to his heart's content beyond the boundaries of the four seas. By his spiritual powers concentrated, he is able to protect all creatures from calamities, afflictions and plagues, and to make the yearly harvest rich and bountiful.[10]

Chuang Tzŭ puts this myth in the mouth of Chieh Yü, a famous hermit of the state of Ch'u, a contemporary of Confucius.[11] On the nature of this myth Chuang Tzŭ lets another hermit make the following observation:

> I think this is sheer insanity. I refuse to believe a word of it! . . . The story is too "big," indeed, too fantastic to be true. It is simply bombastic and absurd. When I listened to this talk of Chieh Yü, I remained completely dumfounded. For his words struck my ears as something limitlessly far-off, just like the infinitude of the Milky Way. In any case, the story seems very remote from our ordinary talk. It does not come near the understanding of ordinary men.

The myth looks so bizarre just because the man who listens to it does not approach it on the mythopoeic level of discourse. The critical remark made by the recluse ("It does not come near the understanding of ordinary men,") shows that he is well aware that Chieh Yü's talk evolves on a different level of discourse from that of daily conversation. In spite of this awareness, the recluse does not know how to understand the meaning of the story in terms of the mythopoeic level of discourse, to which it properly belongs. In order that he might be able to understand the story in terms of the mythopoeic level, he must have already seen in the ecstatic dimension of consciousness the very source from which spring forth visionary images of this kind. The minimum requirement is that the story, as soon as it is heard, should conjure up in the mind of the listener, and that in the same spiritual dimension of consciousness, a series of images of a similar nature. The listener, in short, must *live* the same images.

The following anecdote shows the same kind of semantic confusion between the mythopoeic and the ordinary level of discourse in a more intellectual form. The *dramatis personae* this time are Chuang Tzŭ himself and his friend Hui Tzŭ, the dialectician. The discussion centers around Chuang Tzŭ's thesis that the True Man has no emotion.

> [Chuang Tzŭ:] The "sacred man" [that is, the True Man] has the physical form of a man, but he has no human emotion. Since he happens to have the form of a man, he does live among other human beings as one of them. But since he has no human emotion, "right" and "wrong" cannot have access to him. Ah how insignificant and small he is, insofar as he belongs to common humanity! But infinitely great is he, insofar as he stands unique in perfecting Heaven in himself.
>
> [Hui Tzŭ:] Is it at all possible that a man should be without emotions?
>
> [Chuang Tzŭ:] Why not?
>
> [Hui Tzŭ:] But if a man lacks human emotions, how could he be called a "man"?
>
> [Chuang Tzŭ:] The Way has given him human features. Heaven has given him his bodily form. How, then, should we not call him a "man"?
>
> [Hui Tzŭ:] But since you call him a "man," it is inconceivable that he should lack human emotions.
>
> [Chuang Tzŭ:] What you mean by "emotion" is different from what I mean by the same word. When I say "he is without emotion," I mean that the man does not let his inner self be perturbed by distinctions between good and evil, and that he conforms to the heaven-given nature of all things, never trying artificially to increase his vital energy.[12]

As mentioned above, the discussion is here carried on in a sober, intellectual atmosphere on the meaning of the words "man" and "emotion," so that there might seem to be almost no reference to the mythopoeic level of discourse. In fact, however, behind Chuang Tzŭ's concept of a "man without human emotion" there lies hidden the cosmic image of Man which finds its proper place only in the domain of mythopoeic experience. That is to say, even when he is engaged in an intellectual dialogue with a sophist-logician at the rational level of discourse, Chuang Tzŭ never forgets to determine the connotations of his key terms in the light of, and in reference to, the images with which these words are intimately associated at the mythopoeic level of discourse. It is but natural that Hui Tzŭ, who has no access to such a semantic dimension of words, should find himself utterly unable to understand what Chuang Tzŭ really means to say.

VII

Turning now to the structure of the mythopoeic level of discourse itself, we would like to begin by giving an example which would seem to be most apt to disclose the fundamental difference between it and what we have proposed to call the mythical or mythological level of discourse. We shall first examine the mythical image of Chaos as it is given by the author of the *Shan Hai Ching*, the *Book of Mountains and Seas*, one of the most important source books of Chinese mythology, in which are given descriptions of mythological monsters that are believed to live in mountains and seas. We shall then compare it with the same mythical image of Chaos as treated by Chuang Tzŭ.

In the *Book of Mountains and Seas*, Chaos (*hun tun*) appears as a hideous monster-bird having no features on the face.

> Three hundred and fifty miles further to the West there is a mountain called Heaven Mountain. The mountain produces much gold and jade. It produces also blue sulphide. The River Ying takes its origin here, and it wanders southwestward until it runs into the Valley of Boiling Water.
>
> Now in this mountain there lives a divine Bird whose body is like a yellow sack, as red as burning fire, that has six legs and four wings. The Bird is completely amorphous [*hun tun*, "chaos"], having no eyes, no feature. But the Bird is very good at singing and dancing.

The bird is said to "have no face," that is absolutely no features on its face: no eyes, no nose, no mouth. It is *hun tun*, the Chaos. Its close association with shamanism is clear from the fact that this featureless monster is described as being "very good at singing and dancing." In ancient China, as in many other places, singing and dancing were magical means for inducing in the shaman-priest the state of ecstasy, and of calling down spirits from the world above.[13] This would imply that the blank face which the monster-bird turns toward us is a mythological presentation of the Void as experienced by the shaman in the state of trance. Interpreted in this way, the myth of the Bird-Chaos is nothing but a myth of shamanistic origin, presenting in a very crude form an essential part of the visionary experience of the ecstatic shaman: the vision of the world of Being as the face of Chaos.

Now we turn to Chuang Tzŭ's myth of Chaos. It immediately springs to the eye that his myth of Chaos is no longer a simple myth reproducing the ecstatic vision of the shaman. For here, as we have remarked above, the very evolvement of imagery *is* the evolvement of philosophical thinking. The whole process may be characterized as philosophizing through the creation of images.

> The name of the Emperor of the South Sea was Brief [*shu*]. The name of the Emperor of the North Sea was Momentary [*hu*]. The Emperor of the central empire was called Chaos [*hun tun*]. Once, Brief and Momentary met in the empire of Chaos, who treated both of them with utmost hospitality. Thereupon, Brief and Momentary deliberated together over the way in which they might possibly repay his kindness.
>
> "All men," they said, "are possessed of seven orifices for seeing, hearing, eating, and breathing. Chaos alone does not possess any orifice. Come, let us bore some on his face!"
>
> They went on boring one orifice every day, until on the seventh day Chaos died.[14]

The process of philosophizing which underlies this myth is not difficult to bring to light. The empire of the Emperor Chaos, the Featureless, evidently refers to the domain of absolute Unity, the ontological plane where all phenomenal distinctions become merged and interfused into one. It is the highest metaphysical state in which all things are "chaotically" one, as they are seen by the spiritual eye of the True Man at the utmost limit of "sitting-in-oblivion" (*tzo wang*).

The "sitting-in-oblivion" is a special technique of meditation described in detail by Chuang Tzŭ.[15] To put it in a nutshell, it is a technique of Taoist yoga consisting in the complete withdrawal of the senses from all external objects, the total elimination of the ego-consiousness, and finally bringing the mind into the state of pure Nothingness. This is what is called by the Taoists variously as "illumination," "losing the ego," and "chaotification of the mind." And as the mind goes through this process of *ekstasis*, or self-realization, phenomenal things lose the objective distinctions among themselves until finally all are brought back to their original metaphysical undifferentiation, a state where a butterfly is no longer distinguishable from Chuang Chou. This state, at once subjective and objective, is what is designated by the word *chaos*.

Now the domain of the Emperor Chaos is the central empire placed between the southern empire of Brief and the northern empire of Momentary. The very names of these two Emperors suggest that theirs is the domain of phenomenal things, characterized by the precariousness and transiency of existence. It is also an ontological domain where all things are clearly distinguished one from the other, where a butterfly can never be Chuang Chou and Chuang Chou never a butterfly.

The two Emperors come to visit the Emperor Chaos. They immensely enjoy the hospitality of Chaos. But since they are "brief" and "momentary," they cannot stay long in his empire. That is to say, the mind enjoys the state of *ekstasis* only momentarily. The two Emperors retire to their quarters: there they make a fatal decision: as a token of gratitude they decide to go back to Chaos, to bore orifices on his featureless face; which kills him. This means that the mind which had a momentary glimpse into the "chaotic" unity of all things did not realize that the featureless face of Being was the real, the original face of the things, that the Chaos was the Reality of all realities.

The crucial point of this myth is the problem of how the consciousness which has once lost itself in the state of ecstasy and has thereby completely lost sight of all essential distinctions among things, should return to itself and to the dimension of phenomenal differentiations. From the point of view of a Chuang Tzŭ, what was done by the two Emperors after the brief visit to Chaos was certainly not right. That is to say, the return of normal consciousness and the corresponding return to the phenomenal world must be made in a totally different way.

VIII

The right kind of the return of consciousness that has just been mentioned is given by Chuang Tzŭ a masterly mythopoeic description in the celebrated image of the Cosmic Wind. Note that the Cosmic Wind, or as Chuang Tzŭ calles it, the "sound of the heavenly wind," is not to be imagined as something separate and distinguished from the (no-) consciousness of the True Man itself. Subjectively it is nothing other than the mind of the contemplative True Man as it resumes its normal function of differentiating one thing from another. Objectively, it is the Absolute, the "chaotic" Unity, as it goes on differentiating itself into the phenomenal forms of the "ten thousand things." The passage, be it noted in passing, is unanimously acknowledged to be one of the masterpieces in classical Chinese Literature.

> The Great Earth [that is, Nature] eructates; and the eructation is called Wind. As long as the eructation does not actually occur, nothing happens.

But once the wind rises, all the hollows of the trees begin to raise ringing shouts.

Listen! Do you not hear the trailing sound of the wind as it approaches, blowing from afar? The trees in the mountain forests rustle, stir, and sway. Then all the hollows and holes of huge trees measuring a hundred arms's stretches around begin to give forth different sounds. There are holes like noses, like mouths, like ears. Some of them are square like crosspieces upon the pillars. Some are round as cups. Some are like mortars. Some are like deep ponds; some are like shallow basins.

[The sounds they emit are accordingly various:] some roar like torrents dashing against the rocks. Some hiss like flying arrows. Some growl, some gasp, some shout, some moan. Some sounds are deep and muffled. Some sounds are sad and plaintive.

As the first blast of wind goes away with a light trailing sound, there comes the second blow with a deep rumbling sound. To a gentle wind the hollows answer with faint sounds. To a violent gust they answer with sharp sounds.

But once the raging gale has passed on, all the hollows and holes remain void and soundless. You see only the boughs swaying silently, and the tender twigs gently quivering. . . .

One and the same Wind blows on the ten thousand hollows in ten thousand different ways, and makes each hollow produce its own peculiar sound, so that each imagines that itself produces that particular sound. But who, in reality, is the one who makes the hollows produce various sounds?

The passage here translated is in fact nothing other than a symbolic and picturesque presentation of the whole gist of Chuang Tzŭ's metaphysics. Let us remark first of all that according to Chuang Tzŭ the Cosmic Wind has no sound of its own. The "sound of Heaven" (*t'ien lai*) is soundless; it is inaudible. What is audible to our ears are the ten thousand sounds produced by the hollows of the trees. They are not the sound of Heaven; they are but the "sound of Earth" (*ti lai*).

The "sound of Earth" which is actually audible to our physical ears differs from one hollow to another. Thus the dimension of the "sound of Earth" is the dimension of Multiplicity. But, Chuang Tzŭ argues, one must hear the soundless "sound of Heaven" behind the various sounds of Multiplicity. Rather, in hearing the "sound of Earth," one *is* really hearing nothing other than the "sound of Heaven." The infinitely various sounds which the hollows emit are no other than the one "sound of Heaven."

As the "sound of Heaven," which is in itself absolute Nothingness—or Void (*hsü*), as Chuang Tzŭ sometimes calls it—acts upon the hollows which are in themselves "void" and "nothing," the latter become activated and emit divergent sounds in such a way that they "imagine that it is they themselves that emit these sounds." They do not know that they are simply serving as different loci in which the soundless "sound of Heaven" actualizes itself in a myriad of audible sounds.

But man, as long as he hears these sounds as so many different sounds, is not actually hearing the "sound of Heaven." Chuang Tzŭ throughout his book urges man to hear the "sound of Heaven" which remains one in all, and which, remaining always one, diversifies itself in an infinity of real sounds. Only then could man be said to have succeeded in boring orifices on the featureless face of the Emperor Chaos without making him lose his life.

We shall bring our discussion to a close by briefly analyzing the ontological structure of Chaos, which has been the main concern of this paper. For that purpose let us begin by recalling that in reference to the philosophical status of Chaos we have in the course of our discussion often used the term "nothingness." In fact the term serves well as an English counterpart of the Chinese word *wu*, meaning literally "non-existence," which, it is well known, is one of the key terms of both Lao Tzŭ and Chuang Tzŭ. But a caution is needed in identifying Chuang Tzŭ's "Chaos" with "nothingness," unless we use the latter term in rather a loose sense, for, strictly speaking, there is a certain respect in which the two must be distinguished from one another.

Nothingness, taken in its absolute sense, would signify objectively a metaphysical stage of the Absolute to be reached only by the "negation of the negation of the negation of existence."[17] Subjectively, it would refer to the absolute and total annihilation of consciousness which is experienced at the extreme limit of *ekstasis*. It thus corresponds to a transcendental metaphysical-epistemological stage called by Lao Tzŭ the "Mystery of mysteries" (*hsüan chih yu hsüan*) that lies beyond even *wu* ("non-existence") and *yu* ("existence").

Now the important point for our particular purpose is that Nothingness in such an absolute sense represents, in the philosophical system of Chuang Tzŭ, only the ultimate point of Chaos, not the whole of it. Certainly, Chaos *is* ultimately pure and absolute Nothingness. But the latter does not exhaust the whole of Chaos. If Chaos were solely pure Nothingness, it would not allow of being represented as anything whatsoever of a positive nature, be it "chaos." The word "chaos" (*hun tun*) itself suggests the shadowy existence of an infinite number of things in a state of undifferentiation, an interfusion of all things. It is true that Chuang Tzŭ calls it the Village of There-is-Absolutely-Nothing (*wu ho yu chih hsiang*).[18] That is to say, there is absolutely "nothing" here to be distinguished as "anything" particular. But it is, on the other hand, at least a "village," no matter how strange and fantastic a "village" it may be; it is a metaphysical region formed by all things in a state of complete interfusion.

Thus in the philosophical system of Chuang Tzŭ, Chaos is to be considered not so much Nothingness itself in its absolute sense as the very world of Being or Multiplicity, our world of empirical reality, as it appears to the spiritual eyes of the True Man when he views it from the vantage point of absolute Nothingness. Chaos in this sense is not sheer negativity. Quite the contrary, it is the plenitude of Being in its true reality. As such it has a peculiar structure of its own. Chaos may thus be represented as the lower half, so to speak, of absolute Nothingness. It is the face of Nothingness turned toward the empirical world. At this stage the world of Being is seen by the ecstatic man beyond the confines of time and space. In his view, all temporal and spatial categories that are produced by the language-determined thinking of ordinary men lose their essential determinations. There is for example no distinction here between the past, the future, or the present. "It was" refers exactly to the same state of affairs as "it is" or "it will be." To say "here" is the same as to say "there."

What is more important to observe about this situation is that when, in this atemporal and aspatial dimension, a peculiar form of thinking arises in conformity with the very structure of the dimension, an entirely new kind of Time and an entirely new kind of Space emerge out of the depths of Nothingness and become reflected in the "chaotified" mind of the True Man. Otherwise expressed, the content of his unusual metaphysical experience evolves itself in entirely new forms in the dimension of unusual Time and Space. Let us, for the sake of theoretical convenience, designate these latter as "metatemporal Time" and "metaspatial Space" respectively. They may as well be called mythopoeic Time and mythopoeic Space. In any case, they have a remarkably different structure from "time" and "space" as ordinarily understood. The distinguishing marks of their structure precisely form the most central part of Chuang Tzŭ's philosophy.

The metatemporal Time is called by Chuang Tzŭ himself the Transmutation of Things (*wu hua*). The Transmutation, in Chuang Tzŭ's sense, represents an aspect of the decisive importance of the metaphysical structure of the world as it appears to the "chaotified" mind of the True Man. It refers to a metaphysical dimension in which all things are ultimately found to be "transmutable" to one another. What is meant here is an absolutely free transmutation, which may conveniently be expressed by the formula: " *a* becomes *b*, *c*, *d*, . . ."; "*b* becomes *a*, *c*, *d*, . . ."; "*c* becomes *a*, *b*, *d*, . . ."; and so forth. A butterfly freely changes into Chuang Chou; Chuang Chou freely becomes a butterfly, or indeed anything else. Everything becomes everything else. The situation is comparable to an imaginary case in which an infinite number of mirrors standing face to face go on reflecting one another indefinitely, without any obstruction.

This cosmic Transmutation of Things is apparent only to the "chaotified" mind which has ceased to observe any essential distinctions between the things. The "chaotified" mind is a mind that is no-mind; it is a state of consciousness in which the ego has lost its self-identity. In correspondence with this subjective disappearance of ego-consciousness, all the objects of perception and intellection also lose their self-identities. Since in this dimension all things are liberated from their essential limitations, they are free to be transmuted into each other.

This process of everything becoming everything else, insofar as it is considered a *process of becoming*, is doubtlessly of a temporal nature. It is Time. Yet on the other hand, since this fluid state involves *all* things, and since, moreover, all things are here essenceless and therefore indistinguishable from one another, the process viewed as an all-comprehensive whole is in reality a static state rather than a temporal state of *becoming*.

The metaspatial Space is but the reverse side of what has just been described as the metatemporal Time. For since in this dimension *all* things, as we have seen, are deprived of their essential self-identity and are transmutable to one another, they cannot but ultimately become merged into an absolute Unity. In this perspective, "*a* becomes *b*, *c*, *d* . . ." would have no other meaning than "*a* is (from the very beginning) *b*, *c*, *d*,. . . ." In point of fact, in this cosmic state of fluidity and amorphousness, *becoming* makes no real sense. For all are One eternally and forever.

The absolute Unity is in a certain sense Space because in it are contained all things, albeit in the state of ultimate undifferentiation.

But since these things are in reality non-entities and therefore occupy no "space," their being together does not occupy any "space." The metaspatial Space is mythopoeically presented by Chuang Tzŭ as the Village of There-is-Absolutely-Nothing or the Wilderness-of-the-Limitlessly-Wide (*Kuang mo chih yeh*).[19]

Notes

1. In the present paper I shall not go into details about the problem of the shamanistic origin of Taoism, a problem which is in itself a very interesting one and which I have already dealt with elsewhere: *Key Philosophical Concepts in Sufism and Taoism*, Part Two (Tokyo, 1967), pp. 1–24, and *"The Absolute and the Perfect Man in Taoism," Eranos-Jahrbuch*, vol. 34 (Zürich, 1968).
2. Cf. Izutsu, "Absolute and Perfect Man," pp. 426 ff.; on the logical aspect of Chuang Tzŭ see also A. C. Graham, "Chuang-tzŭ's Essay on Seeing Things as Equal," *History of Religions*, vol. 9 (Chicago, 1969–70), pp. 137–159.
3. Chuang Chou is the real name of Chuang Tzŭ; the latter simply means, Master Chuang.
4. *Chuang Tzŭ Chi Shih*, ed. Kuo Ch'ing Fan (Peking, 1961), p. 112. All quotations in the present paper are made from the "Interior Chapters" (*nei p'ien*) of the *Chuang Tzŭ*, which, being most probably from his own pen, represent the thought of Chuang Tzŭ in its most authentic form.
5. "Abnormally big but [just because of its extraordinary bigness] quite useless" is an expression used by Hui Tzŭ, the above-mentioned dialectician, in his criticism of Chuang Tzŭ's thought; cf. *Chuang Tzŭ*, bk. 1, p. 36.
6. *Ch'i Hsieh*, meaning that cosmic harmony which equalizes (i.e., brings back to the original "chaotic" unity) all things, is a name invented by Chuang Tzŭ. *Ch'i Hsieh* is also said to be the name of the fictitious author of the book.
7. *Chuang Tzŭ*, bk. 1, pp. 2–4.
8. Mention has earlier been made of this masterpiece of shamanistic poetry, cf. section II.
9. In fact Chuang Tzŭ himself says in his book that such cases often occurred to him, cf. bk. 1, pp. 36–40.
10. *Chuang Tzŭ*, bk. 1, pp. 30 ff.
11. It is interesting to observe that this hermit is a man of Ch'u, just like the shaman-poets of the above-mentioned *Elegies of Ch'u*. The state of Ch'u was the greatest center of shamanism in ancient China.
12. *Chuang Tzŭ*, bk. 5, pp. 217, 220–222.
13. For more details about this point cf. Izutsu, *Key Concepts*, pp. 18–19.
14. *Chuang Tzŭ*, bk. 7, p. 309.
15. Cf. Izutsu, *Key Concepts*, pp. 66 ff.; Professor Chang Chung-yuan, "Process of Self-realization" in *Creativity and Taoism*: *A Study of Chinese Philosophy, Art, and Poetry* (New York, 1963), pp. 123–168, in which the author gives a masterly description of the technique of "sitting-in-oblivion" as it was developed by the Taoists.

16. *Chuang Tzŭ*, bk. 2, pp. 45–50.
17. For a detailed explanation of this seemingly strange phrase see Izutsu, *Key Concepts*, pp. 94–97, and *Absolute and Perfect Man*, pp. 426–428.
18. *Chuang Tzŭ*, bk. 1, pp. 39–40.
19. Ibid.

Toshihiko Izutsu

THE PARADOX OF LIGHT AND DARKNESS IN THE *GARDEN OF MYSTERY* OF SHABASTARÎ

Inna li-Allâh sab'în alf ḥijâb
min nûr wa-ẓulmah

Verily God is hidden behind seventy thousand
veils of Light and Darkness

I

THIS PAPER, A STUDY OF THE STRUCTURE OF METAPHORICAL THINKING IN Islamic mysticism (Sufism), will trace this type of thinking back to its experiential origin, that is to say, by observing the very process by which archetypal metaphors arise out of the transcendental awareness of Reality. The study will analyze, for this particular purpose, two of the key metaphors of Sufism, light (*nūr*) and darkness (*ẓulmah*) in their paradoxical interactions, as they appear in the *Gulsham-e Râz* of Shabastarî and as they are philosophically explicated by Lâhîjî in his celebrated commentary upon this poem.

Maḥmûd Shabastarî (or Shabistarî) is one of the most famous Persian mystic-philosophers, or "theosophers," of the fourteenth century (d. 1320 A.D.). The *Gulshan-e Râz*, or the *Garden of Mystery*, is a long philosophic poem which is not only a unanimously recognized masterpiece of Shabastarî's, but is also given a very high place in the whole history of Persian literature.

The importance of the *Garden of Mystery* has induced a number of distinguished thinkers to write commentaries upon it, the most important of which is the *Mafâtîḥ al-I'jâz fî Sharḥ-e Gulshan-e Râz*[1] by Lâhîjî, whose thought I shall examine in the following, together with that of Shabastarî himself. Muḥammad Gîlânî Lâhîjî (d. probably 1506–7) was an outstanding Sufi master of the dervish order called Nûrbakhshîyah, and the most famous of the successors of the master Nûrbakhsh. His commentary has been studied for centuries not only as the best commentary upon the *Garden of Mystery*, but also as one of the most lucid, systematic expositions of Sufi philosophy written in Persian.[2]

II

As a convenient starting point for the discussion of our problem, let us begin by inspecting the classical definition of metaphor given by Aristotle in his *Poetics*. It runs: "Metaphor consists in giving the thing a name that belongs to something else; the transference being either from genus to species, or from species to genus, or from species to species, or on grounds of analogy."[3] Of the various possible forms of semantic transference mentioned here by Aristotle, it is in modern times the last one, namely the transference based on the observation of analogy, that is usually thought of when one speaks of metaphors.[4]

Thus, in accordance with this understanding, we may say that a metaphor is a linguistic sign which has a proper, conventionally established reference to a thing (A) being used in reference to something else (B) on the ground of some structural similarity observed between A and B. That is to say, we have a metaphor whenever a word is used in a double role, pointing at the same time to two different things (A and B), the first being its literal or conventional meaning and the second its non-conventional or figurative meaning. As Paul Henle says: "A word is an *immediate sign* of its literal sense and a *mediate* sign of its figurative sense."[5]

If such is the correct understanding of "metaphor," the Sufi use of the word *light* (*nûr*), for example, clearly constitutes a metaphor. For in the particular context of Sufi terminology, the word *light* still retains its literal sense, which it indicates in ordinary, daily circumstances: physical light. But it refers at the same time to a certain unusual spiritual experience peculiar to a certain phase of mystic life, and there is—at least from the subjective viewpoint of the Sufi who experiences it—an undeniable structural analogy between the two experiences.

However, again from the subjective viewpoint of the Sufi who actually uses the word *light* in reference to some aspects of his transcendental experience of Reality, the whole thing would appear as highly problematic. The problem of metaphor, in other words, is for him not as simple as might be imagined from the Aristotelian definition of it. For the Sufi, to begin with, is firmly convinced that if there is at all anything in the world that might be fully entitled to be called light, it is the spiritual light as he experiences it, not the physical counterpart of it. Physical light, even the light of the sun, let alone artificial light, is for him too weak to be real. So overwhelmingly strong is the light which he sees with his "eye of spiritual vision" (*'ayn al-baṣîrah*). Compared with the latter kind of light, the physical light can be called "light" only as a figure of speech. The Illuminationist (*ishrâqî*) metaphysics of Suhrawardî[6] provides a remarkable example of philosophizing on the basis of the spiritual light as experienced by the mystics as the supreme metaphysical reality.

Thus, linguistically speaking, we are here in the presence of an unusual case in which the so-called literal meaning of a word turns into a figurative meaning, while what is ordinarily taken as figurative or metaphorical is found to be "real." In this particular context, the word *light* functions as an *immediate sign* for the spiritual light and as a *mediate sign* for the physical. So much so that from a linguistic point of view we might even say that the very occurrence of semantic transformation of such a nature in human consciousness marks the birth of a real mystic.

Obviously, then, at the very source of this kind of unusual use of words there is an original intuition of Reality. From this original intuition there develops an original form of thinking. The latter is clearly typified in Sufi poetry and philosophy. In reference to this phenomenon, it is often said that the poets and mystics express or describe the contents of their intuition by means of metaphors. This observation is certainly right in so far as it is made from the standpoint of ordinary language usage. For the word *light* coming out of the mouth of a mystic, for example, *is* a metaphor from such a point of view. But we have already established above that this is after all nothing but an outsider's view. Seen from the inside, that is, in terms of the inner structure of the transcendental consciousness, the so-called metaphor used by the mystic is not a metaphor in the ordinary sense of the word.

In order to have a real insight into the matter we must keep in mind the following point: it is not the case that an extraordinary vision comes first to a mystic, and that then he tries to describe it through a metaphor or a series of metaphors. Quite the contrary, the vision *is* itself the metaphor or metaphors. There is no discrepancy here between the level of the original vision and the level of its metaphorical expression. There is in this respect no room for free choice for the mystic with regard to the "metaphor" to be used. When a mystic uses the word *light*, for example, in describing his vision of Reality, he has not chosen it for himself from among a number of possible metaphors. Rather, the metaphor has forced itself upon him, for light is simply the concrete form in which he sees Reality. It is but natural that such a state of affairs should develop in the mystic a very peculiar thought pattern, if it is to formulate itself verbally in the dimension of the intellectual and philosophical activity of the mind. It is this kind of pattern that the present paper intends to analyze under the name of "metaphorical thinking in mysticism."

III

It is to be remarked that the pattern of thoughts typical of mystical philosophy originates in an experience known to the Islamic mystics as the stages of *fanâ'* ("annihilation") and *baqâ'* ("survival"), an ontological and metaphysical experience of an extraordinary but neatly delineated nature, which occurs at the transcendental level of awareness.[7] And the philosophical thinking here in question evolves out of a fundamental metaphysical vision which is an immediate product of the *fanâ'-baqâ'* experience.

At the stage of *fanâ* there is absolutely no consciousness of anything whatsoever—no object to be seen, no ego to see—not even the awareness of there being nothing. So naturally there is at this stage no possibility for the emergence of an image.

At the stage of *baqâ'*, however, as the mind awakes to the existence of things—including the perceiving subject itself—and begins to resume its normal functioning, various images tend to emerge in the consciousness. These images, especially the most archetypal of them, are not for the Sufi mere subjective illusions or phantasms. They are, on the contrary, so many objective forms in which Reality discloses itself, hence the great importance attached to the basic function of imagery in the evolvement of thought in Islamic mysticism. In fact, thinking in and through images is in this context almost the only authentic form of thinking. For an image here is not a symbol indicating something beyond itself; rather, it is the indicator of its own self. It *is* a reality. Looked at from the outside, however, this type of thinking cannot but appear as "symbolic" and "metaphorical."

The images of light and darkness are constantly met with in the writings of Sufis, whether in prose or poetry. They are among the most representative of the archetypal images of Sufism in the sense that they are natural, immediate self-expressions of a root experience of the absolute Reality. The root experience—the basic structure of which will be made clear as we proceed—manifests itself most naturally in the form of the light-darkness imagery. The images themselves form an integral part of the root experience. They are not symbols by means of which Sufis try to express something entirely different. They are not metaphors as normally understood, although in fact they *are* metaphors from the viewpoint of common sense and ordinary language. If we want to place emphasis on this latter aspect of the matter, we may call the root experience itself a "metaphorical experience" in the sense that light and darkness are basically and originally there as two of its constituent factors.

Within the framework of metaphysical thinking peculiar to the school to which Shabastarî and Lâhîjî belong, the Absolute or Reality at its highest stage is conceived as "pure existence." What is conceived metaphysically as existence (*wujûd*) coincides with what is grasped in terms of the root experience as light (*nûr*). In this context existence *is* light. It is not the case that there is a reality called existence which bears striking similarities with light as we know it in the empirical world and which, therefore, is properly to be indicated by the metaphor of light.

The theosophic position taken by Suhrawardî the Illuminationist shows this point in the most conspicuous form. Suhrawardî places exclusive emphasis on the light as a root experience. From such a point of view, the very conception of light *as* existence deprives the fundamental experience of its fundamentality and rationalizes it into something abstract. Thus in his view *existence* is nothing but a rational "metaphor" for light. *Existence*, in short, is for him an abstract concept which the human intellect has fabricated. This Suhrawardian position is known in the history of Persian thought as the *i'tibârîyah*, "fictitiousness" or ultimate unreality, of existence.

On the contrary, in the school of the unity of existence (*waḥdat al-wujûd*), supported by Shabastarî and Lâhîjî, emphasis is laid on existence. They readily admit that the absolute reality as a matter of immediate experience is certainly light. But, they argue, when one remembers the ontological plenitude which one feels in this kind of experience, one cannot but take the position that the light is existence itself. In fact, even as a matter of immediate experience there is absolutely no discrepancy between *light* and *existence*. Rather, existence is a "luminous reality" (*ḥaqîqah nûrânîyah*); it is itself a reality of the very nature of light. Thus it comes about that in this school the word *light* is often used as if it were a metaphor for existence. In reality, however, even in this school, *light* is only seemingly a metaphor.

IV

In the matter that has preceded, one point stands out as deserving special attention before we set out to analyze the paradox of light and darkness. This paradox, when elaborated rationally, will inevitably result in an ontological *coincidentia oppositorum* of Unity and Multiplicity. It will take on the form of a very peculiar paradoxical relationship of identity in the character of the distinction between the Absolute and pehnomenal things. Thus it would appear as if the paradox of light and darkness were a "metaphorical" presentation of the ontological *coincidentia oppositorum*. In truth, however, it is the former that is the basis while the latter is but a philosophical elaboration of the former.

The very first opposition of light and darkness which we encounter in the theosophic world view of Shabastarî-Lâhîjî is that between absolute existence (*hastî-ye muṭlaq*)[8] and the phenomenal world. As is clear from what has been said earlier, absolute existence is the same as absolute light (*nûr-e muṭlaq*),[9] so all phenomenal things are relegated to the region of darkness (*ẓulmah*). The phenomenal world is the world of our ordinary empirical experience, the world of Multiplicity, the ontological dimension in which an infinite number of things seem to exist self-subsistently, being distinguished one from the other by their own essential demarcations.

This world of Multiplicity is darkness in two different senses. First it is darkness in the sense that it is *in itself* nothing and nonexistence (*'adam*). Because of this fundamental nothingness (*'admîyat-e aṣlî*),[10] the world and all individual things in the world remain forever in darkness; the word "fundamental" (*aṣlî*) in the above phrase means that nothingness is woven into the essential structure of the phenomenal world and is therefore never separable from it.

It is this aspect of Multiplicity that Shabastarî refers to by the word "black-facedness" (*siyah-rû'î*). "No phenomenal thing," he says, "whether in the external world or in the internal, ever leaves the state of black-facedness."[11] The expression "black-faced," besides the meaning of blackness and darkness, implies shame, disgrace, and infamy. It is therefore a very apt metaphor for the purely negative aspect of all phenomenal things. Everything in this empirical world is "black-faced." Everything is literally "nothing" and is therefore in an extremely low and disgraceful position. Note that "black-facedness" *is* a metaphor in the ordinary sense of the word; it is not an archetypal metaphor like light and darkness.

Since there is no intermediary ontological state conceivable between existence and nonexistence, and since, moreover, existence is the Absolute, it is only natural that the world of phenomenal things, as something different and distinguishable from the Absolute—for the phenomenal world is *not* the Absolute—should be nonexistence.[12] Every phenomenal thing is in this respect sheer "non-thing" (*lâ-shay'*). The world is naturally experienced by the mystic as a field of pure darkness.

We have just said that every phenomenal thing is "nothing" insofar as it is something distinguishable from the Absolute, insofar as it is "other" (*ghayr*) than the Absolute. In truth it is this qualification ("insofar as . . .") that is going to play a crucial role in the paradox of light and darkness. It is the very beginning of this ontological paradox.

Certainly everything in the phenomenal world is, essentially speaking, nothing and is therefore darkness. That, however, does not exhaust the whole structure of a phenomenal thing. For *in a nonessential way*, everything in this world is "something." Otherwise there would be no perception, be it even an illusion, of a *phenomenal* thing.

The phenomenal world of Multiplicity is essentially sheer darkness. But there is at the same time a certain respect in which this fundamental darkness turns into an apparent light. The world is light. Otherwise expressed, darkness phenomenally appears as light. This is the first paradox which we run into in our factual encounter with the world of Being.

The empirical world, insofar as it is phenomenally apparent to our senses, must be said to be a region of light. All things in fact loom up out of their original darkness in the dim light of existence. They do exist, and to that extent they are illumined. But theirs is a dim light because it is not the light of their own; it is a borrowed light, a feeble reflection coming from the real Source of light. "The whole world becomes apparent by the Light of the Absolute" (Shabastarî).[13]

It is important for our purpose to observe the highly paradoxical nature of the verse just quoted. "The whole world"—that is the world of Multiplicity which, as we have already seen, is in itself sheer darkness —"becomes apparent"—becomes illumined and thereby turns into light—"by the Light of the Absolute." This means that the very darkness of the phenomenal world is a product of light, and that, paradoxically enough, the very coming-into-being of the darkness constitutes by itself the birth of the phenomenal light.

The whole process will best be understood in terms of the metaphysics of the unity of existence (*waḥdat al-wujûd*) which is the result of a philosophical systematization of the fundamental experience of light and darkness. We must remark first of all that light in this context is not a stable thing, that it is, on the contrary, the incessant *act* of the effusion of creative energy from the ultimate source, which is the Absolute which, again, is pure existence. From this ultimate source the light of existence (*nûr-e wujûd*) is incessantly being effused in the form of the self-manifestations (*tajallîyât*) of the Absolute. From this point of view, the phenomenal things are but determined and limited forms of the one single all-comprehensive light of existence. "Existence which is observable in this world is but a derivation and reflection of the Light of Existence which is the Absolute."[14] In this sense every phenomenal thing, being in itself a nonreality and darkness, *is* a reality and light. Thus the emergence of darkness *eo ipso* marks the emergence of light.

V

The fact that the phenomenal world is in itself sheer darkness is not apparent to the physical eye. Quite the contrary, man ordinarily and naturally tends to see the phenomenal world as light: nothing else is visible to him. The truth is that the phenomenal light is visible to the physical eye as light simply because it is an extremely feeble light, because instead of being pure, it is a mere reflection, a reflected image. Light in its absolute purity is too brilliant to be visible. It dazzles the eye; it is darkness. This is another paradox of light and darkness, the real structure of which will be clarified later on.

The phenomenal light, because of its being a reflection, is often called in Islamic mysticism *ẓill*, "shadow." It is a shadow cast by the sun of Reality upon the reflecting surface of nonexistence. "Just as a shadow becomes visible by the activity of Light, and just as it is a non-thing if considered in itself without any reference to its source, so does the world become apparent by the Light of real Existence; it is a non-thing and Darkness if considered in its own essence."[15] The underlying idea is that it is only through the shadow, indirectly, that man can see pure light. But what is more relevant to our immediate topic is that man is actually far from having even this kind of indirect perception of pure light.

The phenomenal world is visible, we have said, because of its reduced light. But precisely because it is so clearly visible to us it tends to act as an insulating screen between our sight and what lies beyond it. This is the second sense in which the world of Multiplicity is said to be darkness. It is darkness because it casts a black veil (*ḥijâb*) over the light of Reality. We are here confined in the region of the "darkness of Multiplicity" (*târîkî-ye kathrat*). We see Multiplicity, only Multiplicity; we cannot see the absolute Unity of Existence hidden behind the impenetrable veil of Multiplicity. Our sight stops at the phenomenal surface of the things. This idea is poetically expressed by Shabastarî in this verse: "Under the veil of every single atom there is hidden the enlivening beauty of the face of the Beloved."[16] The human tragedy is that most men are not aware even of the hidden presence of the Beloved behind the curtain.

Briefly restated in ontological terms, the whole situation at this stage will be somewhat as follows. Everything in this world is, as we have repeatedly pointed out, essentially and in itself "nothing." But insofar as everything is a determined form in which existence manifests itself, it is a reality. Everything thus has two "faces," negative and positive. In its negative aspect, it is perishable and perishing; it is fundamentally ephemeral. In its positive aspect it is imperishable and everlasting. The Qur'ânic verse, "All things are perishable, except His Face,"[17] is often interpreted by the mystics in this sense. Says Lâhîjî: "Every phenomenal thing has two faces. Its face of non-existence [*wajh-e nîstî*] is forever perishing, while its face of existence [*wajh-e hastî*] forever remaining."[18]

But here again we come across an ontological paradox. The paradox consists in the fact that of these two "faces" it is the ephemeral and perishable (which is in itself "nothing") that appears to man's eyes as "something" solidly established on the ground of existence. The negative protrudes itself as if it were the positive. And that which is really positive is completely lost sight of. The positive aspect of a thing in which it is a self-manifestation and self-determination of absolute existence (that is, absolute light) sinks into darkness. For as long as man sees a thing as a "thing," man can never see the Thing that lies behind it.

The idea of the veil, however, is in reality of a more complicated structure, because it contains in itself other basic paradoxes. One of them is the following. We have just said that the phenomenal world works as an impenetrable veil concealing the Absolute behind it; the Absolute is not visible because of the veil. But on reflection we easily discover that this is a very inexact description of the real ontological situation. For as we have seen above, the veil and the Absolute are not two different things: the veil is the external epiphany of the Absolute. From this point of view we must say that when man sees the veil, he is actually seeing nothing other than the very Absolute. In other words, the veil qua "veil" does cause obstruction to man's sight and prevents him from seeing the Absolute, but in its epiphanic form the veil is rather an immediate presentation of the Absolute itself. We must go a step further and say that the Absolute is so nakedly apparent to man's sight that it is not visible—another paradoxical situation in which light appears as darkness. As Shabastarî says: "The whole world of Being is the beams of the absolute Light. The Absolute remains hidden because it is so clearly manifest."[19] Explicating this idea Lâhîjî remarks: "Covering necessarily causes concealment, but it often happens also that the extremity of exposure causes concealment. Do you not see? In the middle of the day, when the sun is immediately exposed to view, the eye does not see the sun itself because of the excessive exposure of its light. In the same way, the Light of the existential Oneness,[20] because of its excessive exposure, remains invisible, being hidden in the very brilliancy of its own."[21]

"What a stupidity!" Shabastarî exclaims, "To search for the burning sun with the light of a candle, in the very midst of the desert!"[22] The burning sun does not conceal itself; it is there in the sky, fully exposed, fully in sight. There is no veil to obstruct the view. The phrase "in the very midst of the desert" suggests that the whole world of Being is a vast plain where there is absolutely no hindrance to the sight. Yet man is vainly searching for the sun with a candle in hand: the candle symbolizes human reason.

But the paradox of the veil has not yet reached its end. As we have already remarked, it is an empirical fact that the world of multiplicity is for the majority of men a veil concealing the metaphysical dimension of absolute Unity. That is to say, as long as man considers the phenomenal things as self-subsistent and essentially existent entities, man can never hope to have an immediate vision of the Absolute which then conceals itself behind its own innumerable phenomenal forms. On the other hand, however—and here we observe another aspect of the paradox—it is precisely because of the actual existence of the veil that man can see the Absolute no matter how indirect, vague, and indistinct the vision may be. Of course he sees principally—and in most cases exclusively—Multiplicity. But it may happen that he has a vague feeling that he is in the presence of Something beyond. In such a case, it is through the veil of phenomenal things that he sees the light of the Absolute. Otherwise, the light is too strong to be seen. Says Shabastarî: "The eye has no power to stand the dazzling light of the sun. It can only see the sun as reflected in the water."[23]

Ontologically speaking, the water which, intervening between the eye and the sun, plays the role of a mirror, at the same time reducing the excessive radiancy of the sun, is the essential nonexistence of the things. It is only through the intermediary of this "mirror of non-existence" that existence becomes visible to our eyes. "Non-existence [*'adam*] is the mirror of absolute Existence [*hastî-ye muṭlaq*], for it is in non-existence that the reflection of the radiancy of the Absolute becomes visible."[24]

It is to be remarked in this connection that in the metaphysical system of *waḥdat al-wujûd* (the "unity of existence") the nonexistence which constitutes the essence of the phenomenal world begins to appear at a higher stage than that of the phenomenal world, namely at the stage of the "eternal archetypes" (*a'yân thâbitah*). Rather, it is the non-existence of the eternal archetypes, properly speaking, that first reflects the pure light of the Absolute. What is observable at the stage of phenomenal things is nothing but an indirect, and therefore extremely weakened, reflection of this primary reflection.

The eternal archetypes, corresponding to what the philosophers call quiddities (*mâhîyât*, sg. *mâhîyah*) and resembling in many respects the Platonic Ideas, are in this school of thought conceived as the primary archetypal forms of things as they exist in the dimension of Divine Consciousness. As such they do exist in this particular dimension, but from the point of view of external, empirical existence they are non-existent, and remain forever nonexistent. And since it belongs to the very nature of nonexistence to stand opposed, in a certain sense, to existence, the eternal archetypes confront pure existence. The latter is reflected in this nonexistent mirror, or the nonexistent mirrors, and the existential light immediately appears diversified in accordance with the diversification of the mirrors.[25] The eternal archetypes are often called shadows; that is to say, they are essentially darkness and yet, in relation to the pure existence which they reflect, they are light. The appearance of the concrete things in the darkness of the phenomenal dimension is but a reflection of the pure light that has already been reflected in the dark mirror of the eternal archetypes.

VI

We shall now turn to a more subjective aspect of the problem and pursue the paradox of light and darkness in particular connection with the gradual development of the transcendental consciousness in the mystic who actually experiences the successive stages of the same paradox.

The whole process may briefly and in a provisional way be described as follows. When the Absolute (which is no other than pure light) appears in its uncontaminated unity to the consciousness of the mystic, all phenomenal distinctions disappear into darkness: no more consciousness of the perceiving subject; no more consciousness of the perceived objects. This is the mystic stage of *fanâ'*, annihilation. The most salient paradoxical point at this stage is that by the full appearance of light in the consciousness all things disappear instead of appearing. Light in this respect is the cause of darkness. Yet, on the other hand, by the very fact that all things become deprived of their individual determinations and become obliterated from the consciousness—including this very consciousness from which they are obliterated—the whole world turns into a limitlessly vast ocean of light. And out of the depth of this ocean of light all the things that have once totally disappeared into darkness begin to emerge resuscitated and regain their individual determinations, being in themselves darkness but this time fully saturated with the pure light of existence. This is the mystic stage technically known as the stage of *baqâ'*, survival in and with God.

The stage of *bagâ'* is ontologically designated by the word *jam'* which literally means "gathering." *Gathering* is opposed to *farq* or "separating." This latter word refers to the ordinary empirical state in which the phenomenal things are separated and distinguished first from each other, and then from the Absolute. In this dimension man normally sees only the phenomenal world, and considers the Absolute—if man at all becomes aware of the existence of something beyond the phenomenal world—as the entirely "other" (*ghayr*).

In contrast to this, gathering, that is, unification, is the stage at which all the separate things are seen reduced to their original existential unity. All things, beginning with the self-consciousness of the mystic, disappear from the ken. The light is extinguished, the light of the phenomenal world. There remains only absolute Unity. There is not even the consciousness *of* the Unity, for there is no trace here of any consciousness. The whole universe *is* Unity. And the Unity is light, but at the same time it is the Darkness of the phenomenal world.

Out of the unfathomable abyss of this light-darkness, the mystic cries out, "I am the Absolute!"[26] The reference is to the famous al-Ḥallâj who, because of this and similar "blasphemous" utterances, was executed in 922. Concerning this particular utterance of al-Ḥallâj, Lâhîjî remarks: "He is one of the 'people of intoxication' [*arbâb-e sukr*] who in the state of inebriation disclose the divine secrets which are manifested to their purified minds. Since in that state they have no ego-consciousness [*az bî-khudî*, literally "because of without-self-ness"] they cannot keep concealed whatever appears to them. Hence the 'I am the Absolute!' of al-Ḥallâj. The utterance indicates that when the mystic traveling back to God through the way of self-purification goes beyond the region of Multiplicity and becomes annihilated and absorbed into the ocean of Unity, he discovers himself to be completely identical with the ocean of Reality of which he has been [in his ordinary consciousness] but a single drop. He is then a 'man of intoxication'. If he, in that state of inebriation suddenly cries out: 'I am the very Ocean itself!' because of his egolessness, we should not be surprised."[27]

VII

It is remarkable that in the process of the development of mystic consciousness light and darkness succeed one another, light itself being transformed into darkness and darkness itself being transformed into light. This process of interchange between light and darkness reaches the most crucial point with the appearance of an extraordinary state known as Black Light (*nûr-e siyâh*). Black Light is a very delicate spiritual state into which the mystic enters just before *fanâ'* (annihilation) turns into *baqâ'* (survival). It may be represented as a point which marks the end of *fanâ'* and the beginning of *baqâ'*: it is state shared by both.

As the mystic goes up the way of ascent toward the Absolute-as-such, he finally reaches a point at which he experiences his inner light, that is, his inner spiritual illumination, all of a sudden turning black. As actually experienced by the mystic, it is an epistemological darkness which is of a different nature from the ontological darkness that has been analyzed the foregoing, although, as we shall see presently, there is also an ontological aspect to it.

This epistemological darkness is a darkness caused by the extreme propinquity of the mystic to the Absolute. Says Shabastarî: "An object of sight, when it approaches the eye too closely, darkens the sight, making the eye unable to see anything."[28] This is true not only of the physical eye, but also of the inner eye (*dîde-ye bâṭin*). "As the mystic in his ascent toward God goes beyond all the stages of the Light of Divine self-manifestation through His Names and Attributes [i.e., in the forms of the "eternal archetypes"], and becomes finally well prepared to receive His essential self-manifestation [i.e., God's revealing Himself directly, without any intermediary forms], suddenly the Light of this latter kind of self-manifestation appears to him in the color of utter blackness. Because of his extreme spiritual propinquity to God, the inner eye of the mystic turns dark and becomes powerless to see anything whatsoever."[29]

The mystic, as we have remarked earlier, is now at a stage just preceding the one in which the whole universe will transform itself into a limitless ocean of light. Rather, the darkness which he is now experiencing is *itself* the supreme light. "This Blackness [*siyâhî*] in reality is the very Light of the Absolute-as-such. In the midst of this Darkness there is hidden the water of Life."[30] The "water of Life" means the state of *baqâ'*, the survival in God, the eternal life of existence.

Lâhîjî recounts his own experience of Black Light: "Once, I found myself in a luminous, non-material world. The mountains and deserts were all in various colors of light, red, yellow, white, and azure. The luminous colors were literally fascinating. Under the overwhelming power of this extraordinary experience I was out of myself, I had lost my own self. All of a sudden I saw the whole universe being enveloped in Black Light. The sky, the earth, the air, everything turned into the same Black Light. I become totally annihilated in this Black Light, and remained consciousless. After a while, I came back to myself."[31]

What is subjectively experienced as Black Light corresponds to what is known objectively—that is, ontologically—as the stage of Oneness (*aḥadîyah*), to which reference has earlier been made.[32] It is also called Supreme Blackness (*sawâd-e a'ẓam*). The Oneness is the ontological stage of the Absolute-as-such prior to its manifesting itself in accordance with its inner articulations. Seen from the side of the phenomenal world, it is the supreme ontological dimension in which all empirical distinctions among things become annihilated and in which all things are absorbed into their original Unity, or even beyond Unity into the metaphysical nothingness which, paradoxically enough, is no other than the real plenitude of existence. In its aspect of nothingness this stage is experienced by the mystic as *fanâ'*, while in its aspect of existential plenitude it is experienced as *baqâ'*.

"The mystic," Lâhîjî observes, "does not realize absolute Existence [*hastî-ye muṭlaq*] unless and until he fully realizes absolute Nothingness [*nîstî-ye muṭlaq*]. Nothingness is in itself the very Existence-by-the-Absolute. Absolute Nothingness is revealed only in absolute Existence . . . and absolute Existence cannot be revealed except in the very midst of absolute Nothingness."[33] In short, nothingness (or darkness) is in reality existence (light), and light is in reality darkness.

VIII

Let us begin by reformulating in ontological terms what has just been described in the preceding section so that we might be better prepared to understand the nature of the paradox of light and darkness at its ultimate and highest stage.

The first thing to notice is that everything we perceive in the empirical world has without exception two different ontological aspects: the aspect of absolute reality (*ḥaqîqah*), and the aspect of individuation (*tashakhkhuṣ*) or determination (*ta 'ayyun*).

In the first aspect, everything is a self-manifestation (*tajallî*) of the Absolute; it is the appearance of the Absolute, not "as-such," to be sure, but in a special form peculiar to the locus. It is an epiphany. In this sense everything is God.

In the second aspect, on the contrary, the same thing is considered in terms of its being something independent and self-subsistent. It is something "other" than the Absolute; it is non-God. From this point of view it is called a "creature" (*khalq*) and, philosophically, a "possible" (*mumkin*).[34] The important point is that "individuation" and "determination"—consequently the thing's being independent and self-subsistent—are in truth fictitious (*i'tibârî*) properties that have no fundamental reality of their own and have been imposed upon the thing by the human mind.

Such being the case, the true knowledge of things will be gained, according to Shabastarî-Lâhîjî, only when man (1) leaves the domain of Multiplicity (which is in itself non-reality and non-thing), (2) betakes himself to the domain of Unity (which is Reality-in-itself), and then (3) comes back again to the domain of Multiplicity and witnesses in every individual thing of this domain the Unity (which is the All) as it manifests itself there in its own self-determination. It goes without saying that the second stage in this process refers to the experience of *fanâ'* and the third to *baqâ'*. Says Shabastarî: "[Real] thinking consists in proceeding from non-reality [*bâṭil*] toward Reality [*ḥaqq*]. It is to see the absolute All in every individual thing."[35] Note that Shabastarî here gives a definition of "thinking" (*tafakkur*) as it is understood by the theosophers, which is of a totally different nature from its ordinary definition. What is meant by "thinking" is *kashf*, "unveiling," that is, an immediate intuitive grasp of Reality, as opposed to *istidlâl*, the process of reasoning by which one tries to arrive, on the basis of something known, at something unknown. The first half of Shabastarî's definition is a reference to *fanâ'*, which consists, as Lâhîjî says, in "all the atoms in the world being effaced and annihilated in the beams of the Light of the Divine Unity, as drops of water in the sea."[36] The second half refers to *baqâ'*, in which all the atoms, after having been absorbed into the ocean of Unity—that is, after having been brought back to their original nothingness (*'adam-e aṣlî*)—are again revived as so many epiphanies of one single Reality.[37]

Thus the paradox of light and darkness reaches its culminating point, indicated by the peculiar expression: "bright night amidst the dark daylight" (*shab-e rowshan miyân-e rûz-e târîk*).[38] The structure of what is meant by this paradoxical expression is clarified by Lâhîjî as follows:

> The *bright night* refers to the ontological stage of Oneness [*aḥadîyah*] which is compared to *night* in respect of its being colorless and its absolute non-determination. For, just as in deep night nothing can be perceived, so in the region of the Divine Essence—which is the region where all phenomenal forms are annihilated—there can be no perception, no consciousness. This is due to the fact that the Absolute-as-such, considered in

its purity without any reference to possible relations, is not perceivable. Remember that at this stage every possible relation, every possible determination has been completely effaced.

But this *night* is said to be *bright* on the basis of the fact that in reality [i.e., apart from all consideration of the basic constitution of human cognition] the Absolute is by itself fully manifest and that all things are made apparent by the illumination of its Light.

Amidst the dark daylight refers to the fact that this absolute Unity is manifested in the very midst of Multiplicity, i.e. in all the phenomenal determinations which are, on the one hand, as clearly apparent as daylight and, on the other, as dark as night because of their essential non-reality and Darkness. Multiplicity is apparent, yet at the same time it remains forever hidden.[39]

Lâhîjî repeatedly states that the stage of *baqâ'* is the ultimate stage to which the mystic can attain, and that it is the end of the spiritual journey, there being no further stage beyond it. But sometimes he seems to suggest the existence of a still higher stage which he designates as *fanâ' ba'da al-baqâ'*, that is, the stage of "annihilation after survival."[40] It would be regarded as the second annihilation. In any case what is described by Lâhîjî as the structure of this stage exactly corresponds to what Hua Yen Buddhism in China establishes as the ultimate of all ultimate ontological stages, the celebrated *ji-ji-muge-hokkai*, the "ontological dimension of unobstructed mutual interpenetration of all things." It also represents the extreme limit which our paradox of light and darkness can reach.

We have already seen that in the world view of the *waḥdat al-wujûd* school all things in the empirical world, even the single atoms of them, are each a particular form in which the Absolute manifests itself. Everything is a self-determination of the Absolute. In the terminology of Islamic theology this situation is often described by saying that everything is God as He is manifested in accordance with the essential requirement of a Divine Name. All Divine Names are ontologically the inner archetypal articulations of absolute Existence.

Thus everything in this world reflects in itself, in its own peculiar way, the Absolute. Everything is a mirror in which is reflected the Absolute. On the other hand, however, all things (that are in themselves darkness) are found to be one if they are traced back to the stage of absolute Oneness (which is light). From this point of view, each one of the things is the same as all others; it *is* the All. Thus when one thing reflects the Absolute in the form of one particular Name, it is by that very act reflecting the Absolute in all Names. This implies that in one single thing the Absolute is reflected in thousands of forms.

Says Shabastarî: "Behold, the whole world is a mirror, each one of the things is a mirror. Even in a single atom hundreds of suns are shining."[41] Again, "From one drop of water, if split apart, will hundreds of pure oceans gush forth".[42]

Lâhîjî explicates this point in the following way:

> It has been established that every single Divine Name is in reality qualified by the properties of all other Names, because all the Names are one at the stage of absolute Oneness. The Names are differentiated from each other only by virtue of the secondary particularities of the Attributes and relations. Thus it comes about that every single thing contains in itself all things. In one single grain of mustard-seed there are contained in reality [i.e., if observed apart from its individual determination] all the things that exist in the world. It is only because of its determination that all these things that are contained therein do not come up to the surface. Thus the mystic sees all things in everything. This is what is called the "mystery of Divine self-manifestations" [*sirr-e tajallîyât*].[43]

Here we are in the presence of the splendor of the paradox of light and darkness. The paradox weaves out a magnificent tapestry in which numberless lights and darknesses intersect each other and interpenetrate in such a way that the whole universe is presented as a multidimensional and intricately shaded Temple of Light.

IX

We shall conclude this paper by discussing, in terms of the paradox of light and darkness, the position in the cosmos occupied by man. This will make an apt conclusion because man is the very embodiment of this cosmic paradox. Man in fact is represented in the metaphysical system of Shabastarî-Lâhîjî as the "intermediary stage [*barzakh*] between Light and Darkness."[44] Moreover, the very paradox of light and darkness is actualized only through the consciousness of man. In this sense man is the center of the cosmic paradox.

As we have often observed, the phenomenal world is the world of Multiplicity, and as such it is a domain of darkness. Man, who is a microcosmos (*'âlam-e ṣaghîr*) in the sense that all the prehuman ontological stages are realized in him, is the extremity of Multiplicity. That is to say, man is the ultimate limit of darkness.

At the same time, however, man is an individual (*shakhṣ*) in the real sense of the word. He is "one" just as the Absolute is One. Thus in this particular respect there is a certain structural similarity observable between the Absolute and man. For the Absolute is One in its essence, many in its attributes; man is also one in his personal individuality while being many in his properties, actions, and functions. This fact—that man comprises in himself "unity" and "multiplicity"—enables him to intuit through his own structure the cosmic paradox of Unity qua Unity being Multiplicity and Multiplicity qua Multiplicity being Unity.

"The very first thing that Man realized," Lâhîjî says, "is his own personal determination which is both the last of all the ontological stages in the 'descending arc' of the circle of Existence, and the very first of all the stages in the 'ascending arc' of the same circle. Thus the ontological stage of Man is called the 'appearance of the first light of the dawn' [*matla' al-fajr*], because Man represents the end of the Darkness of Night [*nihâyat-e ẓulmat-e shab*] and the beginning of the Light of the Day of Unity [*bidâyat-e nûr-e rûz-e waḥdat*]."[45] Man is, in short, the *barzakh* between light and darkness. The whole cosmic drama of light and darkness is enacted in his mind.

Notes

1. Muḥammad Gîlânî Lâhîjî, *Mafâtîḥ al-I' jâz fî Sharḥ-e Gulshan-e Râz*, Kayvân Samî'î, ed. (Tehran, 1956).
2. Henry Corbin, for instance, describes it as "une véritable somme de soufisme en persan." See his "Symboles choisis de la roseraie du mystere," *Trilogie Ismaélienne* (Téhéran and Paris, 1961), vol. 3, p. 28.
3. Aristotle *Poetics* (trans. Bywater). 1457b–1458a.
4. Cf. Paul Henle, ed., "Metaphor," *Language, Thought, and Culture* (Ann Arbor, Mich., 1965), chap. 7.
5. Ibid., p. 175.
6. Shihâb al-Dîn Yaḥyà al-Suhrawardî (1153–1191), one of the greatest mystic-philosophers of Persia, was known for his philosophy of light. Cf. Seyyed Hossein Nasr, "Suhrawardi and the Illuminationists," in *Three Muslim Sages* (Cambridge, Mass., 1964), pp. 52–82.
7. The structure of the *fanâ'* and *baqâ'* will be explained in detail later on in connection with the problem of the paradoxical relation between light and darkness.
8. *Hastî* is a Persian word corresponding to the Arabic *wujûd*; both mean exactly the same thing; "existence."
9. Lâhîjî, p. 104.
10. Ibid., p. 98.

11. *Gulshan-e Râz*, v. 126. The original word for "phenomenal thing" here is *mumkin*, i.e., "possible." The numbering of the verses throughout this paper is based on the text of *Gulshan-e Râz* as it is reproduced in the Tehran edition of Lâhîjî's commentary (cf. n. 1).
12. Lâhîjî, p. 72.
13. *G.R.*, v. 115.
14. Lâhîjî, pp. 72, 89.
15. Ibid., p. 110.
16. *G.R.*, v. 165.
17. "Kullu shay'in hâlikun illa wajha-hu," XXVIII, 88.
18. Lâhîjî, p. 99.
19. *G.R.*, v. 97.
20. *Aḥadîyah*, "absolute oneness," as distinguished from *wâḥidîyah*, "oneness" (meaning the comprehensive "unity" of all things), constitutes in the metaphysical system of Lâhîjî the highest stage of the Absolute qua existence.
21. Lâhîjî, p. 72.
22. *G.R.*, v. 94.
23. Ibid., v. 131.
24. Ibid., v. 133.
25. Cf. Lâhîjî, pp. 104–106.
26. *G.R.*, v. 25: "Out of the ocean of Unity a mystic cried out: I am the Absolute!" (*ana al-Haqq*)
27. Lâhîjî, p. 29.
28. *G.R.*, v. 122.
29. Lâhîjî, p. 95.
30. *G.R.*, v. 123.
31. Lâhîjî, p. 96.
32. Cf. n. 20.
33. Lâhîjî, pp. 100, 102–103.
34. Ibid., p. 9.
35. *G.R.*, v. 72.
36. Lâhîjî, p. 50.
37. Ibid., p. 51.
38. *G.R.*, v. 128.
39. Lâhîjî, p. 101.
40. Ibid., p. 115.
41. *G.R.*, v. 145.
42. Ibid., v. 146.
43. Lâhîjî, p. 115.
44. Ibid., p. 10.
45. Ibid.

F. W. Wentzlaff-Eggebert

JOY IN THIS WORLD AND CONFIDENCE IN THE NEXT: ON MYSTICISM AS SPECULATION IN THE WORKS OF DANIEL von CZEPKO

POETRY MAY REMAIN BURIED FOR A LONG TIME, FOR MANY GENERATIONS and for whole eras, until a certain constellation in time brings it to life again. After World War I the poetry of the seventeenth century, scarcely recognized until then, was raised to the dignity of "baroque poetry." H. Wölflin's new method of art-historical interpretation was responsible for this apt designation, one which was further substantiated between 1930 and 1935 by such scholars as Walter Unus. It was during the same period that the poetic works of Daniel von Czepko first came to light and were made accessible to literary research by Werner Milch, whose death was so sadly premature.

I well remember one of my conversations with Werner Milch in which he spoke highly of Czepko's juxtaposition of joyous affirmation of this world and serene confidence in the next, a characteristic that is clearly discernible throughout everything this poet wrote. It was the striving for clarity of thought, hand in hand with a mounting certainty of faith that, in Milch's view, transcended the day and age of this Silesian poet. Because of these resources of spiritual strength, the then almost unknown baroque poet seemed to both Milch and myself "powerful and exemplary."

Today we sense an even closer kinship with the literature of the baroque era than did the generation that followed upon World War I. Later and more fully developed research is not the only reason for this. A few lines from Opitz's "Trostgedicht in Widerwärtigkeit des Krieges" ("Poem of Consolation in Hideous Times of War"), or Andreas Gryphius' "Feurige Freystadt" ("Fiery Freystadt") bring home to us so poignantly the immediate precariousness of life that they remain almost indelibly in our minds. In those slow and stately alexandrines and anguished sonnets we find forebodings that are valid in our day because in two successive wars "earthly vanities" did indeed turn to dust and ashes. Today we are even prepared to lend a serious ear to some of those homilies that show us how the "hopeless futility" of human existence was interpreted and overcome three hundred years ago. In short, much of Daniel von Czepko's work still has power to move us because this juxtaposition of reason and faith gives us such a clear image of a strongly developed personality. During the Thirty Years War (1618–1648), that major crisis in German history, seventeenth-century man learned to endure the polarity between the precariousness of this life and hope in the life to come, and to experience that polarity at such a profound level that the end of life offered a prospect of perfect security in faith. Today we admire this as a victory over the antithesis felt to exist in life.

To the baroque mind, the world to come was the sole yardstick of the value of this world. Death was seen as the gateway from one realm into the other. Little was said of "the void," or only in a quite different sense, that of the origin of spirit. This world received its light from the world to come, and the world to come was seen as "the counterpole of vanity." The two realms lay facing one another, and the connecting bridge was not life but the act of death. Yet, prior to that, this life was to be lived, and baroque man lived it joyously, perhaps precisely because in no century did the "Triumph of Death" ride in such majestic procession as in the seventeenth. Worldly joys were sought and found, in feast days, in love, in friendship, in conversation, each of which marks off one of the areas from which life, despite the daily threat of death, drew its strength. Lighthearted enjoyment joined hands with solemn reflection, awareness of momentary grace with expectations of eternity, and all these experiences and meditations combined to form a view of God and the world that bore the simultaneous imprint of tradition and the spiritual climate of the day.

Such was the world of Daniel von Czepko. Born in 1605 near Liegnitz in Silesia, the son of a Protestant clergyman, by 1623 he had already moved to Leipzig to study medicine, and later he moved to Strasbourg to study law. Here he became acquainted with the humanistic circle whose pivotal point was Mathias Bernegger. Toward this figure all eyes were turned, and he exerted a strong influence over Czepko. Side by side with the national humanism of Strasbourg, another formative force acquired significance for him: the Lowlands pietistic movement, the ripples of which spread as far as this Strasbourg circle. Later, when

Czepko had completed his years of study, years also of chivalrous escapades, this pietistic movement directed him to the Silesian circle of like interests that had formed around Valentin Weigel, Christoph Köler, and Abraham von Franckenberg, among whom a deep and personal devotionalism became a self-imposed obligation. Even his later encounter with pansophy in no way affected his firmly anchored Lutheran piety, from which he never wavered even in his exploration of mystical experience.

The force of Czepko's personality makes itself felt throughout his work. His writing is invariably self-oriented yet at the same time self-critical, emphatically rationalistic yet in matters of faith strongly emotional although never ecstatic or exalted. The joys of this world prompt the same sense of responsibility in him as the expectations of the world to come. He duly played his part in the world as a member of court society, as a lawyer, as an adviser to his prince, who later conferred upon him the aristocratic title of von Reigersfeld. Czepko demanded respect, and he knew how to secure it for himself wherever his rank failed to elicit voluntary recognition. In life as in poetry, his command of the forms accruing to him from tradition, yet nevertheless chosen for a given moment, remained absolute. Thus in his epic "Coridon und Phyllis," a conventional specimen of occasional poetry, verbal splendor unfolds in its entirety. When poured into rigid figurative conventions, the familiar images seem to have congealed in their accumulation and affectation. But when, as in his secular poetry, he raised love to the status of a human value, this rigidity disappeared. Here Czepko tested his reflective powers on one of life's genuine values, and he succeeded in producing serious poems of meditation in which a personal tone breaks through, thrusting aside fanciful conceits and intricate ornamentation. This gallant artistry now appears solely in the artful arrangement of words and no longer in the content. Thus in a poem from the cycle "Angefangener und vollendeter Ehestand" ("Wedlock Begun and Perfected"), which, although beginning as an occasional poem, ends as a personal statement on a supreme value, the points of departure and completion are to be found in the words "one another."

  Therefore
This Daniel and this Anna Catharina
  will love one another.
  They look at one another:

And look into one another as they administer God
to one another,
They honor one another:
And take from one another that which they keep
with one another,
They want one another:
And grant one another that which they desire
from one another,
And nevermore will they be able to part
from one another:
Even when they die, they will not die,
For their life consists not in the body but
in love,
Which knows naught of dying. . . .[1]

VAIN FLIGHT FROM LOVE

Here the emotional experience of love finds artfully structured expression, and we see how far Czepko managed to transcend purely formal style even in a secular occasional poem. As with most poets of that century between the Reformation and the Enlightenment, a statement of such a personal and solemn nature seldom made its appearance in so pure a form of self-orientation. Generally speaking, in his gallant poetry ("Coridon und Phyllis," "Zwey Rollen verliebter Gedancken" ["A Lover's Thoughts in Two Roles"], "Unbedachtsame Einfälle" ["Random Ideas"]), Czepko remained beholden to the forms of a gay and frivolous social culture or verbose formal verse. But even here he appears as an independent, speculative spirit uniting the play of metaphors with a reflectiveness fraught with fine differentiation, and for whom words in all their potential of ingenious ambivalence expand in image-studded expressive style. Again and again in these poems we find the rudiments of a psychologizing observation of love that elsewhere in the seventeenth century are almost stifled by the traditional wealth of metaphor. A sense of the bittersweet joys in amorous encounter that derives from personal experience is raised to the level of universal experience.

By fleeing I'll not find flight,
When I through wind and ocean
My course do set in motion,

Still follows me that light.
Through hill, vale, wooded place,
Constant I see before me
That gentle form and face.
Myself I should then flee from,
For, filled with lover's anguish,
Dwells in my heart thy image,
'Tis that I must be free from.[2]

Despite its dependence on common Petrarchan metaphors, it is precisely this simple expression of vain flight from love, extending into the realm of timeless utterance, in which we sense its closeness to today's lyrical poetry.

It is true, of course, that among Czepko's contributions to the "social" poetry that obeyed the conventions of the time—and these contributions represent a very considerable portion of his total output—such well-integrated verses remain for the most part as yet undiscovered. The image of a poet transcending his own day and suffering unjust oblivion in ours does not emerge until we turn to his spiritual writings which, apart from a few songs, have come down to us in prose and epigrams.

Even in his Strasbourg student days Czepko had already begun his attempt to pinpoint the position of self in the world by turning his gaze toward the world to come. *Supra illum nemo est, qui supra fortunam est*, we read in the dedication of the epigrams to Venator. His search reinforced his awareness of his own value within the larger scheme of things. Perception of self was to him the supreme and ultimate goal, especially during the years of solitude in the Silesian countryside. In a letter written in Latin to Christoph Köler we read sentences that throw a clearer light on the image of Czepko in his spiritual individuality and originality.

> I derive much joy from the solitude of country life. After associating so much with my Silesian friends, I have found in this joy a friend who seems to take the place of all of them for me. Do you ask who he may be? It is myself, for I am beginning to become my own friend. . . . It is with myself that I converse. . . . Many people search for others and in so doing neglect themselves. And all those who do not conduct a dialogue with themselves fail ultimately to arrive at self-perception. Yet it is this that harbors the supreme Treasure.

Such phrases, when they do occur in the baroque era, rarely have more behind them than a claim to the recognition of the silent personality in court society, where such turning away from the world is often intended as public evidence of the emanations of a philosophical spirit. In Czepko's case this self-observation was to be taken seriously. His pen has left us reflections on his past that testify to the steady strengthening of his religious views. Invariably we find self-contemplation to be the focal point of a system of thought that expands toward the infinite, and hence to the world beyond. We would know even more about this if many of Czepko's notes had not gone up in flames in the campfires of bivouacking soldiers.

Czepko's personal devotionalism was undoubtedly influenced by his reading of the Spanish and German medieval mystics. At the time, within the circle of the Silesian nobility, Czepko was living "inwardly" and trying in this way to create—for himself and presumably for his aristocratic friends as well—a "counterpole" to the general sense of the transitory nature of life. The two concepts of "inwardness" and "counterpole," besides occurring frequently in his work, provided the titles to two collections of epigrams from which many of his thoughts later found their way into his now famous "Trostschrift" ("Words of Consolation") and his "Sechshundert Schlussreime" ("Six Hundred End-Rhymes"), thus influencing Angelus Silesius in his writing of "Der cherubinische Wandersmann" ("The Cherubic Wanderer").

Although Czepko's dependence on Spanish and German mystical texts must remain a field for future scholars to explore, we find ourselves responding today to the forcefulness with which a man of the baroque era, in the midst of the Thirty Years War, fortified his position vis-à-vis God and the world within his own self and thus protested the increasing instability of religious values.

DEATH, MAN, AND GOD UNITED IN TRANQUILLITY

For Czepko the certainty of God's sheltering presence sprang from the consciousness of the divine origin of his soul. It was in his soul that he perceived the "Kingdom of God within," and in the truth of his divine origin he found the "counterpole of vanity." This was the positive element in his speculations: that through introspection he achieved tranquillity of the self and chose this tranquillity for himself and his friends as the point of departure for his consolations in those unsettled times. This was no static quietism, but a dynamic penetration of the darkness surrounding his generation's state of faith that had been undermined by the sufferings of war. This "Kingdom of Heaven within" reveals itself only to those who achieve a profounder understanding of God in the tranquil contemplation of their own being and follow the shining radiance of God to a point just this side of infinity.

> Halt, whither goest thou? Thou mayst not Heaven-ward,
> Not the delight of the world, the sun's fair travell'd course.
> Come with me into thyself. Thou hast—self once perceived—
> Far more than sun and world and Heav'n can embrace.
> Look inward, fellow man, thou find'st thyself without death:
> Delight without world: light without sun: without Heav'n, God.[3]

The deeper meaning of this call to the human self lies in the words: "Come with me into thyself . . . look inward . . . thou find'st thyself without death." Only by evaluating human existence in terms of its divine origin can we achieve true peace in earthly life, that tranquillity of the soul (*tranquilitas animi*) that alone makes life bearable.

> Rest is the loftiest work that ever God hath thought,
> Creating all, Himself as Rest He wrought,
> Each separate thing cries: Rest.[4]

But man can only participate in this loftiest work of God's if he turns his gaze inward and contemplates his own being with eyes closed.

> O man, I show thee: Gaze into thee, such peace:
> Yet wilt thou truly see it, then close both eyes.[5]

Czepko knew the limits of the mystical vision. He sounded a clear warning against penetrating the "fierce heat" that surrounds God and ". . . splits all that approaches it into a thousand fragments." Too many have soared off in "ecstasy" into the divine sphere and in so doing have met their earthly downfall. Czepko's speculative spirit knew a different way:

> Stay, there's no need to search: Naught find'st thou
> here or there
> Know they self wisely, Himself God comes to thee.[6]

For the withdrawal of the soul into itself Czepko found many poetic images and meditative variations whose purpose is to give sharper definition to the origin of that counterforce from which man derives a "counterpole of vanity," to which Czepko devoted a special collection of epigrammatic couplets. This constitutes the first step from introspection toward world-perception. Self and the law governing the world can only be experienced in their profound relationship when "truth" triumphs over "vanity" and the wider contrasts between internal and external, world and Heaven, man and God, are reconciled within the dimensions of a man's own soul.

> Thou handful of ash and dust, is God to use thy thinking—
> God, thy source of joy—to guide His eternal order?[7]

Czepko did not derive his acknowledgment of the eternal order from the overall concept of *fortuna* prevalent in the baroque era. Apparent though this fact is here, it is clearest of all in his confrontation with death. Although in his eyes dying had its place in the eternal order of things, he had his own personal way of contemplating the event of death. He did not—like the "Ackermann aus Böhmen" ("The Plowman from Bohemia," ca. 1400)—question the lawfulness of death's power over man, nor did he accept it—like Luther—as a natural law whose power is outmatched by the still higher power of the divine grace of the Redeemer; rather, as a poet of his time, he inquired after the origin of death and recognized in death the one and only bridge to eternity. The origin and end of the soul meet in human death.

> Death justifies itself and has its origin in Heaven. It is an eternal order whence, as life flows, so death joins its power to life, so that the two form never-ending witness to the eternity flowing within itself. One cannot exist without the other.[8]

Death, man, and God are conceptually united in "tranquillity." However, man in this world cannot enter into truly permanent tranquillity because "constant inconstancy" makes union impossible with this God whose very center is tranquillity. Only death, because it leads from the turbulence of the world into the tranquillity created by God, can bring about true union with God. Thus Czepko entered the broad realm of mystical speculation on the nature of the soul and the soul's union with its origin.

For him there was but one substance in man that is not compounded and innately antithetical. That is the soul. Its origin and its end remain forever in God. Dying enables the soul to make its longed-for journey back to its origin. The motif of the *unio mystica* (mystical union) appears here in the course of a speculation on the nature of the soul and its continued existence after earthly death. Drawing on these thoughts Czepko created an abundance of genuine words of consolation in a work written on the death of the sister of his patroness, a member of the Czigan family. Nowhere else in Czepko's writings do we find such a timelessly valid offer of consolation. The human soul remains the focal point of his meditations; it is from the soul that all consolation issues.

> The soul is without ceasing in God and perceives God not in His goodness, not in His truth, but as He is, what He is. The soul perceives Him in union and transcends, searches for, the meaning of union. Where God is, there is the soul, and where the soul is, there is God.[9]

The fact that in this passage he employs a purely mystical motif—that of the birth of the soul in Master Eckhart's terms—does not signify overmuch at this point, because shortly afterward Czepko justifiies the then current conception of the continued existence of the dead by citing their spiritual "virtues," in particular the exemplary display of love during their lifetimes. But it is with this word "love" that his real speculation on "oneness" with God, and hence on the *unio mystica*, begins. After death the human soul is absorbed in the All-Oneness of God, for this union is brought about by God's "love" for the human soul.

> Now God Himself is naught but love, therein lies His Godhood, His being. But ye must know that He loves naught but the soul, and loves Himself in the soul, and causes His work and His being to be born in the soul, and transforms the soul into Himself in and through love and encloses and conceals His eternal being in the soul.[10]

Yet wisdom in matters concerning life and death also speaks from the "Sexcenta Monodisticha" ("Six Hundred Monodistichs"), the collection of two-line rhymed sense-units that greatly influenced the religious aphoristic writing of the baroque era, especially that of Angelus Silesius. Here the structure of the rhymed alexandrine, with its caesura in the middle of the long line, often of serial or antithetical word-constructs, contributes toward a special forcefulness. All the values recognized in the "Consolatio" acquire in these epigrams a special significance as approaching logical reasoning. The result is brief poetic works of art which make us forget their origin in mystical speculation and which create a basis for an outlook that makes joy in this world and faith in the next appear quite reconcilable in our lives.

Sense must move to reason, reason to faith move,
Faith move to love, and thus thou canst improve.[11]

A strong religious attachment to faith forms the basis for this confidence in a spiritually governed human existence on earth. This sustained contemplation of death, which in Czepko never rested, began by leading him to an emotionally intensified conception of union in the sense of the *unio mystica*. Now, with the synthesis of sense, thought, and faith completed, the tranquil path through this world into the realm of the world to come appears assured. The image of the human soul is now filled with that divine power of love that goes back to and penetrates its origin and makes the union of divine and human existence possible in this life.

The soul of faith is love: without soul all is dead.[12]

[*Translated from the German by Leila Vennewitz*]

Notes

The following are the quotations cited in German by the author and rendered into English by the translator of this essay. No attempt has been made to use a corresponding early seventeenth-century form of English spelling, although the customary elisions, rhyme schemes, and word transpositions of that period have been used where possible and appropriate. For primary and secondary sources, *see* F. W. Wintzlaff-Eggbert, *Deutsche Mystik zwischen MiHelalter und Neuzeit*, 3rd. ed. (Berlin: Verlag Walter de Gruyter, 1969), pp. 333, 391.

Also werden
Dieser Daniel und diese Anna Catharina
einander lieben.
Sie sehen einander an:
Und sehen ineinander, wie sie Gott einander versehen,
Sie verehren einander:
Und nehmen voneinander, was sie miteinander behalten,
Sie wünschen einander:
Und gewehren einander, was sie voneinander begehren,
Und nimmermehr wird voneinander trennen können:
Auch wann sie sterben, werden sie nicht sterben,
Denn ihr Leben bestehet nicht im Leibe, sondern
in der Liebe,
Die von keinem Sterben weiss.

2. Durch fliehn entflieh ich nicht,
Wenn ich durch Wind und Wellen

Gleich meinen Lauf wil stellen,
Folgt doch das schöne Licht;
Durch Berge, Thal und Wald
Seh ich stets vor mir gehen
Die freundliche Gestalt.
Mich müst ich selber fliehn,
Dieweil hier steckt im Hertzen
Dein Bild voll Liebes Schmertzen
Dem ich mich wil entziehn.

3. Halt an, wo wiltu hin? Du darffst nicht Himmel an,
Nicht, wo die Zier der Welt, der Sonnen schöne bahn:
Komm mit mir in dich selbst. Du hast, erkennstu dich:
Ja mehr als Sonn und Welt und Himmel schleust in sich,
Schau in dich, lieber Mensch, du findest dich ohn Tod:
Die Zier ohn Welt: den Glantz, ohn Sonn: ohn Himmel, Gott.

4. Ruh ist das höchste Werck, das iemals Gott bedacht,
Da, als er schuff, hat er sich selbst zur Ruh gemacht,
Ein jedes Ding schreyt: Ruh.

5. O Mensch, hier zeig ich dir, schau in dich, diese Ruh:
Doch willtu sie recht sehn so schleuss beyd' Augen zu.

6. Bleib, es bedarff es nicht: Nichts suchst du für und für,
Nihm deiner weisslich wahr, Gott selber kommt zu dir.

7. Du Hand voll Asch und Staub, Sol Gott nach deinem Dencken
Gott, der dich seelig macht, sein ew'ge Ordnung lencken?

8. Der Tod bestehet vor sich und hält seinen Ursprung vom Himmel. Es ist eine ewige Ordnung, aus der wie das Leben fliesset, so der Tod seine Macht mit dem Leben verknüpffet, dass die Zwey unaufhörliche Wort Zeugen sind der in sich fliessenden Ewigkeit. Eines ist ohne das andere nicht.

9. Sie ist ohn Unterlass in Gott und nihmt nicht Gott, als er gut, nicht als er wahr ist, sondern als er ist, das er ist. Sie nihmt in der Einigung und geht durch, sucht, was die Einigung sey. Wo Gott ist, da ist die Seele, und wo die Seele ist, da ist Gott.

10. Nun ist Gott an ihm selber nichts als Liebe, in der liegt seine Gottheit, sein Wesen. Das must ihr aber wissen, dass er nichts liebet als die Seele, und liebet sich selbst darinnen und gebieret in die Seele sein Werck und Wesen, und wandelt die Seele in sich in und durch die Liebe und verschleust und verbirget sein ewiges Wesen in der Seele.

11. Der Sinn muss in Vernunfft, Vernunfft in Glauben gehn,
Der Glauben in die Lieb, und so kanst du bestehen.

12. Des Glaubens Seel ist Lieb: Ohn Seel ist alles todt.

LIST OF CONTRIBUTORS

BAYS, GWENDOLYN M.

Studied at Agnes Scott College, Decatur, Georgia, Emory University, Atlanta, Georgia. Ph.D. Yale University. Fulbright scholar to the Sorbonne. Studies in German Literature at the University of Heidelberg.

Present position: Professor of French, Clarion State College, Clarion, Pennsylvania.

Books: *The Orphic Vision* 1964.

BRENCH, ANTHONY C.

Born September 3, 1935 in Reading, Berkshire U.K.

Studied at Bristol University.

Present position: Lecturer, Department of French, University of Glasgow.

Books: *The Novelists' Inheritance in French Africa*, O.U.P. London, 1967.
Editor: *Writing in French from Senegal to Cameroon* (critical anthology), O.U.P. London 1967.
Coeditor: *French English/Anglais Francais* (Collins Language Dictionaries), Collins, London & Glasgow 1969.
In preparation: *Jean Malonga: écrivain congolais*, for F. Nathan (Littérature africaine) Paris; (Revised) *Bibliography of African Literature*, Institute of African Studies, University of Ibadan with M. Amosu and P. Young).

DAVIS, CHARLES TWITCHELL

Born April 29, 1918 at Hampton, Virginia.

Studied at Dartmouth College, University of Chicago, Ph. D. New York University, 1951.

Present position: Professor of English; Chairman, Afro-American Studies Committee, The University of Iowa.

Books: *E. A. Robinson: Selected Early Poems and Letters*. New York, 1960; *A New England Girlhood* (by Lucy Larcom), New York 1961; The American Experience Series: "The World of Primal Thought," *Whitman, the Poet*, ed. J. C. Broderick, Belmont, California 1962; "Poetry: 1910–1930," *American Literary Scholarship, An Annual, 1963*, ed. J. Woodress, Durham, North Carolina 1965; "Image Patterns in the Poetry of Edwin Arlington Robinson," *Appreciation of Edwin Arlington Robinson*, ed. R. Cary, Waterville, Maine 1969; "Robinson's Road to Camelot," *Edwin Arlington Robinson: Centenary Essays*, ed. E. Barnard, Athens, Georgia 1969.

Coeditor: *Walt Whitman's Poems*, New York University Press 1955 (with Gay Wilson Allen); *On Being Black: Writings by Afro-Americans from Frederick Douglass to the Present*, Greenwich, Conn. 1970 (with Daniel Walden).

HARRIS, WILSON

Born 1921 in British Guiana.

Studied in British Guiana.

Present position: Commonwealth Fellow in Caribbean Literature, University of Leeds.

Books: *Palace of the Peacock*, London 1960; *The Whole Armour*, London 1962; *The Secret Ladder*, London 1963; *Heartland*, London 1964; *The Eye of the Sacrecrow*, London 1965; *Tumatumari*, London 1968; *Ascent to Omai*, London 1970; *The Sleepers of Roraima*, London 1970; *The Age of the Rainmakers*, London 1971; *Tradition, the Writer and Society*, London and Port of Spain 1967 (a collection of critical essays).

HIRST, DÉSIRÉE

Born 1922 in Colombo, Ceylon.

Studied at St. Mary's Convent, Cambridge, Famborough Hill and St. Hilda's College, Oxford.

Present position: Lecturer in English, University of Wales, University College of Swansea, since 1964.

Books: *Hidden Riches, Traditional Symbolism from the Renaissance to Blake*, Eyre & Spottiswoode, London & New York 1964.

HOPPER, STANLEY ROMAINE

Born March 22, 1907 in Fresno, California.

Studied at the University of Southern California, Boston University School of Theology, Harvard University, University of Zürich, Mansfield College, Oxford, England, Ph.D. Drew Theological School, Drew University, 1936, and D.D. Allegheny College, 1963.

Present position: The Bishop W. Earl Ledden Professor of Religion, Syracuse University.

Books: *The Crisis of Faith*, 1944; *The Book of Jeremiah*: Exposition for the "Interpreter's Bible," Vol. 5, 1956.
Editor: *Spiritual Problems in Contemporary Literature*, Peter Smith, Gloucester, Mass. 1958.
Coeditor: *Interpretation: The Poetry of Meaning*, Harbinger Books, New York 1967 (with David L. Miller).
Chapters in Books: "The Future of Religious Symbolism," in *Religious Symbolism*, ed. by F. Ernest Johnson, Kennikat Press, Port Washington, New York 1955; "Augustine's Manichean Writings" in a *Companion to St. Augustine*, ed. by Roy Battenhouse, Oxford University Press, 1955; "On the Naming of the Gods in Hölderlin and Rilke," in *Christianity and the Existentialists*, ed. by Carl Michalson, Charles Scribner's Sons, New York 1956; "Camus: The Argument from the Absurd," in *Christian Faith and the Contemporary Arts*, ed. by Finley Eversole, Abington Press, Nashville, Tenn. 1957.

IZUTSU, TOSHIHIKO

Born May 4, 1914 in Tokyo, Japan.

Studied at Keio University, Tokyo.

Present position: Full Professor, McGill University, Montreal.

Books: *Language and Magic*, Tokyo 1956; *God and Man in the Koran*, Tokyo 1964; *The Concept of Belief in Islamic Theology*, Tokyo 1965; *Ethico-Religious Concept in the Qur'ân*, Montreal 1966; *The Key Philosophical Concepts in Sufism and Taoism*, 2 vols., Tokyo 1966–67; *Sabzawari: Sharḥ-I Manẓûmah*, editor, Tehran 1969; *The Concept and Reality of Existence*, Collected Papers, to appear in 1971 in Tokyo.

JACOBI, MARIO

Born August 27, 1925 in Leipzig, Germany.

Studied at the École Normale de Musique in Paris and at Guildhall School of Music and Drama in London. Ph.D. University of Zürich, Diploma in analytic psychology at the C.G. Jung-Institut, Zürich.

Present position: active in private practice, lecturer at the C.G. Jung-Institut, and lecturer at the Institut für angewandte Psychologie, Zürich.

Books: *Grundsätzliche Ueberlegungen zur Violinpädagogik*, Zürich 1964.

MERKELBACH, REINHOLD

Born June 7, 1918 in Grenzhausen, Germany.
Studied at the University of Hamburg. Ph.D. 1947.
Present position: Professor of Classical Philology, University of Cologne.

Books: *Untersuchungen zur Odyssee*, München 1951; *Die Quellen des griechischen Alexanderromans*, München 1954; *Roman und Mysterium in der Antike*, München 1962; *Griechisches Leseheft zur Einführung in Paläographie und Textkritik*. Göttingen 1965 (with Helmut von Thiel); *Lateinisches Leseheft zur Einführung in Paläographie und Textkritik*, Göttingen 1969 (with Helmut van Thiel).
Coauthor: *Hesiodus* (Die Hesiodfragmente auf Papyrus), Leipzig 1957; *Isisfeste in griechische-römischer Zeit; Daten and Riten*, Meisenheim am Glau 1963 (with M. L. West); *Fragmenta Hesiodea*, Oxford 1967 (with F. Solmsen and M. L. West); *Hesiod* (Oxford Classic Text), Oxford 1970 (with Helmut van Thiel).
Coeditor: *Studien zur Textgeschichte und Textkritik*, Köln 1959, Dedicated to G. Jackmann (with H. Dahlmann); *Beiträge zur klassischen Philologie*, Meisenheim am Glau (a series containing 36 volumes) 1960–; *Papyrologische Texte und Abhandlungen*, Bonn (a series containing 13 volumes). 1968– (with L. Koenen). *Zeitschrift für Papyrologie und Epigraphic*, Bonn (7 vols.).

NAMBIAR, ODAYAMADATH KUNJAPPA

Born August 10, 1910 at Tellicherry, Kerala State, India.
Studied at Presidency College, Madras, India.
Present position: Before retirement, Professor of English and head of postgraduate department of English studies at Bangalore University's Central College. Appointed by the Indian Universities Grants Commission for research and teaching at postgraduate level under the scheme for the utilization of the services of outstanding teachers. In 1971, invited to teach Indian literature to a group of American students at the Callison College study center at Bangalore in an experimental program in area studies conducted by the University of the Pacific, Stockton, California.

Books: *Last of the Perumâls*, Calicut; *Portuguese Pirates and Indian Seamen*, Bangalore 1955; *The Kunjalis—Admirals of Calicut*, Bombay 1963; *Walt Whitman and Yoga*, Bangalore 1966; ". . . I hear the Hindoo . . ." (further essays on Whitman), Bangalore.
Editor, *Sreyas*, Bangalore.
To be published: *Yoga in the Temple* (a Hindu view of the symbols and ritual of Freemasonry); *New Light on Yoga.*

PONSOYE, PIERRE

Born in 1915 in Nîmes, South France.

Studied medicine at Montpellier and Marseilles.

Present position: Medical Counsel for the Parisian section of the Social Security Administration.

Books: *L'Esprit, Force biologique*, Montpellier 1944; *L'Islam et le Graal*, Paris 1957. Essays: "Saint-Bernard et la Règle du Temple," *Etudes Traditionnelles*, No. 364, Mars-Avril 1961, Paris; "Intelletto d'Amore," *Etudes Traditionnelles*, No. 370, Mars-Avril 1962 and No. 371, Mai-Juin 1962.

SANDERS, JO

Born October 22, 1941 in Cedar Rapids, Iowa.

Studied at the University of Iowa, the University of Oklahoma, at Middlebury and at the University of Nottingham in England.

Present position: Ph.D. candidate in German, The Pennsylvania State University.

SCHIMMEL, ANNEMARIE

Born April 7, 1922 in Erfurt, Germany.

Studied at the University of Berlin. Ph. D. In Islamics 1941. Habilitation in Arabistic and Islamology at the University of Marburg Jan 12, 1946.

Present position: Prefessor of Indo-Muslim Culture, Harvard University.

Books: *Indices of the Chronicles of Ibn Iyas*, Istanbul 1945; *Die Bildersprache Eschelaladdin Rumis*, Walldort 1949; *Edition of the Sirati Ibni Khafif, i Shirazi, Ankara* 1955; *Dinler Tarinin Giris* (Introduction into History of Religions), Ankara 1955; *Gabriel's Wing, A study into the religious ideas of Sir Muhammad Iqbal*, Leiden 1963; *Pakistan, Ein Schloss mit tausend Toren*, Zuerich 1965; *Islamic Calligraphy*, Leiden, 1970; *Orientalische Dichtung in Uebersetzungen Friedrich Rueckerts*, Bremen 1963.
Translations: Muhammad Iqbal, *Javidname=Buch der Ewigkeit* (German poetry), München 1957; Muhammad Iqbal, *Botshaft des Ostens* (German poetry) Wiesbaden 1963; Muhammad Iqbal, *Persischer Psalter* (Selections of his Persian, Urdu, and English writings), Köln 1968; Ibn Khaldun, *Ausgewählte Abschnitte aus der Muqaddima*, Tübingen 1951; *Lyrik des Ostens* (the Near Eastern part), München 1950; al-Halladsch, *Märtyrer der Gottesliebe* (translations of his poetry and prose as well as from later poets who allude to him), Köln 1969; John Donne, *Nacktes denkendes Herz*, Köln 1969.
Co-editor: Arabic Cultural Magazine *Fikrun Wa Fann*, Hamburg, since 1963.

SILBERSCHLAG, EISIG

Born on January 8, 1903 in Stryj, Austria.
Studied at the University of Vienna. Ph.D. 1926.
Present position: Professor of Hebrew Literature, Hebrew College and Visiting Professor, Emmanual College in Boston.

Books: (poetry): *Bi-Shevilim Bodedim*, New York 1931; *Aleh, Olam, be-Shir*; *Kimron Yamai*, Jerusalem, 1959; (criticism): *Tehiyah u-Tehiyah be-Shirah*; (plays): *Sheva Panim le-Havah*, Tel Aviv 1942; *Bi-yeme Isabella*, New York, 1939–41.
Translations: *Berenice*, Tragedy in Five Acts by Carl de Haas, translated from German into Hebrew, New York 1947; *Poems of Love* by the Byzantine poet, Paulus Silentiarius, translated from Greek into Hebrew, Tel Aviv 1962; *The Eleven Comedies of Aristophanes*, translated from Greek into Hebrew, Jerusalem and Tel-Aviv, 1967.
Monographs: *Hebrew Literature: An Evaluation*, New York 1959; *Saul Tschernichowsky—Poet of Revolt*, Cornell University Press 1968.
Coeditor: *Sefer Touroff*, Boston 1938; *Hatekufah*, vols. 30–31, 32–33, New York 1946–47.
Coeditor: *Poet Lore* (periodical), Boston 1939.

STRELKA, JOSEPH P.

Born May 3, 1927 in Wiener Neustadt, Austria.
Studied at the University of Vienna. Ph.D. 1950.
Present position: Professor of German, State University of New York at Albany.

Books: *Der Burgundische Renaissancehof Margarethes von Österreich und seine literarhistorische Bedeutung*, Wien 1957; *Kafka, Musil, Broch und die Entwicklung des modernen Romans*, Wien 1959; *Rilke, Benn, Schönwiese und die Entwicklung der modernen Lyrik*, Wien 1961; *Brecht, Horvath, Dürrenmatt: Wege und Abwege des modernen Dramas* Wien 1963; *Brücke zu vielen Ufern: Wesen und Eigenart der österreichischen Literatur*, Wien 1966; *Vergleichende Literaturkritik: Zu den Prinzipien und Methoden einer neuen Literaturtheorie*, Bern-München 1970; *Die gelenkten Musen: Dichtung und Gesellschaft*, Soziologische Problemstellungen der Literaturewissenschaft, Wien 1971.
Editor (book series): *Yearbook of Comparative Criticism*, University Park and London, since 1968 (4 vols. to date); *Penn State Series in German Literature*, University Park and London, since 1971; *Deutshe Literatur im Exil seit 1933* (with Professor John Spalek), State University of New York at Albany, Bern, since 1972.
Editor (books): *Gedichte Margarethes von Österreich* (First publication of a 16th-century manuscript), Wien 1954; *Traum und Verwandlung* (Anthology of the works of Ernst Schönwiese), Graz and Wien 1961; Felix Grafe, *Dichtungen* (First complete edition of the collected works,) Wien 1961; *Das zeitlose Wort: Eine Anthologie österreichischer Lyrik von Peter Altenberg bis zur Gegenwart*, Graz and Wien 1964; *Aufruf zur Wende: Eine Anthologie neuer Dichtung*, Wien 1965; *Der Engel vom westlichen Fenster* (Anthology of the works of Gustav Meyrink), Graz and Wien 1966; *Moderne Amerikanische Literaturtheorien* (with Professor Walter Hinderer), Frankfurt am Main 1970.
In preparation: Ausgewählte Werke von Gottlieb Leon.
Textbooks: *Lügendichtung* (with Harold von Hofe), New York 1966; *Vorboten der Gegenwart: Nietzsche, Freud, Marx, Einstein* (with Harold von Hofe), New York 1967.

WENTZLAFF-EGGEBERT, FRIEDRICH WILHELM
Born June 16, 1905 in Freist (Krs. Stolp in Pommern).
Studied at the University of Berlin. Ph.D.
Present position: Ordentlicher Professor für deutsche Philologie and Director of the Deutsche Institut, University of Mainz.

Books: *Deutsche Mystik zwischen Mittelalter und Neuzeit*, Berlin 1919; *Das Problem des Todes in der deutschen Lyrik des 17, Jahrhunderts*, Leipzig 1931; *Dichtung und Sprache des jungen Gryphius*, Berlin 1936; *Andreas Gryphius lateinische und deutsche Jugenddichtungen*, 1938 (2. Auflage 1965); *Studien zur Lebenslehre Taulers*, Berlin 1939; *Opfer und Schicksal in Hölderlins "Hyperion" und "Empedokles,"* Strassburg 1943; *Heinrich Seuse, Sein Leben und seine Mystik*, Lindau 1947; *Die Dicthung des Bodenseegebietes, Ein Überblick*, Lindau 1949; *Schillers Weg zu Goethe* (2. Auflage 1963), Tübingen 1949; *Kreuzzugsdichtung des Mittelalters*, Berlin 1960; *Der Hoftag Jesu Christi 1188* in Mainz, Wiesbaden 1962; *Deutsche Literature im späten Mittelalter*, 3 Bde 1971 (Mit Texten).
Deutsche Literaturzeitung für Kritik der internationalen Wissenschaft, Berlin 1880–.

YOUNG, PETER
Born in 1941 in England.
Studied at the University of Durham at King's College, Newcastle.
Present position: Lecturer (høgskolektor) in English at a new regional college in Norway, where he is setting up a department of English.

Books: Co-editor (since 1967) of the projected *Dictionary of West African English*.
Periodicals: Co-editor (from 1968–70) of the journal *Ibadan Studies in English*.

INDEX OF NAMES